3

38.85
100k

D0709466

Strategy Assessment and Instruction for Students with Learning Disabilities

NATIONAL UNIVERSITY
LIBRARY RIVERSIDE

STRATEGY ASSESSMENT AND INSTRUCTION

FOR STUDENTS WITH LEARNING DISABILITIES

From Theory to Practice

Edited by
LYNN J. MELTZER
Institute for Learning and Development

pro·ed

8700 Shoal Creek Boulevard
Austin, Texas 78758

© 1993 by PRO-ED, Inc.

All rights reserved. No part of this book may be
reproduced in any form or by any means without
the prior written permission of the publisher.

Printed in the United States of America

Library of Congress Cataloging-in-Publication Data

Strategy assessment and instruction for students with learning
    disabilities : from theory to practice / [edited by] Lynn Meltzer.
        p.   cm.
    Includes bibliographical references.
    ISBN 0-89079-540-1
    1. Learning disabled children—Education—United States.
    2. Learning disabled—Education—United States.   3. Learning
    disabilities—United States—Diagnosis.   I. Meltzer, Lynn.
    LC4705.S77   1992
    371.9′0973—dc20   91-48272
                                                             CIP

pro·ed

8700 Shoal Creek Boulevard
Austin, Texas 78758

1   2   3   4   5   6   7   8   9   10   96   95   94   93   92

To Peter, Colin, and Danny for their support, endurance, and humor

and

To Jack and Thelma for helping me to pursue my goals

Contents

Contributors **ix**

Foreword by Joseph K. Torgesen **xiii**

Preface by Lynn J. Meltzer **xix**

PART 1 Issues in Strategy Use: Prospects and Problems

1 Learning Disorders and the Flavors of **5**
Cognitive Science
D. Kim Reid

2 The Origin of Strategy Deficits in Children with **23**
Learning Disabilities: A Social Constructivist Perspective
C. Addison Stone and Lydia Conca

3 Principles and Procedures in Strategy Use **61**
H. Lee Swanson

4 Strategy Use in Students with Learning Disabilities: **93**
The Challenge of Assessment
Lynn J. Meltzer

PART 2 Language, Attention, and Motivation: Their Impact on
Strategic Learning

5 Automaticity, Word Retrieval, and Vocabulary **141**
Development in Children with Reading Disabilities
Denise Segal and Maryanne Wolf

6 Strategy Training for People with Language-Learning   **167**
Disabilities
Elisabeth H. Wiig

7 Achievement-Related Beliefs in Children with   **195**
Learning Disabilities: Impact on Motivation
and Strategic Learning
Barbara Licht

8 Learning Disabilities and Attention Deficits   **221**
in the School Setting
Sally E. Shaywitz and Bennett A. Shaywitz

PART 3 Academic Competencies and Strategy Instruction

9 Approaches to Strategic Reading Instruction Reflecting   **247**
Different Assumptions Regarding Teaching and Learning
*Annemarie Sullivan Palincsar, Judith Winn, Yvonne David,
Barbara Snyder, and Dannelle Stevens*

10 Teaching Writing Strategies to Students with   **271**
Learning Disabilities: Issues and Recommendations
Steve Graham and Karen R. Harris

11 Mathematics Assessment and Strategy Instruction: **293**
An Applied Developmental Approach
Bethany Roditi

PART 4 Strategy Instruction and Classroom Demands

12 The Investigation of Setting Demands: A Missing   **325**
Link in Learning Strategy Instruction
*M. Lewis Putnam, Donald D. Deshler, and
Jean B. Schumaker*

13 Closing Thoughts on Strategy Instruction for   **355**
Individuals with Learning Disabilities: The Good
Information-Processing Perspective
*Michael Pressley, John G. Borkowski, Donna Forrest-Pressley,
Irene W. Gaskin, and Debra Wile*

Index   **379**

Contributors

John Borkowski, PhD
Department of Psychology
University of Notre Dame
Notre Dame, IN 46556

Lydia Conca, PhD
Kramer Middle School
81 Fiske Hill Road
Sturbridge, MA 01566

Yvonne David, MEd
University of Michigan
Program in Education and
Psychology
1360 SEB
610 East University Drive
Ann Arbor, MI 48109

Donald D. Deshler, PhD
Institute for Research in
Learning Disabilities
Robert Dole Human
Development Center,
Room 3061
University of Kansas
Lawrence, KS 66044

Irene Gaskins, EdD
Benchmark School
2107 Providence Road
Media, PA 19063

Steve Graham, EdD
University of Maryland
Department of Special
Education
College Park, MD 20742

Karen R. Harris, EdD
University of Maryland
Department of Special
Education
College Park, MD 20742

Barbara G. Licht, PhD
Florida State University
Department of Psychology
Tallahassee, FL 32306-1051

Lynn J. Meltzer, PhD
Institute for Learning and
Development
One Courthouse Lane
Chelmsford, MA 01824
and Tufts University
Eliot-Pearson Department of
Child Study
Medford, MA 02155

Annemarie Sullivan Palincsar, PhD
University of Michigan
Educational Studies
1360F SEB
610 East University Drive
Ann Arbor, MI 48109

Michael Pressley, PhD
EDHD Benjamin Building
University of Maryland
College Park, MD 20742

Donna Forrest-Pressley, PhD
Kennedy Institute School
Johns Hopkins University
Medical Center
Baltimore, MD 21205

M. Lewis Putnam, PhD
Department of Exceptional
Education
University of
Wisconsin–Milwaukee
P.O. Box 413
Milwaukee, WI 53201

D. Kim Reid, PhD
University of Northern Colorado
Greeley, CO 80639

Bethany N. Roditi, PhD
Institute for Learning and
Development
One Courthouse Lane
Chelmsford, MA 01824

Jean B. Schumaker, PhD
Institute for Research in
Learning Disabilities
Robert Dole Human
Development Center,
Room 3061
University of Kansas
Lawrence, KS 66044

Denise E. Segal, PhD
Laboratory for Child Language
and Dyslexia Research
Tufts University
Eliot-Pearson Department of
Child Study
Medford, MA 02155

Bennett A. Shaywitz, MD
Yale University School of
Medicine
Department of Pediatrics
333 Cedar Street
New Haven, CT 06510

Sally E. Shaywitz, MD
Yale University School of
Medicine
Department of Pediatrics
333 Cedar Street
New Haven, CT 06510

Barbara Snyder, MA
Michigan State University
Counseling, Educational
Psychology and Special
Education
Erickson Hall
East Lansing, MI 48823

Dannelle Stevens, MEd
Whitman College
School of Education
Walla Walla, WA 99362

C. Addison Stone, PhD
Learning Disabilities Program
Department of Communication
Sciences & Disorders
Northwestern University
2299 Sheridan Road
Evanston, IL 60208-3560

H. L. Swanson, PhD
School of Education
University of California
Riverside, CA 92521

Elisabeth H. Wiig, PhD
Boston University, Professor
Emirita
7101 Lake Powell Drive
Arlington, TX 76016

Debra Wile, MEd
Benchmark School
2107 Providence Road
Media, PA 19063

Judith Winn, PhD
University of
Wisconsin–Milwaukee
School of Education
Department of Exceptional
Education
P.O. Box 413
Milwaukee, WI 53201

Maryanne Wolf, EdD
Laboratory for Child Language
and Dyslexia Research
Tufts University
Eliot-Pearson Department of
Child Study
Medford, MA 02155

Foreword

By Joseph K. Torgesen

In reviewing the range of topics and depth of coverage in this book, I am both amazed and gratified at the progress we have made in our understanding of strategic processing inefficiencies in children with learning disabilities. This is a topic that was not a formal part of the literature on learning disabilities prior to 1977! Yet, in this volume we have extensive documentation of the strategic processing difficulties of children with learning disabilities across a broad range of important academic tasks. Even more significantly, this book provides discussions of intervention programs and assessment procedures that make practical contributions to the treatment of children, adolescents, and adults with learning disabilities.

Since its formal inception as an independent area of research and practice in 1963, the field of learning disabilities has consistently struggled with two fundamental problems. The first of these issues involves validation of the hypothesis that learning disabilities are neurologically based, and hence represent a "genuinely handicapping condition." The second major challenge to the field has involved developing methods of effective identification and intervention for individuals with learning disabilities.

Four extremely important developments have been made in the field over the past 18 years that represent fundamental contributions in meeting each of these areas of challenge. First, new methods and research addressing the heterogeneity of the LD population have given us a greater formal appreciation of the variability that exists among individuals with learning disabilities. We have begun to recognize that progress in clarifying the concept of learning disabilities cannot be made as long as our research approaches do not take seriously the possibility that distinct subtypes of learning disabilities exist. Second, we now have at least one widely accepted, and well supported theory that identifies the specific neurological base of a relatively common type of learning disability, phonological reading disabilities. This theory makes a genuine contribution toward validating the concept of learning disabilities because it focuses on a specific academic problem, identifies the underlying and specific processing limitations causing the academic problem, locates the neurological basis for the processing limitations, and proposes a specific etiology for the neurological impairment.

The third great contribution to our field in the last 18 years has been development of knowledge and theory about the strategic processing inefficiencies of children with learning disabilities. As is manifest in this volume, knowledge in this area has led to significant new approaches to assessment and intervention that promise to help students with learning disabilities be much more effective in compensating for their processing weaknesses and managing their intellectual capacities in ways that will lead to better learning. One of the themes of this volume is the importance of bridging the gap between theory and practice. The critical changes in the field that allow this theme to be so well developed in this book is the movement of research on strategic processes in children with learning disabilities from the laboratory to the classroom. A natural consequence of this movement is that research on both assessment and intervention becomes more sensitive to the actual contexts in which learning occurs. Research that is embedded within a realistic context supports the development of assessment procedures that are more clearly linked to instruction, and it ensures that instructional procedures themselves will be more likely to succeed within the day-to-day realities of the classroom.

The fourth major development in our field, which is supported by extensive work from developmental psychology, is our increased understanding of the consequences of early failure in school for the child's motivational, attitudinal, and intellectual development. We also have a much better understanding of the ways in which early failure produces different learning environments for good and poor learners. This understanding is well documented in this book, and it is beginning to inform some of the newer methods of instruction that are discussed within these pages.

From the perspective of these four major contributions to our field, the importance of this volume is easily apparent. It brings together, with a focus on application, the most recent developments within two of these areas. The book's attempt to bridge the gap between theory and practice is important, because knowledge about strategic processing inefficiencies, and understanding of the educational consequences of early failure experiences, are directly useful in meeting the second fundamental challenge to the field. That is, they contribute directly to the development of more effective assessment and intervention methods for children with learning disabilities.

One of the few questions about strategic processing inefficiencies in children with learning disabilities that is deliberately not addressed in this volume is the question of etiology, or causality. This omission is certainly a correct one, as we have very little evidence on which to base hypotheses about the origins of strategic processing difficulties. Further, given the book's focus on the application of knowledge for more effective assessment and intervention techniques, a discussion of causes, particularly neurophysiological ones, is not likely to produce immediate benefits at this point. As a link between the content of this book and traditional conceptualizations of learning disabilities, it seems useful to indicate a possible *range* of causal models in this area. These causal alternatives are not mutually exclusive. In fact, it would be consistent with current views about the heterogeneity of children with learning disabilities to propose that there might be several types (with reference to primary cause) of strategic processing difficulties in these children.

Information from a variety of sources suggests at least three plausible causes for the inefficiencies in strategic information processing that are frequently observed in children with learning disabilities. First, these difficulties in coordinating and integrating multiple processes and skills on complex tasks may arise from immature or damaged development of the brain centers that are required for such coordination. Such a view would be consistent with the observation that sometimes children, with little previous history of failure in school, begin to experience severe difficulties when first confronted with complex academic tasks such as writing book reports, solving math word problems, taking notes, or understanding complex texts. This view would identify strategic processing inefficiencies as another expression of neurological difficulties in children with learning disabilities. There is also the possibility, as is considered in the chapter by Addison Stone in this volume, that difficulties in strategic information processing arise in some children because of certain communication and instruction patterns in the home. Specifically, patterns that do not lead children to discover their own problem-solving abilities or to assume responsibility for monitoring their own behavior are likely to interfere with the process of discovering and applying effective learning strategies in school.

In direct contrast to both of these hypotheses that suggest causes for strategic inefficiency outside the school experience itself, is the idea that strategic processing inefficiencies may be a result, rather than an initial cause, of school failure. There are several possible mechanisms by which early and chronic failure on one or more specific academic tasks (e.g., reading) may lead to failure to develop normal strategic processing abilities. First, as is suggested in the chapter by Barbara Licht, early failure has profound motivational and attitudinal consequences. If, for example, children withdraw effort from school tasks, particularly new or difficult tasks, they are less likely to discover the strategies that are effective on these tasks. Thus, early loss of motivation for achievement in school, or lack of persistence on school tasks, can lead to a reduced repertoire of learning and performance strategies, which, in turn, can limit ability to adapt successfully to new tasks.

A second variant of the hypothesis that strategic processing inefficiencies can result from early school failure derives from the fact that strategic efficiency on a given task is strongly related both to content knowledge related to the task and to efficiency of operation of the component subskills required by the task. For example, a child may appear to be strategically inefficient on two-digit addition problems because of the need to divert too much processing energy to adding the single digits within the problem.

The final variant within the general idea that strategic processing inefficiencies may result from early school failure comes from the analysis of student-teacher communications among "good" and "poor" students. As is suggested in the chapters both by Stone and by Palincsar, Winn, David, Snyder, and Stevens, teachers communicate differently with students who are having difficulty with basic subjects such as reading. In general, their communication patterns with these children are not as supportive of the development of sophisticated strategies or self-monitoring skills as they are with students who are doing well in school.

From this analysis, it is apparent that causal explanations for the strategic processing inefficiencies of children with learning disabilities are likely to be very complex. One factor that must be considered in any speculation about causality is that the strategic inefficiencies of children with learning disabilities encountered to date are all subject to modification through careful instruction and practice. Although our view of causality may lead us to place different emphasis on prevention versus remediation, for example, there is no question that appropriate instruction can have a positive impact on strategic inefficiencies that are properly identified.

The essential importance of this book is that it discusses the methods we can use to identify and ameliorate strategic information processing difficulties in children with learning disabilities. If special and regular educators, as well as parents, become sensitive and skilled in the identification, prevention, and remediation of strategic processing inefficiencies, we will have come a long way toward helping children and adults with learning disabilities achieve satisfying and productive lives both in and out of school.

Preface

By Lynn J. Meltzer

> The last thing one discovers in writing a book is what to put first.
> (Blaise Pascal, 1623–1662)

The genesis and development of the discipline of learning disabilities have been influenced by the cross-fertilization of a multiplicity of orientations and ideas, the fusion of which has sometimes been incomplete. From the 1960s through the 1980s, this hybrid field looked for guidance and support to some of its more pedigreed predecessors such as educational psychology, mental retardation, and neurology. After establishing its right to exist independently, the field of learning disabilities needed to repair and consolidate the definitions and concepts that provided the foundation for its continued existence. The 1990s have heralded such a focus and have resulted in a move to transcend definitional arguments and to improve specific methods for the identification and teaching of students who manifest these difficulties in learning.

A new and exciting phase has begun in the growth of the discipline of learning disabilities, which has become a melting pot for research and theory from diverse areas such as cognitive psychology, developmental psychology, educational psychology, and the neurosciences. Among the most exciting developments are the recent convergence of these different perspectives and the move away from the isolationist and territorial nature of these viewpoints. Conceptualizations of learning disabilities that have emphasized discrete processing deficits have been replaced by the heterogeneity paradigm, which recognizes that learning disabilities comprise multiple interacting characteristics. There has also been increasing recognition that the manifestation of learning disabilities is affected by the complex interactions of the individual's cognitive status, motivation, and level of background knowledge with environmental influences such as the complexity of the curriculum and the style of teaching. Recent work in learning disabilities has also been influenced by metacognitive research on normal achievers, which has demonstrated the importance of organization, planning, and self-regulatory strategies for spontaneous, independent learning. Since the mid–1980s the impact of metacognition on special education has become more evident, particularly in the domains of theory and practice (Wong, 1987). This is reflected in the currently accepted view that students with learning disabilities frequently use different processing routes for accessing information and that they may often display inflexible and inefficient strategies for problem solving and learning (Meltzer, 1991; Meltzer, Solomon, Fenton, & Levine, 1989; Swanson, 1988, 1989; Torgesen, 1978). Students with learning disabilities have been characterized as "actively inefficient learners" who cannot easily access and coordinate multiple mental processes and who also have difficulty with self-regulatory processes such as monitoring, checking, and revising their solutions (see review in Swanson, 1989). Their difficulties span a continuum ranging from effortful, strategic processing to automatic processing that occurs without effort (Swanson, 1989). It is the combined influence of these deficits that often prevents students with learning disabilities from performing at the level of which they are intellectually capable.

Metacognitive and strategy deficits may account for the discrepancy between intelligence and performance, a discrepancy that has been the traditional benchmark for defining and measuring learning disabilities. The discrepancy definition has recently been the focus of a great deal of debate, and there has been considerable disagreement about the role of IQ in the definition of learning disabilities (see JLD, 1989, special issue). The debate has, in turn, stimulated discussion about appropriate methods of assessment with sharp controversy about Siegel's contention that IQ tests should be cast from their current pedestal as the central measures for identifying learning disabilities (Graham & Harris, 1989; Siegel, 1989). Currently, there is greater acceptance of the view that diagnostic decision making can no longer be based on a few absolute test scores but must instead rely on a multidimensional assessment approach and must take account of the context in which learning occurs (Graham & Harris, 1989). This highlights the importance of transcending the limitations of assessments that typically focus on determining eligibility for special education services. Assessment procedures are needed that evaluate how, why, and what children learn with the goal of developing alternative methods to improve classroom instruction. Such diagnostic approaches should account for developmental changes as well as curriculum effects in the classroom setting and must address the quality and efficiency of students' problem-solving and learning strategies (Meltzer, 1991, chap. 4 of this volume). Such assessment systems will eventually help to broaden the range of measurement approaches and to ensure closer links between identification and intervention. These improved methods of identification will, in turn, impact on research and theory as the field continues to wrestle with etiological issues such as the relative importance of higher versus lower order processes as causes of learning disabilities.

Developmental and curriculum effects exert a critical influence on the manifestation of learning disabilities and need to receive more attention in current assessment and teaching approaches. Students' learning profiles frequently change over time as a function of the interactions among their particular developmental strengths and vulnerabilities and the demands of the curriculum. Learning disabilities may remain latent for many years as students rely on their strengths to compensate for their underlying weaknesses, and their deficits may emerge only in the form of academic and/or social difficulties during critical transition times in the curriculum. At these times a mismatch is provoked between the child's skills and strategies and the demands of the learning environment (Meltzer, 1991). Certain transition times in the academic curriculum—namely, first grade, fourth grade, junior high school, high school, and college—can be particularly challenging and problematic. At these times, new and more complex tasks are introduced that require greater coordination and integration of multiple skills and strategies; for example, complex writing requirements, book reports, and multiple-choice tests.

The chapters in this volume present a wide range of perspectives within the unifying framework of a model of strategic learning. It is hoped that this volume will eventually help to narrow the lingering gap between research and practice and to enhance our paradigms as well as our specific methods for identifying and teaching these students with learning disabilities.

Goals of This Volume

In light of the recent surge of interest in strategic learning in students with learning disabilities, a number of major themes are interwoven throughout this volume; these themes are represented by the four parts of the book. The first theme addresses the importance of moving away from a static model of learning disabilities and from diagnoses and teaching that imply permanent deficits. Instead, the emphasis is on dynamic and holistic models that account for students' learning strategies and contain specific implications for teaching and treatment. There is an emphasis on the critical connections among theory and practice, and the necessity of improving the linkages among different assessment and teaching approaches. Traditionally, assessment has remained separate from instruction and ability and achievement tests have not adequately informed instruction (Campione, 1989). In the current volume there is an emphasis on the continuous spiral that connects process-oriented assessment with classroom-based teaching as reflected in the Assessment for Teaching paradigm (Meltzer, 1991; Roditi, chap. 11 of this volume). The second theme that characterizes this volume addresses the roles of language, attention, motivation, and self-esteem as they impact on strategic learning. The third theme addresses the wide variety of methods for teaching specific strategies to students with learning disabilities in the areas of reading, writing, spelling, and mathematics. These methods range from the Vygotskian approach and the cooperative teaching model of Palincsar to the more structured teaching strategies of Deshler and his colleagues. Finally, discussion focuses on the necessity of incorporating strategic instruction in the classroom setting as well as the implications for teacher training.

Discussions of learning disabilities in the 1990s inevitably raise a number of issues and questions relating to definition, etiology, and identification. Are learning disabilities neurologically based or primarily influenced by environmental factors? What are the critical developmental factors that influence learning disabilities, and how do developmental variables interact with the curriculum to unleash previously latent learning disabilities? Can we continue to embrace models that emphasize isolated processing deficits or should we focus on higher order processing difficulties? Alternately, is it important to recognize the complex interactions among these different variables and the influence of isolated processing deficits on cognition and knowledge acquisition? How do we differentiate learning disabilities from attention deficit disorders, and is such a distinction of great importance? Finally, what are the implications for assessment and teaching practices? This volume represents the viewpoints of a variety of well-respected theoreticians, researchers, and practitioners who provide a range of answers to many of these questions and who pose additional controversial questions that reflect the ongoing evolution of the field of learning disabilities.

The unifying theme of these chapters is the view that strategic learning is critical for academic success and that many students with learning disabilities are characterized by inefficient and inflexible strategies that prevent them from functioning at the level of their potential. I hope this volume will help to further our understanding of the complexities of learning disabilities and will stimulate more ecologically valid research that will eventually improve the effectiveness of existing assessment and teaching methods. Ultimately, these improved techniques will ensure that students with learning disabilities are able to function at the level of which they are intellectually capable.

Acknowledgments

I would like to thank the staff at PRO-ED and particularly Dr. Jim Patton, my editor, for his many helpful comments and suggestions and for his commitment to the cohesion and successful completion of this volume. My appreciation to my colleague and friend Dr. Bethany Roditi, whose encouragement, creative ideas, and good humor helped me to weather the challenges of completing this volume for publication. I would also like to acknowledge my colleagues from the Boston Children's Hospital for their help and support during the early years of my research on strategic learning: Drs. Melvin D. Levine, Terence Fenton, and Edward Moroney. Finally, my thanks to the many children and families whose struggles with the day-to-day pressures of their learning problems have taught me so much about the importance of patience, persistence, tolerance, and faith.

References

Campione, J. C. (1989). Assisted assessment: A taxonomy of approaches and an outline of strengths and weaknesses. *Journal of Learning Disabilities, 22,* 151–165.

Graham, S., & Harris, K. R. (1989). The relevance of IQ in the determination of learning disabilities: Abandoning scores as decision makers. *Journal of Learning Disabilities, 22,* 500–503.

Journal of Learning Disabilities, 22. (1981). [Special Issue].

Meltzer, L. J. (1991). Problem-solving strategies and academic performance in learning disabled students: Do subtypes exist? In L. Feagans, E. J. Short, & L. J. Meltzer (Eds.), *Subtypes of learning disabilities* (pp. 163–188). Hillsdale, NJ: Erlbaum.

Meltzer, L. J., Solomon, B., Fenton, T., & Levine, M. D. (1989). A developmental study of problem-solving strategies in children with and without learning difficulties. *Journal of Applied Developmental Psychology, 10,* 171–193.

Siegel, L. S. (1989). IQ is irrelevant to the definition of learning disabilities. *Journal of Learning Disabilities, 22,* 469–478.

Swanson, H. L. (1988). Information processing theory and learning disabilities: A commentary and future perspective. *Journal of Learning Disabilities, 20,* 155–166.

Swanson, H. L. (1989). Strategy instruction: Overview of principles and procedures for effective use. *Learning Disability Quarterly, 12*(1), 3–14.

Torgesen, J. K. (1978). The role of non-specific factors in the task performance of learning-disabled children: A theoretical assessment. *Journal of Learning Disabilities, 10,* 27–35.

Wong, B. Y. L. (1987). How do the results of metacognitive research impact on the learning disabled individual? *Learning Disability Quarterly, 10,* 189–195.

PART 1

Issues in Strategy Use: Prospects and Problems

In recent years increasing attention has been devoted to the role of strategy deficits in learning disabilities, partly as a result of the documented importance of metacognitive and problem-solving strategies for independent learning in normal achievers (Brown, Bransford, Ferrara, & Campione, 1983; (Pressley, Symons, Synder, & Cariglia-Bull, 1989; Pressley, Woloshyn, Lysynchuk, Martin, Wood, & Willoughby, 1990). This interest in strategic learning has also stemmed from the research findings that students with learning disabilities often have difficulty with the efficient, flexible access and utilization of strategies (Torgesen, 1978; Swanson, 1988, 1989; Meltzer, 1984, 1991). Theories of strategy deficits in these students have reopened the debate about the relative importance of higher versus lower order processes for learning. Undergirding these discussions are the different theoretical orientations regarding the origins of strategy deficits and the manner in which they manifest in students with learning disabilities. Other issues of central importance to these discussions relate to the most appropriate methods for identifying and assessing strategic learning. The chapters in this first part of the book address theoretical issues with an emphasis on the implications of theory for assessment and teaching practices.

In the first chapter Kim Reid reviews the historical roots of the information processing perspective and the significance of social constructivist and cooperative learning methods for students with learning disabilities. Within the framework of the constructivist perspective, she discusses the importance of instructional approaches such as cooperative learning, reciprocal teaching, and cognitive developmental education.

In the second chapter the theoretical approaches that are reviewed by Kim Reid are elaborated on by Addison Stone and Lydia Conca, who discuss the major assumptions of the social constructivist perspective. Their chapter focuses primarily on Vygotsky's theories and the implications for learning disabilities. They review the evidence regarding the social origins of strategy deficits in children with learning disabilities and focus in particular on parent and teacher interactions with these students. Finally, they discuss the findings that students with learning disabilities are not challenged appropriately because their deficits and needs are often overestimated by the adults in their environments.

In the third chapter Lee Swanson reviews the definition of strategies and discusses the rationale or "why" of strategy instruction, thereby providing a context for the research on strategy use in students with learning disabilities. He provides a rationale for strategy instruction and its importance for addressing the difficulties students with learning disabilities experience when they are required to access information flexibly, efficiently, and in a planful fashion. He emphasizes eight principles of strategy instruction and summarizes a number of his own studies that demonstrate the importance of these principles.

In Chapter 4 Lynn Meltzer focuses on the importance of developing dynamic, process-oriented assessment approaches that evaluate strategy use in problem solving and learning areas. The chapter addresses the need for methods to evaluate cognitive flexibility, efficiency of strategic learning, and the interface between automaticity and problem solving in the learning disability population. An alternative model of assessment is proposed that integrates diagnosis and teaching and goes beyond the current reliance on isolated scores and static tests. Central to this theme is a discussion of the Assessment for Teaching model (Meltzer, 1991; Roditi, chap. 11 of this volume), a paradigm that connects process-oriented assessment with classroom-based teaching.

The theme that emerges from these chapters is the importance of reducing the gap between theory and practice and the necessity of improving existing techniques for assessment and intervention among students with learning disabilities.

References

Brown, A. L., Bransford, J. D., Ferrara, R. A., & Campione, J. (1983). Learning, remembering and understanding. In P. H. Mussen (Ed.), *Handbook of child psychology* (Vol. 3, pp. 77–166). New York: Wiley.

Meltzer, L. J. (1984). Cognitive assessment and the diagnosis of learning problems. In M. D. Levine & P. Satz (Eds.), *Middle childhood: Development and dysfunction* (pp. 131–152). Baltimore: University Park Press.

Meltzer, L. J. (1991). Problem-solving strategies and academic performance in learning disabled students: Do subtypes exist? In L. V. Feagans, E. J. Short, and L. J. Meltzer (Eds.), *Subtypes of learning disabilities* (pp. 163–188). Hillsdale, NJ: Erlbaum.

Pressley, M., Symons, S., Snyder, B. L., & Cariglia-Bull, T. (1989). Strategy instruction research comes of age. *Learning Disability Quarterly, 12,* 16–30.

Pressley, M., Woloshyn, V., Lysynchuk, L. M., Martin, V., Wood, E., & Willoughby, T. (1990). A primer of research on cognitive strategy instruction: The important issues and how to address them. *Educational Psychology Review 2*(1), 1–58.

Swanson, H. L. (1988). Information processing theory and learning disabilities: A commentary and future perspective. *Journal of Learning Disabilities, 20,* 155–166.

Swanson, H. L. (1989). Strategy instruction: Overview of principles and procedures for effective use. *Learning Disability Quarterly, 12*(1), 3–14.

Torgesen, J. K. (1978). The role of non-specific factors in the task performance of learning-disabled children. A theoretical assessment. *Journal of Learning Disabilities, 10,* 27–35.

1

Learning Disorders and the Flavors of Cognitive Science

D. Kim Reid

Over the last decade, an extraordinary number of papers addressing philosophical and theoretical issues have appeared in journals on learning disorders. Beginning in the early 1900s, a growing perception of behaviorism's inability to explain the complexities of human behavior led a number of insightful scholars to seek experimental methods for going beyond the then exclusive focus on observable behaviors. It was not until the early 1950s, however, that the prevailing zeitgeist in America shifted (Mandler, 1985). Researchers in philosophy, psychology, sociology, psycholinguistics, and artificial intelligence, for example, seemed to recognize almost simultaneously that more satisfying explanations of human knowing and learning were dependent on understanding nonobservable, enabling, and mediating behaviors. The amalgam of these alternative positions has become known as cognitive science (or sometimes generally as information processing) and has increasingly attracted scientists interested in learning disorders. As with any meld of diverse entities, however, a number of "flavors" of this new approach to the study of human behavior have resulted. It is partly because of the shifting zeitgeist and partly because of the widespread failure to become aware of these sometimes rather substantial differences in flavor that so many papers on the theory and philosophical underpinnings of learning disorders have emerged.

For the most part, all nonbehavioral perspectives were regarded as "theme and variation on an information processing approach" (Reid, 1988a, p. 418). A more careful reading, however, indicates that, although the differences have seldom been emphasized, the flavors of the new cognitive science that have emerged in the learning disorders literature are surprisingly diverse (Bruner, 1986, chronicled a number of interacting theoretical forces, but only three have predominated in the study of learning disabilities). One flavor may indeed be referred to as information processing, but much of the work that has been subsumed under the information processing label is really constructivism, and some represents an ecological (contextual or comparative psychology) approach. The purpose of this chapter is to argue that the study of learning disorders and the treatment of students who exhibit such disorders will be better served if we distinguish among these flavors of cognitive science.

Behavioral Roots

Traditionally, persons interested in learning disabilities have been disinterested in theory. As the early medical (or underlying abilities) model was repudiated in favor of behaviorism, operants dominated the scientific study of learning disorders.[1] As a result, there was less concern with understanding the nature of learning disorders than with treating them. The treatment of choice was educational.

Because teachers' control of operants was thought to bring about desired learning behaviors in their students, complex processes (e.g., reading and arithmetic) were analyzed into component skills. These skills were ordered in what was assumed to be a hierarchical progression and taught from the bottom of the hierarchy (i.e., the group of skills presumed to be easiest) upwards, step by step through levels of the hierarchy, to more and more complex behaviors (i.e., those composed of a number of "easier" skills). Reward structures and reward schedules were carefully manipulated. Token economies flourished. There was a strong focus on materials and tests. Lessons were devised by analyzing the tasks to be learned. They were planned solely by the teacher and in advance of instruction.[2]

---

[1]Skinner (1966) defined *operants* as a class of behavior bearing probability relations with environmental events that occur after instances of members of that class.

[2]Today, theory suggests that lessons be designed to capitalize on the student-generated goals and subgoals that arise during learning encounters and to interact with students' moment-to-moment understandings and reactions in ways that modify their representation of and approaches to the problem. See the section later in this chapter on ecological approaches.

Consequently, pupils with and without special needs were taught the same sets of prescribed exercises. What was *individualized* was the presentation of those exercises at the students' own rates. By remediating specific content deficiencies directly (i.e., teaching components of target behaviors), instructors expected to "cure" disorders by eliminating gaps in knowledge (Kronick, 1988). What happened, however, was that the special needs students learned more slowly and repeatedly practiced the lower level skills. Often, so much practice of the least complex skills was needed that there were few opportunities for these students to engage in the more meaningful, higher level skills. The consequence was that the essential nature of instruction for able and less able students diverged.

When children with learning disorders became adolescents and then adults with learning disorders, it became apparent that these instructional practices were inadequate. As critics became increasingly vocal (both from within the field and from without) and cognitive science developed to the point where applications to children and special populations became feasible (Kail & Bisanz, 1982), the ranks of non-behaviorists swelled. Researchers called for the adoption of the information processing framework to give the study of learning disorders a scientific base (cf. Swanson, 1987), but educators, for the most part, continued past practices. Did this new cognitive science have important implications for teaching? If so, what were they and how should they be implemented? In the absence of clear direction for change, many materials manufacturers and special educators struggled with lending precision to methods for analyzing tasks and manipulating operants. Others tried to apply disparate research findings from information processing studies as they became available. Attempts to include strategic behaviors in the behavioral curriculum provide one example of this piecemeal approach.

Information Processing

Just as behaviorism emerged at the turn of the century as an antidote to the problems associated with introspectionism, so information processing emerged 30 to 40 years later as an answer to the limitations of behaviorism. Behaviorists' rejection of theory was rooted in their objection to mentalism—the assignment of hypothetical explanations to the functions that determine and guide observable behavior. They believed that the only "real" behavior was physical and that psychology would ultimately be reduced to physiology. This position, however, was inadequate to explain complex human functions, and so behavioral characteristics in the form of little *r*s and *s*s were assigned to the theoretical notions advanced. Information processing "substituted for the (often vague) physiological mechanisms the mental mechanisms necessary for a full theoretical analysis" (Mandler, 1985, p. 4). Paving the way was a collection of mentalistic constructs: the concept of the unconscious articulated by Freud, imageless thought described by the Wurzburg school, structured perception introduced by the Gestalts, a schema-based theory of memory advanced by Bartlett and influential to later works by Craik and Broadbent, the constructivism of Piaget and Vygotsky, and the psychophysical tradition embodied in psychophysics and experimental psychology.

Perhaps the earliest comprehensive, widely accessible discussion of information processing was provided by Lachman, Lachman, and Butterfield (1979). They defined the area of study for information processing as "the way man collects, stores, modifies, and interprets environmental information or information already stored internally" (p. 7). Information processing theorists want to know how information is acquired, how it is accessed, and how it is used in every facet of human activity. They believe that the activities necessary to collect, store, access, and use information define cognition and serve as the basis for oral and written language as well as creative thought. Many also believe that these activities constitute the essential characteristics that distinguish humans from other animals and consequently undergird emotion, personality, and social interaction.

Capitalizing on modern technology, information processing theorists study human cognition using computer metaphors that describe information representation and processing in an inherently active system. Perceptual, memory, and executive control processes were first represented in "serial boxes" connected by arrows and later, as intellectual connections were reestablished with the *dynamic* processes of the German and French traditions, as parallel or cascading processes, indicating the simultaneous and interactive nature of various subprocesses and routines. Heuristics and strategies were also borrowed as the artificial intelligence community attempted to test well-articulated aspects of theories by writing computer programs to model them. Mandler (1985) argued that information processing is "a way of looking at the world, a framework for thinking, *not* a theory" (p. 19).

Because information processing requires such elaborate specification, however, this view embraces many of the same reductionist principles as behaviorism. Indeed, some have argued that relabeling *input* and *output* in the flow charts as *S* and *R* makes the similarities obvious. There are, however, some very real advantages to the information processing approach: First, environmental stimuli are recognized as noise until humans selectively apply sophisticated procedures to create the meaningful structures that appear in consciousness and behavior (i.e., the organism is regarded as inherently active). Second, the aim is to understand how the *system* of processes, analogous to *mind* rather than individual cells, operates. Finally, in pursuit of this aim, important achievements—memory systems, stages of processing, and operating strategies—have attracted scholars across a wide range of disciplines, and the resultant foment has been richly productive.

Despite these achievements, however, information processing remains an unsatisfactory account of human performance. Brown (1979) noted that a system "that cannot grow, or show adaptive modification to a changing environment, is a strange metaphor for human thought processes which are constantly changing over the life span of the individual and the evolution of the species" (p. 100). Neisser (1976) also lamented the lack of emphasis on accommodation. He argued that programs of human functioning modeled on computers fail to represent the effects of a complex environment with coherent properties of its own, properties that sometimes vary from one environment to another and sometimes remain invariant. Neisser (1985) further remarked that the typical information processing experiment tests a hypothesis about an internal mechanism against its competitors, taking cognition completely out of context. Experiments that are unnatural and arbitrary cannot account for the important interactions that occur in life. For a critique of information processing that is directly related to its application to learning disorders, see Gavelek and Palincsar (1988).

Although information processing may not be *the* answer to our needs for theoretical grounding, it certainly has a role to play in generating knowledge about the nature of learning disorders. This perspective has taught us a great deal about how people process information in real time and the types of processing difficulties experienced by persons with learning disorders. We have learned a fair amount about their difficulties with representation, elaboration, strategic behaviors, and mneumonic processes.[3]

These analyses obviously carry implications for instruction—the need for clear exposition, the importance of teaching the means to accomplishing instructional goals, the necessity of linking current with

---

[3]A rich source of the work using an information processing framework to investigate questions related to learning disorders is the *Journal of Learning Disabilities*, beginning in 1987. It is important to note, however, that few of these articles disentangle constructivist from ecological from true information processing positions. The new text by Reid, Hresko, & Swanson (in press) does describe some of these distinctions. For a very convincing argument that laboratory studies can elucidate and enrich the interpretation of studies conducted within the ecological framework (and vice versa), see Gelfand (1985).

past information, and so forth. How the findings can be applied directly to educational interventions, however, remains unclear. If children have difficulty with short-term memory, do we teach them to remember or should we provide memory supports while we teach them to read? If children do not read well, should we teach them a set of strategic behaviors? The research suggests that children probably will not use those strategies spontaneously when they read (see Reid, 1988b, for a review), even if they can demonstrate that they have learned each of the strategies in isolation. It appears that other flavors of cognitive science may be more helpful in the design of instructional environments.

Constructivist Theories

Of the many mentalistic advances that occurred to prepare for the transition from behaviorism to the new cognitive science, one of the most influential was the constructivism of Piaget and, more recently, Vygotsky. They were among the first scientists to attack the tenets of behaviorism. Not only did they share a whipping boy, each considered the other a worthy opponent—admiring, critiquing, and, in the process, being influenced by his work. Although their exchange of papers was centered on discussions of language and egocentrism, at the heart of their differences lay the question of whether children are inherently social beings. Piaget's mission was to generate a biologically oriented explanation of human cognitive development. He, like Freud, viewed humans as essentially and initially self-serving biological organisms. Through interactions with a separate, often resistant environment, humans construct their own knowledge and, in the process, gradually come to be socialized. Vygotsky's dialectical perspective, on the other hand, assumed that infants are socialized and socializing from birth. Consequently, he viewed development as a process of constructing shared meanings by internalizing social models, first ineptly and then with greater and greater skill, eventually leading to conscious awareness and free will.

Biological Constructivism

Piaget became world famous as a very young man because of three books (original French editions 1927, 1936, and 1937; English editions 1930, 1952, and 1954, respectively) he wrote detailing observations of the development of infants and young children. With the behaviorists he shared the desire to produce a data-based description of the development of human knowledge by simply laying out "the facts"—in contrast to the more popular armchair philosophizing or introspectionism of his day. As his critic Vygotsky was quick to point out, however, it is not possible to organize a complex data base without using implicit assumptions about human behavior in an integrating framework. Consequently, Piaget became a theory builder in spite of himself.

With reductionism (and consequently behaviorism) as his foil, Piaget (1971, 1977) ultimately schematized the course of psychological development as an extension of biological development, as a dialectical (resulting from the interplay of assimilation and accommodation) and augmentative (because the dynamic interchanges inherently characteristic of living systems always lead to growth) spiral. At the base of the spiral are a few instinctive behaviors and reflexes that, through integration and differentiation during exercise as the infant interacts with its environment, gradually and systematically enlarge the baby's set of possibilities for responding. Once a response is acquired, the baby is able to interpret a wider array of stimuli. As continued activity leads to the organization of increasingly complex systems of behavior, the spiral widens. Dialectical interplay among developing cognitive systems becomes, like the interplay between specific assimilations and accommodations, another driving force of knowledge acquisition (Inhelder, Sinclair, & Bovet, 1974). All interactions are, however, governed by the laws of the growing system as a whole.

Piaget believed that children's responses to questions about information they had been taught were contaminated by the use of verbal propositions the children did not really understand. For this reason, he was careful to study the development of concepts that are not taught in school (e.g., conservation, seriation, class inclusion).[4] His work, therefore, ignored the effects of the social environment.

Social Constructivism

In the decade between 1924 and 1934, Vygotsky (original Russian edition 1934; English edition 1987) lauded Piaget's chronicling of the course of child development and agreed with his vitalistic and holistic (rather than behaviorism's mechanistic and reductionistic) stance. He argued that development is not a process of an individual's moving from idiosyncratic to socialized thought. Vygotsky instead saw socialization as the *source* of knowing. First, he believed that new abilities

---

[4]For an extended discussion of biological constructivism, see Gallagher and Reid (1983), the only comprehensive account of Piaget's later works, emphasizing the mechanisms of development and change (available in English).

are spawned and nurtured during interactions with others (most often a caretaking adult) in the context of a particular task. Only gradually are these abilities internalized by the child, primarily through the vehicles of shared experience and language. Second, he argued that, although some elementary functions are essentially biological as Piaget suggested, all higher cognition is mediated by socially constructed systems such as language and mathematics.

Vygotsky also disagreed about the role that instruction plays in development. Unlike Piaget, he conceived of instruction in its broadest sense, including informal exchanges as well as formal teaching. Because language is the primary vehicle for internalizing thought, it does not matter that the scientific concepts taught in school are learned initially only as verbal propositions. In fact, that is their strength. Because they are verbal, they begin as part of an organized system of thought and gradually are understood in relation to the concrete phenomena that the concept represents. Everyday concepts (including those Piaget studied), on the other hand, are generated "outside of an ordered system and move upward only slowly toward generalization" (Vygotsky, 1987, p. 168).

Vygotsky's research indicated that there is a higher level of conscious awareness with scientific concepts and that their acquisition is followed by a rapid improvement of performance with everyday concepts. In sum, an increased level of knowledge leads to enhanced scientific thinking which, in turn, enriches spontaneous behavior. *Instruction leads development.* Consequently, what children can do alone tells very little about what they know. What they can do when engaged in meaningful activity with adults, however, is a sensitive index, referred to as the *zone of proximal development,* that enables us to judge better both what they know and what they are ready to learn.[5]

Stone and his colleagues (1985; Stone & Wertsch, 1984) have suggested that the higher functions Vygotsky defined as involving reflective awareness and deliberate control amount to what we now call strategic or metacognitive functions. Indeed, it is clear from their writings that developmental psychologists who initially promoted the study of strategic behaviors were influenced by both Piaget and Vygotsky (cf. Brown, 1975; Flavell, 1985). The concept of metacognition has roots in constructivism.

There are several reasons why metacognitive, especially strategy, studies were perceived by the learning disabilities community primarily as part of the information processing literature. One reason is

---

[5]See the chapters by Palincsar and Stone in this volume (chaps. 9 and 2, respectively) for more detailed descriptions of Vygotsky and subsequent workers' social constructivism as it relates to learning disorders.

coincidental: The study of strategic behaviors and the introduction of information processing occurred at approximately the same time. Second, American researchers used rigorous, quantitative research techniques, rather than the more qualitative structural analyses associated with Piaget's *méthode clinique.* Another reason may be that cognitive behavior modification (CBM) with its emphasis on self-monitoring skills became popular in the treatment of attention deficit disorders. CBM is continuous with the behavioral, learning theory tradition. Similarly, many researchers have assumed the executive processes in an information processing model to be essentially identical to metacognition, and, indeed, many strategy studies have been carried out within an information processing framework. Finally, all three flavors of cognitive science, because they described learning as a process of assimilation rather than association, were widely perceived as a single, unified theory.

An Appropriate Role for Constructivism

Reid (in press-a) and Reid, Knight-Arest, and Hresko (1981) have argued that constructivism has the *potential* to contribute realistic and educationally relevant data about learning, because it focuses on the spontaneous organizing activity of the student over time and on the interactions between that student and the objects, persons, and/or events in the environment (Piaget, 1977, 1978). But, although such single-subject or group studies are rich and instructive, they do not provide much direct information about interpersonal and/or sociocultural effects.

Although any number of interesting questions can be researched from a constructivist perspective, it seems to be particularly well suited to educational studies and interventions. Perhaps Poplin's (1988b) treatise is the best argument advanced to date for the use of constructivist principles in education. Her work is a significant departure from behavioral and information-processing–based applications of strategy instruction and is based instead on what she calls holistic/constructivist principles: (a) Learning is the construction of meaning; (b) the individual is self-regulating and self-preserving; (c) the best predictor of what will be learned is what is already known; (d) error plays an important role in learning; (e) feelings affect learning; (f) learning is enhanced when people trust those they are learning from; and, finally, (g) the belief that learning is a primary human function—it does not require coercion (Poplin, 1988a). Although these principles lead to a conception of education that is substantially different from what we currently offer, it is consonant with the tenets of constructivism, particularly biological constructivism as it was conceived by Piaget. Basing their work on Vygotsky's social constructivism, Stone and Wertsch (1984) as well as Brown (Brown & Campione, 1986; Brown & Palincsar, 1982), Palincsar (Palincsar, 1986, Palincsar & Brown, 1984, 1986), and their colleagues (cf. Englert & Lichter, 1982; Pearson & Gallagher, 1983; Thomas, Englert, & Gregg, 1987) have generated and tested powerful intervention techniques for students with learning disorders. These techniques—for example, reciprocal teaching (Palincsar & Brown, 1984) —require that students and teachers share the responsibility for completing a task. They place a high premium on metacognitive functions.

In reciprocal teaching, group members take turns being teacher. "Teaching" means asking questions, clarifying confusions or misinterpretations, predicting what is likely to follow in the text, and summarizing what has been learned. The goal is always knowledge acquisition. Because the task is performed collaboratively, strategies one student uses to complete the task are modeled for others, while differences in expressed understandings help participants confirm or modify old ideas. This method complies to a great extent with Poplin's criteria that students learn to take control of their learning activities, that there are alternative routes to goal achievement and an appreciation for wrong answers, and that there is no reduction of the content to exercises on presumably additive subskills (see the discussion earlier in this chapter on behavioral roots). An overview of this perspective is given in Palincsar's chapter in this volume (chap. 9).

It is interesting that Poplin (1988a, 1988b) overlooked these interventions, because she too failed to differentiate between strategy instruction that conforms to an information processing perspective and that which is contextually embedded. Although Brown, Palincsar, et al. support explicit instruction in specific strategies, they do not treat strategies as skills to be taught in isolation. Instead, each emerges naturally in contexts in which its use is required for satisfactory performance.[6] Undoubtedly, however, Poplin would urge more autonomy for the students and a more child-receptive, although not necessarily more passive, role for the teacher.

Another instructional format that is gaining widespread acceptance as a result of the interactional focus of social constructivism is cooperative learning (cf. Palincsar, Brown, & Martin, 1987). Reciprocal teaching is inherently collaborative because it requires that students share ideas and monitor each others' performances. Other forms of cooperative learning include peer tutoring and arrangements wherein students work jointly on a project, are tested individually, and are

---

[6]For an extended discussion of this comparison, see Reid (1988b).

given a group grade. These arrangements are easy to implement and have been found to produce results superior to more competitive classroom structures.

Reid (1989) speculates that cooperative learning arrangements may be particularly well suited to the instruction of students with learning disorders, because they (a) replicate the social context of natural learning, (b) promote self-efficacy, (c) provide level-appropriate models of information processing, (d) foster meaningful construction, and (e) address some of the most frequent information processing difficulties of persons with learning disorders (e.g., improving the ability to process information in working memory, to access information from long-term memory more efficiently, to acquire knowledge more rapidly, and to compensate for capacity limitations).

Assessment practices have also been addressed from within the constructivist perspective. Reid (1991) provides an overview of the careful analyses of the child's action sequences that dominate the most modern Piagetian assessment practices, whereas Campione (1989) detailed the specifics of "assisted assessment," a set of procedures based on social constructivist principles that examine the student's behavior within the zone of proximal development. Meltzer (1987) devised an assessment approach that is an outgrowth of both information processing and constructivist perspectives. These assessment approaches are characterized by their emphasis on the processes children use to attain knowledge, rather than on some quantitative representation of how much they know.

Ecological Approaches

Vygotsky's constructivism has recently gained wide acceptance in part because it represents one of the approaches to human cognition that emphasizes the study of the organism in its environment. It is not, however, the only ecological movement in psychology. For example, a small group of scientists known as ethologists (Lorenz, 1981) have argued that it is impossible to understand any piece of behavior without considering its context and its adaptive significance: Animals must be studied in their natural habitats, because each species fits neatly into its own ecological niche.

Unlike the behaviorists' assumption that general learning principles could be established that would adhere across species, the ethologists found that there were striking differences in the learning abilities of different species, of different animals within the same species, of the same animal in different situations, and of the same animal at different points during its life span. Because many types of natural learning fail to appear in laboratory settings, ethologists concentrate on field studies. Furthermore, unlike the information processing tradition, ethology is not model oriented. It is, however, just as scientific: This "behavioral biology" has links to neurobiology and genetics. Similar premises and methodologies have been advanced by ecologists, neo-Gibsonians, and others interested in animal cognition.

> The ecological approach . . . [takes] the environment seriously, focusing on cognition in ordinary settings. To study concept formation, one begins with an analysis of everyday concepts; to study perception, one begins with visual control of action in cluttered environments; to study memory, one begins with the kinds of things people ordinarily remember. Such an approach usually forces the researcher to look at temporally extended stimulus variables and behavior that occurs over time, rather than at brief flashes and momentary responses popular in information processing research. It also implies a concern with cognitive development and cognitive change, including both the changes due to age and those that come with the acquisition of skill—i.e., with learning itself. Most important, perhaps, is that ecological psychologists are generally reluctant to construct models or to postulate hypothetical mental events. Too often, they believe, those hypotheses have substituted for careful analysis of the real environment and the real events that occur in it. (Neisser, 1985, p. 21)

In the ethological movement or other ecological movements, the general principles that guide the research are more important than any theoretical perspective. (Recall that Mandler argued the same is true of information processing.) Shlechter and Toglia (1985) suggested that ecologically valid studies are defined by their focus on "the contextual relationships which exist among the organism, its cognitive behaviors, and the environment" (pp. 12–13). This emphasis on the macro-environment and the interdependencies of organismic, functional, and environmental effects constitutes a radical departure from both information processing and constructivist studies.

Although Brown (1979) has catalogued some of the ways the findings of ecological studies have complemented developmental psychology, few studies have been conducted among individuals with learning disorders that treat human learning as an adaptation to a natural environment with significant properties that have an impact on the learner. Arguments such as that advanced by Swanson (1988) that "broadening the information processing variables influencing the learning process" (p. 290) would lead to a rapprochement between the mechanistic and ecological traditions fail to respect the fundamentally conflicting premises (e.g., reductionism vs. holism) on which these flavors of cognitive science are based: Contextualism *cannot* be reduced to information processing. Although chocolate and strawberry may be mutually enhancing, they cannot be mixed together into one flavor without changing the nature of both.

Studies that have treated learning disorders as adaptations to significant environmental influences have frequently been associated with and reported in arguments for a paradigm shift to holism—a profoundly ecological position. Heshusius (1989), for example, reviewed a group of separate studies showing that observation of students in their natural environments can lead to explanations of their behavior that could not emerge in laboratory studies. Students who were labeled retarded on the basis of test scores, for example, turned out to be intelligent enough to plot their way out of a 24-hour supervised institution! Similarly, capable students were thought to be disabled learners because they adopted the goals of *not* working, *not* learning, and *not* cooperating in school. Finally, a group of "nonreading" and "nonwriting" high school students rewrote their history text when they were able to cast events in a personally meaningful light.

The instructional design changes that have resulted from whole language orientations in literacy instruction in mainstream and increasingly in special education settings are also ecologically sound—as is reciprocal teaching. Although information processing has enabled us to describe and understand the nature of many specific learning difficulties, there is no reason to assume that instruction must remediate such acknowledged deficits one by one.

Cognitive developmental instruction (Reid, 1988b) capitalizes on all aspects of the physical and social environment as they interact with the constantly shifting intellectual, affective, and motivational characteristics of the student. Cognitive developmental interventions

> are nearly always carried out in context and utilize higher order, meaningful information. Reading is taught with text that incorporates examples of whatever is to be learned rather than with word cards or exercise sheets. Handwriting and spelling are taught in the context of meaningful writing experiences—such as essays, reports, and letters—rather than as repetitive, copying assignments. Arithmetic is practiced using real-world problems rather than isolated facts. It is only when the information is both meaningful and contextualized that the procedural and conditional aspects of knowledge can be acquired. (pp. 62–63)

Furthermore, instruction is designed to provide an opportunity for learners to apply their knowledge, skills, strategies, interests, expectations, and so forth, as the starting point for achieving closer and closer approximations of expert performance. Student ownership and self-control constitute the suprastructure within which all instructional negotiations occur. Organismic, functional, and environmental effects are free to interact and are attented to conjointly in cognitive developmental instruction.

Postbehavioral Perspectives and Learning Disorders

As Bruner (1986) recently noted, psychological theories are not so much right or wrong as they are a question of "congruence with values that prevail in the culture" (p. 135). Ironically, one interesting phenomenon that contributed to the widespread acceptance of information processing theory was its appeal to adherents of biological constructivism. When the predominant orientation in the study of learning disorders was behaviorism, assimilation theorists were virtually disenfranchised, considered some small group doing research in "Piagetian theory"—interesting perhaps as a chapter for an edited volume, but certainly irrelevant to the mainstream. Because information processing was an assimilation theory easily comprehended by former behaviorists, however, it provided a vehicle for expressing a child-centered, cognitive position on learning disorders (cf. Reid, 1988b; Reid & Hresko, 1981). Information processing became the intersection of sets that added vitalism to what remained an essentially reductionist model. Now that the primary concerns among scientists interested in learning disorders have shifted from materials and lessons to the child's activity (Brown, Bransford, Ferrara, & Campione, 1983) and it is widely accepted that the human organism is inherently active and self-regulating, there appears to be a receptive forum for a new look at constructivism (e.g., Poplin, 1988a, 1988b), especially social constructivism (e.g., Brown & French, 1979). But whether it be social constructivism or an ecological approach, most researchers have now recognized the importance of studying human cognition in situ.

An analogy may serve to better illustrate this point. Doise (1987) recently criticized experimentation in American social psychology for attempting to explain social behavior in terms of processes that occur within an individual, partially neglecting interpersonal effects and almost entirely neglecting the connections between those and societal structures and processes. He argued that experimental results are influenced not only by the characteristics and activities of the individual, but also by interpersonal and situational variables, one's social position, and the beliefs, values, and norms associated with societal order.

Consequently, he called for an interdisciplinary, multilevel approach to social psychology experimentation.

A similar criticism might be leveled at research on learning disorders. Much of the existing literature has been directed toward processes that occur within the individual—the research task for which information processing appears to be best suited. Relatively few studies have addressed interpersonal variables, and fewer still have examined larger, environmental effects. What work has been done, has addressed each of these variables separately, although clearly they operate in tandem. This point is particularly important to the *treatment* of learning disorders: In the educational setting, all levels of variables operate in microcosm.

An ecological view is particularly important to the stance adopted by the proponents of holism who oppose (a) the behaviorism that still dominates special education assessment and instructional practices and (b) the reductionist, mechanistic information processing framework for research and theory building. The Vygotskian and other ecological approaches currently beginning to have an increased impact on the study of learning disorders in a variety of fields of inquiry are also consonant with the holistic point of view. Although holists are less enamored of quantification than the majority of American scientists, it appears that many trends apparent in American cognitive science are, with the obvious exception of the information processing perspective, coalescing with other movements within the new paradigm.

Conclusions

The study of learning disorders has been as much a part of the changes taking place in our conceptions of the purposes and goals of science as have many other areas of inquiry. Our work has increasingly become inter- or cross-disciplinary as well as multilevel. We have exchanged a focus on proximal, observable stimuli for interests that are proximal, organismic, and distal; observable and nonobservable; and contextually interdependent. Given that the exciting innovations in the assessment and treatment of learning disorders have been generated from nonbehavioral principles, it seems remiss that the majority of schools continue to cling to a system of instruction that embodies the simple S–R principles described earlier in this chapter. Where the results of our labors are actually being delivered to the population we profess to serve, we seem to be least accurate in our understanding of human nature and human learning—and vanilla is, most often, still the only flavor.

References

Brown, A. L. (1975). The development of memory: Knowing, knowing about knowing, and knowing how to know. In H. Reese (Ed.), *Advances in child development and behavior* (pp. 104–152). New York: Academic Press.

Brown, A. L. (1979). Learning and development: The problems of compatibility, access and induction. *Human Development, 25,* 89–115.

Brown, A. L., Bransford, J. D., Ferrara, R. A., & Campione, J. C. (1983). Learning, remembering, and understanding. In J. H. Flavell & E. M. Markman (Eds.), *Handbook of child psychology* (Vol. 3, pp. 77–166). New York: Wiley.

Brown, A. L., & Campione, J. C. (1986). Psychological theory and the study of learning disabilities. *American Psychologist, 41,* 1059–1068.

Brown, A. L., & French, L. A. (1979). The zone of potential development: Implications for intelligence testing in the year 2000. *Intelligence, 3,* 253–271.

Brown, A. L., & Palincsar, A. S. (1982). Inducing strategic learning from texts by means of informed, self-control training. *Topics in Learning and Learning Disabilities, 2,* 1–17.

Bruner, J. (1986). *Actual minds, possible worlds.* Cambridge, MA: Harvard University Press.

Campione, J. C. (1989). Assisted assessment: A taxonomy of approaches and an outline of strengths and weaknesses. *Journal of Learning Disabilities, 22,* 151–165.

Doise, W. (1987). *Levels of explanation in social psychology.* Cambridge, England: Cambridge University Press.

Englert, C. S., & Lichter, A. (1982). Using statement-pie to teach reading and writing skills. *Teaching Exceptional Children, 14,* 164–170.

Flavell, J. H. (1985). *Cognitive development.* Englewood Cliffs, NJ: Prentice-Hall.

Gallagher, J. M., & Reid, D. K. (1983). *The learning theory of Piaget and Inhelder.* Austin, TX: PRO-ED.

Gavelek, J. R., & Palincsar, A. S. (1988). Contextualism as an alternative worldview of learning disabilities: A response to Swanson's "Toward a metatheory of learning disabilities." *Journal of Learning Disabilities, 21,* 278–281.

Gelfand, H. (1985). The interface between laboratory and naturalistic cognition. In T. M. Shlechter & M. P. Toglia (Eds.), *New directions in cognitive science* (pp. 276–293). Norwood, NJ: Ablex.

Heshusius, L. (1989). The Newtonian mechanistic paradigm, special education, and contours of alternatives: An overview. *Journal of Learning Disabilities, 22,* 403–415.

Inhelder, B., Sinclair, H., & Bovet, M. (1974). *Learning and the development of cognition.* Cambridge, MA: Harvard University Press.

Kail, R., & Bisanz, J. (1982). Information processing and cognitive development. In H. W. Reese (Ed.), *Advances in child development and behavior* (pp. 45–81). New York: Academic Press.

Kronick, D. (1988). *New approaches to learning disabilities: Cognitive, meta-cognitive, and holistic.* Philadelphia: Grune & Stratton.

Lachman, R., Lachman, J. L., & Butterfield, E. C. (1979). *Cognitive psychology and information processing: An introduction.* Hillsdale, NJ: Erlbaum.

Lorenz, K. Z. (1981). *The foundations of ethology.* New York: Springer-Verlag.

Mandler, G. (1985). *Cognitive psychology: An essay in cognitive science.* Hillsdale, NJ: Erlbaum.

Meltzer, L. J. (1987). Abstract reasoning in a specific group of perceptually impaired children. *Journal of Genetic Psychology, 132,* 185–206.

Neisser, U. (1976). General, academic and artificial intelligence. In L. Resnick (Ed.), *Intelligence* (pp. 78–120). Hillsdale, NJ: Erlbaum.

Neisser, U. (1985). Toward an ecologically oriented cognitive science. In T. M. Shlechter & M. P. Toglia (Eds.), *New directions in cognitive science* (pp. 17–32). Norwood, NJ: Ablex.

Palincsar, A. S. (1986). The role of dialogue in scaffolded instruction. *Educational Psychologist, 21,* 73–98.

Palincsar, A. S., & Brown, A. L. (1984). Reciprocal teaching of comprehension fostering and comprehension monitoring activities. *Cognition and Instruction, 1,* 117–175.

Palincsar, A. S., & Brown, A. L. (1986). Interactive teaching to promote independent reading from text. *Reading Teacher, 39,* 771–777.

Palincsar, A. S., & Brown, A. L., & Martin, S. M. (1987). Peer interaction in reading comprehension instruction. *Educational Psychologist, 22,* 231–253.

Pearson, P. D., & Gallagher, M. C. (1983). The instruction of reading comprehension. *Contemporary Educational Psychology, 8,* 317–344.

Piaget, J. (1930). *The child's conception of physical causality.* London: Kegan Paul.

Piaget, J. (1952). *The origins of intelligence in children.* New York: International Universities Press.

Piaget, J. (1954). *The construction of reality in the child.* New York: Basic Books.

Piaget, J. (1971). *Biology and knowledge: An essay on the relations between organic regulations and cognitive processes.* Chicago: The University of Chicago Press.

Piaget, J. (1977). *The development of thought: Equilibration of cognitive structures.* New York: Viking Penguin.

Piaget, J. (1978). *Success and understanding.* Cambridge, MA: Harvard University Press.

Poplin, M. S. (1988a). Holistic/constructivist principles of the teaching/learning process: Implications for the field of learning disabilities. *Journal of Learning Disabilities, 21,* 401–416.

Poplin, M. S. (1988b). The reductionist fallacy in learning disabilities: Replicating the past by reducing the present. *Journal of Learning Disabilities, 21,* 389–400.

Reid, D. K. (1988a). Reflections on the pragmatics of a paradigm shift. *Journal of Learning Disabilities, 21,* 417–420.

Reid, D. K. (1988b). *Teaching the learning disabled: A cognitive developmental approach.* Boston: Allyn & Bacon.

Reid, D. K. (1989). The role of cooperative learning in comprehensive instruction. *The Journal of Reading, Writing, and Learning Disabilities—International, 4,* 229–242.

Reid, D. K. (1991). Assessment strategies inspired by genetic epistemology. In H. L. Swanson (Ed.), *Handbook on the assessment of learning disabilities: Theory, research, and practice,* (pp. 249–263). San Diego: College-Hill.

Reid, D. K., & Hresko, W. P. (1981). *A cognitive approach to learning disabilities.* Austin, TX: PRO-ED.

Reid, D. K., Hresko, W. P., & Swanson, H. L. (in press). *A cognitive approach to learning disabilities.* Austin, TX: PRO-ED.

Reid, D. K., Knight-Arest, I., & Hresko, W. P. (1981). Cognitive development in learning disabled children. In J. Gottlieb & S. S. Strichart (Eds.), *Developmental theories and research in learning disabilities* (pp. 104–154). Baltimore: University Park Press.

Shlechter, T. M., & Toglia, M. P. (1985). Ecological directions in the study of cognition. *New directions in cognitive science* (pp. 1–15). Norwood, NJ: Ablex.

Skinner, B. F. (1966). *The behavior of organisms: An experimental analysis.* Englewood Cliffs, NJ: Prentice-Hall.

Stone, C. A. (1985). Vygotsky's developmental model and the concept of proleptic instruction: Some implications for theory and research in the field of learning disabilities. *Research Communications in Psychology, Psychiatry, and Behavior, 10,* 129–152.

Stone, C. A., & Wertsch, J. V. (1984). A social interactional analysis of learning disabilities remediation. *Journal of Learning Disabilities, 17,* 194–199.

Swanson, H. L. (1987). Information processing theory and learning disabilities: An overview. *Journal of Learning Disabilities, 20,* 3–7.

Swanson, H. L. (1988). Comments, countercomments, and new thoughts. *Journal of Learning Disabilities, 21,* 289–298.

Thomas, C. C., Englert, C. S., & Gregg, S. (1987). An analysis of errors and strategies in the expository writing of learning disabled students. *Remedial and Special Education, 8,* 21–30.

Vygotsky, L. S. (1987). *Thinking and speech.* In R. W. Rieber & A. S. Carton (Eds.), *The collected works of L. S. Vygotsky, Vol. 1, Problems of general psychology* (pp. 39–288). New York: Plenum.

2

The Origin of Strategy Deficits in Children with Learning Disabilities: A Social Constructivist Perspective

C. Addison Stone
Lydia Conca

Since Torgesen's seminal argument 15 years ago (Torgesen, 1977), both researchers and educators in the field of special education have accepted a characterization of many children with learning disabilities as being deficient in the acquisition and/or use of cognitive strategies (Swanson, 1989b). Although this view of the child with learning disabilities (LD) has gone a long way toward balancing the previous tendency to postulate process deficits at the root of all problems evidenced by this population, it is not without its own excesses and unanswered questions. One of the most important unresolved issues relates to the origin of strategy deficiencies. Two potentially complementary views on this issue relate strategy deficiencies to motivational

Preparation of this chapter was supported in part by a grant from the National Institutes of Health (Grant No. R01 NS26244-01). We would like to thank Joanne Carlisle for her comments on an earlier draft.

factors (e.g., a pattern of learned helplessness) on the one hand, or to a processing "bottleneck" caused by underlying processing inefficiencies on the other hand (cf. Torgesen & Licht, 1983). In this chapter we explore some issues related to a third view. In particular, we examine the conceptual and empirical issues related to the role of altered social interactions in inefficient cognitive performance. In doing so, the goal is not to argue for the exclusive validity of a single factor. Indeed, as we will argue later, the theoretical framework that guides this discussion can encompass all three factors as contributing causes of strategy deficiencies.

The discussion of these issues will be guided by a social constructivist perspective on human behavior (Forman, 1989; Rogoff, 1990). This perspective, most closely associated with the work of Vygotsky (1978, 1987), views the development of the child as inseparable from social interchanges within a cultural context. This approach has a great deal to offer in an attempt to understand the nature and origins of strategy deficiencies in children with LD. Furthermore, because the most effective intervention is based on a firm understanding of the dynamics of the problem at hand, this perspective may ultimately lead to refinements in our approach to helping the child with LD.

This chapter is divided into four sections. In the first section we provide a context by presenting a brief characterization of strategy deficiencies in the LD population. We also describe current approaches to the study of these issues. In the second section we discuss some of the major assumptions of the social constructivist perspective, focusing mainly on the work of Vygotsky and his students. We also discuss Vygotsky's positions on the nature of childhood exceptionalities and appropriate approaches to intervention. In the third section we examine some of the empirical evidence relevant to the social origins of the strategy deficiencies of children with LD. This includes a review of research on parent-child and teacher-child interaction. In the final section we discuss the implications of the issues raised for future research.

The Child with LD as Strategy Deficient

The view of the child with learning disabilities as strategy deficient has been amply demonstrated over the past 15 years. It is well documented that, as a group, children with LD recruit fewer strategies spontaneously and use strategies less often than same-age nondisabled peers. Now that this general characteristic has gained widespread acceptance, there is movement in the field toward refining the concept of strategic deficiency. An emerging consensus holds that children with LD experience a range of strategy problems rather than a simple failure to deploy strategies (Gerber, 1983; Kolligan & Sternberg, 1987; Swanson, 1987; Torgesen & Licht, 1983; Wong, 1985b).

Characterizations of Strategy Deficiency

The strategic deficiencies shown by individuals with LD fall into at least two general classes. One class includes problems of strategy *selection:* Children with LD often rely on simpler, less efficient strategies compared to same-age nondisabled peers (Conca, 1989; Fleischner, Nuzum & Garnett, reported in Connor, 1983; Graham & Freeman, 1985; Pistono, 1980). A second class of deficiencies includes problems of strategy *execution.* Here, chosen strategies are applied inexpertly: Children with LD sometimes fail to implement strategies in a fluid, controlled fashion, (Ford, Pelham, & Ross, 1984; Swanson, 1983).

Some researchers view children's failure to select and apply strategies efficiently as a failure of metacognition (Paris & Lindauer, 1982: Pressley, Goodchild, Fleet, Zajchowski, & Evans, 1987; Reeve & Brown, 1985; Wong, 1983). Metacognitive failures of this kind may take the form of a failure of knowing when previously used strategies are useful in new situations, knowing when and how to modify well-used strategies when they prove ineffective, and knowing when to abandon them in favor of new, more powerful tools.

One component of metacognition is awareness of one's own skill, and the task goals and strategies needed for efficient performance (Flavell & Wellman, 1977). Some researchers who favor metacognitive explanations propose that strategy acquisition is driven by children's understanding of the purposes strategies serve, the tasks for which strategies are appropriate, and the relative gains and effort involved in using classes of strategies (Borkowski & Kurtz, 1984). This argument suggests that the preference of children with LD for immature strategies reflects a failure to appreciate their value relative to more sophisticated strategies.

Another important component of metacognition comprises executive control functions such as predicting, planning, and checking (Brown & DeLoache, 1978). These routines are also believed to drive strategy acquisition (Reeve & Brown, 1985). For example, the increased tendency of the developing child to analyze a problem to determine whether similarities exist between this and previous problems is believed to maximize chances that previously used strategies are generalized to new situations (Brown, Bransford, Ferrara, & Campione, 1983). This view suggests that children with LD may have difficulty planning sequences of actions attuned to task demands, monitoring actions to determine whether progress toward the goal is made, and adjusting actions accordingly.

Some researchers are reluctant to attribute advances in strategy acquisition to either of these two general factors (Chi, 1978; Naus & Ornstein, 1983). These researchers propose that children's growing knowledge of their world and of language influences the emergence of strategies. Similarly, Swanson (1986) suggested that lack of knowledge on the part of children with LD, or their different representation of that knowledge, may place restrictions on the strategies that can be used.

Most contemporary accounts of strategy acquisition incorporate tenets from both orientations to explain developmental and individual differences in strategy use (Brown et al., 1983; Paris, Lipson, & Wixson, 1983; Swanson, 1984b; Torgesen & Licht, 1983). However, the accounts vary in their emphases, and thus vary in conceptions of the source of developmental and individual differences in strategy use. How normal-learning children profit from experience and subsequently learn to regulate their behavior more efficiently is an issue of much debate. Similarly, why children with LD often fail to recruit and apply strategies efficiently is subject to considerable discussion. Despite ongoing attempts to resolve many issues, there are some points of agreement. Strategy choice is believed to be influenced by children's perceptions of an action's utility and the ease with which the action can be applied. These issues are addressed in the next two sections.

Strategy Utility and Consequences of Previous Behavior

It is widely believed that children's judgments of the adequacy of past actions influence how they meet the demands of future tasks (cf. Brown & Reeve, 1987; Kail, 1979; Pressley et al., 1987). When children engage in goal-directed behavior, they often obtain feedback about how well their behavior served its intended purpose. This feedback furnishes children information about the significance of their actions. Sometimes children perceive actions as useful and worth the time and effort. These actions are likely to be used again. At other times actions are viewed by children as lacking value, or as too time-consuming to be of worth. These actions are likely to be modified or abandoned. Thus, perceptions of a strategy's value and economy are believed to alter children's knowledge about the efficacy of past actions and to set the stage for behavior when similar tasks are encountered again (Paris & Cross, 1983).

This sketch, although overly simplified, is not controversial. Strategy maintenance and strategy transfer are enhanced when children possess knowledge about the value of the strategy for improving performance (Borkowski, Levers, & Gruenenfelder, 1976; Kennedy & Miller, 1976; Moynahan, 1978: Paris, Newman, & McVey, 1982), and judge past performance as adequate (Brown & Barclay, 1976; Lodico, Ghatala, Levin, Pressley, & Bell, 1983). For example, Moynahan (1978) reported that children who correctly assessed that they remembered better and attributed their better performance to the strategy they were using, utilized that strategy more often. Lodico et al. (1983) found that simply prompting 7- and 8-year-old children to assess their memory performance following instructed use of single- and multi-item rehearsal was sufficient to support the transfer of the more effective rehearsal strategy to another task. Children's tendency to evaluate and monitor their performance is therefore believed to provide them important information about the differential utility and applicability of strategies (Pressley et al., 1987; Paris & Cross, 1983). This feedback is thought to have its effect on maintenance and transfer by enriching awareness of the purposes and relative values of classes and strategies (Borkowski & Kurtz, 1984).

Some researchers have proposed that repeated interactions between children and adults are catalysts for learning about the applicability of strategies (cf. Reeve & Brown, 1985; Paris, Newman, & Jacobs, 1985). According to this view, parents, teachers, and friends introduce children to intentional behavior by jointly participating with them in problem solving. For example, in everyday settings, parents often ask questions about misplaced objects and, thus, prompt children to recognize when remembering is important. Through guided interactions such as these, it is believed that children come to realize that their behavior (or the behavior of others) causes successful or unsuccessful outcomes.

The above suggests that the strategic inefficiency demonstrated by some children with LD may be traced to their difficulty using feedback provided by other people or their own behavior. This view is compatible with the claims that children with LD often have difficulty gauging the adequacy of their own performance (Swanson, 1987) and attributing the outcomes of performance to their own behavior (Licht & Kistner, 1986).

Inadequate self-assessments may contribute to failure on the part of children with LD to choose effective strategies. It is often claimed that these children have difficulty monitoring and evaluating their performance. As a consequence some children with LD may derive incomplete or inaccurate knowledge about the purposes and relative values of strategies.

Inadequate self-assessment may contribute to the strategic inefficiency displayed by children with LD in another way. It is often claimed that children with LD attribute task success to factors beyond their control, such as luck or ease of the task, rather than to factors within their control, such as effort (Butkowsky & Willows, 1980; Pearl, 1982). As a consequence, some children with LD may fail to attribute even successful performance to their own behavior (Licht & Kistner, 1986).

Through repeated experience children build beliefs about their own competence, the value of alternate actions, and expectations for success. These beliefs have profound effects on how tasks are approached (Paris & Cross, 1983; Pressley et al., 1987). Failures to appreciate the effects and the relative values of strategies may contribute strategic inefficiency in some children with LD. Still other children with LD, however, may understand the value of a strategy, but find that the effort involved in using the strategy outweighs the benefits.

Strategy Effort and Automaticity

It is commonly assumed that before an action can be used as a strategic means, the component skills that the action comprises must be well mastered in their own right. This proposal is based on work of both American and Soviet researchers (Guttentag, 1984; Smirnov & Zinchenko, 1969). These researchers speculate that the mental effort requirement of strategy use influences strategy selection. According to this view, children's incomplete mastery over the component skills that constitute more effective strategies dispose them to preferring simpler strategies. For example, it is widely claimed that young children are not as adept as older children at repeating to themselves sequences of words in a fluent, controlled fashion. This difficulty is often attributed to young children's difficulty with rapid naming of familiar objects (Dempster, 1981). Young children's difficulty naming successive sets of items is thought to dispose them to using nominal, rote-like naming rehearsal strategies. In contrast, the greater automaticity with which older children can execute these same component skills is believed to contribute to their inclination to rehearse multi-items. An additional factor in increasing strategy sophistication, of course, relates to the integration of component skills into more complex strategies, via either explicit instruction or implicit experience. Thus, developmental progress toward mastering the component skills, as well as the subskill integrations that make up more refined strategies, are thought to contribute to decreases in the mental effort requirement of strategy use.

The above suggests that young children use strategies that are relatively easy to execute, and avoid using strategies that are effortful, challenging, and attention-demanding. It is well documented that children with LD are slow to produce the names of familar objects (Denckla

& Rudel, 1976; Lorsbach & Gray, 1985). Given that the memory strategy of rehearsal requires one to recognize and subvocalize stimulus names quickly and accurately, it stands to reason that these children will need to exert considerable effort to use the strategy. Some children with LD may therefore not only be slow to develop mature memory strategies, but also show a preference for less effective, visually based strategies that circumvent the need to reproduce item names (Conca, 1989; Kastner & Rickarts, 1974; Swanson, 1984c).

Toward an Integrated View of Strategy Deficiencies

Several views regarding the reasons for strategy inefficiency among children with LD have been discussed. One view is that children with LD may not have completely mastered the subcomponent skills that make up effective strategies. Thus, some children with LD may fail to use effective strategies not only because they do not know, understand, or think to use a strategy, but because the strategy requires them to expend relatively large amounts of mental effort, compared to nondisabled peers. A second view is that children with LD may have difficulty using feedback provided by the immediate consequences of their own behavior. Some children with LD may have difficulty assessing the adequacy of previous actions and thus may be slow to acquire knowledge about the purposes and relative values of classes of strategies. Other children with LD may fail to attribute successful performance to their own efforts, and thus fail to appreciate the effects of strategies.

Finally, a third view of strategy deficiency is that some deficiencies may result from impoverished or maladaptive interactions with significant others in their home and school environments. It is this third implication that we will explore in the remainder of this chapter. In the chapter we will examine the utility of a particular theoretical framework that may prove useful in integrating the multiple causal factors discussed above, and in identifying crucial causal factors not highlighted by past frameworks. This framework is referred to below as social constructivism.

The Social Constructivist Perspective

The phrase "social constructivist" characterizes a family of theoretical frameworks that share the central assumption that human development is in large part constituted by the pattern of interactions instantiating one's culture (Rogoff, 1990). Unlike other constructivist frameworks, such as Piaget's, the social constructivist framework places minimal emphasis on a semiautonomous, individualistic constructive process. Instead, it is assumed that the successive cognitive, motivational, and emotional organizations of the developmental continuum are the creation of the complex interplay of individual, institutional, and social interactional factors in a particular historical and cultural context. The best known of these frameworks is that of Lev Vygotsky (1978, 1987; Wertsch, 1985b). In this section we describe selected assumptions of Vygotsky's framework and focus on those aspects of the framework that are most central to a discussion of possible social interactional origins of strategy deficiencies.

Vygotsky on the Nature and Path of Development

Vygotsky's perspective on the nature and development of human functioning differs from other influential perspectives in its central emphasis on the formative role of social relations and culturally defined activities in shaping the path of development. Much of this work has recently become familiar to psychologists and educators, and several good sources are now available, including recent translations of the unabridged edition (Vygotsky, 1987) of what is perhaps Vygotsky's most central book, *Thought and Language* (1962). There are also several excellent secondary sources (e.g., Rogoff & Wertsch, 1984; Wertsch, 1985a, 1985b). In the present context, no attempt will be made to provide a comprehensive picture of Vygotsky's framework. Instead, the discussion concentrates on those aspects of Vygotsky's theory that are central to the application of his general developmental framework to the unique case of exceptional children. The most important concepts in this regard are the distinction between the natural and cultural lines of development, the distinction between elementary and higher psychological functions, the notion of interfunctional connections, the movement from social to individual control of behavior, and the role of language and other semiotic systems and social congentions in fostering development. The following discussion provides a brief description of each of these issues.

Perhaps the most important construct in Vygotsky's account of human development in his distinction between the natural and cultural lines of development. In drawing this distinction, Vygotsky was attempting to separate a set of human capabilities that he believed were biologically based from a set of capabilities that he considered to be cultural products. Examples of functions within the natural line of development include basic sensory capacities, the orienting aspect of attention, and recognition memory functions. In contrast, functions such as selective attention and voluntary memory, assumed by many to be later extensions of natural development, were considered by Vygotsky to be cultural products. Closely related to this distinction is Vygotsky's differentiation between elementary and higher psychological functions. In fact, the examples provided above of the natural and cultural lines of development fit nicely into this distinction as well. In addition to characterizing elementary psychological functions as part of the natural line of development, Vygotsky characterized them as relatively isolated one from the other and as involving no conscious intentionality. In contrast, higher psychological functions were said to be cultural products and to involve the intentional allocation of psychological resources. In addition, higher psychological functions were considered to be, at least in part, the result of increasing interfunctional connections.

As his theory matured, Vygotsky placed increasing emphasis on the notion of connections among psychological functions as a central aspect of later development. In his discussions of this issue, it is possible to distinguish two aspects of this increasing connectivity, although ultimately Vygotsky saw them as manifestations of the same phenomenon. One aspect involves the interrelations amount cognitive functions themselves, and the second involves connections between affective and cognitive functions. The first emphasis is evident in Vygotsky's (1978) discussions of the nature of higher psychological functions, in which he placed considerable emphasis, for example, on the increasing use of verbal mediation to control attention and memory. In later discussions of increasing interfunctional connections, Vygotsky (1987, in press) stressed the importance of relations between affective and cognitive functions in addition to interrelations among cognitive functions themselves. He came to see higher psychological functions as involving a combination of intellect and volition and, in one place, noted that the changing relationship between affect and intellect is "the *most* essential thing in the whole psychological development of a child" (Vygotsky, in press, p. 442). It is important to stress again, however, that for Vygotsky this changing relationship was culturally constituted, rather than a naturally evolving emotional or cognitive maturity.

As is now widely appreciated, Vygotsky emphasized the role of adult-child interactions in the fostering of higher psychological functions.[1]

---

[1]Vygotsky devoted considerable effort to describing the various social mechanisms involved in the development of higher psychological functions. It is impossible to discuss all of these mechanisms in the present context. Instead, the discussion will focus on a subset of the issues most useful in interpreting the discussion to follow on parent-child and teacher-child interactions in children with LD. See Wertsch (1985b) for a useful summary, and Minick (1989) for a historical overview of Vygotsky's evolving views on this issue.

Vygotsky viewed these interactions as constituting a "zone of proximal development" (ZPD) within which the child is stimulated to adopt a more sophisticated perspective on a situation, or to make use of a more sophisticated strategic approach to a task. These interactions, involving parents, teachers, or other significant knowledgeable adults or older children, were seen by Vygotsky as essential sources of development, and it is these interactions that are the focus of the later sections of this chapter. It is important to point out, however, that these interactions form only one subset of the significant sociocultural influences on development. Of equal importance, but less often stressed, are the numerous institutional conventions and practices inherent in the informal day-to-day activities in any society[2] (see Forman, Minick, and Stone, in press, for discussions of this aspect of Vygotsky's work).

Discussions of Vygotsky's views on the role of adult-child interaction in fostering child development are often associated with the metaphor of scaffolding (Palincsar, 1986; Wood, Bruner, & Ross, 1976). The central notion here is that adults provide for children the temporary support they need to accomplish a task beyond their current capabilities, and that, as a result of carefully calibrated support, children gradually take over responsibility for the task. This metaphor captures a great deal of what is inherent in Vygotsky's notion of the ZPD. One central component of the notion often de-emphasized in discussions of scaffolding, however, is the role of language and other semiotic systems in facilitating the transfer of responsibility (Stone, in press). In these discussions, the adult's language is seen, quite reasonably, as one means of providing structural support for the child (via verbal directives). However, Vygotsky saw language as much more than a temporary support in these situations. Instead, he viewed the dialogue between the adult and child as embodying the very strategy to be mastered by the child, and he conceived of the transfer of responsibility as a process of appropriation of the dialogue by the child. Due perhaps to his early death, Vygotsky did not provide an account of the mechanism of this appropriation. Subsequent work by his colleagues and other scholars has led, however, to the beginnings of the specification of these mechanisms. Central to these recent accounts is a focus on the semiotic devices inherent in the dialogue with the ZPD (Stone, 1985; in press; Wertsch, 1985b; Wertsch & Stone, 1985). Thus, if this analysis is cor-

---

[2]Although this issue will not be discussed in any detail, it is possible that the nature of their basic disability, as well as societal accommodations to that disability, might well result for some individuals with LD in a selective exposure to these practices. For example, peer activities that involve oral and written language skills or perceptual-motor skills, such as the school newspaper or organized athletics, might be embarrassing for some children with LD. The implications of this fact warrant examination.

rect, careful attention to the dialogue (both verbal and nonverbal) involved in adult-child interaction is crucial for an understanding of the implications of the interaction (Stone, 1989). We will return to this point later in the chapter.

Vygotsky on Childhood Exceptionalities

Although many of Vygotsky's central assumptions concerning the nature of normal development are now familiar, at least in part, it is less widely known that Vygotsky wrote a great deal about childhood exceptionalities. Indeed, for many years Vygotsky was actively involved in both clinical work and research with a wide range of exceptional children, including those with physical handicaps, emotional disturbance, and mental retardation. Over a 15-year period, he published a large number of papers concerned with both theoretical issues and practical concerns related to the assessment and education of exceptional children (Vygotsky, in press). He viewed his work both as a contribution to a significant social issue and as a window into the dynamics of normal human functioning.

As would be expected, Vygotsky's views on exceptionalities placed considerable emphasis on the role of social factors in both etiology and treatment. In considering the nature of a given exceptionality, Vygotsky made use of his distinction between the natural and cultural lines of development. In describing the symptomatology of a given exceptionality, he was careful to distinguish between what he saw as direct and indirect effects of the handicap. Direct effects were related to those lower level aspects of functioning that constitute the natural line of development. These effects, such as sensory losses, were assumed to be neurologically based. In constrast, impoverished conceptual thinking in deaf persons or strategic deficiencies in individuals with mild retardation were conceived of as indirect effects and as part of the cultural line of development. Such indirect effects were seen as the result of well-intentioned, but misguided social and educational accommodations to the exceptional child.

Vygotsky's writings on exceptionalities emphasized the secondary or socially based aspects of a child's symptomatology. He saw these secondary manifestations as avoidable results of a mismatch between the psychological structure of a child with handicaps and the structure of society. By virtue of being different, exceptional children are treated differently, that is, they are embedded in a different social network. Vygotsky saw this consequence of a handicap as more devastating than the primary disability itself. With respect to blind and deaf children, for example, he believed that "a loss of vision or hearing means, therefore, first and foremost the failure of serious social functions, the degeneration of societal ties, and the disruption of all behavioral systems" (Vygotsky, in press, p. 118). To appreciate the implications of this point from Vygotsky's perspective, it is important to consider his stress on the role of society in providing cultural tools (i.e., social practices, symbol systems) to extend and transform the capacities of the individual. In the case of children with intact elementary processes, there is a naturally evolved match between the child's capabilities and society's supports and challenges. This is not the case for exceptional children. One obvious example used by Vygotsky is the stress placed by society on the use of oral (as opposed to manual, or sign) language for communication and social regulation, and the consequences for deaf children.

Although Vygotsky did not write about the population with LD, his discussion of children with mild retardation provides a useful perspective on strategy deficiencies that is perhaps applicable to many individuals in the population with LD. Vygotsky believed children with MR were more impaired in higher psychological functions than in lower functions, and that this situation was the result of cultural underdevelopment due to lack of educational challenge. He referred to the child with MR as suffering from a "secondary developmental passivity" (p. 238), or a deficiency in "volition" or "will." Thus, he saw mild retardation as both a cognitive and an affective handicap, one that was due, in part, to a mismatch between the exceptional child's needs and the support provided by the societal institutions around the child.

Perhaps Vygotsky's most interesting contribution to a framework for thinking about handicapped individuals is his concept of "compensation." In describing a handicap, Vygotsky stressed that, although a handicap involves certain limitations in functioning (related primarily to deficits in lower level, or elementary functions), it is also a stimulus for reorganization of functions into new, often adaptive functional systems. In addition, the handicap may stimulate intensified advancement or heightened development of other functions (primarily higher psychological functions). In this context, Vygotsky stressed the role of sociocultural experience in the fostering of new interfunctional connections. Thus, at root, his notion of compensation is both a biological and a cultural construct.

Implications for an Examination of the Nature and Treatment of Strategy Deficiencies

In summary, two fundamental principles underlie Vygotsky's views on the nature and treatment of childhood exceptionalities. First, the principle of compensation leads to a view of exceptionality that stresses the role of sociocultural factors in the genesis and treatment of exceptionalities, and that emphasizes the potential for restructuring of the capacities of the exceptional individual. Second, the emphasis on the integral nature of cognitive, affective, and motivational factors leads to a wholistic view of the child. If these principles are accepted as important components of our view of strategy deficiencies, it follows that a discussion of the nature and origins of such deficiencies in the population with LD would benefit from an examination of the role of social and motivational factors. This conclusion is, of course, entirely consistent with the views of numerous other writers (e.g., Torgesen, 1977; Torgesen & Licht, 1983). What a social constructivist position can add, however, is a new set of analytic tools for examining the role of these factors, and a fresh perspective on the key issues in need of additional scrutiny. For example, this perspective places more emphasis on the functional quality of adult-child interactions than on their frequency, or on the mere presence of specific interactional components, such as questions or commands. Similarly, more emphasis is placed on the discourse characteristics of the interactions than on their content, though the latter is clearly important as well. Finally, the Vygotskian perspective provides a conceptual framework for integrating individual and societal issues in the study of disabilities. In the next section, we will illustrate the value of this perspective in the context of a review of existing studies of social influences on the development of strategy deficiencies.

Social Factors in the Etiology of Strategy Deficiencies

Although it does not deny the existence of biologically based exceptional conditions in childhood, the social constructivist perspective places considerable emphasis on the role of sociocultural factors in atypical cognitive development. The present section incorporates a review of research on the instructional environment of the child with LD. In this context, the environment is viewed broadly to include the special education curriculum and its explicit and implicit expectations, teacher-child interaction in both the resource and mainstream settings, and parent-child interaction in the home setting. The goal is to examine the quality of the "instructional" environment provided to the child with LD compared to that provided to a normally achieving child. Then, the discussion will turn to an evaluation of the implications of these differences within the context of the social constructivist perspective.

Parent-Child Interaction

There has been a slow but steady stream of studies of parent-child interaction involving children with LD. The majority of these studies have focused on children with oral language impairments. Most of the studies have involved observations of dyads in semistructured settings, and most have included direct comparisons to dyads including matched normally developing peers. The majority of the studies were not conducted within the social constructivist framework. Indeed, many of the questions posed by, and much of the methodology dictated by, the social constructivist framework have not been directly examined in this work. To highlight the types of issues that might be addressed by social constructivism, the discussion will focus first, in some detail, on one study within this framework. Then, the questions, methodologies, and findings of the other studies can be more easily viewed in that context.

The one study conducted explicitly within a Vygotskian framework was focused on children with language impairment (LI). Sammarco (1984; Wertsch & Sammarco, 1985) contrasted the interactions of six children with LI and six control children with their mothers in the context of a model-copy task. The two groups of children were matched for age, nonverbal IQ on the Hiskey-Nebraska (Hiskey, 1966), and socioeconomic status (SES). All of the children with LI had receptive language disorders. The dyads were videotaped during a 20-minute session, in which the mothers were told to assist their children in making their own copy of a toy airport scene. A model of the scene to be constructed was placed in front of the mother. The scene consisted of a base depicting an airport hangar and runway, and an arrangement of cars, helicopters, and airplanes varying in color and size. The child was given a base and set of vehicles identical to those in the mother's display, as well as several distractor vehicles.

The coding of the mothers' interactive style involved three levels of decisions. First, for each object to be placed in the array, the author coded who was physically responsible for its actual placement in the array. Second, for those pieces placed by the child, Sammarco coded whether or not the mother provided assistance in determining the location of the object (in Vygotsky's terms, whether "self-" or "other-regulation" was involved). Finally, in instances involving other-regulation, the author coded what type of assistance was provided by the mother. Two types of assistance were noted. "Direct" assistance involved instances of explicit directives, such as, "The helicopter goes over here." In contrast, "indirect" assistance involved instructions that presupposed certain aspects of the general "game plan." For example, the mother might ask, "What goes next to the red plane?" a question that presupposes knowledge of the role of the model airport scene in determining the "correct" location of each piece. Sammarco argued that it is instances of indirect assistance that provide the greatest learning challenge for the child, and that lead to maximal learning. A similar argument has been made elsewhere (Stone, 1989; Stone & Wertsch, 1984; Wertsch, 1979).

The results of the study indicated that the LI mothers assumed direct responsibility for placing pieces in the array significantly more often (21% of the pieces) than the control mothers (3%). In addition, the LI mothers took responsibility for checking the model to determine correct object placement significantly more often (39% vs. 0% of the objects).

Sammarco interpreted these findings as indicating that the LI mothers provided more direct assistance than was necessary, thereby depriving their children of significant learning experiences. She also provided other informal evidence of interaction patterns in the LI dyads that may not be conducive to maximal learning. For example, whereas the control mothers tended to lead their children to place all members of a given object class (e.g., helicopters) in their appropriate places in the array before moving to another class, the LI mothers tended to jump from class to class. In a related pattern, when a child with LI failed to select the object specified or implied by the mother's request, the mother either told the child that it was incorrect with no explanation, or abandoned the attempt to place the initially intended object and simply showed the child where to put the one actually picked up. Sammarco termed these behaviors "ineffective other-regulation" and interpreted them as providing "a confusing and disorganized language-learning environment" (Sammarco, 1984, p. 190). In this context, it is important to note that the behaviors of the LI mothers showed no clear relation to their child's performance on an informal measure of task-relevant vocabulary. Thus, it is difficult to argue that the mothers were acting solely in accordance with their sensitivity to their child's need for greater structure. We will address this issue in more detail below.

Several important principles of a Vygotskian approach to analyzing adult-child interaction are evident in Sammarco's study. Of most importance is Sammarco's reliance on a functional analysis of the interaction patterns. Working from a detailed analysis of the goal structure of the task at hand, Sammarco was able to map out crucial subcomponents of the appropriate task strategy, and to track the child's success and the degree of maternal assistance with each subcomponent. The type of assistance was then codable in terms of its fit with the superordinate goal and with the child's immediate needs. Second, the nature of maternal assistance was analyzed in accordance with Vygotskian principles of semiotic medication, with particular emphasis on the communicational contingencies involved (Stone, 1989).

The following pages provide an analysis of other recent studies of parent-child interaction. The goals of this analysis are twofold: first, to provide a summary of recent work in the area and, second, to interpret this work in light of the Vygotskian principles presented earlier and embodied in varying degrees in Sammarco's study. The interactional studies are grouped into two categories: those that involve children termed "language-impaired" (mostly preschoolers), and those that involve children labeled "learning disabled" (mostly school-age children). The separation of the studies of these two groups of children is not intended to imply that the two populations are not related. Indeed, a language impairment can be seen as one specific type of learning disability, one that leads ultimately to significant academic difficulties (Catts, 1989). However, although many children with LD are known to exhibit oral language difficulties, such difficulties are not necessarily present in children with LD. Thus, keeping these studies separate is useful in distinguishing possible relations between child characteristics and interactional patterns.

The results of these studies are discussed in the context of research concerning parental perceptions of children with LD and their instructional needs. This work allows a more direct consideration of the issue of the functional utility of the interactional patterns highlighted in the dyadic studies. The importance of this issue is nicely underlined in recent papers by Schneider and Gearhart (1988) and by Marfo (1990).

Children with Language Impairment.   By definition, children with language impairment (LI) have normal nonverbal intelligence and primary difficulties with language comprehension and/or use. Because of their language difficulties, these children may be at particular risk for differential interactional experiences. Furthermore, these children are identified much earlier than most children with reading and other learning disabilities, and age factors may play an important role in determining the nature of parent-child interactions. Thus, careful attention to studies of this population is important.

In addition to the Sammarco study discussed above, four studies were identified that involved comparisons of parent-child interactions with children with LI and normal developing children matched on relevant child characteristics.[3] As might be expected, these studies repre-

---

[3]Other existing comparative studies of children with LI do not attempt to match groups on nonverbal ability (Cohen, Beckwith, & Parmalee, 1978), or do not include information concerning this variable (Lasky & Klopp, 1982).

sent a wide range of methodologies in terms of the interactional setting and the types of behaviors examined. All but one of the studies used a laboratory setting and a specific interactional context. Thus, the issue of generalizability to unstructured interactions in the home is a difficult one.

The one home-based study (Wulbert, Inglis, Kriegsmann, & Mills, 1975) involved a comparison of 20 children with LI and 20 control children aged 2.8 to 5.7 years. The two groups of children were matched for age, sex, birth order, SES, nonverbal IQ (Leiter), and marital status of the mother. A "handicapped control group" of 20 Down syndrome children was also included. All but two of the children with LI had receptive language delays of at least 1 year, and all 20 had even greater delays in expressive language. The major dependent variable was the Caldwell Inventory of Home Stimulation, a checklist of 48 items rating the quality of the home environment in terms of both physical resources (books, toys, etc.) and interactional patterns. The Caldwell yields scores for six dimensions of the home environment. On five of these six dimensions, the LI group was rated significantly below the normal and handicapped control groups, which did not differ. The greatest differences were on the three scales dealing with mother-child interactions (emotional and verbal responsiveness of the mother, avoidance of punishment, and maternal involvement with the child). It is important to note that none of the Caldwell scores were related to SES in this sample. In discussing the results, the authors note that the LI mothers appeared to have little understanding of their child's developmental status and of ways to promote it. They were also more likely than the mothers in the other two groups to talk about their child in critical tones and to use physical rather than verbal discipline. Finally, the LI mothers were described as engaging in very little interaction with their children.

Unfortunately, very little information is provided by the authors concerning the home observations. Neither the length of the home visit nor the exact settings were noted. Thus, the contribution of factors such as maternal staging or embarrassment is difficult to judge. The inclusion of the control group with handicaps reduces this concern to some extent, however, because one might expect such artifacts to be present in that case as well. Thus, in general, this study provides some support for the existence of different interaction patterns in LI families. The significance of these patterns is difficult to judge, however. The data were based on live observations from unspecified settings, and consisted of global judgments on the part of the project staff. The functional significance of the interactional patterns is therefore impossible to estimate. The authors do, however, paint a very bleak picture of the home environment of the LI sample, one that was not at all evident among the Down syndrome sample.

Sigel and colleagues (Pellegrini, McGillicuddy-DeLisi, Sigel, & Brody, 1986; Sigel, McGillicuddy-DeLisi, Flaugher, & Rock, 1983) conducted what is by far the most comprehensive study of parent-child interactions with children with LI. They compared 5-minute segments of the interactions of both mothers and fathers with their child with LI or normally developing child in the context of two tasks, storybook reading and origami paper folding. The two groups of children were matched on SES, number of siblings, birth order, age, and sex. All of the children with LI had nonverbal intelligence within the average range, as based on the *Wechsler Preschool and Primary Scale of Intelligence* (Wechsler, 1967), but no attempt was made to match the two samples on this variable because the authors wanted to study possible IQ differences as a potential outcome of differing interactional styles. Little information is provided concerning the nature or severity of the children's language difficulties. Parental behaviors were coded on six dimensions, including provision of verbal support and information, nonverbal management and task structuring, and cognitive demand of utterances (e.g., requests for descriptions vs. requests for evaluations).

The interactions of the parents with their children with LI were found to differ from those of the control parents on several dimensions. First, the LI parents were more variable in their interactional style. In general, however, they used more utterances involving "low-level" cognitive demands (e.g., label, describe, demonstrate), whereas the control parents used more "medium-level" demands (sequence, describe similarities or differences). LI parents also used more nonverbal task structuring and attention-maintenance. There were also some indications of factors related to the interactional style of the LI parents. For example, the parents of children with LI who took longer to complete the tasks were less sensitive to their child's mood and ability level. Also, on a parent questionnaire, the LI parents tended to express the belief that children are passive recipients of knowledge. Finally, there was some evidence that the LI parents' interactional style was related to their child's representational abilities, as measured by a series of imagery and memory tasks administered in a separate session.

As a whole, these findings suggest that the parents of the children with LI were less likely to challenge their children in the context of these tasks. Unlike the first study, these findings are based on a detailed functional analysis of the interactions within the context of the task goals. Thus, these findings appear consistent with those of Sammarco (1984) in providing some indication of an instructional environment that is less stimulating than that of the normally developing child. Also, similar to Sammarco's study, the findings of Sigel et al. (1983) suggest that the differing interactional patterns may be due, at least in part, to inaccurate or incomplete parental perceptions of the child's instructional needs.

In contrast to the first two studies, a third large-scale comparison of LI and control parents revealed little evidence of any difference in interactional styles (Cunningham, Siegel, van der Spuy, Clark, & Bow, 1985). The authors compared the interactions of 33 children with LI and 27 control preschool children with their mothers in the context of both free play and structured interactions. The two groups of children were matched on age, sex, and SES. All the children had nonverbal IQs within the average range based on the *Leiter International Perform-ance Scale* (Leiter, 1948), but the IQs of the LI group were significantly lower than those of the control group (as they were in the study by Sigel et al., 1983).

The frequency of specific verbal and nonverbal behaviors was tallied for the mothers and children in six categories each (e.g., mother questions, child responds, mother encourages play, child initiates interaction). The results from the free-play period indicated that the children with LI were more passive, especially following periods of noninteraction on the part of the mother. However, there were no significant differences between the two groups in the frequency of the maternal behaviors coded during the free-play session. During the structured tasks, the control mothers questioned their children more frequently, but there were no differences on the remaining maternal measures.

In interpreting these findings, it is important to consider the nature of the interactional variables coded. Although the coding included indices of the frequency of maternal initiations and responses, the coding system does not appear to have been sensitive to the *nature* of the mothers' behaviors. In contrast, in the studies by Sammarco and by Sigel et al. (1983), the analyses focused on the communicational demands of the mothers' behaviors. Within the context of a Vygotskian framework, this distinction is an important one, because instructional power rests not only on the frequency of interactions, but also on the functional role of those interactions in encouraging new learning.

One other study of children with LI and their mothers also found few significant differences between the interactional styles of LI and control mothers (Scheffel, 1984). The author observed the interactions of 19 children with LI and 10 control 4- to 5-year-old children with their mothers during a storybook activity. The groups were matched for age, and for nonverbal ability on the *Columbia Mental Maturity Scale* (Burgemeister, Blum, & Lorge, 1972). The group with LI included a mix of children with receptive and expressive disorders. Mothers were given a standard children's storybook and asked to read it "with" their child as they might normally do. The formal analyses focued on three aspects of the interactions: the structure of the discourse (number of conversational exchanges), the function (e.g., boundaries, prompts, instructions), and the content (e.g., evaluation, description, explanation) of the utterances composing the discourse.

The analyses revealed no significant differences between the two groups on any of the formal measures of the discourse structure, or on the function or content of maternal utterances. It should be noted, however, that, although Scheffel (1984) did include some measures of the function of maternal utterances, her analyses were not sensitive to the immediate significance of the utterances in the context of the child's behavior. Thus, it is not clear whether or not the maternal utterances functioned differently for the two groups of children.

Some indication that actual differences might have been masked by the coding system can be found in Scheffel's (1984) qualitative discussion of the interactions. She noted, for example, that the LI dyads tended not to sustain interactions over as many moves, and that the children with LI and mothers were less verbally responsive to each other. The LI mothers also tended to make statements that required no response, and to spend more time directing their child's attention and eliciting responses. The author also noted that the control mothers were more likely to describe the attributes or actions of objects and characters in the story. Finally, the control mothers used language to establish cause-effect relations, whereas the LI mothers often failed to elaborate their explanations, or associated causes with inaccurate effects.

Although the findings from the five studies of interactional patterns in LI parent-child dyads (including Sammarco's) are mixed, as a whole they seem to suggest that parents of children with LI are often less demanding of their children than are parents of normally developing children whose language development is proceeding normally. LI parents have been found to provide fewer linguistic and cognitive challenges to their children. Findings regarding differential frequency of interactions have been more mixed, but, as argued above, the functional significance of such interactions may be a more appropriate index of parental stimulation of development.

Children with Learning Disabilities.   Studies focused on interactions of school-identified children with LD and their parents are even less common than those involving children with LI. The literature appears to contain only three studies that provided direct comparisons with a control group matched for IQ and certain other demographic factors.[4] The first study (Campbell, 1975) involved a comparison of the interactions of 13 children with LD, 13 children with hyperactivity, and 13 control boys and their mothers. The three groups of boys were matched for age (8 years), socioeconomic status, and for full scale IQ on the *Wechsler Intelligence Scale for Children* (Wechsler, 1974). All of the boys with LD and hyperactivity were at least one grade behind in reading achievement. The interactions took place in the context of two tasks, block design items and anagrams. The analyses focused on the frequency of seven maternal behaviors, including evaluations, suggestions, encouragements, direct physical help, and comments on task difficulty or mode of approach. The mothers of students with hyperactivity differed from the mothers in the other two groups on several variables, suggesting that the variables were sensitive to some aspects of interactional differences. However, there are no significant differences between the LD and control mothers on any of the measures.

These results provide evidence of similar interactional styles in mothers of boys with LD and control boys. Note that in this study the focus on the analyses was on the functional significance of the maternal behaviors within the context of the specific task. Although the analytic framework was not as fine-tuned as that of Sammarco, (1984; Wertsch & Sammarco, 1985), the methodology does seem similar. One significant limitation of the study, however, is the omission of any information concerning the boys' success at the tasks used, or any analyses of the relation between the child's performance and the mother's assistance. These issues were addressed, for example, in the LI studies conducted by Sammarco (1984) and Sigel et al. (1983). This omission makes it difficult to appreciate the instructional significance of the behaviors studied.

A second study reporting few differences between LD and control mothers focused on interactions in the context of a school-related task (Tollison, Palmer, & Stowe, 1987). The mothers of 15 boys with LD and 16 control boys in the second to fourth grades were observed while they administered two subtests of the KeyMath Achievement Test (Connolly, Nachtman, & Pritchett, 1971) to their sons. All boys had IQs between 85 and 115. The mothers' behavior was coded for the frequency of positive and negative verbal evaluations, encouragement, or directions regarding how to solve problems, as well as positive and negative nonverbal feedback. In addition, the mothers' expectations for their sons' successes and their attributions for the reported performance levels of their sons were also assessed. LD mothers had signif-

---

[4]This review was completed in September 1989.

icantly lower expectancies and provided significantly more negative nonverbal feedback. No other group differences were significant. Thus, in general, the two groups of mothers provided evaluations and encouragement with equal frequency.

In interpreting these findings, it should be noted that the analyses focused more on evaluative feedback and motivational encouragement than on instructional interactions. Thus, the focus is less comprehensive than in the studies reviewed above, and the results have only limited relevance to the issues of instructional dynamics at issue here. This comment is not intended to minimize the importance of motivational encouragement, however. Indeed, as discussed above, the Vygotskian framework places considerable emphasis on this issue.

In contrast to the first two studies, Ditton and colleagues (Ditton, Green, & Singer, 1987) reported significant differences between LD and control parents in the provision of verbal instructions to their children. The sample consisted of 30 students with LD and 30 control students in junior high school and their (self-identified) primary care parent. The two groups were matched for verbal IQ, parental occupation, and family configuration. The parent was asked to describe to the student, via a one-way telephone conversation, how to arrange a set of five Rorschach drawings on a table so as to match the arrangement in front of the parent. Transcripts of the parental instructions were rated by two independent judges as either High or Low in "communication deviance," which included characteristics such as unrelated shifts in content, ambiguous referents, odd word usage, and contradictory messages. This analysis of the parental instructions led to successful prediction of group membership for 87% of the 30 LD and 77% of the control dyads. Thus, the two groups of students appeared to receive instructions varying significantly in clarity.

Although the results of this study are interesting, it, like the majority of those discussed above, falls short of the type of functional analysis dictated by the social constructivist approach. Perhaps the most serious limitation in this regard is the fact that the children were not able to provide feedback to their parents concerning the clarity of the messages and that the parents were not able to observe their child's performance. Thus, the parental instructions could not be contingent on the child's activity.

In general, the findings from these studies of parent-child interaction in LD samples indicate that there is some evidence of differing syles in parents of children with LD than in parents of normal-achieving children. However, the findings are far from definitive. Indeed, the studies reviewed above raise more questions than they answer. In most cases, the studies were not designed to be sensitive to the functional flow of the dyadic interactions, either in terms of the child's moment-to-moment success, or in terms of the communicational dynamics. Thus, it is impossible to estimate the extent to which the patterns of interaction revealed are conducive to new learning. We will discuss the implications of this point for future research in the final section of this chapter.

Summary.   The studies of parent-child interaction reviewed above reflect a wide range of theoretical perspectives and methodological sophistication. This diversity reflects the breadth of interest in the role of such interactions in children's development. In addition, it reflects the relatively undeveloped nature of research in this area. Such research is difficult to conduct. In addition, it is extremely time-consuming to carry out the kinds of functional analyses of interactions that would seem to be most promising.

Although the findings of these studies are mixed, some tentative conclusions appear to be possible. First, those studies that incorporated functional analyses of parental behavior (as opposed to raw counts of behavior types) tend to indicate significant differences in interactional patterns. One difference noted in several studies was the greater cognitive challenge provided by the parents of the normally developing children. This finding was more evident in the studies of children with LI than in those that focused on children with learning disabilities. In general, the findings from the studies of children with LI revealed more consistent evidence of interactional differences. Such a fact might be expected on the basis of the crucial role of oral communication in interactions in our culture. It should be noted, however, that the differences in the findings in the two populations might also reflect the fact that the children with LI tended to be younger than the children with LD studied. Differential interactional patterns might be more frequent at younger ages. In addition, the different findings might be, at least in part, a result of differing methodologies, because functional analyses were more often employed in the LI studies. A resolution of these possibilities must await future research. However, it seems clear that care should be taken to distinguish these issues of age, population, and type of interaction in future research.

One final crucial issue raised by these studies relates to the implications of any differential interactions for fostering children's development. In the case of children with retardation, where such patterns of fewer challenges and more directive interactions have been long noted, it has recently been argued that these interactional differences reflect an adaptation on the parents' part to the special needs of their children (Marfo, 1990; Schneider & Gearhart, 1988). Although this may turn out to be the case in many instances, the studies reviewed above that provide direct evidence relevant to this issue (Sammarco, 1984; Sigel et al., 1983) present findings that suggest that the parents of children with LI may not have a completely realistic perspective on their child's developmental status or needs.

Sammarco's (1984) study is particularly interesting in this regard. Her finding that the parent's behavior was not closely related to the child's knowledge of task-relevant vocabulary, and that LI mothers were often unaware of their child's comprehension difficulties, suggests that the mother's interactions were not dictated by a sensitivity to their child's needs. Also relevant here is Sigel's (Sigel et al., 1983) finding that LI parents tend to view their children as no different from other children in terms of their capabilities for the development of concepts of time, perspective taking, and rules. As noted above, Sigel et al. also found that LI parents were more likely to believe that children in general are passive recipients of knowledge.

In addition to the incidental evidence found in the interactional studies, numerous studies have focused directly on parental attitudes toward their children with LD. Many of these studies have reported evidence of lower expectations on the part of LD parents, as in the study by Tollison et al. (1987) discussed above. (See also Owen, Adams, Forrest, Stolz, & Fisher, 1971; and Bryan, Pearl, Zimmerman, & Matthews, 1982.) Surely, some of these lower expectations are realistic and adaptive (a point made also by Marfo, 1990). However, findings such as those by Sammarco (1984) and Sigel et al. (1983) suggest that parental expectations are not always accurate. Also, as noted by Bryan et al. (1982), these expectations can be self-fulfilling.

Teacher-Child Interaction

In addition to the possible influences of parental interactional styles on the approach to learning of children with LD, interactions with teachers are clearly an additional important arena for social influences on the development of learning strategies. The present section contains a discussion of research on the nature of teacher-student interactions in the mainstream classroom and the resource room setting. Again, our intent is to highlight any differences in the instructional environment of possible relevance to a social constructivist perspective. Before discussing those studies focused specifically on students with LD, we will touch briefly on studies of differential teacher interactions based on individual differences in academic success within the "normally achieving" population.

Studies of Low-Achieving Students.   In recent years, differences in mainstream teachers' treatment of students termed "low" and "high" achievers (defined variously) have been amply documented. Reviews of studies indicate that teachers interact more with high achievers than low achievers. Comparisons also indicate that teachers call on low achievers less often, allow them less time to answer questions, or give them the answer or call on someone else rather than try to improve responses through rephrasing. In addition, teachers criticize low achievers more frequently for incorrect responses, praise them less for successful responses, and generally provide them with less frequent, less accurate, and less detailed feedback (see Good, 1980, and Brophy, 1982, for reviews of this literature). Clearly, differential treatment of this sort could have implications for the effectiveness of instruction, in the short term. Of perhaps greater importance, however, is the possibility of long-term consequences of such interactional patterns. In the context of Vygotsky's framework, these differences would contribute importantly to general developmental issues in the areas of both motivation and higher cognitive skills.

The extent to which similar differences are evident in comparisons of average students and students with learning disabilities is less clear, but there is some evidence to that effect. in the next section, some relevant work will be examined.

Studies of Students with Learning Disabilities.   The majority of studies of classroom interactions involving students with LD focus on time allocation. For example, Haynes and Jenkins (1986) reported that "mildly handicapped" fourth, fifth, and sixth graders (88% LD), spent the majority of their time doing individual seatwork in the resource room, and were likely to receive twice as much demonstration, feedback, and questioning when in mainstream classrooms. Ysseldyke, Thurlow, Mecklenburg, and Graden (1984) found that third- and fourth-grade students with LD spent considerably more time doing independent seatwork in the resource room compared to the regular classroom, had the teacher by their side more often, and received more approval from the teacher.

These findings are suggestive of differential instructional interactions in the mainstream and special education settings, but they do not allow firm conclusions regarding the nature of these differences. Studies of the nature of the contacts between teachers and students provide more insight into classroom practices. The majority of the studies on LD student-teacher interaction occur within mainstreamed settings. The variables most frequently considered are total frequency of contacts and frequency of praise and criticism.

In general, studies have indicated that students with LD, as well as others with mild handicaps have an equal number of contacts with their teachers compared to nonhandicapped students (Richey & McKinney, 1978; Slate & Saudargas, 1986), if not more contacts (Alves & Gottlieb, 1986; McKinney, McClure, & Feagans, 1982; Stipek & Sanborn, 1985; Swanson, 1984c; Thompson, Vitale, & Jewett, 1984; Thompson, White, & Morgan, 1982). Some studies also have suggested that mainstream teachers' verbal contacts are no more negative toward special education students than toward their peers (Alves & Gottlieb, 1986; Swanson, 1984a).

On the surface, these findings appear to conflict with those reported in the preceding section, in which mainstream teachers are usually found to interact more with high achievers than low achievers, and to treat high achievers in a more positive manner (Brophy, 1982; Good, 1980). At least part of the discrepancy in findings may be attributed to the nature of contacts initiated by teachers. Several researchers have reported that teacher-initiated contacts with students with LD pertained more to behavior management than to academic material (Alves & Gottlieb, 1986; Dorval, McKinney, & Feagans, 1982; Thompson et al., 1984, 1982). The data are less consistent regarding teacher initiations that are academic in nature. However, there is some evidence that teachers direct more verbal interactions toward students with LD than toward their average-achieving peers. Swanson (1984a) found that LD teachers (Grades 1 through 6) provided more verbal questions and directives to their students compared to regular teachers. Slate and Saudargas (1986) found that when mainstreamed students with LD (Grades 3, 4, and 5) were engaged in a task, they received more teacher directions than their peers, even though their peers were equally engaged in the same task. Similar findings were reported by Stipek and Sanborn (1985) in a study of 14 preschool children with handicaps (mixed diagnoses, all with approximately a 1-year developmental delay) and 13 underachieving preschool children receiving special educational assistance. The authors reported that teachers offered more unrequested information and assistance during free choice time to the target children than to their nonhandicapped peers. Further, Swanson (1984a) reported that special education teachers were likely to express satisfaction with correct but nonstrategic reponses of students with LD. Such contingencies may encourage passivity. Similarly, Ysseldyke et al. (1984) reported that students with LD received more approval from their special education teacher than did their peers in the mainstream, and that special education teacher approval coincided with passive responding (e.g., listening, waiting, looking at the teacher).

Summary. Two worrisome trends emerge from studies of interactional patterns between students with LD and their teachers. First, teachers may be prone to "overhelp" students with LD, unduly influenced by the special needs of the child. A high level of teacher-initiated interactions may breed passivity and dependence. Children may come to learn that they can rely on adult assistance. They may be robbed of opportunities to think on their own, and persist when faced with difficulty. Swanson (1984a) provided some evidence of this pattern. Students with LD in Swanson's study were more apt to ask questions that required teacher assistance (e.g., "How do I do this problem?") than normal controls, who were more apt to ask narrow questions (e.g. "I read this assignment and answered two questions, but I can't figure out the answer to this question").

The second trend to emerge is that students with LD may receive more praise that is not contingent on satisfactory academic performance and less encouragement for strategic approaches to tasks than their average-achieving peers. This pattern is also potentially worrisome. In an attempt to bolster the self-confidence of students with LD, teachers may offer praise whether or not performance reflects the child's best effort. If praise is noncontingent on achievement or effort, this may favor student passivity and lack of persistence (Licht & Kistner, 1986). Such praise may signal to the child low expectations on the part of the teacher.

Conclusions and Implications

Existing research on the nature of parent and teacher interactions with children with LD provides only partial insight into the origins of the strategy deficiences of these children. There is a scarcity of relevant research, and those studies that do exist are often difficult to interpret, either because of methodological deficiencies or because of the absence of a clear theoretical connection between the variables studied and the outcomes to be inferred.

In general, however, two conclusions are warranted, at least provisionally. First, there is reasonable evidence indicating that both parents and teachers adopt an interactive style that is less challenging to the child with LD than that evidenced in interactions with average-achieving children of comparable age and general ability. This evidence is clearest in the case of parental interactions with preschool children with specific language impairments. Second, the unique interactional patterns do not appear to be simply a result of the parent's or teacher's sensitivity to a greater need for structure on the part of the child with LD. Instead, parental perceptions of the child's skill level or instructional needs suggest that the parents may overestimate the child's needs.

The findings, however, are by no means unequivocal. Several cautions are needed. First, in more than one study, there is considerable variability in the interactions of parents and teachers with children with LD. As with other research on the population with LD, this variability suggests that there may be distinct subpatterns obscured by the general trend. Second, the majority of the studies suffer from certain methodological shortcomings, especially from the perspective of social constructivism. For example, only one of the parent-child studies involved observations in a home environment, and none of the studies capitalized on a naturally occurring instructional interaction. A third limitation relates to the choice of tasks. Several of the studies involved data collected from more than one task (Campbell, 1975; Cunningham et al., 1985; Sigel et al., 1983). In each case, the interactional patterns differed to some degree for the two tasks. For example, in the study by Sigel and colleagues, two of the differences between the interactional styles of LI and control parents were evident on one task but not the other. Related to the task issue is the fact that, although the majority of the studies reviewed controlled in some manner for differences in general ability, none of the studies controlled for task-specific abilities. The influence of this factor on interactional patterns may be profound. For example, turning again to Sigel's study, the fact that it was the book-reading task, not origami, that yielded more salient interactional differences may relate directly to the language difficulties of the children with LI. Thus, although the general pattern of the research is suggestive of some potentially important differences in the interactions of parents and teachers with children with LD, much remains to be learned about the generality of these differences. Furthermore, although it appears that the differences in the interactions of adults with LD and normally achieving children are not entirely adaptive reactions to differing child capabilities and needs, the issues raised above suggest that this conclusion warrants considerably more scrutiny.

If the findings reviewed above are accepted as at least tentative indications of differential instructional experiences for the child with LD, how should they be interpreted? Here, the social constructivist framework offered by Vygotsky becomes important. This framework is consistent with current emphases on an analysis of children's development in terms of increasing mastery of cognitive strategies. Vygotsky emphasized the central place of strategic deficiencies in the profiles of problem learners. However, he placed considerably greater emphasis on the role of social experiences in the etiology of learning problems than is generally accepted today. It is in this context that the research reviewed above gains its significance. If, indeed, there are subtle but pervasive differences in the informal and formal instructional environments provided to children with LD, the implications may extend beyond momentary learning opportunities. A general pattern of strategic deficiencies might result. This possibility highlights the importance of future research on the social world of the child with LD.

Several issues should be considered in designing future studies. First, there is a need to observe interactions in multiple settings and tasks. Although structured laboratory-like settings may be necessary for careful documentation of many interactional patterns, these patterns will need to be verified with more naturalistic observation in the home or school. In either setting, it is not sufficient to focus on interactions in a single task. For example, tasks with objective goals (e.g., puzzles) may accentuate interactional differences that are not so apparent in less structured activities such as free play. Of equal importance for a special population such as individuals with learning disabilities, tasks that involve a given child's area(s) of deficiency (e.g., word games) may lead to interactional patterns that are markedly different from those in more "neutral" tasks (e.g., counting). A second and related point is the need to pay considerably more attention to the match between the task demands and the child's skill level. The match between these variables can, and should, be manipulated to study its influence on the patterns of interaction. Third, it is critical to look closely at the relation between child competence and parental response. Fourth, future researchers must distinguish between the amount and type of assistance provided to children with LD by parents and teachers. As we emphasized above, more or less assistance may not be so important as the quality of the assistance and its match to the child's needs. Studies should focus on the extent to which parents and teachers provide support calibrated to the child's moment-to-moment needs. Also, greater attention must be paid to the discourse characteristics of the interactions. It is this match between the child's needs and the assistance provided that defines the optimal instructional benefits of the zone of proximal development.

Finally, care must be taken to define the particular population at issue. As was noted above, the findings of differential parental interaction patterns are clearer in the case of preschool children with specific language impairments, as compared to school-age children defined in terms of academic underachievement. The relative importance of age and type of impairment needs careful exploration. One final point in this context relates to the type of comparison groups to include. The decision of Wulbert et al. (1975) and of Campbell (1975) to include comparison groups of other children with handicaps seems to be a wise one. These controls allow us to examine the discriminative power of the measures used, and to assess the relation of any distinctive interactional patterns observed to specific child characteristics.

In closing, it should be emphasized that there is a positive aspect to a Vygotskian perspective on children with LD that should not be lost. In Vygotsky's writings on childhood exceptionalities, there is an optimism regarding the potential for "compensation" in the problem learner. Without denying the reality of a biologically based deficiency in some sensory, perceptual, or attentional capacity, Vygotsky emphasized the value of properly orchestrated social experiences in assisting the exceptional child to construct alternative pathways to instructional ends. The challenge in adopting Vygotsky's perspective is in assuring an appropriate "instructional" environment for the child with LD. In this context, the term *instruction* is used, as it was by Vygotsky, to subsume a nexus of formal and informal interactive experiences of both a cognitive and affective nature, in both the school and everyday context. Equally important is attention to the nature of the interactions. As alluded to above, Vygotsky placed considerable emphasis of the role of communicational dynamics in appropriate instruction within the zone of proximal development. At present, the LD field has made some progress in designing instructional programs targeted at specific strategic deficiencies common in children with LD (see the recent special issue of *Learning Disability Quarterly* [Swanson, 1989c]). However, these programs have met with only limited success (Ellis, 1986; Wong, 1985a). Within a Vygotskian framework, two reasons for this limitation are evident. First, little attention has been paid to the communicational dynamics of strategy instruction (Stone, 1989). Second, these programs have been limited to certain highly structured activities in the classroom. Research such as that reviewed in this chapter suggests that interventions targeted at both the informal flow of the classroom and the dynamics of parent-child interactions in early childhood may be equally, or even more, important than formal strategy training in fostering strategic activity in the child with LD. Considerably more research is needed, however, if this potential is to be realized.

References

Alves, A., & Gottlieb, J. (1986). Teacher interactions with mainstreamed handicapped students and their nonhandicapped peers. *Learning Disability Quarterly, 9*, 77–83.

Borkowski, J. G., & Kurtz, B. E. (1984). Metacognition and special children. In B. Gholson & T. Rosenthal (Eds.), *Applications of cognitive developmental theory* (pp. 193–213). New York: Academic Press.

Borkowski, J. G., Levers, S. R., & Gruenenfelder, T. A. (1976). Transfer of mediational strategies in children: The role of activity and awareness during strategy acquisition. *Child Development, 47,* 779–786.

Brophy, J. (1982). *Research on self-fulfilling prophecy and teacher expectations.* Paper presented at the annual meeting of the American Educational Research Association, New York.

Brown, A. L., & Barclay, C. R. (1976). The effects of training specific mnemonics on the metamnemonic efficiency of retarded children. *Child Development, 47,* 71–80.

Brown, A. L., Bransford, J. D., Ferrara, R. A., & Campione, J. C. (1983). Learning, remembering, and understanding. In J. H. Flavell and E. H. Markman (Eds.), *Handbook of child psychology* (Vol. 1, pp. 77–166). New York: Wiley.

Brown, A. L., & DeLoache, J. S. (1978). Skills, plans, and self-regulation. In. R. S. Siegler (Ed.), *Children's thinking: What develops?* (pp. 3–36). Hillsdale, NJ: Erlbaum.

Brown, A. L., & Reeve, R. A. (1987). Bandwidths of competence: The role of supportive contexts in learning and development. In L. S. Liben & D. H. Feldman (Eds.), *Development and learning: Conflict or congruence?* (pp. 173–224). Hillsdale, NJ: Erlbaum.

Bryan, T., Pearl, R., Zimmerman, D., & Matthews, F. (1982). Mothers' evaluations of their learning disabled children. *The Journal of Special Education, 16,* 149–160.

Burgemeister, B. B., Blum, L. H., & Lorge, I. (1972). *Columbia mental maturity scale* (3rd ed.). San Antonio, TX: Psychological Corp.

Butkowski, S., & Willows, M. (1980). Cognitive-motivational characteristics of children varying in reading ability: Evidence for learned helplessness in poor readers. *Journal of Educational Psychology, 72,* 408–422.

Campbell, S. B. (1975). Mother-child interaction: A comparison of hyperactive, learning disabled, and normal boys. *American Journal of Orthopsychiatry, 45,* 51–57.

Catts, H. (1989). Defining dyslexia as a developmental language disorder. *Annals of Dyslexia, 39,* 50–64.

Chi, M. T. H. (1978). Knowledge structures and memory development. In R. Siegler (Ed.), *Children's thinking: What develops?* (pp. 73–96). Hillsdale, NJ: Erlbaum.

Cohen, S., Beckwith, L., & Parmalee, A. (1978). Receptive language development as related to caregiver-child interaction. *Pediatrics, 61,* 16–20.

Conca, L. (1989). Strategy choice by LD children with good and poor naming ability in a naturalistic memory situation. *Learning Disability Quarterly, 12,* 97–106.

Connolly, A. J., Nachtman, W., & Pritchett, E. M. (1971). *The KeyMath diagnostic arithmetic test.* Circle Pines, MN: American Guidance Service.

Connor, F. P. (1983). Improving school instruction for learning disabled children: The Teacher's College Institute. *Exceptional Education Quarterly, 4,* 23–44.

Cunningham, C. E., Siegel, L. S., van der Spuy, H. I. J., Clark, M. L., & Bow, S. J. (1985). The behavioral and linguistic interactions of specifically language-delayed and normal boys with their mothers. *Child Development, 56*, 1389–1403.

Dempster, F. N. (1981). Memory span: Sources of individual and developmental differences. *Psychological Bulletin, 89*, 63–100.

Denckla, M., & Rudel, R. (1976). Rapid automatized naming: Dyslexia differentiated from other learning disabilities. *Neuropsychologia, 14*, 471–479.

Ditton, P., Green, R. J., & Singer, M. T. (1987). Communication deviances: A comparison between parents of LD and NA students. *Family Process, 26*, 75–87.

Dorval, B., McKinney, J. D., & Feagans, L. (1982). Teacher interaction with learning-disabled children and average achievers. *Journal of Pediatric Psychology, 7*, 317–330.

Ellis, E. S. (1986). The role of motivation and pedagogy on the generalization of cognitive training by the mildly handicapped. *Journal of Learning Disabilities, 19*, 66–70.

Flavell, J. H., & Wellman, H. M. (1977). Metamemory. In R. V. Kail & J. W. Hagen (Eds.), *Perspectives on the development of memory and cognition* (pp. 3–33). Hillsdale, NJ: Erlbaum.

Ford, C. E., Pelham, W. E., & Ross, A. D. (1984). Selective attention and rehearsal in the auditory short-term memory task performance of poor and normal readers. *Journal of Abnormal Child Psychology, 12*, 127–142.

Forman, E. A. (1989). The role of peer interaction in the social construction of mathematical knowledge. *International Journal of Educational Research, 13*, 55–70.

Forman, E. A., Minick, N., & Stone, C. A. (in press). *Contexts of learning: Sociocultural dynamics of children's development.* New York: Oxford University Press.

Gerber, M. M. (1983). Learning disabilities and cognitive strategies: A case for training or constraining problem-solving? *Journal of Learning Disabilities, 5*, 255–260.

Good, T. (1980). Classroom expectations: Teacher-pupil interactions. In J. McMillan (Ed.), *The social psychology of school learning.* New York: Academic Press.

Graham, S., & Freeman, S. (1985). Strategy training and teacher versus student-controlled study conditions: Effects on learning disabled students' spelling performance. *Learning Disability Quarterly, 8*, 267–274.

Guttentag, R. E. (1984). The mental effort requirement of cumulative rehearsal: A developmental study. *Journal of Experimental Child Psychology, 37*, 92–106.

Haynes, M. C., & Jenkins, J. R. (1986). Reading instruction in special education resource rooms. *American Educational Research Journal, 23*, 161–190.

Hiskey, M. S. (1966). *Manual for the Hiskey-Nebraska test of learning aptitude.* Lincoln, NE: Union College Press.

Kail, R. (1979). *The development of memory in children.* San Francisco: Freeman.

Kastner, S. B., & Rickarts, C. (1974). Mediated memory with novel and familiar stimuli in good and poor readers. *The Journal of Genetic Psychology, 124,* 105–113.

Kennedy, B. S., & Miller, D. J. (1976). Persistent use of verbal rehearsal as a function of information about its value. *Child Development, 47,* 566–569.

Kolligan, J., & Sternberg, R. J. (1987). Intelligence, information processing, and specific learning disabilities: A triarchic synthesis. *Journal of Learning Disabilities, 20,* 8–17.

Lasky, E. Z., & Klopp, K. (1982). Parent-child interactions in normal and language-disordered children. *Journal of Speech and Hearing Disorders, 47,* 7–18.

Leiter, R. G. (1948). *Leiter international performance scale.* Chicago: Stoelting.

Licht, B. G., & Kistner, J. A. (1986). Motivational problems of learning disabled children: Individual differences and their implications for treatment. In J. K. Torgesen & B. Y. L. Wong (Eds.), *Psychological and educational perspectives on learning disabilities* (pp. 225–255). New York: Academic Press.

Lodico, M. G., Ghatala, E. S., Levin, J. R., Pressley, M., & Bell, J. A. (1983). The effects of strategy monitoring training on children's selection of effective memory strategies. *Journal of Experimental Child Psychology, 35,* 263–277.

Lorsbach, T. C., & Gray, J. W. (1985). *Item identification and memory span performance in learning disabled children.* Paper presented at the annual meeting of the American Educational Research Association, Chicago.

Marfo, K. (1990). Maternal directiveness in interactions with mentally handicapped children: An analytical commentary. *Journal of Child Psychology and Psychiatry, 31,* 531–549.

McKinney, J. D., McClure, S., & Feagans, L. (1982). Classroom behavior of learning disabled children. *Learning Disability Quarterly, 5,* 45–52.

Minick, N. (1989). Mind and activity in Vygotsky's work: An expanded frame of reference. *Cultural Dynamics, 2,* 162–187.

Moynahan, E. (1978). Assessment and selection of paired-associate strategies: A developmental study. *Journal of Experimental Child Psychology, 26,* 257–266.

Naus, M. J., & Ornstein, P. A. (1983). The development of memory strategies: Analysis, questions, and issues. In M. T. H. Chi (Ed.), *Trends in memory development research* (pp. 1–31). Basel, Switzerland: Karger.

Owen, R. W., Adams, P. A., Forrest, T., Stolz, L. M., & Fisher, S. (1971). Learning disorders in children: Sibling studies. *Monographs of the Society for Research on Child Development, 36,* No. 144.

Palincsar, A. S. (1986). The role of dialogue in providing scaffolded instruction. *Educational Psychologist, 21,* 73–98.

Paris, S. G., & Cross, D. R. (1983). Ordinary learning: Pragmatic connections among children's beliefs, motives, and actions. In J. Bisanz, G. L. Bisanz, &

R. Kail (Eds.), *Learning in children: Progress in cognitive developmental research* (pp. 137–169). New York: Springer-Verlag.

Paris, S. G., & Lindauer, B. K. (1982). The development of cognitive skills during childhood. In B. W. Wolman (Ed.), *Handbook of developmental psychology* (pp. 333–349). Englewood Cliffs, NJ: Prentice-Hall.

Paris, S. G., Lipson, M. Y., & Wixson, K. K. (1983). Becoming a strategic reader. *Contemporary Educational Psychology, 8,* 293–316.

Paris, S. G., Newman, R. S., & Jacobs, J. E. (1985). Social contexts and functions of children's remembering. In M. Pressley & C. J. Brainerd (Eds.), *Cognitive learning and memory in children* (pp. 81–115). New York: Springer-Verlag.

Paris, S. G., Newman, R. S., & McVey, K. A. (1982). Learning the functional significance of mnemonic actions: A microgenetic study of strategy acquisition. *Journal of Experimental Child Psychology, 34,* 490–509.

Pearl, R. A. (1982). Learning disabled children's attributions for success and failure: A replication with a labeled LD sample. *Learning Disability Quarterly, 5,* 173–176.

Pellegrini, A. D., McGillicuddy-DeLisi, A. V., Sigel, I. E., & Brody, G. H. (1986). The effects of children's communicative status and task on parents' teaching strategies. *Contemporary Educational Psychology, 11,* 240–252.

Pistono, K. S. (1980). *Certain aspects of problem solving abilities of learning disabled and normal 6- to 7-year-old boys as reflected in external cue incorporation on a memory task.* Unpublished doctoral dissertation, Northwestern University, Evanston, IL.

Pressley, M., Goodchild, F., Fleet, J., Zajchowski, R., & Evans, E. (1987). *What is good strategy use and why is it hard to teach? An optimistic appraisal of the challenges associated with strategy instruction.* Paper presented at the annual meeting of the American Educational Research Association, Washington, DC.

Reeve, R. A., & Brown, A. L. (1985). Metacognition reconsidered: Implications for intervention research. *Journal of Abnormal Child Psychology, 13,* 343–356.

Richey, D. D., & McKinney, J. D. (1978). Classroom behavioral styles of learning disabled boys. *Journal of Learning Disabilities, 11,* 297–302.

Rogoff, B. (1990). *Apprenticeship in thinking: Cognitive development in social context.* New York: Oxford University Press.

Rogoff, B., & Wertsch, J. V. (1984). *Children's learning in the "zone of proximal development."* San Francisco: Jossey-Bass.

Sammarco, J. G. (1984). *Joint problem solving activity in mother-child dyads: A comparative study of language disorder and normally achieving preschoolers.* Unpublished doctoral dissertation, Northwestern University, Evanston, IL.

Scheffel, D. L. (1984). *An investigation of discourse features of mother-child verbal interaction with normal and language-impaired children in the context of story reading.* Unpublished doctoral dissertation, Northwestern University, Evanston, IL.

Schneider, P., & Gearhart, M. (1988). The ecocultural niche of families with mentally retarded children: Evidence from mother-child interaction studies. *Journal of Applied Developmental Psychology, 9*, 85–106.

Sigel, I. E., McGillicuddy-DeLisi, A. V., Flaugher, J., & Rock, D. A. (1983). *Parents as teachers of their own learning disabled children* (Research Rep. No. 83-21). Princeton, NJ: Educational Testing Service.

Slate, J. R., & Saudargas, R. A. (1986). Differences in learning disabled and average students' classroom behaviors. *Learning Disability Quarterly, 9*, 61–67.

Smirnov, A. A., & Zinchenko, P. I. (1969). Problems in the psychology of memory. In M. Cole & I. Maltzman (Eds.), *A handbook of contemporary Soviet psychology* (pp. 452–502). New York: Basic Books.

Stipek, D., & Sanborn, M. E. (1985). Teachers' task-related interactions with handicapped and nonhandicapped children. *Merrill-Palmer Quarterly, 31*, 285–300.

Stone, C. A. (1985). Vygotsky's developmental model and the concept of proleptic instruction: Some implications for theory and practice in the field of learning disabilities. *Research Communications in Psychology, Psychiatry, and Behavior, 10*, 129–152.

Stone, C. A. (1989). Improving the effectiveness of strategy instruction for the learning disabled: The role of communicational dynamics. *Remedial and Special Education, 12*, 35–42.

Stone, C. A. (in press). What's missing in the metaphor of scaffolding? In E. A. Forman, N. Minick, & C. A. Stone (Eds.), *Contexts of learning: Sociocultural dynamics of children's development.* New York: Oxford University Press.

Stone, C. A., & Wertsch, J. V. (1984). A social interactional analysis of learning disabilities. *Journal of Learning Disabilities, 17*, 194–199.

Swanson, H. L. (1983). Relations among metamemory, rehearsal activity and word recall of learning disabled and non-disabled readers. *British Journal of Educational Psychology, 53*, 186–194.

Swanson, H. L. (1984a). Does theory guide practice? *Remedial and Special Education, 5*(5), 7–16.

Swanson, H. L. (1984b). Process assessment of intelligence in learning disabled and mentally retarded children: A multidirectional model. *Educational Psychologist, 19*, 149–162.

Swanson, H. L. (1984c). Semantic and visual codes in learning disabled readers' recall. *Journal of Experimental Child Psychology, 37*, 124–140.

Swanson, H. L. (1986). Multiple coding processes in learning disabled and skilled readers. In S. J. Ceci (Ed.), *Handbook of cognitive, social, and neuropsychological aspects of learning disabilities* (Vol. 1, pp. 203–228). Hillsdale, NJ: Erlbaum.

Swanson, H. L. (1987). Information processing theory and learning disabilities: An overview. *Journal of Learning Disabilities, 20*, 3–7.

Swanson, H. L. (Ed.). (1989a). Learning strategy instruction [Special issue]. *Learning Disability Quarterly, 12*(1).

Swanson, H. L. (1989b). Strategy instruction: Overview of principles and procedures for effective use. *Learning Disability Quarterly, 12*, 3–14.

Thompson, R. H., Vitale, P. A., & Jewett, J. P. (1984). Teacher-student interaction patterns in mainstreamed classrooms. *Remedial and Special Education, 5*(6), 51–61.

Thompson, R. H., White, K. R., & Morgan, D. P. (1982). Teacher-student interaction patterns in classrooms with mainstreamed mildly handicapped students. *American Educational Research Journal, 19,* 220–236.

Tollison, P., Palmer, D. J., & Stowe, M. L. (1987). Mothers' expectations, interactions, and achievement attributions for their LD or NA sons. *The Journal of Special Education, 21,* 83–92.

Torgesen, J. K. (1977). The role of nonspecific factors in the task performance of learning disabled children: A theoretical assessment. *Journal of Learning Disabilities, 10,* 27–34.

Torgesen, J. K., & Licht, B. G. (1983). The learning disabled child as an inactive learner: Retrospect and prospects. In J. McKinney & L. Feagans (Eds.), *Current topics in learning disabilities* (pp. 3–32). Norwood, NJ: Ablex.

Vygotsky, L. S. (1962). *Thought and language.* Cambridge, MA: MIT Press.

Vygotsky, L. S. (1978). *Mind in society.* Cambridge, MA: Harvard University Press.

Vygotsky, L. S. (1987). *The collected works of L. S. Vygotsky: Vol. 1. Problems of general psychology.* New York: Plenum.

Vygotsky, L. S. (in press). *The collected works of L. S. Vygotsky: Vol. 2. Problems of defectology.* New York: Plenum.

Wechsler, D. (1967). *Manual for the Wechsler preschool and primary scale of intelligence.* San Antonio, TX: Psychological Corp.

Wechsler, D. (1974). *Manual for the Wechsler intelligence scale for children.* San Antonio, TX: Psychological Corp.

Wertsch, J. V. (1979). From social interaction to higher psychological processes. *Human Development, 22,* 1–22.

Wertsch, J. V. (1985a). *Culture, communication, and cognition: Vygotskian perspectives.* New York: Cambridge University Press.

Wertsch, J. V. (1985b). *Vygotsky and the social formation of mind.* Cambridge, MA: Harvard.

Wertsch, J. V., & Sammarco, J. G. (1985). Social precursors to individual cognitive functioning. In R. Hinde, A. N. Perret-Clermont, & J. Stevenson-Hinde (Eds.), *Social relationship and cognitive development of knowledge* (pp. 276–293). Oxford: Clarendon Press.

Wertsch, J. V., & Stone, C. A. (1985). The concept of internalization in Vygotsky's account of the genesis of higher mental functions. In J. V. Wertsch (Ed.), *Culture, communication, and cognition: Vygotskian perspectives* (pp. 162–179). New York: Cambridge University Press.

Wong, B. Y. L. (1985a). Issues in cognitive-behavioral interventions in academic skill areas. *Journal of Abnormal Child Psychology, 13,* 425–442.

Wong, B. Y. L. (1985b). Metacognition and learning disabilities. In T. G. Waller, D. Forrest-Pressley, & E. MacKinnon (Eds.), *Metacognition, cognition, and human performance* (pp. 137–180). New York: Academic Press.

Wood, D., Bruner, J., & Ross, G. (1976). The role of tutoring in problem solving. *Journal of Child Psychology and Psychiatry, 17,* 89–100.

Wulbert, M., Inglis, S., Kriegsmann, E., & Mills, B. (1975). Language delay and associated mother-child interactions. *Developmental Psychology, 11,* 61–70.

Ysseldyke, J. E., Thurlow, M. L., Mecklenburg, C., & Graden, J. (1984). Opportunity to learn for regular and special education students during reading instruction. *Remedial and Special Education, 5*(1), 29–37.

3

Principles and Procedures in Strategy Use

H. L. Swanson

Helping students with learning disabilities (LD) to become better strategy users is an important educational goal (e.g., see Pressley, Symons, Snyder, & Cariglia-Bull, 1989). This goal is based on several studies suggesting that the information processing approaches used by students with LD do not appear to exhaust—or even tap—their learning potential (Borkowski, Estrada, Milstead, & Hale, 1989; Kolligian & Sternberg, 1987; Palincsar & Brown, 1984; Swanson, 1989b). For example, the lack of success in the classroom of students with LD, whether in academic or social situations, can be modified in various ways, such as their ability to shift from one strategy to another, to abandon inappropriate strategies, to process information with one strategy and then select another, or even to consider several processing approaches in rapid succession to arrive at a correct solution to a problem. In the spirit of this broad educational goal, the objective of this chapter is to review some strategy instruction principles as they apply to learning disabilities. Some of these principles have been discussed previously (e.g., Swanson, 1989b, 1990, 1991), but are extended and elaborated here. To control for any excessive generalizations or incorrect conclusions on my part, these principles are drawn primarily from some of my own studies. These principles, however, find general support in the cognitive literature.

61

Strategies Defined

A strategy is defined as a set of responses organized to solve a problem. The problems that need to be solved by students with LD vary, but the definition implies that strategy use requires effortful processing. It is assumed that one of the reasons students with LD experience strategic processing difficulties is that they exert little effort in solving problems (see Gelzheiser, Cort, & Sheperd, 1987, for a review). For example, a number of researchers in the field of learning disabilities have converged on the notion that the ability of children with learning disabilities to access knowledge remains inert, unless they are explicitly prompted to use certain strategies (e.g, see Swanson, 1987, for a review). In the area of memory research, children with LD may be taught to (a) organize lists of pictures and words in common categories, (b) rehearse the category names during learning, and (c) use the names and retrieval cues at the time of the test (e.g., see Cooney & Swanson, 1987, for a review). The data suggest that when children with LD are explicitly encouraged to use such strategies on some tasks, their performance improves and thus the discrepancy between general intellectual ability and contextually related deficits is lessened (e.g., Dallego & Moely, 1980; Torgesen, Murphy, & Ivey, 1979; Wong & Jones, 1982).

Embedded in this notion of "processing effort" is the idea that strategy deficiencies represent a continuum from a failure to use a strategy to a failure to use a strategy that is not comparable to the non-LD population. Unfortunately, when one reviews the literature to document strategy deficiencies in children with LD, it is not in terms of this continuum. Rather, the majority of research in the field of learning disabilities has focused primarily on production deficiencies; that is, a focus has been placed on the failure to use strategies rather than on the range of strategies used. Thus, current LD strategy research can be characterized as first demonstrating that students with LD do not adopt a strategy. Then it is demonstrated that the strategy can be trained and performance can be improved. The problem with this line of research is the concern with variables that influence training rather than the nature of the learning disability that necessitates the need for such training. However, the questions about *why* students with LD are strategy-deficient have not been addressed. A focus on *why* is appropriate because the field of learning disabilities has been historically concerned with intra- and interindividual differences—that is, what the child's individual strengths and weaknesses in processing are, and how to match the characteristics of each individual child to the best intervention.

The Why of Strategy Instruction

One possible reason why children with LD need exposure to appropriate strategy training is related to the concept of access. Access refers to the notion that the information necessary for successful task performance resides within the child. Some children (e.g., those who have learning disabilities) are not able to access this information flexibly; that is, efficient processing is limited to a constrained set of circumstances (Campione, Brown, Ferrara, Jones, & Steinberg, 1985; Ferrara, Brown, & Campione, 1986; Swanson, 1986b). Further, some children (e.g., those with learning disabilities) are *not* "aware" of these processes and/or have difficulty consciously describing and discussing their own cognitive activities that allow them to access information. Children with learning disabilities appear to have difficulty accessing and coordinating the information they have available to them. Several studies support the notion and can be summarized as follows: Children with LD experience difficulty with such self-regulating mechanisms as checking, planning, monitoring, testing, revising, and evaluating during their attempts to learn or solve problems (e.g., Bauer & Emhert, 1984; Brown & Palincsar, 1988; Butkowsky & Willows, 1980; Dallego & Moely, 1980; Duffy et al., 1986, 1987; Palincsar & Brown, 1984; Pressley & Levin, 1987; Short & Ryan, 1984; Wong & Sawatsky, 1984; Wong, Wong, Perry, & Sawatsky, 1986). In addition, these children suffer from deficits in mental operations such as the logical organization and coordination of incoming information (Meltzer, Chapter 4 this volume; Swanson, 1988). Such children also perform poorly on a variety of tasks that require the use of general control processes or strategies for solution (see Pressley & Levin, 1987, for a review). Under some conditions well-designed strategy training improves performance (e.g., Borkowski, Weyhing, & Carr, 1988), whereas at other times some general cognitive constraints prevent the effective use of control processes (Baker, Ceci, & Herrmann, 1987; Swanson, 1986a) (see Cooney & Swanson, 1987, for a review). However, training attempts are successful (e.g., Borkowski et al., 1988; Englert et al., in press; McLoone, Scruggs, & Mastroperi, & Zucker, 1986; Palincsar & Brown, 1984) when the training of information processing components includes instructions related to self-evaluation (e.g., predicting outcomes, organizing strategies, using various forms of trial and error), appropriate attributions (beliefs) related to effective strategy use (e.g., Licht, Kistner, Ozkaragoz, Shapiro, & Clausen, 1985), and certain subprocesses that are relatively familiar or automatized (see Pellegrino & Goldman, 1987; Spear & Sternberg, 1987).

Consequently, children with learning disabilities may have ineffective strategies for approaching the complex requirements of academic tasks and may be unable to meet their academic potential. The student with learning disabilities may be characterized as an *actively inefficient learner*—one who either lacks certain strategies or chooses inappropriate strategies and/or generally fails to engage effectively in self-monitoring behavior.

The implication of this strategy research is that the previous research must shift from its focus on isolated processing deficits (e.g., see Stanovich, 1986, related to phonological coding), and must now incorporate findings that suggest that children with LD also suffer from higher order cognitive processing problems. No doubt, it is possible that isolated or specific processing deficiencies influence higher order cognitive processing. It may also be argued, however, that a learning disability may be related to the inefficient regulation or *coordination* of mental processes that are not directly related to a specific processing deficiency (see Swanson, 1985, for a related discussion). It is not the intent of the above comments to suggest that the domain-specific or process-specific models of LD be abandoned, but rather put into perspective. Although the "notion of specificity" is a critical assumption in the field of learning disabilities (Stanovich, 1986), this orientation has generated several competing hypotheses. Further, even if a specific deficit is isolated, as suggested by Paris and Oka (1989), the problem is pervasive over time in its influence on cognition and the acquisition of knowledge. Without denying a specific etiology of LD, there are both theoretical and practical benefits to focusing on higher order processing difficulties of children with learning disabilities.

Advantages of a Strategy Model

Consistent with the above discussion, there are several positive aspects to a strategy oriented perspective on learning disabilities. Two advantages will be listed briefly. First, a strategy model explains *conscious and active rule creation and rule following*. Cognition involves planful activities and a focus on strategies, which allows the teacher to search for underlying "plans" that influence behavior. As stated by Pressley, et al. (1989), comprehensive strategy programs are made up of a number of factors that support active rule creation and rule following. For example, to write an essay the student must plan the essay, translate the plan into a narrative, and review and revise the various steps. In addition, a student must have a complete model of strategy use. Good strategy users have (a) a variety of strategies to accomplish a task,

(b) specific strategies that can be integrated into high-order sequences that accomplish complex cognitive tasks, (c) metacognitive processes to regulate competent performance, (d) appropriate beliefs about the payoffs in the strategies they use, and (e) an adequate knowledge base.

Second, *a focus is placed on what is modifiable*. That is, differences between ability groups are conceptualized in terms of cognitive processes that are susceptible to instruction, rather than fundamental or general differences in ability. For example, in the area of reading, Paris and Oka (1989) argued that although learning disabilities are traditionally conceptualized in terms of "specific" deficits, there are benefits to focusing on strategy instruction. Learning in these students has been diminished (possibly because of processing deficits) in terms of the acquisition of knowledge in the content areas. Strategy instruction provides a focus on domain processes not usually associated with instruction in the classroom. Teaching children with learning disabilities how to select, deploy, and monitor appropriate strategies thereby enables them to regulate the quality of their academic performance.

Strategy Instruction as a Continuum

When a teacher attempts to convert some of the assumptions of the strategy instruction model to actual classroom activities, it is usually in terms of inducing students with LD to become aware of their own cognitive processes (i.e., a focus is placed on metacognition). For example, the training mechanisms favored are those that mediate learning, via the teacher who provides hints, clues, counter examples, probes, and so forth (Borkowski et al., 1988). Adequate learners are those who pose questions to themselves, practice strategies, question their assumptions, provide counter strategies, and so on. However, the reader should be aware that strategy instruction must be conceptualized within an instructional continuum.

At one part of the instructional continuum, the teacher is viewed as a model and interrogator of the child's strategic thinking, as well as someone who engineers instructional activities that influence the child's strategic use of mental resources. As the learner's self-regulatory controls eventually become more internalized, the teacher's level of participation diminishes (e.g., Palincsar & Brown, 1987). At the other end of the continuum, a focus is placed on processing skills and subskills that must be performed automatically (Spear & Sternberg, 1987). It is assumed that the ability to perform deliberate and effortful tasks, such as reading, mathematics, and spelling, requires the automatic and rapid deployment of relevant subskills (see Pellegrino & Goldman, 1987).

When combining both ends of the continuum, appropriate instruction for the child with LD must include moving through a metacognitive training phase in which the learning environment consciously directs, encourages, or elicits learning strategies toward a more automatic and less controlled form of processing. This continuum from highly effortful conscious processing to processing that occurs without awareness, effort, or intention appropriately represents the continuum of difficulties experienced by the student with LD. In short, improvement in the learning ability of children with LD necessitates not only the deployment of strategies, but also an executive mechanism that automatically accesses and combines learning skills (i.e., information processing components) when they are needed.

Given these introductory comments related to strategy instruction, let me now briefly outline some points not usually addressed in development of strategy programs for youngsters with learning disabilities. I will primarily draw on my own research, because these are the studies I know most about, as well as because an analysis of my own studies controls for any overgeneralization I might make from the research of others.

Principles of Strategy Instruction

There are eight principles that must be considered for strategy instruction research to be a major intervention approach in the field of learning disabilities. Some of these principles have been outlined elsewhere (e.g., Levin, 1986, 1988), but are summarized here with particular application to learning disabilities.

1. *Strategies must be considered in relation to a student's capacity.* In some instructional cases, poor strategy use may not provide an adequate explanation of learning disabilities. This is because the learning characteristics, such as deficits in cognitive capacity, may not have been taken into consideration (e.g., Swanson, 1982, 1987b, 1987c; Swanson, Cochran, & Ewers, in press). Before a strategy deficit explanation can provide a comprehensive explanation of instructional effects related to the performance of the child with learning disabilities, the majority of predictions provided below need to be supported.

a. Students with LD who use strategies should show minimal variation in their performance across different tasks that *demand the use of such strategies.* That is, if the child with LD is using a systematic approach, his or her performance should be relatively constant.

b. Students with LD should be specifically prone to disruption of their performances that make demands on higher order processes.

c. Students with LD should be minimally influenced by task parameters that are irrelevant to strategy formation.

d. Students with LD should be specifically influenced by strategy components of instruction, such as feedback.

e. Students with LD should show improved performance when they discover definite strategies for coping with the task.

f. Residual performance and differences between ability groups should be eliminated when effective strategies are acquired and learned.

If these six points are not met, then one may assume that cognitive constraints underlie the performance of students with LD. Swanson (1984a) has conducted three experiments that support the notion that children with LD may suffer processing constraints related to limitations in memory capacity. In these experiments, an intentional free-recall task (children informed of the secondary memory test) was presented after subjects correctly matched to-be-remembered words to a series of anagrams organized semantically, phonemically, or in an uncategorized fashion.

The anagram problem-solving task of the to-be-remembered words involved two degrees of effort. In the low-effort condition, anagrams were scrambled for only the first and second letters; in the high-effort condition, all letters were rearranged. These conditions are similar to those of current cognitive effort studies (e.g., Ellis, Thomas, & Rodriguiz, 1984), in which manipulation of primary task difficulty and subsequent performance on a secondary task is used to infer processing effort. However, task difficulty influences not only how much effort or mental input has been invested, but also the various attentional resources necessary for output (recall). Thus, task difficulty not only influences the intensity or effort of processing during input, but also the availability of attentional resources to transmit information.

The results related to the first experiment are shown in Figure 3.1. The results are unequivocal in showing the individual variations in the facilitative effects of cognitive effort on later retrieval. The results were interpreted as indicating that the poor recall of readers with learning disabilities was related to their failure to activate distinctive features of words from memory, to allocate attentional capacity to elaborate those features, and, in some instances (as found on anagram solutions that included errors), to activate a critical number of word features to fill the allocated attentional capacity. Skilled readers' suc-

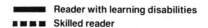

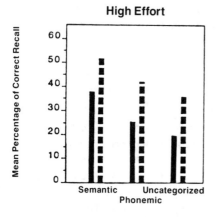

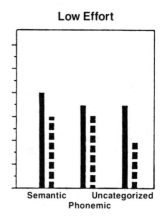

FIGURE 3.1.   Recall as a function of encoding effort.

cessful recall apparently represents some critical number of word features activated during encoding that matched allocated attentional capacity.

In subsequent work (Swanson, 1986a), I have found that skilled readers enhanced their recall by accessing more usable information from semantic memory than did readers with disabilities. Children with disabilities were found to be inferior in the quantity and internal coherence of information stored in semantic memory as well as the means by which it was accessed. This finding is also noted in another study (Swanson, in press), which compared the elaborative encoding strategies of students with learning disabilities, students with mental retardation, gifted students, and normally achieving students. The results suggested that slow learners, normal students, and gifted children improved in performance when they used elaborative strategies as compared with nonelaborative strategies. In contrast, children with learning disabilities were less positively influenced by elaborative strategies, possibly due to excessive demands placed on processing capacity.

The point that is being stressed in these studies is that strategy inefficiencies are not a sufficient explanation for the instructional performance of children with learning disabilities. No doubt, the need for previous studies to explain the instructional deficiencies of children with LD in terms of strategy use may be, in part, a by-product of the efforts to place learning disabilities within a "production deficiency" framework or some other optimistic instructional model. What is needed is instructional research that provides a framework for considering how both processes and capacity interact during instructional interventions. Unfortunately, most LD strategy research, either implicitly or explicitly, has considered cognitive capacity to be a confounding variable, and few attempts have been made to measure its influence.

2. *The use of effective strategies does not necessarily eliminate processing differences.* It is commonly assumed that if children with disabilities are presented a strategy that allows for the efficient processing of information, then improvement in performance is due to the fact that the strategies are affecting the same processes as those of non-disabled students (e.g., Torgesen et al., 1979). This assumption has emanated primarily from studies that have imposed organization on seemingly unorganized material. For example, there is considerable evidence that readers with learning disabilities do not initially take advantage of the organizational features of material (e.g., Dallego & Moely, 1980). When children with learning disabilities are instructed to organize information into semantic or related categories, some studies (e.g., Torgesen et al., 1979) have suggested that their performance is comparable to that of non-disabled students. Some training studies (e.g., Dallego & Moely, 1980; Wong, Wong, & Foth, 1977) have directed readers with disabilities to sort items (rods, pictures) into separate but multiple categories of superordinate information (e.g., pictures that go with furniture, animals, transportation). Such procedures are assumed to increase superordinate classification of information by children with learning disabilities and thereby enhance their ability to automatically access information stored in long-term memory (see Worden, 1985, for a review). Such an interpretation, however, does not adequately explain the fact that residual differences between ability groups still emerge (Wong et al., 1977).

It is possible that instruction that directs children with LD to sort information into categories interacts with various organizational processes. That is, although sorting procedures may produce optimal learning for both ability groups, how certain processes interact may determine if residual differences in recall will occur. To determine if recall differences between ability groups during strategy training reflect the different organizational processing, two experimental phases were implemented in a study by Swanson and Rathgeber (1986). An integrative training phase was presented first, because knowledge of the various organizational classes is a prerequisite skill of elaborative organization (Mandler, 1979). During the integrative phase, children sorted separate word lists according to either semantic, phonemic, or orthographic classes of word features. The sorting of words into distinct features accented the intrastructural (integrative) characteristics of words within each list. After sorting each word class, a memory task assessed the independent effects of each type of word organization on the recall of readers with learning disabilities and on their clustering performance. In the second phase of the study, the elaborative phase, we assessed whether individual differences in recall emerge when the three types of organizations (i.e., semantic, phonemic, orthographic) were merged into an interstructural (elaborative) network. Elaborative organization was assessed on two tasks. One task utilized familiar words from the previous integrative phase, whereas another task used unfamiliar words. When compared to unfamiliar word structures, the more familiar word structures (as presented in the previous integrative phase) were assumed to be more likely to facilitate processes related to elaborative organization.

The organizational processing of readers with learning disabilities, under conditions that direct the encoding of elaborative dimensions (interstructural relationships), is not qualitatively different from that of their age-related counterparts. That is, under conditions that allow for interstructural organization of word classes, the recall of readers with disabilities is like that of nondisabled readers. However, when compared to nondisabled readers, readers with learning disabilities are inferior in their ability to access a comparable amount of information during integrative or intrastructural organizational processing. These recall differences are reflected in the uneven distribution of attention by readers with disabilities to the various intrastructural word organizations. Young readers with disabilities appear to overattend to the intrastructural aspects of words when compared to age-related nondisabled readers, whereas skilled readers process such features without intention or awareness. The diffuse attention (i.e., selective-attention scores below zero) that occurs at the older age for readers with disabilities reflects the fact that when integrative processing places minimal demands on attention, such children may simply fail to process important word features.

There are two important implications related to these results of the study. First, the study does not support current notions suggesting that recall differences between readers with learning disabilities and nondisabled readers are eliminated if both groups are taught to use the same encoding strategy (e.g., Torgesen et al., 1979). Second, not all children with LD take advantage of the integrative and elaborative structure of materials. That is, just because readers with learning disabilities are sensitized to the internal structure of material by sorting activities, does not mean they will make use of it in a manner consistent with the expectation of the experiment.

To further illustrate this finding in a simpler fashion, let us consider a *pilot* study recently completed in an LD classroom (Swanson,

Kozleski, & Stegink, 1987). Two adolescents with learning disabilities who had serious memory and reading (i.e., comprehension) problems, were given two tasks. One task required remembering critical details of various stories read daily from a newspaper column. Immediately after presentation of the story, both students listened to passages and freely recalled idea units. After recall was completed, their taped verbal responses were played back. For each idea unit recalled, the students were asked, "Now how did you remember that?" Student responses were tape-recorded and their responses subjected to a verbal protocol analysis. The coding of verbal "think-aloud" protocols was as follows:

a. *Nonstrategic.* Subjects recalled idea units, but verbalizations were irrelevant or did not reveal an action sequence (e.g., "I must remember it," "It seemed important").

b. *Visual imagery.* Verbal response in which the context associated with the idea unit is a nonverbal referent such as an object, a picture, or a mental image (e.g., "I imagined a basketball court in my mind").

c. *Access to long-term memory.* Verbal responses in which previous experience and/or familiarity with the word or idea is associated with an idea unit (e.g., "I have a friend with the same name").

d. *Advanced organization.* Verbal responses that refer to the structure of the prose, key words in the prose, or related ideas for logically organizing information (e.g., "I remember that from when I wrote the words on paper in the beginning").

e. *Rehearsal.* Verbal responses in which rote repetition or repetitive naming is associated with an idea unit (e.g., "I just keep saying the information over to myself").

f. *Novel encoding.* Verbal responses that emphasized the salience or unfamiliarity of ideas (e.g., "I remember that because it is so unusual . . .").

The second task, which assessed any possible generalization of training effect from the primary task, required the retrieval of information on a social studies assignment. For the strategy phase of instruction, students were provided a sheet of paper that included a visual map (diagram) that would enhance note taking of idea units. It was assumed that the writing of idea units into visual organizational chunks and the linking of these chunks to the title of the passage would encourage verbatim encoding and thereby improve recall. Thus, strategy training involved teaching the students to map (write) on paper the main idea and the supporting idea units of each passage on the space provided on the sheet. The visual organizer (map) was assumed to guide the learner in building a coherent outline or "organizer" of the prose material (see Pressley & Levin, 1986, for a review of the literature on this procedure). Students were instructed to "take notes" on the mapping organizer during the tape-recorded presentation of the prose passage. At the end of the prose passage presentation, students were then instructed to turn over the mapping organizer and recall as many idea units as possible. Procedures followed for the taping and playback that were the same as those used for the baseline phase.

The results of the study are shown in Figure 3.2. Two findings are of importance. First, nonstrategic components characterize baseline performance, whereas components related to rehearsal strategies facilitate cognitive training sessions. These results suggest that treatment effects for readers with disabilities represent a qualitative change in mental processing between the baseline and the treatment phase. Second, and most important, prose recall improved during strategy training, but the student's verbalized strategies were *not* ostensibly related to the treatment condition (i.e., verbalizations related to rehearsal were more frequent compared to verbalizations on imagery). These findings support the notion that isolated or sustaining mental processes may influence or depress disabled readers' prose performance. These processes are not directly related to specific instruction and appear to represent a general activation of simple strategies in the child's repertoire (i.e., rehearsal).

In sum, some studies suggest that performance changes that occur because of strategic instruction may be influenced by interactive processes. Further, these interactive processes may differ between ability groups and/or these processes may underlie performance changes that are not directly related to the process taught during strategy training.

3. *Comparable performance does not mean comparable strategies.* Although the previous principle suggests that different processes may be activated *during* intervention that are not necessarily the intent of the instructional intervention, it is also likely that students with learning disabilities use different strategies on tasks in which they seem to have little difficulty. It is assumed that although children with learning disabilities have isolated processing deficits and require general learning strategies to compensate for these processing deficits, they process information in a way comparable to their normal counterparts on tasks in which they have little trouble. Yet several authors have suggested that there are a number of alternative ways for achieving successful performance (Newell, 1980), and there is some

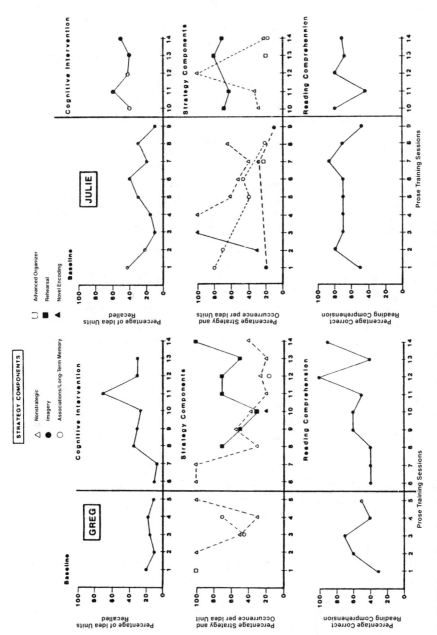

FIGURE 3.2. Recall, mental components, and reading comprehension performance.

indirect evidence that individuals with disabilities may use qualitatively different mental operations (Shankweiler, Liberman, Mark, Fowler, & Fisher 1979) and processing routes (e.g., Swanson, 1986a) when compared to their nondisabled counterparts.

For example, a recent study (Swanson, 1988) found that children with disabilities may use qualitatively different processes on tasks that they have little difficulty performing. Evidence in support of this finding was provided when comparing "think aloud protocols" of children with learning disabilities and nondisabled children on picture arrangement problem-solving tasks.

Students with learning disabilities and normal achieving students were comparable in the total number of mental components used to solve the task and the number of problems solved. However, children with learning disabilities had difficulty in using isolated heuristics (general problem-solving approaches) related to problem representation and deleting irrelevant information. In addition, normal achieving children were better than children with learning disabilities in using strategies that related to evaluation, systematic problem solving, feedback, and pattern extraction. Further, a stepwise regression analysis suggested that the overall mental processing of children with learning disabilities was best predicted by heuristics, whereas nondisabled children's overall mental processing was best predicted by specific strategies. There are two major implications of this finding for strategy intervention research.

First, students with LD and non-LD students have a number of alternative means for achieving successful performance. The idea that a task can be performed with a variety of different mental components is important when designing instructional programs. My findings suggest that the mental processing of children with disabilities is more likely driven by heuristics than by algorithms. No doubt such general methods of problem solving allow them to benefit from general strategy instruction interventions that are not deeply embedded in a particular academic domain. Further, the use of heuristics allows them to perform in the normal range of intelligence. Unfortunately, although these general problem-solving methods have greater generality than algorithms, they also have relatively less power. My findings also suggest that learning disabled children may not understand how explicit strategies or algorithms can be used in task performance. Thus, instructions that help children with LD organize certain mental processes into algorithms may have more applicability to classroom performance than the teaching of heuristics. In my study, children with learning disabilities were able to tag new information and abandon inappropriate algorithms throughout different phases of the task. Likewise, they had relatively little difficulty in accessing various pieces of information to solve a problem. Thus, when compared to nondisabled children, it appears that children with learning disabilities develop strategic thought patterns "actively," although inefficiently. (That is, as indicated in the protocol collected, children with learning disabilities did actively engage in strategy development and use.) These inefficiencies appear to be related to their preferred use of heuristics and suggest that such children with disabilities may be constrained in their ability to use strategies in a flexible manner (see Brown & Campione, 1986, for a related hypothesis).

Second, the protocols for both ability groups tend to reflect thinking that is "multidirectional" rather than linear. This kind of thinking is in contrast to the step-by-step or serial thinking that is followed in some "strategy training packages." Rather, the natural flow of children's thinking reflects a coordination of multiple pieces of information (i.e., subroutines) or multiple operations rather than a step-by-step or component-by-component process. This finding is consistent with other literature on "opportunistic" thinking (e.g., Hayes-Roth & Hayes-Roth, 1979). This suggests that children and adults make decisions related to task performance that do not fit strategically into a completely integrated or hierarchical plan. Further, as individuals make decisions, their problem-solving approach may develop by processes that may not be coherently integrated. However, for some children with learning disabilities, this opportunistic thinking may reflect excessively poor coordination or independent functioning of mental components (also see Swanson, 1984b, 1985, for a related hypothesis). In terms of strategy intervention, a possible instructional goal is one directed at the executive processing or monitoring of various components so that a smooth coordination of information processing occurs during task performance.

In sum, some evidence suggests that comparable performance does not mean comparable strategy use.

4. *Good strategies for non-LD (NLD) students are not necessarily good strategies for LD students.* Strategies that enhance access to procedural and/or declarative knowledge for NLD students will not, in some cases, be well suited for the child with LD and vice versa. For example, in a study by Swanson and Cooney (1987) it was discovered that students who do well in retrieving mathematical facts benefited from strategies that enhanced the access of procedural knowledge, whereas children poor in math benefited from strategies that enhanced declarative knowledge. To further illustrate, Wong and Jones (1982) trained adolescents with LD and NLD adolescents in a self-questioning strategy to monitor reading comprehension. Results indicated that

although the strategy training benefited the adolescents with learning disabilities, it actually lowered the performance of non-LD adolescents. This concept is also illustrated in a study by Dansereau, et al. (1979), in which college students were presented a networking strategy for transforming text material into nodes and links. Control subjects, who were not taught the strategy, showed a typical positive correlation between their grade-point average (GPA) and achievement, whereas for the experimental subjects the GPA and achievement scores were negatively correlated. Not only were the strategy instructions ineffective, they were actually damaging to the high-GPA subjects.

To illustrate this point further with children with learning disabilities, Swanson (in press) presented students with LD, students with mental retardation, gifted students, and average achieving students a series of tasks that involved base and elaborative sentences. Their task was to recall words embedded in a sentence. For example, one type of sentence consisted of a base sentence (e.g., the _____ people smiled), and the children completed the sentence by choosing between the words *happy* and *sad.* The other sentence consisted of a base sentence and a short phrase (e.g., the _____ people smiled at the clown). It was assumed that the elaborative sentence would clarify the significance of the target word and thereby would improve recall performance. The results of the first study suggested that children with learning disabilities differed from the other group in their ability to benefit from elaboration. As shown in Figure 3.3, elaborative sentences benefited all children, except those with learning disabilities. The elaboration requirement placed excessive demands on the executive processing strategies of children with learning disabilities when compared to the

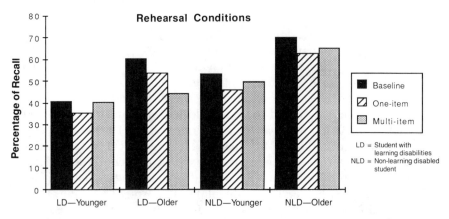

FIGURE 3.3. Percentage of mean recall by rehearsal activity, group, and age.

other ability groups. This assumption was supported in a follow-up study (Swanson, 1989a, Experiment 2) that suggested that encoding difficulty must be taken into consideration when determining strategy effects. The results also suggest that children with disabilities may require additional strategies to bring their performance to a level comparable to that of their cohorts.

In another study (Swanson, Cooney, & Overholser 1989), college students with learning disabilities were asked to recall words in a sentence under semantic and imagery instructional conditions. The stimulus materials were in the form of common and uncommon sentences. Common sentences depicted ordinary scenes (e.g., "The lawyer dropped a magazine in the pond"), whereas uncommon sentences depicted unusual scenes that would not be likely to occur (e.g., "The lawyer floated across the pond on a magazine"). After hearing each sentence, subjects in the imaginal-processing condition were instructed to form an interactive image of three underlined words and then to rate the ease of forming that image. For the semantic-processing condition, subjects were instructed to form a *category* that tied the sentence's three underlined words together and then rate the ease of categorizing those words. A scale from 1 to 5 (1 = very easy, 4 = easy, 3 = moderately difficult, 2 = difficult, 1 = very difficult) was used for both conditions. A cued recall task was then administered. Subjects were asked to respond to the cue by recalling the second and third underlined printed words in the order that they originally appeared in the sentence. These cued-recall procedures were followed for each condition.

The results indicated that readers with disabilities recalled more words for common than uncommon sentences and recalled more words under semantic than imagery-processing instructions. Similarly, skilled readers recalled more targeted words from common than uncommon sentences. In contrast to readers with disabilities, however, skilled readers preferred imagery over semantic processing. Ability groups were comparable during semantic processing, but recall differences in favor of skilled readers occurred during imagery processing. These results support the notion that self-generated imagery instructions for subjects with learning disabilities fail to provide a "distinctive" item representation. Further, the results suggest that bizarre images may actually disrupt the processing of word information by readers with disabilities. Of course, one may argue that the effects of imagery recall are not consistent with the extant literature (e.g., Scruggs, Mastropieri, & Levin, 1987). The poor recall effects related to bizarre imagery, however, are consistent with the notion that internally generated representational images result in variable memory traces. Thus, a self-generated bizarre image does not add much to an already meaningfully interpreted text (Levin, 1981). Regardless, the results clearly suggest that readers with disabilities have difficulty benefiting from instructions that prompt self-generated imagery, whereas skilled readers do not.

In sum, some studies suggest that strategies that are effective for NLD students may, in fact, be less effective for students with LD.

5. *Comparable strategy use may not eliminate performance differences.* In a production deficiency view of learning disabilities, it is commonly assumed that, without instruction, students with learning disabilities are less likely to produce strategies than their normal counterparts. Several studies have indicated that residual differences remain between ability groups, even when ability groups are instructed and/or prevented from strategy use (Gelzheiser 1984; Swanson, 1983, 1987a; Wong et al., 1977). For example, in a study by Gelzheiser et al. (1987) children with LD and NLD children were compared on the basis of their ability to use organizational strategies. After instruction in organizational strategies, children with disabilities and nondisabled children were compared on the basis of their ability to recall information on a posttest. The results indicated that children with learning disabilities were comparable in strategy use to nondisabled students, but were deficient in overall performance.

In another study, Swanson (1983) found that the recall of a group with learning disabilities did not improve from baseline level when trained with rehearsal strategies. Using children with disabilities and nondisabled children, Swanson examined the relationship of memory estimation (children estimate performance prior to performing task) and retrieval knowledge for specific rehearsal strategies in the free recall of unrelated words. At each level, a baseline and two instructional conditions were devised to manipulate the child's rehearsal activity to the task. The baseline condition emphasized spontaneous rehearsal, whereas the two instructional conditions emphasized (a) one-item and (b) multi-item rehearsal. All conditions emphasized that children were to recall words. In addition to comparing recall performance, Swanson assessed children's use of estimated recall ability and retrieval understanding for all instructional conditions so that links between strategic knowledge and rehearsal activity could be examined. Specifically, the experimenter told the children they would be presented a list of items orally and they were to practice learning the words aloud during the interval following the presentation of each item. For the baseline condition, children were told to practice aloud. No particular rehearsal strategy was suggested, because children could practice aloud one item or with any other previous words. Two other trials were given for one-item instructions, and children were told to "say only the presented word once"; for multi-item instructions, children were told to "practice each word with as many of the earlier presented words as possible but to say the newly presented word at least once." After rehearsal instructions were given for each word list, children were asked to examine that list and to estimate how many words they could remember. After an estimation was made, the experimenter presented the lists of words orally. To determine the extent to which rehearsal instructions would lead to effective metamnemonic behavior, the experimenter asked up to four questions in the order given below for all three instructional conditions (questioning ceased after any unambiguous recall strategy was repeated):

a. How did you remember these words?

b. What did you think about when the word list was given?

c. Some children remember by following my instructions, or say or do something different. What did you do?

d. Maybe you did it the way I presented it to you; did you? How did I do it?

The results related to the recall phase are shown in Figure 3.4. As shown in Figure 3.4, readers with learning disabilities were generally inferior in recall to nondisabled readers, even though both ability groups were comparable in rehearsal use. Support for this interpretation comes from the lack of rehearsal activity difference between groups on baseline and multi-item conditions. An inspection of the retrospective reports indicated that readers with disabilities reported a word organization strategy less frequently, thereby suggesting that they analyze words at a more superficial level than skilled readers.

Data on the interrelation of baseline, one-item, and multi-item rehearsal activity; self-estimates of span; and reported strategy provided an interesting interpretation of the inferior recall performance of readers with learning disabilities. Although readers with learning disabilities did not clearly articulate a plan for recalling words, they did in fact use rehearsal activity comparable to nondisabled readers. Thus, one cannot say children with learning disabilities failed to use the appropriate rehearsal activity because they were unaware of the difficulty of the task or could not articulate a mnemonic strategy.

The results of the studies reviewed support the notion that groups of children with different learning histories may continue to learn differently, even when the groups are equated in terms of strategy use.

6. *Strategies taught do not necessarily become transformed into expert strategies.* One mechanism that promotes expert performance

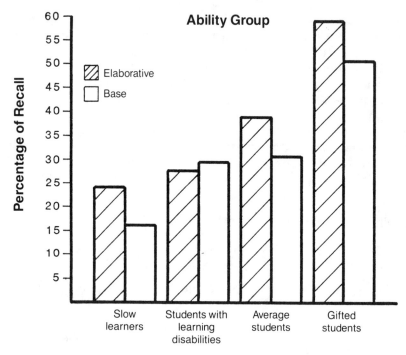

FIGURE 3.4. Recall performance as a function of type of sentence and ability group.

is related to strategy transformation (e.g., Chi, Glaser, & Farr, 1988). That is, it often appears that children who become experts at certain tasks have learned simple strategies and, through practice, discover ways to modify those strategies into more efficient and powerful procedures. In particular, the proficient learner uses higher order rules to eliminate unnecessary or redundant steps to hold increasing amounts of information. The child with learning disabilities, in contrast, may learn most of the skills related to performing an academic task and perform appropriately on that task by carefully and systematically following prescribed rules or strategies. Although children with learning disabilities can be taught strategies, some evidence suggests that the differences between children with learning disabilities and nondisabled children (experts in this case) is that the latter have modified such strategies to become more efficient (Swanson & Cooney, 1985; Swanson & Rhine, 1985). It is plausible that the child with learning disabilities remains a novice because he or she fails to transform simple strategies into more efficient forms.

One study (Swanson & Cooney, 1985) illustrates this point. The researchers assumed that a possible mechanism that permits the retrieval of mathematical facts and procedures is strategy transformation. The dependent measure and strategy transformation conditions are shown in Figure 3.5. The dependent measure is an averaging technique for determining the subject's information "handling" rate for different types of problems. Assuming that strategy transformations occur, each subject was made to perform calculations covering as large a range of arithmetic problems as possible. Problems selected were at least three grade levels below the current mathematical functioning of children with learning disabilities on standardized math tests. Each transformation condition included a minimum of five problems that were as numerically diverse as possible, but arithmetically comparable. Each strategy transformation condition is briefly described and provided below.

Results to answers. This strategy transformation focuses on the extent that children rely on memory retrieval rather than computation.

Reduction to rule. This strategy transformation focuses on the extent to which children identify a set of steps that provide an answer with minimal calculation. These sets of steps require the searching for constant relationships across problems.

Method replacement. Method replacement consists of replacing one procedure with another that more efficiently accomplishes the same result.

Unit building. Unit building consists of grouping mental operations into a single set. This strategy involves memorizing consistent sequences that can be clustered together.

Saving partial results. Saving of partial results is like the unit building transformation in that a focus is placed on reducing computation effort.

Process elimination. Process elimination is comparable to method replacement, except that in a process elimination strategy, a transformation is made of all prior operations. In contrast, method replacement may reuse earlier operations.

Reordering. Reordering refers to the changing of previously learned strategies to reduce task difficulty.

As shown in Figure 3.5, the results of the Swanson and Cooney (1985) study indicate that nondisabled children, in contrast to children with disabilities, are more likely to solve simple arithmetic problems, via the use of processes that involve strategy transformation. Children with learning disabilities are more likely to use strategies they have been taught, yielding lower information handling rates than their nondisabled counterparts.

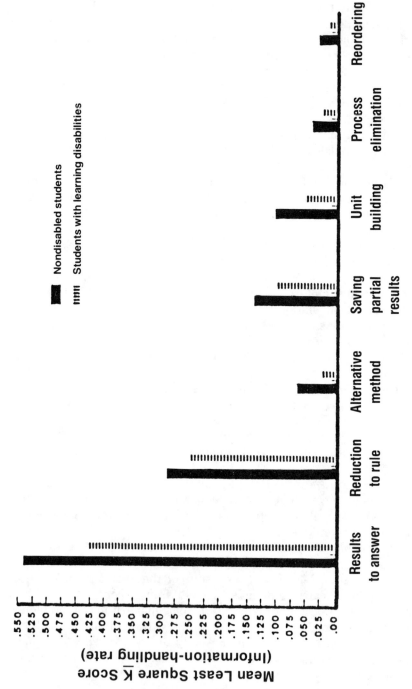

FIGURE 3.5. Transformation performance as a function of ability group.

These preliminary findings suggest that acquired knowledge must undergo changes in specific processes or operations before proficient performance can be obtained.

7. *Strategy instruction must operate on the law of parsimony.* A number of "multiple component packages", of strategy instruction have been suggested for improving functioning of children with learning disabilities. These components have usually encompassed some of the following: skimming, imagining, drawing, elaborating, paraphrasing, mnemonics, accessing prior knowledge, reviewing, orienting to critical features, and so on. No doubt there are some positive aspects to these strategy packages in that:

a. These programs are an advance over some of the studies that you see in the LD literature that focus on rather simple or quick-fix strategies (e.g., rehearsal or categorization to improve performance).

b. These programs promote a domain skill and incorporate procedures that enhance metacognitive skills.

c. The best of these programs involve (1) teaching a few strategies well rather than superficially, (2) teaching students to monitor their performance, (3) teaching students when and where to use the strategy in order to enhance generalization, (4) teaching strategies as a integrated part of an existing curriculum, and (5) including a great deal of supervised student feedback and practice.

The difficulty of such packages, however, at least in terms of instructional intervention, is that little is known about which components best predict student performance. Further, it is difficult to determine why the strategy worked. The multiple component approaches that are typically found in a number of LD strategy intervention studies must be carefully contrasted with a component analysis approach that involves the systematic combination of instructional activities known to have an additive effect on performance.

Thus, the questions arise, What components are necessary for performance improvement, and what components are necessary for maintaining performance? Consider a typical effective strategy intervention program based on a cognitive-behavioral model. In this study (Swanson, 1985, Experiment 1), the daily instructional treatment for junior high school students with learning disabilities followed the verbal modeling procedure outlined by Meichenbaum, (Meichenbaum, 1982; Meichenbaum & Goodman, 1971). Training proceeded according to the following five sequential steps: (a) Student quietly observes the teacher (model) performing a task as the model talks aloud; (b) student performs the same task while the teacher instructs; (c) student performs the task while instructing himself/herself aloud; (d) student performs the task while whispering softly with no teacher prompting; and (e) finally, the student is instructed to perform the task quietly to himself or herself.

In the beginning phases, the teacher models (verbalizes) task-specific and general skills statements. Strategy statements serve to slow down the problem-solving process to assist in error monitoring ("Yesterday I didn't _____ and I missed the answer"), to self-interrogate ("I need to ask myself . . ."), to make predictions ("If I do that I'll be able to . . ."), and to set the stage for self-reinforcement when the corrected response occurs. The error-monitoring component of instruction includes a coping statement from previous sessions (i.e., "I should have asked myself the title of the story, then I would have been able to answer the question"). The specific task self-instruction statement focuses on *identifying* what the child can do (task-specific requirements) to *ascertain* the appropriate knowledge (i.e., ask the teacher, look up the word in the dictionary, study the word list aloud) to *produce* the appropriate response (write the answer in the blank). For example, a typical monologue in this study included the following:

> *Spelling:* "Let's see, what is it I have to do today? *(self-interrogation)*. Later I will need to spell these 10 words correctly *(identify)*. I need to study these words slowly by underlining word families. I need to remember this for the spelling test *(ascertain knowledge)*. This has the vowel-consonant-silent /e/ pattern. From my spelling test yesterday, I missed a word formed like this *(error monitoring)*. I need to ask myself, How is the best way to do this? *(self-interrogation)*. If I remember my word families *(ascertain)*, I won't have to guess on spelling words I'm not sure of. That's easy *(self-reinforcement)*. Even if I don't remember each of the letters of the word to spell, I can remember the word family *(prediction and error monitoring)*. I need to write my words on this piece of paper" *(produce)*.

Which of the above statements or instructional phases are necessary for effective instruction? One approach to answering this question is to have selected components or steps from the package "dropped out" at various points in the training. Such a procedure would allow the teacher to determine which components are necessary to maintain student performance. For example, Swanson (1985; Experiment 2) assessed differential performance of subjects when various instructional stages of the self-instruction model were introduced. This manipulation had a certain social validity about it, because the components of the training procedure were time-consuming in terms of other skills that must be taught. To shorten training periods, it was necessary to separate cognitive-behavioral training steps (e.g., cognitive modeling; subject verbalizes aloud while doing task) across different instructional sessions. That is, the five steps of cognitive-behavioral instruction were separated across sessions.

This separation is shown in Figure 3.6. Steps 1, 2, and 3 included the first three steps of the Meichenbaum and Goodman (1971) procedure discussed earlier (modeling; student performs task while teacher verbalizes; student does task and verbalizes). For Step 3, the modeling and student performance/teacher verbalization steps were eliminated from the cognitive-behavioral procedure. Instead, the child was instructed to do the task and verbalize aloud. The teacher consistently prompted the child if self-statements did not include task-specific and general task components. For Step 4, children were instructed to whisper their self-instructions to themselves. They were provided cue cards with questions to help them remember their self-instructional components. For Step 5, children were instructed for each session "to think about what they had been instructed in the past." They were told to do their thinking to themselves.

The dependent measures in the study were correct math computation and spelling. For both math and spelling performance, the introduction of the various cognitive-behavioral steps improved academic performance and performance was maintained on a related task. The important finding of this study, however, was that the cognitive-behavioral program was efficiently "spread" across sessions, thus making parsimonious use of the components necessary to maintain intervention effectiveness. Another important finding related to strategy intervention is that a major goal of instruction was reached. This goal relates to the utilization of internal speech as a means for generating control over behavior (Vygotsky, 1962). That is, as environmental manipulations by the teacher were lessened, the child assumed major responsibility for using verbal mediation to direct behavior (as shown for Step 5 in Figure 3.6).

The principle demonstrated in the previously reviewed study is that *not* all phases or components of an instructional model are necessary for implementation to positively influence student performance.

8. *Strategies serve different purposes.* Analysis of the cognitive strategy research suggests there is no single best strategy for students with LD within or across particular domains. As reflected in a number of strategy studies to date, research is in pursuit of the best strategy or strategies to teach students with learning disabilities. A number of studies, for example, have looked at enhancing the performance of

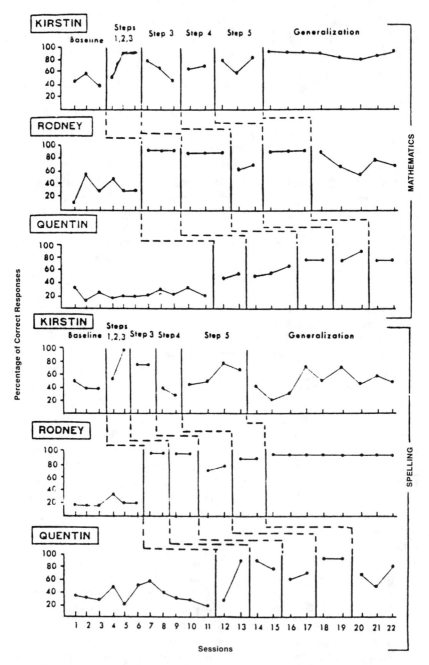

FIGURE 3.6. Math and spelling performance as a function of intervention sessions.

children with LD through the use of advanced organizers, skimming, asking, questioning, taking notes, summarizing and so on. But apart from the fact that students with LD have been exposed to various types of strategies, the question of which strategies are the most effective is not known. We know that in some tasks, such as those that require the memorization of facts, the key word approach appears to be more effective than direct instruction models (Scruggs et al., 1987). However, the rank-ordering of different strategies changes in reference to the different types of learning outcomes expected. Certain strategies, such as previously read material, are better suited to enhancing students' understanding of academic tasks, whereas other strategies are better suited to enhancing students' memory of words or facts. The important point to remember is that there are a number of ways in which different strategies can effect different cognitive outcomes.

Conclusions

Researchers and teachers must follow certain guidelines and principles in their selection of strategies to be taught to students with LD. Strategies are never applied in isolation of person, process, and context. Strategies are always applied to specific materials, in a specific context, with a specific student. When these factors are kept in mind, the strategy model of instruction has much to offer the LD field. I have highlighted only a few of the principles to keep in mind when implementing strategy programs for students with LD. It is hoped that such information will guide models of instruction designed to teach students with LD effective strategy use.

References

Baker, J. G., Ceci, S. J., & Herrmann, N. D. (1987). Semantic structure and processing: Implications for the learning disabled child. In H. L. Swanson (Ed.), *Memory and learning disabilities* (pp. 83–110). Greenwich, CT: JAI Press.

Bauer, R. H., & Emhert, J. (1984). Information processing in reading-disabled and nondisabled children. *Journal of Experimental Child Psychology, 37,* 271–281.

Borkowski, J. G., Estrada, M. T., Milstead, M., & Hale, C. (1989). General problem-solving skills: Relations between metacognition and strategic processing. *Learning Disability Quarterly, 12,* 57–70.

Borkowski, J. G., Weyhing, R. S., & Carr, M. (1988). Effects of attributional retraining on strategy-based reading comprehension in learning-disabled students. *Journal of Educational Psychology, 80,* 46–53.

Bos, C., & Filips, D. (1982). Comprehension monitoring skills in learning disabled and average students. *Topics in Learning and Learning Disabilities, 2*, 79–85.

Brown, A. L., & Campione, J. C. (1986). Psychological theory and the study of learning disabilities. *American Psychologist, 41*, 1059–1068.

Brown, A. L., & Palincsar, A. S. (1988). Reciprocal teaching of comprehension strategies: A natural history of one program for enhancing learning. In J. Borkowski & J. P. Das (Eds.), *Intelligence and cognition in special children: Comparative studies of giftedness, mental retardation, and learning disabilities.* New York: Ablex.

Butkowsky, I. S., & Willows, D. M. (1980). Cognitive-motivational characteristics of children varying in reading ability: Evidence for learned helplessness in poor readers. *Journal of Educational Psychology, 72*, 408–422.

Campione, J. C., Brown, A. L., Ferrara, R. A., Jones, R. S., & Steinberg, E. (1985). Breakdown in flexible use of information: Intelligence-related differences in transfer following equivalent learning performance. *Intelligence, 9*, 297–315.

Chi, M. T. H., Glaser, R., & Farr, M. (1988). *The nature of expertise.* Hillsdale, NJ: Erlbaum.

Cooney, J. B., & Swanson, H. L. (1987). Memory and learning disabilities: An overview. In H. L. Swanson (Ed.), *Memory and learning disabilities* (pp. 1–40). Greenwich, CT: JAI Press.

Dallego, M., & Moely, B. (1980). Free recall in boys of normal and poor reading levels as a function of task manipulations. *Journal of Experimental Child Psychology, 30*, 62–78.

Dansereau, D. F., McDonald, B. A., Collins, D. W., Garland, J., Holley, C. D., Dierkhoff, G., & Evans, S. H. (1979). Evaluation of a teaching strategy system. In H. F. O'Neil & C. D. Spielberger (Eds.), *Cognitive and affective learning strategies* (pp. 3–43). New York: Academic Press.

Duffy, G. G., Roehler, L. R., Meloth, M., Vavrus, L., Book, C., Putnam, J., & Wesselman, R. (1986). The relationship between explicit verbal explanation during reading skill instruction and student awareness and achievement: A study of reading teacher effects. *Reading Research Quarterly, 21*, 237–252.

Duffy, G. G., Roehler, L. R., Sivan, E., Rackliffe, G., Book, C., Meloth, M., Vavrus, L., Wesselman, R., Putnam, J., & Bassiri, D. (1987). The effects of explaining the reasoning associated with using reading strategies. *Reading Research Quarterly, 22*, 347–368.

Ellis, H. D., Thomas, R. L., & Rodriguiz, I. A. (1984). Emotional mood states and memory: Elaborative encoding, semantic processing, and cognitive effort. *Journal of Experimental Psychology: Learning, Memory, and Cognition, 10*, 410–432.

Englert, C. S., Raphael, T. E., Anderson, L. M., Anthony, H., Fear, K., & Gregg, S. (in press). A case for writing instruction: Strategies for writing informational text. *Learning Disabilities Focus.*

Ferrara, R. A., Brown, A. L., & Campione, J. C. (1986). Children's learning and transfer of inductive reasoning rules: Studies of proximinal development. *Child Development, 57,* 1087–1089.

Gelzheiser, L. M. (1984). Generalization from categorical memory tasks to prose in learning disabled adolescents. *Journal of Educational Psychology, 76,* 1128–1138.

Gelzheiser, L. M., Cort, R., & Sheperd, M. J. (1987). Is minimal strategy instruction sufficient for LD children? Testing the production defending hypothesis. *Learning Disability Quarterly, 10,* 267–276.

Hayes-Roth, B., & Hayes-Roth, F. (1979). A cognitive model of planning. *Cognitive Science, 3,* 275–310.

Kolligian, J., & Sternberg, R. J. (1987). Intelligence, information processing, and specific learning disabilities: A triarchic synthesis. *Journal of Learning Disabilities, 20,* 8–17.

Levin, J. R. (1981). On the function of pictures in prose. In F. Pirozzola & M. C. Wittrock (Eds.). *Neuropsychological and cognitive processes in reading* (pp. 203–220). New York: Academic Press.

Levin, J. R. (1986). Four cognitive principles of learning strategy instruction. *Educational Psychologist, 21,* 3–17.

Levin, J. R. (1988). Elaboration-based learning strategies: Powerful theory = powerful application. *Contemporary Educational Psychology, 13,* 191–205.

Licht, B. G., Kistner, J. A., Ozkaragoz, T., Shapiro, S., & Clausen, L. (1985). Causal attributions of learning disabled children: Individual differences that their implications for persistence. *Journal of Educational Psychology, 77,* 208–216.

Mandler, G. (1979). Organization and repetition: Organization principles with special reference to rote learning. In L. Nilsson (Ed.), *Perspective on memory research* (pp. 293–315). Hillsdale, NJ: Erlbaum.

McLoone, B. B., Scruggs, T. E., Mastropieri, M. A., & Zucker, S. F. (1986). Memory strategy instruction and training with learning-disabled adolescents. *Learning Disability Research, 2,* 45–53.

Meichenbaum, D. (1982). *Teaching thinking: A cognitive behavioral approach.* Austin, TX: Society for Learning Disabilities and Remedial Education.

Meichenbaum, D., & Goodman, J. (1971). Training impulsive children to talk to themselves. *Journal of Abnormal Psychology, 77,* 115–126.

Moely, B., Hart, S., Santulli, K., Leal, L., Johnson, I., Rao, N., & Borney, L. (1986). How do teachers teach memory skills. *Educational Psychologist, 21,* 55–71.

Newell, A. (1980). Reasoning, problem solving and decision processes: The problem space as a fundamental category. In R. Nickerson (Ed.), *Attention and performance VIII.* Hillsdale, NJ: Erlbaum.

Oka, E. R., & Paris, S. A. (1987). Patterns of motivation and reading skills in underachieving children. In S. J. Ceci (Ed.), *Handbook of cognitive, social, and neuropsychological aspects of learning disabilities* (pp. 115–145). Hillsdale, NJ: Erlbaum.

Palincsar, A. S., & Brown, A. L. (1984). Reciprocal teaching of comprehension-fostering and monitoring activities. *Cognition and Instruction, 1,* 117–175.

Palincsar, A. M., & Brown, A. (1987). Enhancing instructional time through attention to metacognition. *Journal of Learning Disabilities, 20,* 66–76.

Paris, S. G., & Oka, E. R. (1989). Strategies for comprehending text and coping with reading difficulties. *Learning Disability Quarterly, 12,* 32–42.

Pellegrino, J., & Goldman, S. (1987). Information processing and math. *Journal of Learning Disabilities, 20,* 23–34.

Pressley, M., & Levin, J. R. (1986). Elaborative learning strategies for the inefficient learner. In S. J. Ceci (Ed.), *Handbook of cognitive, social and neuropsychological aspects of learning disabilities* (Vol. 1). Hillsdale, NJ: Erlbaum.

Pressley, M., Symons, S., Snyder, B., & Cariglia-Bull, T. (1989). Strategy instruction research comes of age. *Learning Disability Quarterly, 12,* 3–15.

Scruggs, T. E., Mastropieri, M. A., & Levin, J. R. (1987). Transformational mnemonic strategies for learning disabled students. In H. L. Swanson (Ed.), *Memory and learning disabilities* (pp. 225–244). Greenwich, CT: JAI Press.

Shankweiler, D., Liberman, I., Mark, L., Fowler, C., & Fisher, F. (1979). The speech code and learning to read. *Journal of Experimental Psychology: Human Learning and Memory, 5,* 531–545.

Short, E. J., & Ryan, E. B. (1984). Metacognitive differences between skilled and less skilled readers: Remediating deficits through story grammar and attribution training. *Journal of Educational Psychology, 76,* 225–235.

Spear, L. C., & Sternberg, R. J. (1987). An information-processing framework for understanding reading disability. In S. Ceci (Ed.), *Handbook of cognitive, social and neuropsychological aspects of learning disabilities* (pp. 3–32). Hillsdale, NJ: Erlbaum.

Stanovich, K. (1986). Matthew effects in reading: Some consequences of individual differences in the acquisition of literacy. *Reading Research Quarterly, 21,* 360–387.

Swanson, H. L. (1982). Strategies and constraints—A commentary. *Topics in Learning and Learning Disabilities, 2,* 79–81.

Swanson, H. L. (1983). Relations among metamemory, rehearsal activity and word recall in learning disabled and nondisabled readers. *British Journal of Educational Psychology, 53,* 186–194.

Swanson, H. L. (1984a). Effects of cognitive effort and word distinctiveness on learning disabled and nondisabled readers' recall. *Journal of Educational Psychology, 76,* 894–908.

Swanson, H. L. (1984b). Process assessment of intelligence in learning disabled and mentally retarded children: A multidirectional model. *Educational Psychologist, 19,* 149–162.

Swanson, H. L. (1984c). Semantic and visual memory codes in learning disabled readers. *Journal of Experimental Child Psychology, 37*(1), 124–140.

Swanson, H. L. (1985). Effects of cognitive-behavioral training on emotionally disturbed children's academic performance. *Cognitive Therapy and Research, 9,* 201–216.

Swanson, H. L. (1986a). Do semantic memory deficiencies underlie disabled readers encoding processes? *Journal of Experimental Child Psychology, 41*, 461–488.

Swanson, H. L. (1986b). Learning disabled readers' verbal coding difficulties: A problem of storage or retrieval? *Learning Disability Research, 20,* 3–7.

Swanson, H. L. (1987a). Organization training and developmental changes in learning disabled children's encoding preferences. *Learning Disability Quarterly, 8,* 1–18.

Swanson, H. L. (1987b). Verbal-coding deficits in the recall of pictorial information by learning disabled children: The influence of a lexical system for input operations. *American Educational Research Journal, 24,* 143–170.

Swanson, H. L. (1987c). What learning disabled readers fail to retrieve: A problem of encoding, interference or sharing of resources? *Journal of Abnormal Child Psychology, 15,* 339–351.

Swanson, H. L. (1988). Learning disabled children's problem solving: Identifying mental processes underlying intelligent performance. *Intelligence, 12,* 261–278.

Swanson, H. L. (1989a). Central processing strategy difference in gifted, normal achieving, learning disabled and mentally retarded children. *Journal of Experimental Child Psychology, 47,* 370–397.

Swanson, H. L. (1989b). Strategy instruction: Overview of principles and procedures for effective use. *Learning Disability Quarterly, 12,* 3–15.

Swanson, H. L. (1990). Instruction derived from the strategy deficit model: Overview of principles and procedures. In T. Scruggs & B. Y. L. Wong (Eds.), *Intervention research in learning disabilities* (pp. 34–65). New York: Springer-Verlag.

Swanson, H. L. (1991). Learning disabilities and memory. In B Y. L. Wong (Ed.), *Learning about learning disabilities* (pp. 103–127). San Diego: Academic Press.

Swanson, H. L. (in press). Executive processing in learning disabled readers. *Intelligence.*

Swanson, H. L., Cochran, K., & Ewers, C. (1989). Working memory and reading disabilities. *Journal of Abnormal Child Psychology, 17,* 145–156.

Swanson, H. L., & Cooney, J. (1985). Strategy transformations in learning disabled children. *Learning Disability Quarterly, 8,* 221–231.

Swanson, H. L., & Cooney, J. (1987). *Individual differences in mental arithmetic: Procedural or declarative knowledge.* Paper presented at the meeting of the American Educational Research Association, Washington, D. C.

Swanson, H. L., & Cooney, J. D., & Overholser, J. D. (1989). The effects of self-generated visual mnemonics on adult learning disabled readers' word recall. *Learning Disabilities Research, 4,* 26–35.

Swanson, H. L., Kozleski, E., & Stegink, P. (1987). Effects of cognitive training on disabled readers' prose recall: Do cognitive processes change during intervention? *Psychology in the Schools, 24,* 378–384.

Swanson, H. L., & Rathgeber, A. (1986). The effects of organizational dimensions on learning disabled readers' recall. *Journal of Educational Research, 79,* 155–162.

Swanson, H. L., & Rhine, B. (1985). Strategy transformation in learning disabled children's math performance: Clues to the development of expertise. *Journal of Learning Disabilities, 18,* 596–603.

Torgesen, J. K., Murphy, H., & Ivey, G. (1979). The effects of an orienting task on the memory performance of reading disabled children. *Journal of Learning Disabilities, 12,* 396–401.

Vygotsky, L. (1962). *Thought and language.* New York: Wiley.

Wong, B. Y. L., & Jones, W. (1982). Increasing metacomprehension in learning-disabled and normally-achieving students through self-questioning training. *Learning Disability Quarterly, 5,* 228–240.

Wong, B. Y. L., & Sawatsky, D. (1984). Sentence elaboration and retention of good, average and poor readers. *Learning Disability Quarterly, 6–7,* 229–236.

Wong, B. Y. L., Wong, R., & Foth, D. (1977). Recall and clustering of verbal materials among normal and poor readers. *Bulletin of the Psychonomic Society, 10,* 375–378.

Wong, B. Y. L., Wong, R., Perry, N., & Sawatsky, D. (1986). The efficacy of a self-questioning summarization strategy for use by underachievers and learning-disabled adolescents. *Learning Disability Focus, 2,* 20–35.

Worden, P. E. (1986). Comprehension and memory for prose in the learning disabled. In. S. J. Ceci (Ed.) *Handbook of cognitive, social and neuropsychological aspects of learning disabilities* (pp. 241–262). Hillsdale, NJ: Erlbaum.

4

Strategy Use in Students with Learning Disabilities: The Challenge of Assessment

Lynn J. Meltzer

As we enter the 1990s, a new and exciting zeitgeist has begun to shape the face of assessment in learning disabilities with the gradual convergence of research and theory from different areas such as cognitive psychology, developmental psychology, instructional psychology, educational psychology, and learning disabilities. The winds of change have been blown in by the alternative theories of intelligence proposed by Howard Gardner (1983) and Robert Sternberg (1984), dynamic assessment (Lindz, 1987; Feuerstein, Rand, Jensen, Kaniel, & Tzuriel, 1987), the work on curriculum-based assessment (Deno, 1985; Shinn, 1989; Tindal & Marston, 1990), and the research on the role of metacognition and strategy use in the learning process (Brown & Campione, 1986; Campione, 1989). Most exciting is the recent cross-pollination of these diverse approaches and the move away from the hitherto territorial nature of these different areas of psychology

I would like to thank Bethany Roditi, Lee Swanson, Addison Stone, and Lisa Guarnieri for their very helpful suggestions and comments about earlier drafts of this manuscript. I would also like to express my appreciation to Thelma Segal for help with manuscript preparation.

and education. This chapter and this entire book represent an attempt to bring together these various perspectives and to demonstrate their relevance for the field of learning disabilities.

This chapter provides an alternative approach to the identification and treatment of the population with learning disabilities, and emphasizes the strategies and processes that these students use to problem solve and learn. Discussion focuses on the need to shift from a static model of assessment and from diagnoses that imply permanent deficits toward dynamic forms of assessment that account for students' learning strategies and contain specific implications for treatment. Three major themes are interwoven throughout this chapter. The first theme focuses on recent assessment models that emphasize the process of learning rather than the products or outcomes of learning. The second theme addresses the importance of developing assessment approaches that build on the recent research that conceptualizes students with learning disabilities as inefficient learners and problem solvers who have difficulty shifting strategies flexibly and directing their own behavior. The third theme concerns the important connections between assessment and instruction and the need for assessment methods that go beyond the initial diagnosis and contribute directly to the teaching process. Central to this theme is a discussion of the Assessment for Teaching (AFT) model (Meltzer & Roditi, 1989), a paradigm that emphasizes the continuous spiral that connects process-oriented assessment with classroom-based teaching. Throughout this chapter, assessment and teaching are discussed within the framework of a cognitive-developmental perspective.

Moving Beyond the Security of Traditional Tests: Assessment of Learning Strategies

Assessment has two major goals: identification and prescription. Ideally, the identification goal focuses on determining *what* the child has learned, *how* the child learns, and *why* learning may be delayed or advanced. An understanding of these processes results in an appropriate designation of the child's eligibility for special education or other services. The second major goal, prescription, ideally provides specific teaching strategies that match the child's profile of strengths and weaknesses and suggests directions for remediation and treatment.

Identification of how, why, and what the child has learned is intricately tied to the assessment of both skills and strategies. Accurate determination of academic delays or advances is dependent on an assessment of the student's knowledge base, skill level, and strategies learned in the context of a particular classroom setting. How are academic skills differentiated from academic strategies? To date, there has been considerable variation in definitions of strategic learning, and there is still ongoing discussion and debate. For the purposes of this chapter, a strategy is considered as a process that is consciously devised to achieve a particular goal, whereas a skill is considered as an unconscious, more automatic process (Paris, Wasik, & Turner, 1991). Specifically, skills are defined as "information processing techniques that are automatic and are applied to text unconsciously for many reasons including expertise, repeated practice, compliance with directions, luck, and naive use" (Paris et al., 1991, p. 4). The close-knit relationship between skills and strategies is reflected in the definition of strategies as "skills under consideration" (Paris, Lipson, & Wixson, 1983). In fact, an emerging skill can become a strategy when the skill is used intentionally (Paris et al., 1990). The converse can occur and a strategy can become a skill when it "goes underground" (Vygotsky, 1978).

How are these skills and strategies identified as part of the assessment process? Over the past decade, product-oriented measures, including IQ and standardized achievement tests, have been used almost exclusively for diagnostic purposes and have emphasized the end product of learning while largely ignoring the processes and strategies with which students approach various learning and problem-solving situations. As a result, answers have been obtained to the *what* component of the identification process, whereas the *how* and *why* components of identification have been largely ignored. Reliance on these product-oriented measures such as IQ and achievement tests has characterized the diagnosis of learning disabilities despite increasing criticism of the IQ test over the past decade (Gardner 1983; Sternberg, 1984). In fact, in 1982, Anastasi described IQ as a score that is often misinterpreted as a trait, "descriptive rather than explanatory, excessive in meaning, and fuzzy in implication" (p. 6). Despite the widespread criticism of IQ tests in the cognitive and developmental literature and the frequent calls to develop alternatives, this has remained the cornerstone of the definition of learning disabilities. Only recently, nearly a decade after Anastasi's published criticisms, has there been extensive debate about the role of IQ tests in the definition and assessment of learning disabilities (see special issue of the *Journal of Learning Disabilities*, October, 1989). Siegel (1989) has argued that the discrepancy definition of learning disabilities needs to be abandoned and that IQ is irrelevant to this definition. Siegel has also maintained that IQ subtests have limited value for the differential diagnosis of learning disabilities. In contrast, Graham and Harris (1989) have emphasized that IQ tests should not be abandoned prematurely. Rather, scores should no longer be used as decision makers and learning disabilities should be diagnosed on the basis of multifaceted assessment approaches and professional judgment, with IQ tests constituting one of the measures in this multidimensional assessment array.

In effect, it is important that we not discard the IQ test completely in the attempt to transcend its limitations for diagnosis. More research-based data are needed as the learning disability field continues to grapple with the issue of the relative importance for learning of higher versus lower order processes and the role of central processes and executive functions in learning. It is clear that alternative approaches and measures are needed to assess learning disabilities, and it is critical to go beyond the current reliance on a few absolute test scores. Assessment needs to expand the range of measurement approaches, to take account of the context in which learning occurs, and to rely on a multidimensional assessment system, as proposed by Graham and Harris (1989). It is also critical to recognize the limitations of current assessment goals that often focus on determining eligibility for special education and do not attempt to explore how the child learns or to provide recommendations for modified classroom instruction. Evaluation procedures are needed that effectively combine the three major goals of assessment and determine how, what, and why children learn. In addition, as emphasized by Shinn (1989) and Shinn, Nolet, and Knutson (1990), assessment procedures must be ecological and take account of the quality of the curriculum as well as the instructional methods used in the classroom. In this chapter I address these issues and suggest an alternative approach to assessment of learning disabilities.

Recent clinical and research work in a number of areas has led to the emergence of three separate knowledge bases that are critically important for the development of alternative assessment techniques: work on dynamic assessment approaches in cognitively delayed students, metacognitive research in learning disabilities, and automaticity research in the developmental and cognitive neurosciences. These three conceptual systems provide an invaluable framework for expanding and enhancing current assessment techniques for learning disabilities. The first knowledge base has emerged from recently developed dynamic, process-oriented assessment techniques for evaluating the learning potential of students with fairly severe cognitive impairments (see review in Lidz, 1987). At the core of many of the dynamic assessment approaches are the concept of "cognitive modifiability" and the recognition that intelligence and ability are not fixed but can be changed as a result of formal and informal opportunities to learn, referred to as "mediated learning experiences." The second body of knowledge stems from recent research findings that students with learning disabilities frequently display weaknesses in the efficiency, flexibility, and effectiveness with which they apply strategies to problem solving and learning situations (Meltzer 1991; Swanson, 1988, 1989). The third knowledge base emerges from the research that students with reading and learning problems often demonstrate weaknesses in automatic processing and memory (Denckla & Rudel, 1976; Wolf, 1986).

An ideal evaluation system could best be achieved through the integration of these three bodies of knowledge. This could occur within the framework of a multidimensional assessment procedure that accounts for all facets of a child's functioning. This would combine process measures that assess the how and why of performance with product measures that assess the end product or what of performance. Overall, it is important to evaluate both the higher order executive processes involved in learning and the lower order processes related to the basic skills that need to be automatically remembered to facilitate efficient performance in achievement areas. Identification of the approaches and strategies that students with learning disabilities use to solve particular tasks can provide invaluable insights about an individual student's learning strengths and weaknesses and can contribute to a broader understanding of his or her learning disability. A process-oriented assessment system could also help to detect those students whose learning disabilities are hidden because they use effective problem-solving strategies to compensate for weaknesses in automaticity and basic skill deficits.

In summary, learning disabilities as a distinct discipline has reached a stage where there is a need to move toward the development of process measures that evaluate the strategies as well as the skills that students apply to different problem-solving and learning situations. Such a holistic evaluation system, if anchored in a developmental context, could take account of the changing abilities, skills, needs, and motivational levels of each child as well as the manner in which these characteristics interact with the instructional requirements of the curriculum. In this fashion, instruction can be appropriately matched with each child's specific learning style and needs.

The following section contains a more detailed discussion of the recent research findings that address these problem-solving and metacognitive strategies and their importance for spontaneous, independent learning in students with learning disabilities.

Strategy Use in Students With Learning Disabilites

Over the past few years, there has been increasing emphasis on the role of strategy deficits in learning disabilities, partially as a consequence of the research on normal achievers that has documented the importance of metacognitive and problem-solving strategies for spontaneous, independent learning (Brown, Bransford, Ferrara, & Campione, 1983; Paris et al., 1991; Pressley, Goodchild, Fleet, et al., 1989; Pressley, Woloshyn, et al., 1990). The critical role of strategy use in the complex and interwoven network of processes that guide learning is reflected in current models of thinking (Brown et al., 1983: Sternberg, 1984) and effective strategy use (Borkowski, Johnston, & Reid, 1987; Pressley, Borkowski, & Schneider, 1987; Pressley, Symons, Snyder, & Cariglia-Bull, 1989). Competent thinking, in their views, comprises multiple components that include an appropriate repertoire of strategies, adequate knowledge of these strategies, an understanding of the value of specific strategies for performing particular tasks, and recognition that effort is required to use particular strategies. Students must recognize the importance of strategies such as planning, summarizing, and note taking before they feel personally empowered and motivated to use these strategies in a learning situation (Deshler & Schumaker, 1986; Deshler, Warner, Schumaker, & Alley, 1983; Putnam, Deshler, & Schumaker, this volume; Paris & Winograd, 1990; Pressley et al., 1990).

What are the implications for the population with learning disabilities? "Maladaptive learning patterns" were first identified by Torgesen (1975, 1977, 1978), who proposed that the metacognitive processes of students with learning disabilities operate differently from those of normal achievers and that students with learning disabilities frequently use passive approaches in different learning situations. He suggested that these students often display inefficient cognitive processing and fail to use the strategies they possess. Specifically, he theorized that students with learning disabilities do not develop an awareness of the appropriate store of information necessary for solving particular problems efficiently. They are cognizant neither of the strategies that are appropriate for performing particular types of tasks, nor of the value of specific strategies such as planning and self-checking.

Torgesen's theory (1975, 1977, 1978) provided the foundation for a different view of learning disabilities that emphasized the importance of identifying global, domain-general strategy deficits and did not focus exclusively on identifying weaknesses in specific areas such as memory, perception, language, and attention. During the 1980s, investigators began to move away from the view of students with learning disabilities as sometimes passive learners toward an approach that emphasized the active but inefficient nature of the learning process. In fact, in 1989, Swanson suggested that students with learning disabilities could be considered as "actively inefficient learners" because of their difficulties in a number of areas:

1. Difficulties accessing, organizing, and coordinating multiple mental activities simultaneously or in close succession. These deficiencies are reflected in problems with the integration of the many cognitive processes involved in problem solving and learning (e.g., perception, memory, language, and attention) and the critical subskills involved in reading and writing (see review article by Stone & Michals, 1986; Swanson, 1985, 1987, 1989).

2. Lack of flexibility in the application of strategies even when students have an awareness of the strategies to be used. Limited flexibility is reflected in difficulties shifting strategies readily, problems identifying the salient attributes in different situations while ignoring irrelevant details, and problems shifting from a specific approach to a global plan and back to the specifics (Meltzer, Solomon, Fenton, & Levine, 1989).

3. Difficulties engaging in self-regulatory strategies such as checking, planning, monitoring, and revising, during learning and problem-solving situations (Short & Ryan, 1984; Swanson, 1989), and failure to make efficient use of feedback concerning the relevance of their choices (Dykman, Ackerman, & Ogleby, 1979).

4. Limited awareness of the usefulness of specific strategies for solving particular tasks as well as problems explaining the solutions that they have correctly developed (Meltzer, 1991; Meltzer et al., 1989; Stone & Michals, 1986).

What about specific problem-solving strategies in the learning disability population? Problem solving depends on the efficiency with which attention, memory, and encoding are deployed and integrated (see review by Stone & Michals, 1986). Because some or all of these processes are frequently deficient in students with learning disabilities, the global problem-solving process may also be affected detrimentally. In fact, a number of investigators have noted that students with learning disabilities often exhibit qualitatively different approaches to concept learning tasks and display discrepancies in the accuracy with which they learn (see review article by Stone & Michals, 1986). Specifically, many students with learning disabilities do not use the available information to solve problems (Gerber & Hall, 1981), they may not reason logically with the information provided (Kavale, 1980), and they frequently attend to extraneous details (Lee & Hudson, 1981). They often do not generate new information systematically in problem-solving situations that require flexibility, and they may not make good use of the data they generate to develop or revise their explanations (Stone & Michals, 1986). Further, these students frequently fail to use systematic plans for approaching problems, they may have difficulty identifying relevant details, and they may fail to use feedback to modify their approaches or to self-correct. In summary, the information-processing approaches used by students with learning disabilities frequently do not reflect their intellectual capability. As emphasized by Swanson (1987),

> their lack of success in the classroom, whether in academic tasks or in social interactions, has been demonstrated by their inability to shift from one strategy to another, to abandon inappropriate strategies, to process information with one strategy and then select another, or even to consider several processing approaches in rapid succession in order to arrive at a solution to a problem. (p. 3)

To conclude this section, it is critical to emphasize that all these strategy deficits do not always characterize all students with learning disabilities, nor do they manifest across all learning situations in the same student. In other words, a particular student may display flexibility on certain complex reasoning tasks, yet may be inflexible in an academically oriented learning situation that requires the coordination of different skills and strategies. Similarly, students with learning disabilities may use strategies actively until a specific point in time and may then become overwhelmed and even immobilized by the task demands. They may also become "stuck" in using strategies that were previously helpful but are inadequate for meeting the increasing complexity of new tasks.

Interactions of Strategy Use with Motivation and Self-Concept

The application of effective cognitive and metacognitive strategies is heavily influenced by motivational factors including attributions for success and failure. These motivational components of strategy use have been the focus of considerable research in recent years (Diener & Dweck, 1978, 1980; Chap. 7 by Licht in this volume; Torgesen & Licht, 1983). Findings suggest that children who believe that their difficulties are caused by insufficient ability and factors beyond their control are often less active in their use of problem-solving strategies and tend to avoid challenging tasks because they fear failure (Torgesen & Licht, 1983). Such beliefs in their limited power to control and direct their thinking often results in the development of "learned helplessness" (Licht, see Chap. 7 in this volume); this, in turn, affects the facility with which they select and apply strategies in different situations. In contrast, children who attribute their failure to controllable factors such as insufficient effort are able to sustain their use of problem-solving strategies and may even be challenged by failure to use more sophisticated strategies (Diener & Dweck, 1978, 1980). In students with learning disabilities, attributions are frequently shaped by the effects of chronic school failure which is attributed to uncontrollable factors, such as low ability. Children with learning disabilities are more likely than normal achievers to show lower self-concepts of ability, lower expectations for success, and a greater decrease in their expectations for success as a result of previous failure (Butkowsky & Willows, 1980; Torgesen & Licht, 1983). Children with learning disabilities may therefore enter into a negative cycle in which initial school problems produce maladaptive attributions for success that, in turn, result in the deterioration of active problem-solving strategies. When confronted with difficult tasks, these children may consequently show decreased effort in conjunction with a deterioration in problem-solving strategies (Torgesen & Licht, 1983; see Chap. 7 by Licht in this volume).

Attributions and self-concepts may also influence students' attention and self-reflection as they approach academic work. Attentional variability in turn affects a student's strategy use as has been demonstrated in studies of effective strategy users (Pressley, Symons, et al., 1989). Pressley and his colleagues have shown that good strategy users believe in the importance of shielding themselves from distractions when they are involved in important tasks (Pressley, Goodchild, et al., 1989). Good strategy users resist competing distractions and emotions, they are not impulsive in their application of strategies, and they monitor their performance while using a strategy to evaluate their success in achieving their goal (Pressley, Symons, et al., 1989). These issues are particularly relevant for the population with learning disabilities in view of the low self-concepts and neurologically based attentional weaknesses that often characterize these students. Impulsive children often fail to expend the effort needed to apply a strategy appropriately because of their belief that "the pain of thinking is not worth the effort involved in thinking" (Pressley, 1991; Pressley, Goodchild, et al., 1989). Similarly, impulsive children frequently lack self-regulatory strategies and fail to self-monitor, self-correct, and check the outcomes of their efforts. In fact, errors such as reversals, which are commonly attributed to deficits in spatial memory, may more frequently result from limited self-monitoring, impulsivity, and a failure to deploy the strategies needed to focus on relevant details.

In summary, students' application of appropriate metacognitive strategies is inherently connected with their feelings of empowerment and their resultant willingness to invest the effort necessary to apply strategies for active problem solving and learning. Their ability to attend, to focus, and to orient to appropriate details further affects the efficiency and accuracy of their learning. In fact, the symbiotic relationship between cognition and motivation determines students' academic performance and is one of the cornerstones of good learning. As emphasized by Paris and Winograd (1991).

> Young children and less-skilled learners in particular need to manage their own learning by planning, evaluating, and regulating their performance on academic tasks. They need to set reasonable goals for themselves, persist in the face of failure, and adopt intrinsic standards for success. The cognitive consequence of self-regulated learning is that students become enabled to select and attack problems strategically. The motivational consequence is that students feel empowered to be successful and thereby invest effort in relevant and challenging tasks. These twin concepts summarize many of the virtues of instruction designed to increase students' metacognition about learning. (p. 49)

Automaticity and Strategic Learning

Strategic learning is affected not only by motivation, attention, and metacognition, but also by automaticity. Automaticity interacts with strategy use to affect the efficiency and effectiveness with which students approach problem solving and learning tasks. Students with learning disabilities frequently display weaknesses in automatic processing so that too much time is spent on letter and number identification during reading and math tasks (Denckla & Rudel, 1976; Wolf, 1986). As a result, insufficient processing time can be allocated to the more complex cognitive components such as comprehension in reading (LaBerge & Samuels, 1974; Sternberg & Wagner, 1982; Wolf, 1984) and problem solving in math (Garnett & Fleischner, 1983; Roditi, 1988). Because students with learning disabilities frequently manifest deficits in automatic memory, they may avoid using strategies that require considerable effort (Pressley, Borkowski, & Schneider, 1987). They may use all available attentional resources to decode or to complete basic math operations and may not have any attentional resources in reserve that allow them to attend to the more challenging cognitive components of the tasks. To date, there has been only a limited amount of research that has explored the manner in which automaticity interacts with problem solving to affect achievement in reading and math (Meltzer et al., 1989, 1991; Meltzer et al., Roditi, 1988). More research is needed to begin to partial out the relative influences of these different processes on academic achievement at the various developmental levels. Preliminary data have been obtained in a few of our own recent studies (Meltzer, 1988; Meltzer et al., 1989) and are summarized later in this chapter.

Expanding the Horizons of Assessment: From Dynamic to Curriculum-Based Assessment

Despite the extensive research and theory that has documented the role of strategy use in learning disabilities, there is currently a dearth of assessment methods for evaluating strategy deficits as they interact with weaknesses in automaticity, memory, language, attention, and self-concept in this population. Few tests exist for diagnosing the efficiency and flexibility of strategy use and for assessing their impact on the educational performance of students with learning disabilities.

Recently, a number of approaches have been developed as alternatives to psychometric tasks. Principles derived from these approaches could be used to develop alternative assessment methods for the diagnosis of learning disabilities. These approaches span a continuum ranging from dynamic assessment approaches that emphasize deficits and strengths inherent to the child (e.g., Feuerstein et al., 1980, 1981) to systems that focus on the discrepancy between the performance of the specific child and the performance of other students within the same classroom setting (curriculum-based assessment or CBA) (see Figure 4.1).

I_____I_____I_____

Deficit within individual	Discrepancy between child's performance and curriculum demands	Discrepancy between performance of child and peer group
LPAD (Feuerstein)	Assisted Assessment (Campione)	AFT (Meltzer & Roditi)	CBA (Shinn)

Note. LPAD = learning potential assessment device; AFT = Assessment for Teaching model; CBA = curriculum-based assessment.

FIGURE 4.1. Continuum of assessment approaches developed as alternatives to psychometric methods.

At one end of the continuum, the dynamic assessment approach of Feuerstein focuses on identifying the cognitive modifiability of the child regardless of the curriculum demands (see Figure 4.1). At the other end of the continuum, curriculum-based assessment (CBA) paradigms address the roles of relevant curriculum, instruction, and contextual factors in the manifestation of an academic problem (Deno, 1985, 1989; Shinn & Good, 1992; Tindal and Marston, 1990). CBA approaches de-emphasize the influence of cognitive and developmental processes internal to the child and focus instead on the child's academic performance. Between these two extremes is the Assessment for Teaching (AFT) model which stresses the identification of each child's cognitive and developmental profile, use of metacognitive strategies and the specific match with the requirements of academic tasks.

The following section provides a brief summary of a number of these assessment approaches and a discussion of their relevance for the evaluation of students with learning disabilities.

Dynamic Assessment

Since the 1970s, psychologists working with children with cultural differences and severe cognitive impairments have attempted to develop alternative, dynamic assessment techniques for use with these populations. In fact, in the 1980s, the work of a number of these researchers converged and there were attempts to formalize and standardize what psychologists had previously considered "clinical observations" in their assessments (see review by Lidz, 1987). The purpose of these new diagnostic approaches was to begin to measure the "how" of learning and to assess the responsiveness of students with cognitive impairment to specific intervention strategies. These process approaches were developed because of the belief that it was possible to tap the potential of students with cognitive impairment and to evaluate their ability to profit from specific forms of instruction. A guiding principle was the belief that "individuals with comparable scores on static tests may have taken different paths to these scores, and (that) consideration of those differences can provide information of additional diagnostic value" (Campione, 1989, p. 157).[1]

To date, these dynamic assessment approaches have not been adapted for use with students with learning disabilities. However, these techniques provide an exciting opportunity to discover answers to the

---

[1]The terms *dynamic assessment* and *process assessment* were originally developed and used in a very specific manner by Feuerstein but are now applied in a more general sense to include a broad variety of assessment approaches (see Lidz, 1987, for a review).

questions of how the child with learning disabilities learns, why specific strengths and weaknesses may exist, and how strategy deficits impact on the learning efficiency and effectiveness of this population. With the extensive flexible format modifications of these dynamic measurement approaches may provide a viable procedure for identifying strategic processing in the population with learning disabilities and can begin to extend recent learning disabilities research into the realm of clinical and educational practice.

Two representative process assessment approaches are described briefly below because of their relevance for the assessment of learning disabled students, namely: (a) the learning potential assessment device (Feuerstein, Miller, & Jensen, 1981; Feuerstein, Rand, Hoffman, & Miller, 1980; see chaps. in Lidz, 1987) and (b) process assessment (Meyers, 1987; Meyers, Pfeffer, & Erlbaum, 1985).

It is important to remember that these approaches have been designed to evaluate students with global deficits. Both these approaches emphasize the identification of the "how" of learning and de-emphasize the end product of learning. They incorporate diagnostic teaching where each child is given assistance that is designed to influence performance and to indicate the child's potential for change.

The Learning Potential Assessment Device. The concept of learning potential developed by Feuerstein et al. (1980, 1981) has been at the forefront of alternative, process-oriented perspectives on assessment and has paved the way for the new zeitgeist in diagnostic approaches. His system is considered the cornerstone of dynamic assessment approaches that emphasize the importance of evaluating how a child learns and the processes that contribute to learning success and failure.

At the core of Feuerstein's (Feuerstein et al., 1980, 1981) paradigm is the concept of structural cognitive modifiability in which the goal of instruction is to change the fundamental structural nature of the cognitive processes that determine functioning. His dynamic assessment approach rests on the assumption that individuals are open systems accessible to structural change irrespective of the etiology, severity, or stage of development of the condition (Feuerstein, Rand, Jensen, Kaniel, & Tzuriel, 1987). This view of ability and intelligence therefore challenges the inference of immutability, a goal consistent with the more recent theories of intelligence proposed by Gardner (1983) and Sternberg (1981, 1984).

The major theme of Feuerstein's paradigm is that the "learning potential" of each child can be identified using a test-teach-test approach. Consequently, the test situation is used to teach a particular concept and then to assess the child's understanding of and ability to apply that concept appropriately. This learning potential assessment device (LPAD) has as its theoretical underpinnings the work of Vygotsky whose concept of the "zone of proximal development" emphasizes the important interaction between the child and adult. During this teaching phase of the assessment, an intensive mediated learning experience is provided for the student with the adult shaping the student's performance. Within the framework of the LPAD model, assessment of modifiability becomes more important than prediction, a major goal of traditional assessment practices that rely heavily on psychometric instruments. Feuerstein's system is based on the premise that potential is observable only when it has already developed into performance and that competence cannot be measured on the basis of current psychometric techniques. In fact, Feuerstein noted the paradox that exists in the field where stable and reliable tests are used to evaluate process. Thus, he incorporates into the testing process certain procedures that have been omitted from psychometric tests because they contaminate validity. These procedures include the following:

1. teaching a child a specific concept and evaluating his or her responsiveness

2. providing the child with accurate feedback

3. individualizing the test situation

The model specifies that initial differences in levels of performance among individuals simply indicate the need for greater investment of time and effort on the part of the adult who provides intervention. Therefore, Feuerstein uses "content free" cognitive tasks as part of his test-teach-test approach to help students acquire the specific concepts, operations, and relationships necessary to perform. Content-free tasks have been selected deliberately to assure that any changes that occur in the learning process are permanent, structural, and general to all domains. Do the effects of this training system generalize to academic tasks? Ongoing research programs have yet to demonstrate these effects unequivocally, but findings, to date, are promising.

In conclusion, Feuerstein's dynamic assessment model has changed our approach to testing and has shown that alternatives to standard psychometric techniques can be developed and used effectively. Modifications of this model could provide a critical step forward in the development of process assessment techniques for use with students with learning disabilities. This could, in turn, advance the field of learning disabilities beyond the limitations of norm-referenced tests as well as the current overreliance on diagnostic labels.

Process Assessment. Process assessment (Meyers, 1987; Meyers et al., 1985) bridges the gap between dynamic assessment and other diagnostic teaching approaches, with the major goal to determine how, when, and where a child learns, and why he or she has difficulties (Haywood, Filler, Shifman, & Chatelanat, 1975; Kratochwill & Severson, 1977; Meyers et al., 1985). In addition to cognitive functioning and social-emotional behavior, the characteristics and learning processes of the individual are assessed as he or she interacts with the educational environment. An understanding of the student's learning processes is then used to develop intervention plans for improving the effectiveness of learning. Meyers has emphasized the importance of process assessment methods that account for the cognitive as well as the academic components of learning and that target domain-specific processes. Within this framework, assessment focuses on generating and testing hypotheses that are unique to a particular child and setting. The diagnostician develops and uses different assessment strategies, depending on the specific requirements and characteristics of the individual and the test situation. In other words, Meyers's (Meyers et al., 1985; Meyers, 1987) process assessment approach differs from Feuerstein's LPAD in that there is no attempt to change the child's underlying cognitive processes.

A core component of process assessment is the inclusion of trial interventions to provide a meaningful data base for the development of specific recommendations for home and school management. On the basis of observations and findings obtained from diagnostic teaching, the learning specialist modifies the task characteristics or specific motivational variables, or teaches the missing skills directly to match the task with the child's preferred learning strategies. This is designed to bridge the gap between assessment and instruction by generating information that can be easily translated into effective and appropriate programmatic recommendations.

Meyers's (Meyers, 1987; Meyers et al., 1985) process assessment approach has broad applicability to the population with learning disabilities because of its systematic focus on analysis of the child, the task, and the environment, first individually, and then in interaction with one another. Unfortunately, the test-teach-test system, which characterizes process assessment, is extremely time-consuming and therefore impractical for school psychologists and other clinicians who usually face major time constraints in their work. Further, these clinicians are required to provide some index of the grade level attained by the child in basic academic areas to satisfy eligibility criteria for special education placement. It is therefore critical to begin to develop a more practical assessment system that incorporates many features of dynamic assessment but is less time-consuming and therefore more likely to be adopted by diagnosticians. Development of such diagnostic techniques, based on this model, could have a major impact on the assessment of students with learning disabilities as well as normal achievers. The *Surveys of Problem-Solving and Educational Skills* (Meltzer, 1987) represents one attempt to go beyond the constraints of current measurement procedures while simultaneously addressing the practical needs of diagnosticians in the school setting (see discussion later in this chapter).

Assisted Assessment

The Assisted Assessment approach developed by Campione (1989) extends the basic principles embedded in the approaches of Feuerstein (Feuerstein et al., 1980, 1981) and Meyers (1987) but differs in its emphasis on classroom-based demands as well as transfer of strategies across different settings. One major difference between Assisted Assessment and the other dynamic assessment techniques relates to the structure that is imposed during the assessment. Students are provided with assistance that is designed to influence performance and consequently to indicate the child's potential for change. A second major difference is the emphasis on transfer or generalizability from one task or situation to another. An essential component of such transfer is the student's understanding of a specific principle or rule that is, in turn, dependent on the student's flexible use of that principle. Campione has developed specific procedures to evaluate transfer and has suggested that guided learning and transfer scores are the best individual predictors of learning gains.

The Assisted Assessment model (Campione, 1989) emphasizes the importance of two major steps in the diagnostic process. First, the child is given a series of standardized tests as well as a pretest on the test items. The child is then introduced to various learning and transfer situations. The goal is to assess the amount of instruction required to learn to use a set of rules independently and to apply these rules in new, but related, settings. Thus, students are required to learn new principles and are provided with "titrated instruction, beginning with weak, general hints and proceeding through much more detailed instruction" (Campione, 1989, p. 158). Systematic measurement is used to determine the amount of help needed by students to reach a specific criterion for using rules appropriately, as well as the amount of additional help needed to generalize these rules to new situations. This approach contrasts with that of Feuerstein, whose major objective is to generate a detailed clinical picture of a student by "following promising leads" during the testing situation.

The teaching component of Campione's (1989) approach is conceptually anchored in a Vygotskian perspective. He described this system as an attempt to provide for the gradual transfer of thought from the adult to the child within the zone of proximal development. One example of this diagnostic-teaching model is reciprocal teaching (Palincsar & Brown, 1984; see Chapter 9 in this volume). Reciprocal teaching of reading and listening comprehension skills consists of guided practice within a group for the purpose of fostering reading comprehension. This procedure enables each student to lead a portion of the discussion which, in turn, reveals his or her level of competence. For example, groups of students and their teachers take turns as they lead a discussion relating to a particular text. The major focus of their discussion centers on specific comprehension-fostering activities, namely, questioning, summarizing, predicting, and clarifying. As a result, the teacher can obtain "on-line diagnosis" (Campione, 1989) as well as instruction that is appropriate for the student's specific needs. The social support provided by the group yields a context for learning that ensures that new skills are learned in a meaningful manner. Overall, then, Campione's Assisted Assessment approach differs from the other dynamic assessment approaches on the basis of the amount of structure imposed on the student during the diagnostic process and the relative emphasis on the child's cognitive characteristics.

How applicable are these dynamic assessment approaches to the evaluation of students with learning disabilities? As we enter the 1990s, dynamic assessment stands at the crest of the wave of a new Zeitgeist that slowly, but with ever-increasing force, appears to be changing the form of our evaluation procedures just as Piaget's theory has permanently changed our views of developmental psychology. Although dynamic assessment approaches were developed for use with students with cultural differences and students with severe cognitive impairments, their applicability to students with learning disabilities is self-evident. Dynamic assessment is still not widely used with students with learning disabilities, possibly because of the lengthy time periods needed to work with each child and because many of these procedures have not yet been adapted for use in a less intense fashion.

The slow rate at which these techniques have been adopted has also been influenced by the political split between school psychologists and teachers. These professionals still view themselves as performing different roles and are frequently threatened by suggestions that they coordinate their efforts more closely as they work with students. Nevertheless, there have been many recent calls for school psychologists to change their roles and assessment practices (Shinn et al., 1990). With the increasing emphasis on implementation of the regular education initiative and the resultant move to mainstream special education students, these barriers will hopefully be eroded and alternative assessment techniques more widely adopted.

The challenge of the 1990s is to ensure that we begin to modify and use these alternative assessment and teaching techniques to enhance our understanding of all students, in particular students with learning disabilities. In doing so, it is critical to develop more pragmatic approaches that are less time-consuming and allow for a long-term working relationship between diagnosticians and teachers. Curriculum-based assessment techniques, discussed below, represent a move in this direction and an attempt to evaluate each student's performance in relation to the demands of the classroom environment.

Curriculum-Based Assessment

Curriculum-based assessment (CBA) methods are based on the assumption that a learning deficit is not inherent to the child but instead represents a discrepancy between the academic performance of the child and the performance of his or her peer group. Development of CBA resulted from a call to develop ecologically valid measures that would incorporate measures of the instructional setting. CBA focuses on the evaluation of three major areas: quality of the curriculum, quality of the teaching methods, and the academic performance of the child in comparison with his or her peer group. Within the CBA model, psychometric assessment of each child's cognitive and developmental profile does not play a critical role, as the emphasis is on educability rather than a search for pathology (Deno, 1989; Shinn, 1989; Tindal & Marston, 1990). Curriculum-based measurement (CBM), one form of curriculum-based assessment, is theoretically anchored in a problem-solving model and was originally conceptualized and researched by Deno (1985) and Deno, Mirkin, & Chiang (1982). CBM consists of a set of measurement procedures for quantifying student performance in reading, spelling, math computation, and written expression (Shinn et al., 1990). CBM identifies learning problems on the basis of a discrepancy between a particular student's performance and the performance of same-grade peers on grade-level tasks. In other words, evaluation centers on the discrepancy between the performance of the particular student and his or her peer group rather than the discrepancy between ability and achievement within the same student.

CBM measures incorporate a number of characteristics that are considered critical for monitoring student progress (Jenkins, Deno, & Mirkin, 1979). These characteristics include the following: (a) anchored in the curriculum, (b) brief to allow frequent administration by teachers,

(c) many forms, (d) inexpensive, and (e) sensitive to student improvement over time. CBM consists of short, timed samples of students' performance on academic tasks that are used in the typical classroom in a particular school at a specific time of the year. These performance samples are obtained in word recognition, spelling accuracy, math facts (e.g., multiplication, division, for older students), math problems, and ability to write a story (Shinn, 1989). For example, reading is evaluated on the basis of a word list which is read for 1 minute as well as a number of passages, each read for 1 minute. These performance samples are used to compare each student's current rate of progress with previous performance in the basic skill areas.

In summary, curriculum-based assessment methods provide a different alternative to standardized assessment techniques. They also yield evidence that reliable measures can be developed that are less time-consuming than standardized assessment techniques and meaningful for diagnostic decision making. Assessment techniques for students with learning disabilities begin to incorporate some of the major principles of CBA. It is also important to ensure that the role of higher order cognitive and metacognitive processes are not ignored in the attempt to focus on basic academic skills. Learning disabilities assessments must continue to address each child's neurological, developmental, and educational profile and determine the interactions among that child's profile of strengths and weaknesses and the demands of the curriculum. Currently, practical diagnostic systems are needed to determine how the metacognitive processes of students with learning disabilities operate and the extent to which a learning disability reduces the flexibility of strategy use. Each of the assessment approaches discussed above suggests alternatives for the development of process-oriented evaluation procedures for students with learning disabilities. One attempt to develop an assessment approach that integrates some of the principles of dynamic assessment, CBA, and standardized psychometric measurement is discussed below.

Strategy Assessment and Dynamic Assessment: Applications to Learning Disabilities

In response to this need for new assessment techniques for students with learning disabilities, our recent research and clinical work has resulted in the development of an alternative assessment paradigm, the Assessment for Teaching (AFT) model (Meltzer, 1991; Meltzer & Roditi, 1989) as well as a diagnostic inventory, the *Surveys of Problem-Solving and Educational Skills* (SPES) (Meltzer, 1987). Both the AFT model and the assessment inventory build on recent theoretical models of intelligence (Gardner, 1983; Sternberg, 1981, 1984) as well as the dynamic and curriculum-based assessment approaches discussed above. The AFT model emphasizes the importance of a systematic, strategy-oriented assessment system that addresses the close connections among automaticity, problem-solving strategies, and educational performance in accordance with recent research (see chaps. in this volume by Kim Reid, Lee Swanson, Michael Pressley).

Within the framework of the AFT paradigm, assessment is conceptualized as a systematic process designed to identify each child's unique profile of strengths and weaknesses in the various problem-solving and learning areas. There is an emphasis on the interactions among each child's developmental, cognitive, and educational skills and strategies as well as the overall curriculum expectations. The AFT model also addresses the importance of using educationally relevant problem-solving tasks in conjunction with academic tasks such as reading and math. This allows the diagnostician to observe whether students problem solve efficiently and accurately, to determine whether they adjust their strategies on the basis of the task demands, and to develop an understanding of their strengths and weaknesses in cognitive as well as educational areas. The model stresses the roles of automaticity in academic areas, strategic planning, monitoring of errors, and self-corrections, as well as students' awareness of and explanations of their strategies. Students' responses are observed systematically in conjunction with flexible probing by the examiner. This ensures a practical and time-effective assessment procedure that can be used by practitioners in clinical and school settings.

The AFT model differs from the dynamic assessment approaches discussed above in terms of its emphasis on the role of the curriculum and its match with the child's developmental and cognitive profile. The AFT model is also broader than CBA because of its focus on the interactions among the child's cognitive, developmental, and educational characteristics rather than an exclusive emphasis on the educational expectations of the classroom. Finally, this model of assessment is criterion-referenced and is broadly linked with grade-level expectations but does not rely on absolute scores as does standardized testing. Within the framework of the AFT model, assessment is an ongoing process that informs teaching so that instructional methods can be continually refined to meet the needs of each child. Identification of each student's unique profile of strengths and weaknesses in cognitive and educational areas allows the teacher to provide challenges that students can meet and that occur within the zone of proximal development. Effective strategy instruction is targeted to each student's areas of strength and also addresses his or her areas of weakness. Effective strategy instruction therefore depends on an accurate understanding of a student's learning profile and helps teachers to ensure that students develop broader based cognitive knowledge about a particular strategy, understand when and where to use that strategy, and begin to monitor their own use of strategies.

Within the conceptual framework of the AFT model, the *Surveys of Problem-Solving and Educational Skills* (SPES) have been designed to merge the dynamic and process approaches to assessment with the strategy-oriented views of learning disabilities. The SPES (Meltzer, 1987; Meltzer et al., 1989) comprises a series of diagnostic tasks that evaluate the cognitive and educational strategies that appear to be dysfunctional in students with learning disabilities. The SPES also assess the level of automaticity acquired in different academic areas, specifically, reading, writing, spelling, and math. The SPES is divided into two sections: the Survey of Problem-Solving Skills (SPRS) and the Survey of Educational Skills (SEDS). The Survey of Problem-Solving Skills provides critical information about the child's strategies for approaching nonacademic tasks; their impact on educational performance is explored during administration of the Survey of Educational Skills (SEDS). This system emphasizes the importance of identifying *how* children solve problems, not only their final solutions. Strategic planning, monitoring of errors, and self-corrections are also assessed. Based on the student's profiles on both these surveys, educational recommendations are generated that take account of the student's strengths and weaknesses in problem-solving and educational areas. Data from both objective performance and interview probes are combined to provide information about a number of aspects of thinking and problem-solving, as well as their impact on academic performance.

The problem-solving and educational tasks incorporated in the SPES are based on a paradigm of strategic learning that emphasizes the major components of strategy use that appear essential for learning: efficiency, flexibility, methods, styles, and the ability to justify the solutions provided (see Figure 4.2). These components of strategic learning focus on identification of students' understanding of task instructions, their ease in formulating strategies, their ability to identify salient details, and the flexibility with which they shift problem-solving approaches. During administration of the SPES tasks, the child is required to introspect and to reflect on the strategies he has used by explaining how he/she solved a problem, describing retrospectively his/her thoughts while solving a problem, or thinking aloud while solving a particular problem. A brief description of each component of the SPES model follows.

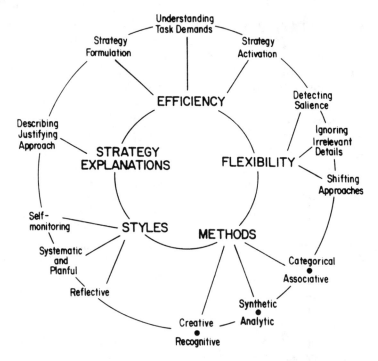

FIGURE 4.2. Problem-solving strategies and learning difficulties: a paradigm. From Meltzer, L. J. (1987). Examiner's manual, *Surveys of Problem-Solving and Educational Skills (SPES)*. Cambridge, MA: Educator's Publishing Service, Inc. Reprinted with permission.

Efficiency of Strategy Selection

Efficient strategy selection underlies effective planning, self-monitoring, and organization. Students also need to believe that well-chosen strategies produce efficient performance (Borkowski, Carr, Rellinger, & Pressley, 1989). As was discussed above, students with learning disabilities often do not structure tasks spontaneously and have difficulty activating specific strategies at the appropriate times (see Torgesen, 1982; Torgesen & Licht, 1983, for reviews). The academic difficulties experienced by many students with learning disabilities may result, in large part, from their inefficient use of strategies so that their performance is compromised and does not reflect their many strengths. Assessment techniques generally do not incorporate measures of students' efficiency in applying strategies. Furthermore, traditional measures of performance speed are not appropriate for evaluating strategy efficiency because bright students may use very efficient strategies, even though they spend a considerable amount of time planning their responses (Sternberg, 1984). Observational ratings may be a better system for evaluating efficiency of strategic learning; the SPES therefore incorporates such ratings.

Flexibility of Strategy Selection

The second major component of the SPES paradigm addresses the flexibility with which students solve problems. As was discussed above, research on strategy instruction and generalization of instruction indicates that flexible use of a principle or rule is a critical index of the individual's understanding of that principle (Campione, 1989). An important component of organizational skills is the ability to shift flexibly from one strategy to another to detect salient details and to ignore irrelevant information (Brown et al., 1983). Most learning tasks require the individual to shift from the specific details to a global plan and back to the specifics (Hayes-Roth & Hayes-Roth, 1979). Further, tasks such as reading comprehension require the student to apply and combine different strategies and to prioritize information on the basis of the different goals, text structures, and content requirements of various reading tasks. As was discussed above, students with learning disabilities often lack flexibility in their strategy use (Meltzer et al., 1989), which may contribute in large measure to their struggle with reading comprehension, written reports, studying, and note taking. For these reasons the SPES includes items that assess flexibility of strategy use in different cognitive and academic tasks.

Methods of Applying Strategies

The ability to organize and integrate information using global categories is critical for successful academic performance. For example, reading comprehension, report writing, and study skills all require students to identify major themes, to categorize information, to devote less attention to irrelevant details, to integrate and prioritize complex information, and to organize ideas sequentially. The SPES therefore includes items that assess a student's ability to identify superordinate categories, to organize information on the basis of global themes, and to prioritize.

Styles of Applying Strategies

Self-monitoring and planning, which are prerequisites for performance in learning and social situations, facilitate the child's capacity to "think about thinking" or to apply metacognitive strategies (Brown et al., 1983). These self-regulatory strategies are critical determinants of effective reading and studying (Brown & Palincsar, 1982). The SPES therefore includes items that evaluate the consistency with which students spontaneously apply self-monitoring and self-checking strategies.

Strategy Explanations

This component deals with the student's self-awareness and ability to articulate the strategies he or she has used to solve a problem. Discrepancies have been noted between students' ability to verbalize self-monitoring knowledge and the actual self-monitoring that they display in their performance (Cavanaugh & Borkowski, 1980). The SPES therefore includes items that require students to explain the strategies they have used to reach specific solutions or judgments.

The SPES

Based on this paradigm, the tasks incorporated in the Surveys of Problem-Solving and Educational Skills (SPES) (see tables 4.1 and 4.2) evaluate the connections among problem-solving strategies, learning processes, automaticity, and educational performance (Meltzer, 1987; Meltzer et al., 1989).

As is evident from Table 4.1, the Survey of Problem-Solving Skills consists of a set of predominantly nonlinguistic tasks that incorporate geometric patterns as stimuli and a set of linguistic tasks that include isolated words and vocabulary as stimuli. The tasks are grouped in two clusters on the basis of factor analytic studies: (a) measures of pattern analysis and memory, and (b) measures of flexibility in conceptualizing and organizing themes.

The problem-solving tasks assess students' efficiency, flexibility, methods, and styles of reasoning in conjunction with their ability to justify and explain their solutions. Ratings identify strengths and weaknesses in self-monitoring skills, reflectivity, organization, planning, and fluency of verbal explanations. The educational tasks shown in Table 4.2 assess performance in the four basic academic skills—reading, writing, spelling, and mathematics. Each skill is evaluated within the framework of a multidimensional model where task complexity increases systematically from an emphasis on automatic memory toward greater emphasis on the integration of underlying subprocesses.

On both these surveys, a systematic rating system guides the assessment procedure and is used to generate educational recommendations through analysis of the performance profiles and error patterns of each

TABLE 4.1
The Survey of Problem-Solving Skills: Description of the Six Problem-Solving Tasks

Task	Description	Focus
Nonlinguistic Tasks		
Series Completion (Pattern Analysis and Memory)	Series of geometric patterns that change according to a specific rule. Students complete the series by selecting the correct solution from a multiple-choice array.	Measures the ability to identify salient features of the task and to ignore irrelevant details.
Categorization (Conceptual/Thematic Flexibility)	Five geometric patterns, from which students must identify the three patterns that share the most common features. The two excluded items share some similar features but differ in other respects.	Assesses the ability to organize nonverbal information and to recognize that some patterns can belong to multiple categories.
Matrix Completion (Pattern Analysis and Memory)	Matrix format with complexity of items increasing by steps through the addition of visual details.	Measures spatial organization, attention to salient details, and pattern analysis.
Linguistic/Verbal Tasks		
Category Shift (Conceptual/Thematic Flexibility)	Four pictures or words that can be sorted in two different ways. A superordinate and an associative category are derived. Explanations are required.	Measures the ability to shift flexibly from one strategy to another. Identifies the student's awareness of the strategy used and his or her explanation of the answer.
Sequential Reasoning (Pattern Analysis and Memory)	Rote sequences that must be completed (e.g., numbers, letters, days of the week, months of the year). These rote sequences are often problematic for students with learning difficulties because of deficits in automaticity.	Measures automatic memory for sequences, working memory, and inferential reasoning.
Classification (Conceptual/Thematic Flexibility)	Word pairs that must be categorized.	Assesses categorization and verbal abstraction.

From Meltzer, L. J. (1987). Examiner's manual, *Surveys of Problem-Solving and Educational Skills (SPES)*. Cambridge, MA: Educator's Publishing Service, Inc. Reprinted with permission.

TABLE 4.2
The Survey of Educational Skills (SEDS): Description of the Educational Tasks

Task	Description	Focus
Reading		
Sight Vocabulary	48 sight words from Dolch word list	Measures automatic word recognition
Decoding isolated words	6 grade-appropriate words for Grades 1–9	Detailed analysis of error patterns
Comprehension-recall/formulation	Silent reading passages for Grades 1–9	Systematic documentation of oral narrative in terms of main ideas, details, total or partial recall, inferences, etc.
Comprehension-structured questions	Silent reading passages for Grades 1–9	Structured questions address recall of main ideas, details, sequence, vocabulary, inferences

Reading comprehension is assessed by comparing oral recall of the story with answers to structured questions to identify organization, ability to shift from main ideas to details and understanding of the major themes, ability to prioritize.

Task	Description	Focus
Writing		
Automatic alphabet production	Timed alphabet production	Evaluates pencil grasp, efficiency, and fluency of writing on a rote memory task.
Sentence production (dictation and read-and-remember)	Grade-level sentences	Evaluates motor planning, spatial organization, symbol production using items with step-wise increase in memory load.
Creative writing	Write about a picture or suggested topic	Evaluates motor planning, spatial organization, symbol production compared with more structured tasks; also evaluates language use, cohesion, organization

The writing inventory compares performance across a number of simple writing tasks that increase in complexity in a stepwise fashion, involve different modes of input and output, and place different demands on memory. The mechanical components of writing are evaluated by comparing performance across the different tasks on a number of the same dimensions, viz: fluency, mechanics, spatial organization. Language usage, ideational fluency, cohesion are also assessed using creative writing samples from the test situation and the classroom.

(continued)

Task	Description	Focus
Spelling		
Spot the correct spelling	Grade-level sentences with 3 possible spellings for a word in a multiple-choice format	Recognition memory
Spell isolated words	Dictated words at grade level	Retrieval memory
In-context spelling	Spelling accuracy during creative writing—review samples from the SEDS and the classroom	

Comparison of spelling accuracy across tasks that incorporate an increasing demand on memory.

Task	Description	Focus
Mathematics		
Automatized operations	Timed mental arithmetic to assess speed on addition, subtraction, multiplication, division	Rapid, automatic memory for basic math facts
Computation	Grade-level math: paper-and-pencil tasks	
Concepts and application	Grade-level word problems	Understanding of math symbol system; ability to analyze word problems and to compute.

student. The functional profiles that are constructed from administration of both the problem-solving and the educational tasks can be matched with remedial and teaching techniques. In other words, the multiplicity of performance patterns that characterize students with learning disabilities constitute the marker variables for identifying these different learning profiles.

Work toward validating the SPES has focused on comparison studies of students with learning disabilities and normal achievers, studies of developmental differences on the problem-solving and educational tasks, and investigations of the power of tasks for predicting performance in the areas of reading, written language, and math (Meltzer, 1991; Meltzer, Fenton, Ogonowski, & Malkus, 1988; Meltzer et al., 1989; Meltzer, Roditi, & Fenton, 1986). Three of these studies will be summarized briefly below. For all these studies, the sample consisted of 626 9- to 14-year-olds, divided into 342 normal achievers and 284 students with learning disabilities. Six problem-solving tasks from the SPRS were administered in conjunction with a number of educational tasks from the SEDS. Multiple regression analyses were applied to determine which combinations of problem-solving strategies were associated with different academic outcomes in students with learning disabilities and in normal achievers.

Problem-Solving Strategies in Students With and Without Learning Disorders.   The first study which is detailed elsewhere (Meltzer et al., 1989), was designed to compare students with and without learning disabilities on the basis of their performance on the SPES problem-solving tasks. In summary, findings indicated that the prevalence of problem-solving difficulties varied as a function of group membership and that significantly more students with learning disabilities displayed difficulty on the problem-solving tasks. These group differences were similar across three age levels, namely, 9- to 10-year-olds, 11- to 12-year-olds, and 13- to 14-year olds. Data also indicated that deficits on one or two of the eight problem-solving tasks did not have a detrimental effect on learning. However, deficits on more than two of the eight problem-solving tasks were associated with an increased incidence of learning disabilities. Discriminant analyses indicated that different problem-solving profiles characterized the group with learning disabilities and the normal achievers. Findings revealed that students with learning disabilities displayed significantly greater difficulty than normal achievers on a task in which they were required to shift among categories and to display flexibility in their use of strategies (category shift task).

Problem-Solving Strategies as Predictors of Academic Achievements.   The second study was designed to examine whether different measures of reading comprehension elicited different problem-solving strategies in students with learning disabilities as compared with normal achievers. Reading comprehension was assessed on the basis of (a) structured questions and (b) the student's ability to retell the story in his or her own words. These two methods were contrasted because both are used in classroom settings to assess the understanding of text. In standarized tests, structured questions generaly constitute the format for assessing reading comprehension. Oral retell methods are widely used in the classroom setting, yet they are not incorporated in standardized tests. This study therefore determined whether the specific method of measuring reading comprehension elicited different performance for the same reading passage in students with learning disabilities and normal achievers. Results are detailed elsewhere (Meltzer, Solomon, & Fenton, 1987) and are summarized briefly below.

When the group of students with learning disabilities was combined with the normal achievers, results of regression analysis indicated that cognitive flexibility was critically important for reading comprehension as measured on the oral retell tasks. This finding revealed the importance of flexible thinking and the ability to shift strategies to prioritize the major themes and supporting details when reading text. When the two groups were considered separately, different results emerged. In the normal achievers, the same four problem-solving tasks predicted reading comprehension on both measures, and the multiple regression coefficients were very similar. Further, for the two different measures of reading comprehension, the problem-solving tasks were entered into the regression equation in the same order. This was not the case for the group with learning disabilities. Here, the relative importance of the problem-solving variables differed, depending on the particular measure of reading comprehension. Specifically, in the group with learning disabilities, cognitive flexibility was the most important predictor of reading comprehension as measured on the basis of oral formulation. In contrast, when structured questions were used to assess comprehension in the group with learning disabilities, understanding of verbal concepts was most important. These findings suggested that students with learning disabilities relied on different problem-solving strategies to derive meaning from text depending on whether they were asked structured questions or were required to summarize the text in their own words. Reading comprehension questions provided structure and focused the attention of students with learning disabilities on specific information, whereas oral retell methods required these students to impose their own structure on the material, a process with which they experienced difficulty. In contrast, normal achievers relied on similar processes to comprehend text regardless of the external structure provided by the specific measure of reading comprehension. These findings highlight the importance of using alternative assessment techniques to evaluate students with learning disabilities so that their difficulties can be more effectively identified in relation to a variety of educational tasks. These results also reveal the importance of structuring and organizing text for students with learning disabilities so that they can eventually learn how to impose this structure independently.

In a second part of this study, math performance was the outcome, and students with learning disabilities and normally achieving students were compared on the basis of the extent to which their problem-solving profiles predicted math performance. In the group with learning disabilities, the category shift task was entered first into the regression equation, which again revealed the critical role played by cognitive flexibility in relation to academic performance. The matrices task, a measure of spatial reasoning, contributed the second largest proportion of variance to the prediction of math performance. In the group of normal achievers, cognitive flexibility assumed lesser importance than sequential reasoning, a measure of automatic memory for rote sequences, working memory, pattern analysis, and cognitive reasoning. These findings suggested that normal achievers relied more extensively on their store of knowledge, memorization, and verbal reasoning for successful math performance. In contrast, students with learning disabilities relied more heavily on cognitive flexibility and spatial reasoning, possibly to overcome weaknesses in their ability to memorize basic math facts (see Chap. 11 by Roditi in this volume).

Automaticity, Problem-Solving, and Academic Achievement in Students.   The third study addressed the relative importance of automaticity and problem-solving processes for reading and math performance. Interest in this relationship stemmed from the research findings discussed above that have documented automaticity deficits in students with reading and learning disabilities (Denckla & Rudel, 1976; Wolf, 1986). To date, there has been no answer about the fundamental question of the relative importance of lower order automaticity and higher order problem-solving tasks for the academic performance of students with learning disabilities. Do these students rely more extensively on cognitive and problem-solving strategies to bypass their automaticity deficits? Alternately, is the attainment of automaticity even more critical for these students with learning disabilities in view of their deficiencies in certain strategies?

In this study, automaticity was measured on the basis of fast, automatic, and fluent performance (FAF) in simple skills that should have been memorized by rote by the fourth grade and that are considered prerequisites for reading and mathematics. Tasks were designed to be ecologically valid and were similar to those used in classroom settings. Specifically, the FAF reading measure consisted of Dolch sight words at or below the second-grade readability level. The FAF mathematics measure consisted of simple math computations that were presented orally and required the student to respond rapidly and fluently. The FAF writing measure was a timed alphabet task.

Results of this third study indicated that automaticity, cognitive flexibility, and sequential reasoning influenced performance differently in two academic domains, reading and mathematics. These findings are detailed elsewhere (Meltzer, Fenton, & Solomon, 1984; Meltzer, Fenton, Ogonowski, & Malkus, 1988) and will be summarized here. In brief, results of backwards regression analysis indicated that in the learning disability group, automatic memory for sight vocabulary was the first variable entered into the reading regression equation for comprehension. In contrast, in the group of normal achievers, cognitive flexibility was entered first. Further, different problem-solving tasks predicted reading performance in the two groups, with measures of pattern analysis playing a critical role for the students with learning disabilities and measures of categorization and cognitive flexibility being more critical for the normal achievers. In other words, slow decoding speeds interacted with problem-solving to affect the reading comprehension of the students with learning disabilities. In contrast, the normal achievers were able to rely more heavily on reasoning and flexible strategy use to make sense of the text they were reading.

When math performance was the outcome, rapid and automatic computation was the most important predictor in both the group with learning disabilities and the normally achieving group. Problem-solving strategies also contributed a significant proportion of the variance to the regression analyses, with sequential reasoning most relevant for math computation and problem solving. This revealed the importance of working memory, cognitive flexibility, and pattern analysis. These results highlight the importance of helping students with learning disabilities to strive for automaticity in the earlier grades, with additional opportunities for reasoning and flexible strategy use as they attempt to solve math items.

In summary, the findings from these studies emphasize the complex interrelationships among automatic memory and the different problem-solving strategies that underlie the various facets of academic learning. The importance of understanding each student's profile of strengths and weaknesses in problem-solving and learning areas is highlighted by these results. Hopefully, the AFT model and the approach used in the SPES can provide a catalyst for the further development of broad and all-encompassing assessment techniques that incorporate many of these components of information processing and result in improved methods for the evaluation and teaching of students with learning disabilities.

Assessment of Organizational Strategies and Study Skills

From the fourth grade onward, students are challenged with increasingly complex writing requirements and a curriculum that emphasizes the application of organizational strategies. This shift in the curriculum results in a greater need for effective organizational and planning strategies, flexibility in applying strategies to different reading and writing tasks, a willingness to relate new information to already-acquired knowledge, and more consistent application of self-monitoring and self-correcting strategies. As the length and volume of material increases, academic success becomes more dependent on students' awareness of the importance of specific strategies and their readiness to apply these strategies to different tasks. Application of effective study skills requires that the child understand and appropriately allocate time, prioritize information, detect main ideas, ignore less relevent details, use a specific and deliberate plan to aid learning, and determine that a particular strategy is effective. Of even greater importance are the building blocks for independent learning; namely, planning, organizational strategies, and study skills. Application of effective organizational strategies (e.g., outlining, note taking, and mnemonic aids) is critical for success in content subjects. Success in content areas is also heavily dependent on effective reading comprehension strategies because students must match their encoding processes with the overall task objectives and must concentrate on understanding the text while simultaneously performing the multiple operations necessary to learn. Reading for meaning, completion of complex writing tasks, and studying all depend on students' ability to understand the purpose of reading, to modify their reading rates in relation to the task demands, and to shift strategies flexibly (Reid & Hresko, 1981).

As yet, many assessment techniques have not been developed for systematic evaluation of the organizational strategies necessary for reading, written language, and studying. In fact, most measures of study skills focus on high school and postsecondary settings and items address the prediction of academic performance, screening for study skills courses, and counseling students about their study skills (Schulte & Weinstein, 1981; Weinstein, Zimmerman, & Palmer, 1988). Most methods rely on self-report and require students to evaluate the effectiveness of their own learning. They emphasize students' use of consistent and regular study habits and do not assess their reliance on active learning styles. To address these gaps, the *Learning and Study Strategies Inventory* (LASSI) (Weinstein et al., 1988) has been developed to evaluate students on the basis of their use of strategies such as self-evaluation, organization, the ability to seek out information, rehearsal, self-testing, and the application of test strategies. In a critique of existing study skills instruments, Pressley et al., (1990) noted that many of these scales are difficult to interpret because students differ in their understanding of items (e.g., "I have trouble making inferences"). Pressley et al. noted the greater value of items that tap strategic processing more directly (e.g., "I learn new ideas by relating them to ideas I already know"). At this time, it is clear that there is a need to develop diagnostic procedures that directly assess each student's ability to organize information, read for meaning, prioritize, outline, and summarize. Such procedures should incorporate direct observations of the strategies students use to study.

In our own clinical work with high school and college students referred to the Institute for Learning and Development, we have developed informal methods to evaluate note-taking and outlining strategies on the basis of a lecture format and presentation of complex reading material. Note taking from a reading passage is compared with note taking from an oral lecture format along the dimensions of efficiency, accuracy, and organization. Students are then required to summarize the information based on their notes. A comparison of the student's outline with his or her summary and with the original material provides important diagnostic information about that student's strategies for planning, organizing information, and differentiating major themes from supportive details. Evaluation also focuses on the student's ability to transform information, to memorize and rehearse information while simultaneously reducing multiple details into summary format, to attend, and to orient to salience. Ongoing work is directed toward refining these assessment techniques and systematizing criteria for analyzing students' organizational strategies. Such tasks will enhance the instructional implications of diagnostic assessments and will increase their ecological validity. Hopefully, future research will focus on the development of more criterion-referenced measures for assessing study strategies directly. These measures are important for identifying each student's ability to study, track homework, organize papers during school, and coordinate the multiple requirements of school and home.

Integrating Assessment and Classroom Instruction

The growing awareness of metacognitive theory has resulted in increasing acceptance of the importance of developmental changes for the learning process and greater recognition that children are active learners. There has also been a shift from a focus on the importance of materials and tasks toward an emphasis on the roles of learners and their specific activities. As part of this changing zeitgeist, the cognitive-developmental approach to learning and instruction has been more widely accepted (Reid, 1988), with its emphasis on the interactions between the child's developmental status and the cognitive and metacognitive components of educational performance. Currently, there is greater recognition that

it is not enough to acquire knowledge, for children must learn how and when to utilize it. What they do in an instructional negotiation will be controlled by what they think about doing, by their understanding of the goal, and by what they know of the material to be learned and the most efficient ways to operate on it. (Reid, 1988, p. 23).

These complex relationships among the child's knowledge base and specific abilities constantly change over the course of development and interact with curriculum demands. As a result, there are continually shifting but symbiotic relationships among the learner characteristics, the learning activities, the materials to be learned, and the critical task components (Reid, 1988). These interactions exert a critical impact on the manifestation of learning disabilities so that a previously dormant learning problem may reveal itself only when there is a mismatch between the child's learning profile and attributions, and the demands of the learning environment. In other words, the learner characteristics are no longer well matched with the learning activities, tasks, and materials. Changes in grade level and in the curriculum often result in the introduction of more complex tasks that require greater coordination of skills and strategies. These transitions may reveal the hitherto hidden weaknesses of a particular student with learning disabilities who lacks spontaneous and automatic access to his or her knowledge base and who also struggles to coordinate the multiple skills, processes, and strategies necessary to learn effectively. Because of the importance of these interactions among the learner, the materials, and the purpose for learning, assessment and instruction must account for the student's skills, strategies, attributions, and level of motivation, as well as the student's understanding of the task demands, the purpose for different learning activities, and his or her knowledge of the environmental constraints and requirements.

The implications for instruction are self-evident: Children's performance must be continually re-evaluated so that, at different points in time, their learning efficiency can be improved in relation to the instructional demands and not in relation to a static view of their ability levels. Recent work on classroom-based assessment provides an important model for this integrated assessment-teaching approach (see Tindal & Marston, 1990). Methods of diagnosis and teaching must take account of the fact that development also results in the organization and refinement of strategic behavior and the abandonment of partially effective strategies in favor of more efficient approaches to different situations. Instruction for students with learning difficulties should therefore address the acquisition of automaticity in basic skills in conjunction with explicit teaching of task-appropriate strategies, practice in the monitoring and regulation of these strategies, and explanations of the importance of these strategies (Brown & Palincsar, 1982; Reid, 1988). Effective strategy instruction within the classroom setting usually requires learners to become aware of their own strategies, to pose questions to themselves, to practice strategies, and to check and self-monitor (see chapters in this volume by Putnam, Deshler, & Schumaker; and by Pressley et al.). Successful strategy instruction usually promotes direct explanations of strategies, addresses metacognitive as well as motivational factors, and enhances peer interaction and cooperation. Students are taught to focus on process as well as content and to use strategies flexibly and selectively.

Strategy instructional approaches can be grouped according to two theoretical viewpoints: (a) the Vygotskian perspective that effective thinking develops through social-instructional interactions with adults and that strategies can be taught indirectly and (b) the direct explanation approach that metacognition needs to be taught directly (e.g., Deshler & Schumaker, 1986; Deshler et al., 1983; Duffy et al., 1986). Both direct and indirect approaches to the instruction of metacognitive strategies promote five goals (Paris, Wasik, & Turner, 1991). First, students must develop a sense that they personally own the information they read and write. Second, instruction must be developmentally appropriate to their skills and interests. Third, students must be taught to recognize the structure of tasks and must be given a meaningful context for learning. Fourth, effective instruction must promote collaboration and sharing of effective strategies among peers and teachers. Finally, control must be transferred to students so they can gradually take responsibility for their own learning.

Vygotskian Approach

The Vygotskian approach emphasizes the role of the adult who initially controls the learning situation by providing teaching and guided instruction for the child. Through the process of "scaffolding" (Palincsar, 1986; Stone, 1989), the adult gradually fades this explicit instruction as the child or less experienced learner gains the necessary expertise. Eventually, the learner internalizes the instructions and self-directed verbalizations. Scaffolding therefore enhances students' awareness of strategies with sets of procedures that indirectly promote strategic learning. Cooperative learning techniques are methods of indirect strategy instruction that provide students with opportunities to model, discuss, and evaluate their strategic learning. For example, in the reading and writing areas, peer conferences and group reading allow students to plan, revise, edit each others' work, and discuss the content and process of reading.

Vygotsky's concept of "compensation" is also relevant for understanding the scattered profiles of strengths and weaknesses that characterize students with learning disabilities. From his perspective, disabilities always involve certain limitations in functioning and they also stimulate the reorganization of functions so that students can compensate for their deficits and develop competence in other areas. Students with learning disabilities may therefore use effective learning strategies to bypass certain difficulties in one situation yet may evidence significant difficulties in another situation where they are unable to compensate. To what extent have Vygotsky's theories influenced instructional practice in remedial and classroom settings? Stone (1989) suggested that remediation of strategies is often ineffective because the social dynamics of the adult-child interaction are frequently ignored. Similarly, in the classroom setting, scaffolded instruction does not often occur because it demands considerable investment of teacher time to provide ongoing informal diagnosis of each student's progress and difficulties and consequent redirection of teaching (Harris & Pressley, in press). Vygotsky's notion of the "zone of proximal development" therefore has major implications for the understanding and teaching of students with learning disabilities, and it is important that techniques based on his theory are incorporated into remedial and regular classroom settings.

Direct Explanations of Strategies

Direct explanation theorists (Deshler & Schumaker, 1986; Duffy et al., 1986) emphasize explicit instruction to a greater extent than Vygotsky. These approaches present carefully sequenced instruction and frequent direct explanations of the strategic processes required to complete specific tasks. Five critical elements of direct instruction have been described by Winograd and Hare (1988), namely:

1. Strategy explanations must be meaningful to students.

2. Students must understand why the strategy should be learned and the potential benefits of using such a strategy.

3. Teachers must explain the strategies on a step-by-step basis.

4. Students must understand the contexts and situations where specific strategies are appropriate.

5. Students must learn to evaluate their use of strategies so they can monitor and self-correct; this allows them to plan, evaluate, and regulate their own thinking.

Strategic learning is heavily dependent on the students' motivation to use a particular strategy, the value placed on that strategy, and recognition of the appropriate context for using a strategy. Strategic learning also rests on students' recognition of their own competence and control, as well as their self-confidence (see Chap. 13 by Pressley et al. in this volume). Strategy instruction generally does not comprise a single strategy, rather, several cognitive and metacognitive strategies are arranged in a manner that facilitates task completion (see Chap. 12 by Putnam, Deshler, & Schumaker in this volume). Deshler and his colleagues (Deshler & Schumaker, 1986; see Chap. 12 by Putnam et al. in this volume) have developed a stepwise process for strategy instruction that involves the following: (a) Test the student to determine current learning habits, (b) describe the learning strategy, (c) model the strategy, (d) verbally rehearse the strategy, (e) practice on controlled materials, (f) provide feedback, and (g) posttest.

Deshler and Schumaker (1986) have also developed a range of mnemonic strategies to help students to memorize the strategies and steps needed for effective reading comprehension, studying, note taking, and so on. Instruction is designed to teach students to learn more effectively and more efficiently and to help them recognize the value of specific strategies so that they can invest the effort necessary to use these strategies. Deshler's approach also teaches students to reinforce themselves for success. As they begin to attribute their success to their effortful use of strategies, they develop greater control over their own learning which, in turn, reduces their level of learned helplessness.

Conclusions

What are the implications of these techniques for the cyclical relationship between assessment and instruction? Evaluation must direct the teaching of skills and strategies so that strategies can be applied flexibly and efficiently in all settings, regardless of the relationship between the student and the particular teacher. An understanding of each student's metacognitive beliefs, expectations with regard to thinking and learning, and attributions for success and failure can help in the development of a more comprehensive profile of each individual's strengths and weaknesses. Such an understanding can be derived from assessment techniques that are process oriented, and focus on identification of the efficiency, flexibility, and effectiveness of each student's strategy use.

The most challenging component of effective strategy instruction is to ensure that students with learning disabilities apply strategies flexibly and learn to generalize these strategies across tasks and settings. To ensure this transfer, students with learning disabilities must be taught to analyze the task demands, monitor the effectiveness of their strategy use, and develop personal beliefs about the relevance of specific strategies (Swanson, 1989). Strategy instruction for students with learning disabilities is effective when it addresses task-specific and general aspects of learning, is well-matched to the student's knowledge base, and helps students to rely on a large repertoire of alternative strategies. Effective strategy instruction is therefore integrally linked with the teacher's understanding of a student's specific profile of strengths and weaknesses, an understanding that results from appropriate evaluation procedures.

To conclude, the past decade has witnessed significant progress in the understanding of learning disabilities. The educational implications of these research findings have recently become more evident in the practice setting and have begun to influence assessment and teaching procedures. Hopefully, the 1990s will witness a revolution in the design of alternative evaluation systems and will herald new and exciting advances that ensure that students with learning disabilities are able to function at the level of which they are capable. To quote Churchill:

> This is not the end.
> It is not even the beginning of the end.
> But it is perhaps the end of the beginning.
> (November 10, 1942)

References

Anastasi, A. (1982). *Psychological testing* (5th ed.). New York: Macmillan.

Borkowski, J. G., Carr, M., Rellinger, E., & Pressley, M. (1990). Self-regulated cognition: Interdependence of metacognition, attributions, and self-esteem. In B. F. Jones & L. Idol (Eds.), *Dimensions of thinking and cognitive instruction*. Hillsdale, NJ: Erlbaum.

Borkowski, J. G., Johnston, M. B., & Reid, M. K. (1987). Metacognition, motivation, and controlled performance. In S. Ceci (Ed.), *Handbook of cognitive, social, and neuropsychological aspects of learning disabilities* (Vol. 2, pp. 147–173). Hillsdale, NJ: Erlbaum.

Brown, A. L., Bransford, J. D., Ferrara, R. A., & Campione, J. (1983). Learning, remembering and understanding. In P. H. Mussen (Ed.), *Handbook of child psychology* (Vol. 3, pp. 77–166). New York: Wiley.

Brown, A. L., & Campione, J. C. (1986). Psychological theory and the study of learning disabilities. *American Psychologist, 41,* 1059–1068.

Brown, A. L., & Palincsar, A. S. (1982). Inducing strategic learning from texts by means of informed self-control training. *Topics in Learning and Learning Difficulties, 2,* 1–18.

Butkowsky, I. S., & Willows, D. M. (1980). Cognitive-motivational characteristics of children varying in reading ability: Evidence for learned helplessness in poor readers. *Journal of Educational Psychology, 72,* 408–422.

Campione, J. C. (1989). Assisted assessment: A taxonomy of approaches and an outline of strengths and weaknesses. *Journal of Learning Disabilities, 22,* 151–165.

Cavanaugh, J. C., & Borkowski, J. G. (1980). Searching for metamemory-memory connections: A developmental study. *Developmental Psychology, 16,* 441–453.

Denckla, M. B., & Rudel, R. (1976). Rapid "automatized" naming (R.A.N.). Dyslexia differentiated from other learning disabilities. *Neuropsychologia, 14,* 471–479.

Deno, S. L. (1985). Curriculum-based measurement: The emerging alternative. *Exceptional Children, 52,* 219–232.

Deno, S. L. (1989). Curriculum-based measurement and special education services: A fundamental and direct relationship. In M. Shinn (Ed.), *Curriculum-based measurement: Assessing special children* (pp. 1–17). Guilford Press.

Deno, S. L., Mirkin, P. K., & Chiang, B. (1982). Identifying valid measures of reading. *Exceptional Children, 49,* 36–45.

Deshler, D. D., & Schumaker, J. B. (1986). Learning strategies: An instructional alternative for low achieving adolescents. *Exceptional Children, 52*(6), 583–590.

Deshler, D. D., Warner, M. M., Schumaker, J. B., & Alley, G. R. (1983). Learning strategies intervention model: Key components and current status. In J. D. McKinney & L. Feagans (Eds.), *Current topics in learning disabilities* (pp. 245–283). Norwood, NJ: Ablex.

Diener, C. I., & Dweck, C. S. (1978). An analysis of learned helplessness: Continuous changes in performance, strategy, and achievement cognitions following failure. *Journal of Personality and Social Psychology, 36,* 451–462.

Diener, C. I., & Dweck, C. S. (1980). An analysis of learned helplessness: II. The processing of success. *Journal of Personality and Social Psychology, 39,* 940–952.

Duffy, G. D., Roehler, L. R., Meloth, M. S., Vavrus, L. G., Book, C., Putnam, J., & Wesselman, R. (1986). The relationship between explicit verbal explanations during reading skill instruction and student awareness and achievement: A study of reading teacher effects. *Reading Research Quarterly, 21,* 237–252.

Dykman, R. A., Ackerman, P. T., & Ogelby, D. M. (1979). Selective and sustained attention in hyperactive, learning disabled, and normal boys. *Journal of Nervous and Mental Disease, 167,* 288–297.

Feuerstein, R., Miller, R., & Jensen, M. R. (1981). Can evolving techniques better measure cognitive change? *The Journal of Special Education, 15*(2), 201–270.

Feuerstein, R., Rand, V., Hoffman, M., & Miller, R. (1980). *Instrumental enrichment: An intervention program for cognitive modifiability.* Baltimore: University Park Press.

Feuerstein, R., Rand, Y., Jensen, M. R., Kaniel, S., & Tzuriel, D. (1987). Prerequisites for assessment of learning potential: The LPAD model. In C. Schneider Lidz (Ed.), *Dynamic assessment* (pp. 35–51). New York: Guilford Press.

Gardner, H. (1983). *Frames of mind: The theory of multiple intelligences.* New York: Basic Books.

Garnett, K., & Fleischner, J. E. (1983). Automatization and basic fact performance of normal and learning disabled children. *Learning Disability Quarterly, 6,* 223–230.

Gerber, M. M., & Hall, R. J. (1981). *Development of orthographic problem solving strategies in learning disabled children* (Tech. Rep. No. 37). Charlottesville: University of Virginia, Learning Disabilities Research Institute.

Graham, S., & Harris, K. R. (1989). The relevance of IQ in the determination of learning disabilities: Abandoning scores as decision makers. *Journal of Learning Disabilities, 22,* 500–503.

Harris, K., & Pressley, M. (in press). The nature of cognitive strategy instruction: Interactive strategy construction. *Exceptional Children.*

Hayes-Roth, B., & Hayes-Roth, F. (1979). A cognitive model of planning. *Cognitive Science, 3,* 275–310.

Haywood, H. C., Filler, J. W., Shifman, M. A., & Chatelanat, G. (1975). Behavioral assessment in mental retardation. In P. McReynolds (Ed.), *Advances in psychological assessment* (Vol. 3, pp. 31–51). San Francisco: Jossey-Bass.

Jenkins, J. R., Deno, S. L., & Mirkin, P. K. (1979). Measuring pupil progress toward the least restrictive environment. *Learning Disability Quarterly, 2,* 81–92.

Kavale, K. A. (1980). The reasoning abilities of normal and learning disabled readers on measures of reading comprehension. *Learning Disability Quarterly, 3,* 34–45.

LaBerge, D., & Samuels, S. J. (1974). Toward a theory of automatic information processing in reading. *Cognitive Psychology, 6,* 293–323.

Lee, W. M., & Hudson, F. G. (1981). *A comparison of verbal problem-solving in arithmetic of learning disabled and non-learning disabled seventh grade males* (Tech. Rep. No. 43). Lawrence: University of Kansas, Institute for Research in Learning Disabilities.

Lidz, C. (1987). *Dynamic assessment.* New York: Guilford Press.

Meltzer, L. J. (1984). Cognitive assessment and the diagnosis of learning problems. In M. D. Levine & P. Satz (Eds.), *Middle childhood: Development and dysfunction* (pp. 131–152). Baltimore: University Park Press.

Meltzer, L. J. (1987). *The surveys of problem-solving and educational skills (SPES).* Cambridge, MA: Educator's Publishing Service.

Meltzer, L. J. (1991). Problem-solving strategies and academic performance in learning disabled students: Do subtypes exist? In L. V. Feagans, E. J. Short, & L. J. Meltzer (Eds.), *Subtypes of learning disabilities* (pp. 163–188). Hillsdale, NJ: Erlbaum.

Meltzer, L. J., Fenton, T., Ogonowski, M., Malkus, K. (1988). *Automaticity, cognitive strategies and academic achievement in students with and without learning disabilities.* Paper presented at the Annual Meeting of the American Educational Research Association, New Orleans.

Meltzer, L. J., Fenton, T., & Solomon, B. (1984, August). *Automatization and abstract problem-solving as predictors of academic achievement.* Paper presented at the meeting of the American Psychological Association, Toronto, Canada.

Meltzer, L. J., & Roditi, B. (1989). *Assessment for teaching: An alternative approach to the diagnosis of learning disabilities.* Unpublished manuscript.

Meltzer, L. J., Roditi, B., & Fenton, T. (1986). Cognitive and learning profiles of delinquents and learning disabled adolescents. *Adolescence, 21*, 581–591.

Meltzer, L. J., Solomon, B., & Fenton, T. (1987). *Problem-solving strategies in children with and without learning disabilities.* Paper presented at the 95th Annual Convention of the American Psychological Association, New York.

Meltzer, L. J., Solomon, B., Fenton, T., & Levine, M. D. (1989). A developmental study of problem-solving strategies in children with and without learning difficulties. *Journal of Applied Developmental Psychology, 10*, 171–193.

Meyers, J. (1987). *The training of dynamic assessment. In C. Lidz (Ed.), Dynamic assessment 1987* (pp. 403–425). New York: Guilford Press.

Meyers, J., Pfeffer, J., & Erlbaum, V. (1985). Process assessment: A model for broadening assessment. *The Journal of Special Education, 19*(1), 73–89.

Palincsar, A. S. (1986). The role of dialogue in providing scaffolded instruction. *Educational Psychologist, 21*, 73–98.

Palincsar, A. S., & Brown, A. L. (1984). Reciprocal teaching of comprehension-fostering and monitoring activities. *Cognition and Instruction, 1*, 117–175.

Paris, S. G., Lipson, M. Y., & Wixson, K. K. (1983). Becoming a strategic reader. *Contemporary Educational Psychology, 8*, 293–316.

Paris, S. G., Wasik, B. A., & Turner, J. C. (1991). The development of strategic readers. In P. D. Pearson (Ed.), *Handbook of reading research* (2nd ed.). New York: Longman.

Paris, S. G., & Winograd, P. (1990). How metacognition can promote academic learning and instruction. In B. Jones & L. Idol (Eds.), *Dimensions of thinking and cognitive instruction*. Hillsdale, NJ: Erlbaum.

Pressley, M. (1991). Can learning-disabled children become good information processors? How can we find out? In L. V. Feagans, G. J. Short, & L. J. Meltzer (Eds.), *Subtypes of learning disabilities: Theoretical perspectives and research* (pp. 137–162). Hillsdale, NJ: Erlbaum.

Pressley, M., Borkowski, J. G., & Schneider, W. (1987). Cognitive strategies: Good strategy users coordinate metacognition and knowledge. In R. Vasta

& G. Whitehurst (Eds.), *Annals of Child Development* (Vol. 5, pp. 89–129). New York: JAI Press.

Pressley, M., Goodchild, F., Fleet, J., Zajchewski, R., & Evans, E. D. (1989). The challenges of classroom strategy instruction. *Elementary School Journal, 89,* 301–342.

Pressley, M., Symons, S., Snyder, B. L., & Cariglia-Bull, T. (1989). Strategy instruction research comes of age. *Learning Disability Quarterly, 12,* 16–30.

Pressley, M., Woloshyn, V., Lysynchuk, L. M., Martin, V., Wood, E., & Willoughby, T. (1990). A primer of research on cognitive strategy instruction: The important issues and how to address them. *Educational Psychology Review, 2*(1), 1–58.

Reid, D. K. (1988). *Teaching the learning disabled: A cognitive developmental approach.* Needham, MA: Allyn & Bacon.

Reid, D. K., & Hresko, W. P. (1981). *A cognitive approach to learning disabilities.* New York: McGraw-Hill.

Roditi, B. (1988). Automaticity, cognitive flexibility, mathematics and problem solving: A longitudinal study of children with and without learning disabilities (Doctoral dissertation, Tufts University, 1988). *Dissertation Abstracts International, 49,* 2396B.

Schulte, A. C., & Weinstein, C. E. (1981). Inventories to assess learning strategies. In C. E. Weinstein (Chair), *Learning strategies research: Paradigms and problems.* Symposium presented at the annual meeting of the American Educational Research Association, Los Angeles.

Shinn, M. R., & Good, R. H. (1992). CBA: An assessment of its current status and prognosis for its future. In J. Kramer (Ed.), *Curriculum-based assessment: Examining old problems, exploring new solutions.* Englewood Cliffs, NJ: Erlbaum.

Shinn, M. R. (1989). Identifying and defining academic problems: CBM screening and eligibility procedures. In M. Shinn (Ed.), *Curriculum-based measurement: Assessing special children* (pp. 90–129). New York: Guilford Press.

Shinn, M. R., Nolet, V., & Knutson, N. (1990). Best practices in curriculum-based measurement. In A. Thomas & J. Grimer (Eds.), *Best practices in school psychology* (2nd ed.), (pp. 287–308). Washington, DC: National Association of School Psychologists.

Short, E. J., & Ryan, E. B. (1984). Metacognitive differences between skilled and less skilled readers: Remediating deficits through story grammar and attribution training. *Journal of Educational Psychology, 76,* 225–235.

Siegel, L. S. (1989). IQ is irrelevant to the definition of learning disabilities. *Journal of Learning Disabilities, 22*(8), 469–478.

Sternberg, R. J. (1981). The evolution of theories of intelligence. *Intelligence, 5,* 209–230.

Sternberg, R. J. (1984). What should intelligence tests test? Implications of a triarchic theory of intelligence for intelligence testing. *Educational Researcher, 13,* 5–15.

Sternberg, R. J., & Wagner, R. K. (1982). Automatization failure in learning disabilities. *Topics in Learning and Learning Disabilities, 2,* 1–11.

Stone, C. A. (1989). Improving the effectiveness of strategy training for learning-disabled students: The role of communicational dynamics. *Remedial and Special Education, 10,* 35–42.

Stone, C. A., & Michals, D. (1986). Problem solving skills in learning disabled children. In S. J. Ceci (Ed.), *Handbook of cognitive, social and neuropsychological aspects of learning disabilities* (Vol. 1, pp. 291–315). Hillsdale, NJ: Erlbaum.

Swanson, H. L. (1985). Assessing learning disabled children's intellectual performance: An information processing perspective. In K. Gadow (Ed.), *Advances in learning and behavior disabilities,* (pp. 225–272). Greenwich, CT: JAI Press.

Swanson, H. L. (1987). The influence of verbal ability and metamemory on future recall. *British Journal of Educational Psychology, 53,* 179–190.

Swanson, H. L. (1988). Information processing theory and learning disabilities: A commentary and future perspective. *Journal of Learning Disabilities, 20,* 155–166.

Swanson, H. L. (1989). Strategy instruction: Overview of principles and procedures for effective use. *Learning Disability Quarterly, 12*(1), 3–14.

Tindal, G. A., & Marston, D. B. (1990). *Classroom-based assessment: Evaluating educational outcomes,* Columbus, OH: Merrill.

Torgesen, J. K. (1975). Problems and prospects in the study of learning disabilities. *Review of Child Development Research, 5,* 385–440.

Torgesen, J. K. (1977). The role of nonspecific factors in task performance of learning disabled children: A theoretical assessment. *Journal of Learning Disabilities, 10,* 27–34.

Torgesen, J. K. (1978). The role of non-specific factors in the task performance of learning-disabled children: A theoretical assessment. *Journal of Learning Disabilities, 10,* 27–35.

Torgesen, J. K. (1982). The learning-disabled child as an inactive learner: Educational implications. *Topics in Learning and Learning Disabilities, 2,* 45–51.

Torgesen, J. K., & Licht, B. (1983). The learning-disabled child as an inactive learner: Retrospects and prospects. In J. McKinney & L. Feagans (Eds.), *Current topics in learning difficulties* (Vol. 1, pp. 3–31). Norwood, NJ: Ablex.

Vygotsky, L. S. (1978). *Mind in society.* Cambridge, MA: Harvard University Press.

Weinstein, C. E., Zimmerman, S. A., & Palmer, D. R. (1988). Assessing learning strategies: The design and development of the LASSI. In C. E. Weinstein, E. T. Goetz, & P. A. Alexander (Eds.), *Learning and study strategies: Issues in assessment, instruction, and evaluation* (pp. 25–39). New York: Academic Press.

Winograd, P., & Hare, V. C. (1988). Direct instruction of reading comprehension strategies: The nature of teacher explanation. In C. Weinstein, E. Goetz, &

P. Alexander (Eds.), *Learning and study strategies: Issues in assessment, instruction and evaluation* (pp. 121–139). San Diego, CA: Academic Press.

Wolf, M. (1984). Naming, reading and the dyslexias: A longitudinal overview. *Annals of Dyslexia, 34,* 87–115.

Wolf, M. (1986). Rapid alternating stimulus naming in the developmental dyslexias. *Brain and Language, 29,* 360–379.

PART 2

Language, Attention, and Motivation: Their Impact on Strategic Learning

The chapters in this part of the book examine a number of critical processes that impact in significant ways on the efficiency and flexibility with which students with learning disabilities access and utilize problem-solving and learning strategies. Language, automaticity of word-retrieval, attention, and motivation are representative processes. These chapters do not provide exhaustive coverage of such influences but hopefully convey a clear message that strategy deficits and strategic intervention cannot occur in isolation and need to be addressed within a broader, multifaceted context.

In Chapter 5, Denise Segal and Maryanne Wolf focus on the automaticity and word-retrieval problems of students with language and reading disorders, as evidenced in lengthy and often deficient access and retrieval processes. They summarize a 10-year longitudinal investigation that explored the early predictive value of word retrieval tasks for later reading performance. They also discuss lexical strategies that children use to compensate for their word-retrieval problems and a pilot treatment program based on an analysis of successful lexical strategies.

In Chapter 6, Elizabeth Wiig discusses language and communication strategy training and emphasizes that language-learning disabilities result in part from inflexible and inefficient cognitive-linguistic strategies. She suggests that we begin to move away from traditional models of language therapy, which consist of 20-minute pullout sessions and do not focus on the development of strategies or procedural knowledge. Instead, she emphasizes the importance of a process- and strategy-directed model of language intervention that fosters strategic communication and can be expanded to specific subject areas such as writing, science, and social studies to ensure relevance for students.

In Chapter 7, Barbara Licht addresses the achievement-related beliefs of students with learning disabilities and their expectations and attributions for success and failure. She reviews the findings that children with learning disabilities are more likely than their peers to believe that their abilities are low and that their efforts will not pay off. Licht explores the research on the achievement-related beliefs of students with attention deficits and conduct disorders, a discussion of direct relevance to the following chapter by Shaywitz and Shaywitz. Finally, discussion addresses the question as to why some children with learning disabilities manage to bypass their weaknesses and to achieve success despite continuing difficulties, a phenomenon with major implications for remediation and teaching.

In Chapter 8, Sally Shaywitz and Bennett Shaywitz examine the characteristics of students with attention deficit disorder (ADD) and they contrast this group with those students who exhibit learning disabilities and conduct disorders. They conclude that these are separate disorders that may co-occur and that further research is needed to explore the efficacy of the different treatment options.

The major theme that emerges from these chapters concerns the heterogeneous nature of learning disabilities and the importance of using a multifaceted perspective for diagnosis and teaching. The chapters also highlight the importance of understanding the distinctions between attention deficit disorders (ADD) and learning disorders, particularly in view of the recent increase in the prevalence of diagnoses of attention deficit disorders (Safer & Krager, 1988). These issues are also critical to consider in light of the fact that the self-regulatory deficits that characterize so many students with learning disabilities may be linked with subtle attentional weaknesses which are not so extensive as to warrant a diagnosis of ADD. Clearly, further research is needed to explore the complex relationships among weaknesses in attention, organization, and self-monitoring as well as their impact on self-esteem.

References

Safer, D. J., & Krager, J. M. (1988). A survey of medication treatment for hyperactive/inattentive students. *Journal of the American Medical Association, 260,* 2256–2258.

5

Automaticity, Word Retrieval, and Vocabulary Development in Children with Reading Disabilities

Denise Segal
Maryanne Wolf

U nable to retrieve the target word *accordion,* Kevin, a bright 10-year-old boy with specific reading difficulties, promptly responded, "Lawrence Welk weigh-a-ton." With similar aplomb he rattled off "united horse" for a pictured unicorn, "Eskimo icehouse" for *igloo,* and "advertisement medium" for *label.* Although the linguistic sophistication and whimsy displayed here may be uncommon, word-finding problems in individuals with learning disabilities are widespread, particularly among children with language impairment and reading disabilities (Denckla & Rudel, 1976a, 1976b; German, 1984;

We are grateful to Sister M. Martina of St. Clement's School and Rob Kahn of the Landmark School, and both their faculties, for their help with this study. We thank Jennifer Keates and Corinne Lewkowicz for their assistance in all phases of the work.

We also wish to acknowledge the very generous support of The Educational Foundation of America for funding the intervention research discussed here.

Rubin & Liberman, 1983). Rudel (1983) wrote that the most typical characteristic of dyslexic children, outside of reading difficulties, is some form of "subtle dysnomia" or word-finding disorder. (In this chapter we will use the general term *reading disability* except when reporting research in which the population is specifically defined as *dyslexic*. In those cases, the authors' terms will be used.)

Beyond the metaphoric talents and the underlying word-finding problems in Kevin's responses, however, is a phenomenon seldom described and only partially understood: *novel compound formation*. This process is a compensatory strategy used by some children for filling "lexical gaps" (Clark, 1982). Typically, the child combines two or more morphemes to form novel words. Novel words are defined here as labels not used in the English language for the particular stimulus involved: for example, "screw horse" for *unicorn* (Wolf & Segal, 1989).

It is our belief that individual lexical stratgies such as compound formation have direct implications for the construction of more general remedial strategies for certain language difficulties. We hypothesize that such a set of strategies may generalize to improvements in reading performance. In this chapter we discuss two kinds of strategies applied to a population of children with learning disabilities: (a) lexical strategies (conscious or unconscious) used by children when encountering problems finding the precise word and (b) programmatic remedial strategies based, in part, on an analysis of successful lexical strategies when word-retrieval breakdown occurs.

Toward these ends, a 10-year research program, based on our work on the connections between word-retrieval processes and reading disability, will be described briefly, emphasizing those aspects that focus on lexical strategies. Second, a review of other treatment programs designed to improve word-finding and/or reading skills is presented. Third, these two bodies of research are connected in a first attempt to conceptualize a treatment approach for word-finding problems in the context of reading disorders.

Research Background: The Relationship Between Word-Retrieval and Reading Processes

The research program to be presented here began with the exploration of one fundamental hypothesis: that the time and subprocesses used to access and retrieve a verbal label in the act of naming are intrinsically related to the time and subprocesses used to access and retrieve a word in the process of reading. In other words, the first prediction is that the two systems intersect in particular ways. Second, if they intersect at the level of various subcomponents, then the naming[1] or word-retrieval system, which is learned early in development, offers a unique window or vantage point for probing particular subprocesses that will later be used in the reading system.

To pursue these questions, a three-stage research program was begun. In Phase I, a componential model of the word-retrieval process was constructed, based on work in cognition and the neurosciences. Intersections with the reading process were hypothesized, based on work in reading theory. In Phase II, a cross-sectional study was conducted to explore (a) the relationship between specific word-retrieval and specific reading tasks and (b) the power of retrieval tasks to differentiate readers with reading disabilities from average readers. Phase III consisted of a systematic, longitudinal investigation of these issues. This phase was also designed to evaluate (a) the early predictive capacities of word-retrieval or naming tests for later reading performance and (b) questions such as the role of automaticity and vocabulary.

Rationale

The rationale for studying connections between word-retrieval and reading processes is based principally on work in the acquired aphasias and the developmental dyslexias. The first reason concerns the structural similarities between naming and reading systems (see models by Goodglass, 1980; Wolf, 1979, 1982, 1986). Both systems[2] require a range of interacting operations that include attention, memory, temporal processing, visual perception, conceptual knowledge, and phonological, semantic, and articulatory processes. The second reason involves the ease and usefulness of tests of naming for probing language dysfunction, particularly in the aphasias (Goodglass, 1980; Goodglass & Kaplan, 1972).

Third, the examination of naming deficits in children has proven to be an important window into normal language development and language disruption (Kail & Leonard, 1986; McGregor & Leonard, 1989), particularly in the developmental dyslexias (Gleason & Wolf, 1988; Katz, 1986; Murphy, Pollatsek, & Well, 1988). For example, the fre-

---

[1]In this chapter the terms *word retrieval*, *word finding*, and *naming* are applied synonymously and refer to the entirety of the processes used for finding and articulating a single word across all contexts. These general terms are to be distinguished from the more specific terms, *lexical access*, *lexical storage*, and *lexical retrieval*, which refer to particular stages or subcomponents of the system.

[2]The naming system also possesses important other characteristics, such as automaticity and relative dissociation from IQ.

quently noted subtle dysnomia that has been identified in readers with dyslexia appears in a variety of forms ranging from slowed naming access speed to generative naming problems (Bowers, Steffy, & Tate, 1988; Denckla & Rudel, 1976a, 1976b; Spring & Davis, 1988; Swanson, 1989). These findings point directly to the possible connections between early naming abilities and later reading performance.

Phase I

The major goal in this phase was to pull together from various bodies of research (e.g., aphasiology, experimental psychology, psycholinguistics) what we know about the time it takes to name a word (Cattell, 1886; Oldfield & Wingfield, 1966) and the processes necessary for naming to occur. More as an ongoing heuristic than any completed theoretical model, a multicomponential model was first constructed. Second, the model's depicted components and influencing factors were used as the basis for the selection of a battery of instruments, capable of systematically probing disruption in the developing naming and reading systems (for details, see Wolf, 1979).

Phase II

In this phase, two questions were examined: (a) the relationship between the battery of naming measures and three forms of reading—word recognition, oral reading, and silent reading comprehension—and (b) the extent to which a word-retrieval battery could differentiate average readers from readers with severe impairment. In a cross-sectional study of 64 children from 6 to 11 years (32 average readers, 32 readers with severe impairment), results indicated a strong general relationship between the word-retrieval battery and the reading measures. Second, results demonstrated that all measures except those emphasizing receptive vocabulary and visual perception differentiated reading groups at all ages.

Two findings were particularly noteworthy. The receptive vocabulary measure began to differentiate children with reading disabilities in the 10- to 11-year age group. In addition, naming measures that emphasized speed appeared particularly powerful in both correlational findings and group differentiation.

The first finding underscores two important issues: Young children with reading disabilities do not appear to have differences related to normal achievers in receptive vocabulary knowledge, but may well develop them over time. As discussed by Chall (1983), Curtis (1987), and Perfetti (1985), there appears an "interconnectedness" between vocabulary and reading development. Further, as described by Stanovich (1986), a reciprocal relationship may exist between the two areas such that underlying deficits in reading may impede later vocabulary growth, which, in turn, exacerbates the original reading problem. To tease apart the roles of vocabulary development and rate of processing and to investigate the early predictive power of the batteries, a longitudinal research program was begun in Phase III.

Phase III

This phase was a 5-year longitudinal effort to chart (a) the development of key word-retrieval processes and their ability to differentiate average readers from readers with severe reading disability[3]; and (b) the potential of retrieval processes to predict specific reading operations. Subjects included children from kindergarten through Grade 4, thus covering all early stages of reading development (Chall, 1983; Frith, 1985).

Subject Description

In recent studies, criteria for classification have been changing to confront a singularly difficult question in reading disability research, namely, deficit specificity. That is, are there truly specific deficits in the child with severe reading disabilities, most often defined as the dyslexic child (Ellis, 1985, 1987; Stanovich, 1988), or is there simply a continuum of poor and very poor readers (Seidenberg, Bruck, Fornarolo, & Backman, 1985)? One approach to specificity is to compare the dyslexic group with what Gough and Tunmer (1986) described as "garden-variety" poor readers: that is, children who are reading at similar poor levels but are not categorized as dyslexic because of their depressed IQ scores. As Stanovich (1988) stated, the inference is that if garden-variety poor readers and readers with dyslexia differ in cognitive subprocesses, they are arriving at reading through alternate (i.e., different) routes. In the last 5-year analyses, therefore, readers

---

[3]The criteria for reading impairment classification were the following: (a) a grade equivalent score 1.5 years or more below grade expected score at the end of Grade 2 on either the *Gray Oral Reading Test* or the Gates-MacGinitie comprehension test; (b) teacher recommendation; and (c) no known neurological, emotional, intellectual, or environmental factors underlying the failure. The criteria were selected to conform both to standard definitions of dyslexia (see Rudel, 1983; Vellutino, 1979) and to important issues in longitudinal research with younger dyslexic children (see discussions in Fletcher et al., in press; Wolf & Goodglass, 1986).

with severe impairment were divided into readers with dyslexia and "garden-variety" poor readers (see criteria in Wolf & Obregon, 1989).

Major Findings

A series of longitudinal studies was conducted at the end of both Grades 2 and 4. This chapter summarizes studies relevant only to lexical compensatory strategies.[4] These include (a) studies on automaticity or rate of processing, (b) studies on vocabulary versus retrieval issues, and (c) an analysis of the strategies themselves.

1. Automaticity Rate.   To assess specific or general problems in the development of automaticity or speed of processing, four studies were undertaken. Wolf, Bally, and Morris (1986) and Wolf (1986) examined naming access speed for different kinds of basic symbolic material and found reading group differences each year of the study. Most children with dyslexia in kindergarten and Grade 1 were slow in naming graphological (i.e., numbers, letters) and nongraphological (i.e., colors, objects) stimuli, but by Grade 2, some readers with dyslexia were significantly slower only on graphological stimuli. Rate differences on these very routinized symbols were maintained for Grades 3 and 4 (Wolf & Obregon, 1989) and Grade 7 (Roditi, 1988), indicating fundamental differences in the time it takes for children with dyslexia to retrieve the most basic verbal information. Results of other researchers (Spring & Davis, 1988; Swanson, 1989; Wolff, Michel, & Ovrut, 1989) indicate that naming access speed problems are both specific to readers with dyslexia and also persist well into adulthood for large subgroups of children with dyslexia.

These findings also point to another possible source of word-retrieval problems, that is, a temporal processing deficit that impedes the rapid activation and/or integration of subprocesses underlying systems like naming. If there is a failure in a timing mechanism or processor, basic cognitive-linguistic systems will function at a slower rate of processing information, and automaticity that should develop in particular subprocesses will be impeded. If, in addition, any *specific* area(s) of developmental delay or disruption occur(s) (e.g., phonology, working memory), there will undoubtedly be exaggerated consequences for the smooth development and functioning of interactive, complex systems like word-retrieval and reading. Pivotal in any treatment approach, therefore, is the issue of the possible contribution of these lower level,

---

[4]For studies on prediction, Wolf, 1986; bilingualism, Novoa & Wolf, 1984; child psychopathology, Wolf, 1985.

process-limiting differences in readers with dyslexia (see also Verbal Efficiency Theory in Perfetti, 1985).

2. Vocabulary and Lexical Development versus Retrieval Deficits. An ongoing question in the dyslexia literature concerns the nature of lexical development, that is, whether retrieval problems on specific confrontation naming tests are (a) persistent across development; (b) based on underlying, blatant vocabulary problems; or (c) based on more subtle problems in storage such as the increasing development of meaning for individual words (Segal, 1989). To begin to address these questions several studies were conducted. The first study (Wolf & Goodglass, 1986) evaluated the confrontation or picture-naming problems of children with dyslexia often noted by clinicians. One fundamental problem, however, was to distinguish between a child's lack of receptive vocabulary knowledge and a dysfunction in accessing or retrieving that knowledge. Based on more than 4,000 children's naming errors, a multiple-choice component was designed for an existing confrontation naming test, *The Boston Naming Test* (BNT) (Kaplan, Goodglass, & Weintraub, 1983). Results from this multiple-choice component of *The Boston Naming Test* (Kaplan, Goodglass, & Weintraub, 1983) and from the *Peabody Picture Vocabulary Test* (Dunn & Dunn, 1981) suggest that young children with dyslexia from kindergarten to Grade 2 have problems in *retrieval* of lexical knowledge rather than in basic-level vocabulary knowledge.

More recently (Wolf & Obregon, 1989), data from Years 4 and 5 of the study were analyzed. Results indicated (a) that significant differences between reading groups in confrontation naming ability persist into Grade 4 and, in fact, become more profound; and (b) that these deficits cannot be explained simply as deficits in general, receptive vocabulary knowledge.

In a recent study, Wolf and Segal (1989) attempted to ferret out more subtle dimensions of lexical development in the early 5- to 7-year period, a time before reading can affect vocabulary knowledge. An unexpected finding in the Wolf and Goodglass (1986) study of confrontation naming was the salience and predominance of novel or innovative compounds. These creative compound words were produced when children either did not know a word or could not retrieve it. In the current study the goals were to explore (a) whether these creative "gap-filling" utterances are a common part of lexical development; (b) whether children with dyslexia might use them more frequently because they have more word-finding problems; and (c) whether the structure and content of the utterances could give clues to retrieval versus vocabulary deficit questions. Another issue was whether very young children with dyslexia have more subtle lexical difficulties that are undetected by standard vocabulary tests and not based on later reading problems (Segal, 1989).

Toward these goals, three areas were compared between the two groups of children: (a) frequency of compound formation; (b) use of perceptual versus functional features in the compound structure; and (c) use of coined derivatives ("er") versus noun + noun compounds. Interest was in the developmental course of novel compound formation during this period and in whether novel compound formation develops differently, potentially as a compensatory strategy, in children with dyslexia as a whole or in some individuals with dyslexia. It was assumed that functional compounds (e.g., "desert milk-giver" for *cactus*) and coined derivatives—that is, one English word plus the coined derivative "er" (e.g., "ice picker upper" for *tongs*)—involve a more sophisticated strategy than perceptual compound formation (e.g., "porcupine tree" for *cactus*). In other words, functional compounds indicate partial knowledge about the word's meaning, whereas perceptual compounds are based only on the physical features of the object (see Winner, 1988).

These findings demonstrate that both average children and children with dyslexia used novel compounds as gap-filling strategies. Most important, readers with dyslexia as a whole produced significantly more novel compounds, "er" forms, and functionally derived compounds. The average readers used more perceptual strategies suggesting more limited vocabulary knowledge for the difficult words. Together, these results support previous findings that children with dyslexia were experiencing word-finding problems based more on word-retrieval difficulties than on any simple lack of vocabulary knowledge.

Of most relevance for this chapter, one large subgroup of children with dyslexia appeared to use novel compounds as a compensatory function for word-retrieval difficulties. In other words, this subgroup used these compounds far more than both other readers with dyslexia and average readers. For some, fully one-third of their errors were made up of such responses as "map ball" for *globe* or "myth horse" for *unicorn*. Such responses reflected not only a wealth of semantic information about the target, but also a kind of linguistic flexibility, characteristics we believe to be important for remedial strategies.

What this study did not address is the underlying source of the word-finding problems, for example, whether phonological processes (e.g., Katz, 1986; Rubin & Liberman, 1983) or semantic elaboration problems (e.g., Kail & Leonard, 1986; McGregor & Leonard, 1989) are the basis for these difficulties. We will address each of these possible sources of breakdown. Most important, it is key to understand in future work the implications of a systematic use of gap-filling strategies and the role of such factors as vocabulary depth and linguistic flexibility in predicting reading and language breakdown. For example, in the intervention study to be described, the pivotal goal is to investigate how these compensatory strategies for retrieval might work together within a program based on the development of vocabulary depth, accuracy, and fluency (Beck, Perfetti, & McKeown, 1982).

Phase IV.   A direct outcome of these studies of confrontation naming is the fourth and most recent phase of the present research program. The major goals are to examine the relationship between word-retrieval difficulty and vocabulary development and the interconnectedness of both to reading failure. The aims are (a) to assess and to distinguish word-retrieval and vocabulary deficit areas with greater precision than previously; (b) to attempt to remediate retrieval difficulties through a vocabulary–retrieval-rate improvement approach; and (c) to determine whether improvement in these language and rate processes generalizes to improved reading performance.

The present focus is on several major areas that may underlie many word-retrieval difficulties in children with reading disabilities: more subtle vocabulary-based problems, retrieval problems, broad rate-based problems, and combinations of all three. The program is directed to these areas. (Other problem sources such as perception, phonology, memory, and learning styles are outside the scope of this investigation; see Meltzer 1984, and Chap. 4 in this volume for discussions of learning strategies.) A more thorough discussion of the present remedial approach will conclude this chapter and will integrate major principles and issues that are raised in the next section's review of treatment efforts.

General Intervention Studies

Dyslexia intervention studies have proven as difficult to design and assess as the population is to define. It is, therefore, not surprising that studies are both few in number and equivocal in outcome (see, e.g., Gittelman & Feingold, 1983). The reasons for the inconclusive findings are as varied as the population: ineffective treatment methods, inadequate definitions, inadequate control groups, a lack of alternate treatment groups for comparison, and failure to account statistically for developmental issues and heterogeneity (e.g., type, severity, and duration of the disorder) (Lovett, Ransby, Hardwick, & Johns, in press).

This section begins with a brief summary of key issues in intervention—heterogeneity and generalization. Next, major approaches to intervention are detailed and include several studies specific to word-retrieval difficulty. The goal in this section is not to evaluate these studies, but to underscore important principles within them for the present intervention program.

The Issue of Heterogeneity

The issue of heterogeneity in dyslexia has long plagued researchers as well as clinicians involved in remediation efforts. As one more attempt to deal with this issue, researchers in the last decade have attempted subgroup classification, where fairly homogeneous subgroups of children with reading disabilities are identified on the basis of varying tasks and skills (e.g., Boder, 1973; Mattis, French, & Rapin, 1975). Subgroup classification efforts have, however, encountered considerable problems (see Morris, Blashfield, & Satz, in press) for reasons varying from definitions and statistical procedures to the tasks chosen for classification of the subgroups.

One promising direction is to examine putative subgroup differences in remedial contexts. As Lovett, Benson, and Olds pointed out (1988), the few studies that have investigated interactions between subtypes and remediation are limited by small sample sizes and lack of randomization in sampling. Their own study was an exception to this. They examined the different individual responses of a heterogeneous group of children with reading disabilities to two intervention programs. They identified four dimensions of importance both for remedial outcome and for subgroup classification: word-recognition skills, visual naming speed, phonological processing (including pseudoword reading and spelling), and language ability (including word knowledge, syntax, and inference comprehension).

The Issue of Generalization

A second study by Lovett and her colleagues underscores the importance of understanding generalization issues. Lovett et al. (in press) asserted that generalization is "at the heart of instructional theory" (p. 30), but that the general cognitive mechanisms by which average learners use and apply new knowledge are little understood. Theories differ widely; for example, Brown and Campione (1984) suggested that a less able learner may store new knowledge without much elaborative processing and thus may not perceive analogous contexts for applying this knowledge. According to other researchers, however, drawing on specific instances plays a more important role in acquiring new information (see review in Lovett et al., in press).

At issue is whether intervention should be specifically focused (e.g., on specific vocabulary items) or whether it should emphasize broader contexts or processes (Fey, 1988; Sternberg, 1987). It is not surprising that both item-specific learning (e.g., Brooks, 1988) and rule-learning (Morrison, 1980) have been emphasized as major problems among children with reading disabilities. For example, Lovett et al. (in press) found that improvement following intervention with children with reading disabilities was actually greater for exception words than for words taught by pattern learning. They explained their results as a function of greater practice time spent on individual exception words.

These studies raise the important question of whether children with reading disabilities have a "reduced tendency to perceive invariance or to learn rules at several different levels of the language system" (Lovett et al., in press, p. 30), and if so, whether such deficits are amenable to treatment. Such a conclusion runs contrary to conventional teaching approaches which emphasize a pattern that can be generalized across words. Still other researchers have argued for a better understanding of the *flexible application* of rules (see Kamhi, 1988), an issue that will play an important role in our intervention considerations.

Phonology-Based Studies

Perhaps the most prominent hypothesis in reading disorders research today is that children with reading disabilities are deficient in some form of phonological processing (Bryson & Werker 1989; Liberman, Liberman, & Mattingly, 1980). There is a great deal of evidence that deficient phonological awareness may cause at least one major type of developmental reading disability (Bradley & Bryant, 1985; Lovett et al., 1988; Stanovich, 1986). Ability in phonemic analysis may play a role in the development of efficient word decoding (Bowey & Patel, 1988), but it is not yet clear whether it is phonological blending (Wagner & Torgesen, 1987), phonemic segmentation deficits (Lovett, Warren-Chaplin, Ransby, & Borden, 1987), or both that affect word-recognition skills. In addition, morphological and syntactic rule knowledge have been found to be deficient in readers with dyslexia (Siegel & Ryan, 1984; Vogel, 1985), which may interact with deficient phonological awareness (Barron, Palmer, & Lovett, 1988).

Despite the importance of phonological processes, few extensive phonological treatment studies have been conducted. Of these, several have involved preschool training. For example, Bryant, Bradley, Mac-

Lean, and Crossland (1989) and Lundberg, Frost, and Peterson (1988) demonstrated that early training in rhyming and alliteration has significant benefits for later reading. Both Olson and Wise (1988) and Vellutino and Scanlon (1987) found improvement using segmentation training, whereas Gittelman and Feingold (1983) found significant improvement in reading for children with reading disabilities by training phonics and word-recognition skills.

In a study of word-retrieval difficulty in third graders, Rubin, Rotella, and Schwartz (1988) found improved performance following training in phonemic analysis and cue generation, where children were taught to identify initial sounds and rhymes and manipulate word segments.

A central issue in phonological treatment is the relative insensitivity of current standardized tests in the assessment of posttreatment effects (Lovett et al., 1987), because these tests sample only a limited number of words at any one level of achievement. A similar argument was made by Curtis (1987) concerning standardized vocabulary test measures.

It is somewhat paradoxical that although the major explanatory thrust in the literature is on phonology, far greater remedial efforts have been made in the semantic arena. This situation is, perhaps, inevitable because treatments are often geared to older children clearly identified as having reading disabilities. These children may well have begun with phonological problems, but have developed multilayered problems at later ages (e.g., phonological and semantic-based).

Semantic-Based Vocabulary Studies

Most would agree that the child's evolving knowledge of word meaning is a principal factor in reading comprehension (Chall, 1983; Curtis, 1987). Indeed, Chall and Curtis regard the difficulty of the words in a text to be "the best single predictor of the difficulty that a student will experience in understanding that text" (Curtis, 1987, p. 45). Nevertheless, although most semantic intervention studies have resulted in improved vocabulary knowledge, only equivocal findings are reported in the improvement of reading comprehension (see Beck et al. 1982).

Such frustrating conclusions may be based, in part, on assessment issues such as limitations in existing tests (Curtis, 1987). For example, Curtis contended that standardized reading vocabulary tests elucidate only the difference "between at least *some* knowledge about a word's meaning and *little or no* knowledge" emphasis added (p. 44). Thus, only a moderate amount of knowledge about the word's meaning is sufficient to answer an item correctly on most standardized measures (Cronbach, 1943).

Predictably, there is little agreement about the best approach to teaching word meanings (Curtis, 1987). Nagy and Herman (1987) argued that explicit training in vocabulary is inherently limited simply because of the vast number of words to be learned. Other issues revolve around the *level* of word knowledge being taught (Beck, McKeown, & Omanson, 1987; Beck et al., 1982); the use of contextual training (Kameenui, Carnine, & Freschi, 1982; Sternberg, 1987); and the use of strategies in organizing material into semantic categories to enhance memory (Bauer & Embert, 1984). Pressley, Levin, and McDaniel (1987) found that learning mnemonic techniques promotes remembering but not inference about undefined vocabulary items, whereas learning from context (Sternberg & Powell, 1983) promotes inference but not retention of word meanings.

The upshot of these diverse issues and conclusions appears to be that more direct instruction may be advocated when comprehension is poor (Curtis, 1987), whereas incidental learning through frequent reading (e.g., Nagy & Herman, 1987) may be best for the general student without problems. A series of successful studies by Beck and her co-workers indicates the use of a direct instruction approach. For example, Beck et al. (1982) investigated the effect of intensive vocabulary instruction on reading comprehension and demonstrated improvement in semantic knowledge and in speed of lexical access.

More specifically, Beck et al. (1982) proposed that semantic processes involved in reading comprehension require *accuracy* (knowing word meanings), *fluency* (rate or speed of lexical access), *richness* (semantic network connections), and *decontextualized knowledge* of words. They proposed that to understand the meaning of a word, we must consider its "commonly accessed meaning components" and "its connection with other concepts demanded by the context" (p. 507). On this basis, instruction may require exploring each word's "meaning and related ideas to yield a deep knowledge of words" (p. 508).

Beck et al. (1982) described levels of lexical access as (a) unknown, (b) acquainted, and (c) established. Words can be taught within classroom texts according to these three tiers: that is, frequent, varied encounters with the word rather than the usual "basic acquaintance" (Beck et al., 1987). Beck et al. (1987) suggested that discrepancies in previous studies may have arisen because *levels* of word knowledge were disregarded and because a high level of word knowledge may be required for text comprehension. They also demonstrated the power of extending the program beyond the classroom in what they call their "Word Wizard" approach (p. 154). (For a somewhat different emphasis on levels of word knowledge, see Kameenui, Dixon, & Carnine, 1987).

Kameenui et al. (1987) made a set of distinctions about internal lexical strategies that have important implications for any intervention program that teaches unknown words to children. They distinguished among derived knowledge (encountering a word in context and figuring out its meaning), prompted recall (allowing the context to prompt recall of a word not fully familiar), and unprompted recall (ability to identify meaning independent of context).

Relatively few semantic-based studies deal directly with word-finding problems in children with dyslexia and language impairment. Except for the work of Leonard and his colleagues (Kail & Leonard, 1986; McGregor & Leonard 1989), these studies have focused on retrieval rather than on levels of word knowledge. A frequent component has been the use of cues and semantic strategies (German, 1988). For example, Wiig and Semel (1980) used semantic classification skills to improve semantic organization, to increase cuing strategies, and to decrease dysfluencies and word substitutions.

A clear exception to this group of studies is work by Kail and Leonard (1986) with children with language impairment. They advocated providing a "richer base of information concerning a word's meaning" (pp. 1–2), and they cautioned against simply teaching strategies of retrieval without adding to the child's knowledge of the word to be retrieved. In a study with four children, McGregor and Leonard (1989) proposed that word-finding difficulties may stem from two sources (a) elaboration, where words are not well established in the lexicon or are represented in a less elaborate form; and (b) retrieval, where children use less efficient "algorithms" for retrieving word names. They found that a combined emphais on elaboration and retrieval led to the greatest improvement in word-finding skills. Such an "elaboration plus retrieval" approach, we believe, may well come closest to incorporating the notion of levels of vocabulary knowledge used by Beck et al. (1982) within a program for word-finding problems.

The present focus extends this conceptualization of elaboration to include the manner in which the word alters its meaning according to its linguistic context (see Segal, 1986b, 1986c). For example, Segal (1986a) found that children from 6 to 12 years, when required to reflect on the meanings of words, assigned different meanings relative to their ages and to the other words in the linguistic context. Children's knowledge of a word's meaning is bound to the task, to the word, and to the context in which the word occurs (Segal, 1986a). An integration of these conceptual frameworks encompasses the principal features of a desired treatment program which will be detailed in the final section.

Educational Implications: Toward an Intervention Program for Word-Retrieval Deficits

As stated from the outset, a primary goal in writing this chapter was to conceptualize an intervention program that builds vocabulary, word-retrieval, automaticity, and reading skills in children with reading disabilities. From this literature review, several principles emerge for such a program. First, the principles of generalization of learning and heterogeneity should be taken into account. Second, there must be an emphasis on a rich (i.e., elaborated) and established vocabulary base for true accuracy in the retrieval of words. Third, the smooth retrieval from this base must be rapid and fluent. Fourth, if either accuracy or fluency is impeded, strategies that are based on lexical richness (i.e., vocabulary depth, phonological development) and flexibility should be incorporated to enhance retrieval, general communicativeness, and reading.

Intervention Program

We will now describe our first efforts at applying such principles in an ongoing pilot study. Our beginning goals were to increase accuracy in the retrieval of words; rate or fluency of word retrieval; and richness and elaboration in vocabulary usage in different contexts. Beyond this, our aim was to examine whether progress in these areas generalizes to reading. The pilot study consisted of three phases: (a) an assessment phase with 30 children with dyslexia and 30 control average readers; (b) an intervention phase with the children with dyslexia; and (c) a posttest phase with the children with dyslexia.[5]

Before describing the components of each phase, two qualifications are necessary. First, an ideal program would emphasize phonology as well as the above goals. Due to the limits on a pilot study, phonological training was restricted to exercises that simultaneously reinforce phonological knowledge and retrieval accuracy. Second, given the inconsistent nature of word-retrieval difficulties and the heterogeneity found in the population with reading disabilities, individualized programs are obviously best-suited to tailor the program to the specific needs of the child. The constraints of pilot research, however, mandate a group approach to test out initial hypotheses. Future work will place greater emphasis on phonological aspects and individualization.

---

[5]Our present study is being carried out at Landmark School for Dyslexic Children.

Assessment Phase

In the assessment phase, the following information was collected:

1. Retrieval speed for basic symbolic information (see Wolf et al., 1986);

2. Accuracy in receptive vocabulary for ostensive (concrete) and non-ostensive[6] (abstract) words and identifying the appropriate use of the word in varied contextual[7] phrases;

3. Accuracy and depth in expressive vocabulary for ostensive and non-ostensive words in a variety of tasks[8];

4. Basic word-recognition skills;

5. Reading comprehension, fluency, and accuracy. (See the appendix to this chapter for specific examples of how levels of word knowledge are assessed across various tasks.)

Intervention Phase

In this phase, teachers were trained to administer the intervention program as part of their daily language routine over a brief, intensive period (e.g., three to four half-hour periods per week for 2 months).

1. *Design Features of the Program*

    a. *Selection of Words.* The focus was on both strategies for learning new words and in-depth instruction for specific words. Age-appropriate words were selected from standardized tests, and the standardized information about these words was combined with a systematic, nonstandardized assessment of the same words. Useful everyday words (highly pertinent within the school program), were added from children's readers. As in the assessment

---

[6]Nonostensive words have been less frequently focused on in previous studies but constitute a large portion of the child's vocabulary, and because they are not easily depicted pictorially, the child has the added difficulty of not being able to visualize them (Segal, 1986a).

[7]A child's failure to retrieve words may stem from his or her limited depth of knowledge (Kail & Leonard, 1986) for that word; for example, knowledge of the word may be limited to specific contexts (Segal, 1986a). Thus, we cannot assume that once a child has learned the word in one linguistic context, he or she is automatically able to generalize its use to all possible contexts. It is of particular interest, therefore, to examine the expanding depth of specific words by controlling for different, developmentally evolving contexts.

[8]Tasks included confrontation naming, definitions, formulating sentences with the word and with multiple meanings where appropriate, drawing associations, providing synonyms.

phase, these words were grouped according to *levels* of knowledge (Beck et al., 1982) (see the appendix).

b. *Evaluation.* A randomly selected control group of children with reading disabilities who received no treatment were included in each age range to evaluate the outcome of treatment (see Gittelman & Feingold, 1983). Furthermore, factors within words were controlled to test for generalization. This was achieved by training only half the pretest words and including words (from the same semantic fields) from the children's texts in the intervention and posttest phases.[9] Dividing the words into groups for assessment (see McGregor & Leonard, 1989) is advocated when the word pool is sufficiently large.

2. *Specific Intervention Strategies*

a. *Flexibility, Fluency and Accuracy.* The first component of treatment was geared to word-finding strategies rather than content issues like vocabulary depth and rate. German (1988) described three word-finding patterns: slow/accurate, slow/inaccurate, and fast/inaccurate. A little-discussed implication of these patterns is the need to teach linguistic flexibility so that the child can draw on a compensatory strategy as quickly as possible. Thus, a pivotal aspect of the program was to develop explicit awareness in children when they experience a word-finding difficulty so they can seek alternative strategies.

This aspect of the program was based on our unexpected observations of what young average readers and children with dyslexia do when they cannot find a word. As mentioned earlier (Wolf & Segal, 1989), we found that some children with dyslexia use novel compounds spontaneously to compensate for their word-finding difficulties. Part of this program was designed to make available as quickly as possible a range of compensatory strategies, including innovative word-coining. This was accomplished through word games and language exercises that were simultaneously aimed to teach children automaticity in rate of retrieval: for example, free word association within a fixed time limit, verbal fluency, and rapid naming drills (see Stacey, 1985).

A caveat about this feature of the program concerns those children with dyslexia who already produce a relatively large number of innovative compounds and who exhibit a creative,

---

[9]Other variables such as priming effects from task to task, the number of treatment sessions, the number of words taught, and so on, are important features that must receive careful consideration in any program.

flexible process in their use of words. For this group, their very flexibility can have two faces with regard to accuracy. Segal (1989) suggested, on the one hand, that there may be an inability to generalize an individual word to varied linguistic contexts (this implies a lack of real flexibility, or excessive rigidity); on the other hand, there may be excessive flexibility with a lack of appropriate constraints. That is, the child fails to take into account the boundary(ies) of the word's meaning, thereby over-extending the meaning of the word in specific contexts. The present goal was to teach the child to impose selective constraints in the use of a word in particular linguistic contexts.

b. *Strategies for Richness.* In both the assessment phase and in previous work (Wolf & Segal, 1989), we found that some subjects spontaneously used a variety of compensatory strategies when approaching the vocabulary tasks. On this basis, it was advocated that these and other strategies be incorporated in the intervention phase. These strategies included (a) *phonological strategies* such as cuing, the use of rhymes, and alliteration exercises (see Bradley & Bryant, 1985); (b) *visual strategies* that employ the use of imagery (e.g., Thompson, Hall, & Sison, 1986, with Broca's aphasia patients); (c) *semantic strategies, circumlocution, and innovative word-coining.* The latter category included the broadest range of exercises. Examples are (a) analyzing words according to morphophonemic principles; (b) defining words; (c) reporting on personal experiences pertaining to words; (d) reflecting on the meanings of words and offering explanations for their uses in different contexts; (e) viewing words within broad categories (e.g., action words, emotion words, mental state words) and narrower superordinate categories; and (f) identifying multiple meanings for words. These strategies require flexibility to maintain both the flow and rate of communication (see Wolf & Segal, 1989). Thus, throughout, there is an emphasis on having a pool of possible alternatives to draw on, ranging from synonyms and circumlocutory alternatives to divergent verbal responses.

A note of caution is important when teaching an array of alternatives to any group of children with dyslexia. It is well-documented that word-finding difficulties frequently result in secondary behaviors, such as interjection of stereotyped meaningless phrases, overuse of circumlocutions and of words that lack specificity, borrowed word formations (words invented or extended by analogy), redundancies, and repetitions (German, 1988; Wiig & Semel, 1980). It is important to create a careful balance for each individual child between drawing on compensatory strategies (e.g., circumlocutions) to preserve communication and discouraging their use when they impede rate and accuracy.

Posttest Phase

This phase is in process and involves (a) readministering the original test battery; (b) testing related and unrelated words in the vocabulary portion of the battery (to evaluate generalization); and (c) maintenance. Ensuring maintenance of what has been taught during intervention has been emphasized frequently (McGregor & Leonard, 1989). McKeown, Beck, Omanson, and Perfetti (1983) advocated the "Word Wizard" approach, whereby children earn points for using previously taught words outside of the classroom. Components of this approach are incorporated in the last phase of our program.

Summary

To summarize, the present intervention effort represents an incorporation and extension of previous research in a variety of areas. Our approach is dominated by an emphasis on the building of vocabulary, retrieval, and rate skills, based in part on the older age of our population. An essential next step in future intervention work, particularly with younger children, lies in combining our insights with phonological training approaches. For the present, we hope the reader shares our curiosity to discover the possibilities and the limits of an approach that sets as its principle goal the deepening of words and a lightness in their use (Calvino, 1988).

Appendix

Evaluation of performance is based on rate, conventional accuracy scores, and levels of word knowledge. Overall scores are obtained in each tested area and for the child's response for each word across all tasks. Specific examples of levels of word knowledge follow.

1. *Unknown level:* The child may have no knowledge of the word, that is, he or she cannot identify the word from a pictorial array and is unable to define it, for example, to contemplate is "to confiscate-contemplate evidence—what police do with evidence."

2. *Acquainted level:* The child may have a receptive knowledge of the word without being able to use or define that word. For example, a

child may be able to identify a *tripod* from an array of four alternative pictures but define it as "A peapod with three peas in it"!

3. *Established level:* The child is able to provide a clear definition of the word indicating established knowledge, for example, a *volcano* is "a mountain where molten lava from inside the earth erupts."

References

Barron, R. W., Palmer, S. M., & Lovett, M. W. (1988). *Phonemic awareness and the origins of the decoding deficit in less skilled readers: A subtype analysis.* Paper presented to the First Annual Conference on Research and Theory in Learning Disabilities, the Pennsylvania State University, University Park, Pennsylvania.

Bauer, R., & Embert, J. (1984). Information processing in reading disabled and nondisabled children. *Journal of Experimental Child Psychology, 37,* 271–281.

Beck, I. L., McKeown, M. G., & Omanson, R. C. (1987). The effects and uses of diverse vocabulary instructional techniques. In M. G. McKeown & M. E. Curtis (Eds.), *The nature of vocabulary acquisition* (pp. 147–163). Hillsdale, NJ: Erlbaum.

Beck, I. L., Perfetti, C. A., & McKeown, M. G. (1982). Effects of long-term vocabulary instructions of lexical access and reading comprehension. *Journal of Educational Psychology, 74,* 506–521.

Boder, E. (1973). Developmental dyslexia: A diagnostic approach based on three atypical reading-spelling patterns. *Developmental Medicine and Child Neurology, 15,* 663–687.

Bowers, P., Steffy, R., & Tate, E. (1988). Comparison of the effects of IQ control methods on memory and naming speed predictors of reading disability. *Reading Research Quarterly, 23,* 304–319.

Bowey, J. A., & Patel, R. K. (1988). Metalinguistic ability and early reading achievement. *Applied Psycholinguistics, 9,* 367–383.

Bradley, L., & Bryant, P. E. (1985). *Rhyme and reason in reading and spelling.* Ann Arbor, MI: University of Michigan Press.

Brooks, L. R. (1988). Decentralized control of categorization: The role of prior processing episodes. In U. Neisser (Ed.), *Concepts and conceptual development: Ecological and intellectual factors in categorization.* Cambridge, England: Cambridge University Press.

Brown, A. L., & Campione, J. C. (1984). Three faces of transfer: Implications for early competence, individual differences, and instruction. In M. Lamb, A. Brown, & B. Rogoff (Eds.), *Advances in developmental psychology* (Vol. 3, pp. 143–192). Hillsdale, NJ: Erlbaum.

Bryant, P. E., Bradley, L., MacLean, M., & Crossland, J. (1989). Nursery rhymes, phonological skills and reading. *Journal of Child Language, 16*(2), 407–428.

Bryson, S. E., & Werker J. F. (1989). Toward understanding the problem in severely disabled children. Part 1: Vowel errors. *Applied Psycholinguistics, 10*, 1–12.

Calvino, I. (1988). *Six essays for the next millenium.* Cambridge, MA: Harvard University Press.

Cattell, M. (1886). The time it takes to see and name objects. *Mind, 2*, 63–65.

Chall, J. S. (1983). *Learning to read: The great debate.* New York: McGraw-Hill.

Clark, E. (1982). The young word-maker: A case study of innovation in the child's lexicon. In E. Wanner & L. R. Gleitman (Eds.), *Language acquisition: The state of the art* (pp. 1–67). Cambridge, England: Cambridge University Press.

Cronbach, L. J. (1943). Measuring knowledge of precise word meaning. *Journal of Educational Research, 36*, 528–534.

Curtis, M. E. (1987). Vocabulary testing and vocabulary instruction. In M. G. McKeown & M. E. Curtis (Eds.), *The nature of vocabulary acquisition* (pp. 37–51). Hillsdale, NJ: Erlbaum.

Denckla, M. B., & Rudel, R. G. (1976a). Naming of objects by dyslexic and other learning-disabled children. *Brain and Language, 3*, 1–15.

Denckla, M. B., & Rudel, R. G. (1976b). Rapid automatized naming (R. A. N.): Dyslexia differentiated from other learning disabilities. *Neuropsychologia, 14*, 471–479.

Dunn, L., & Dunn, L. (1981). *Peabody picture vocabulary test–Revised.* Circle Pines, MN: American Guidance Service.

Ellis, A. W. (1985). The cognitive neuropsychology of developmental (and acquired) dyslexia: A critical survey. *Cognitive Neuropsychology, 2*, 169–205.

Ellis, A. W. (1987). On problems in developing culturally-transmitted cognitive modules: Review of P. H. K. Seymour, *Cognitive analysis of dyslexia. Mind and Language, 3*, 242–251.

Fey, M. E. (1988). Generalization issues facing language interventionists: An introduction. *Language, Speech and Hearing Services in Schools, 19*(3), 272–281.

Fletcher, J. M., Espy, K. A., Francis, D. J., Davidson, K. D., Rourke, B. P., & Shaywitz, S. E. (in press). Comparisons of cut-off score and regression-based definitions of reading disabilities. *Journal of Learning Disabilities.*

Frith, U. (1985). Beneath the surface of dyslexia. In K. Patterson, J. Marshall, & M. Coltheart (Eds.), *Surface dyslexia* (pp. 301–330). London: Erlbaum.

Gates, A., & MacGinitie, W. (1978). *Gates-MacGinitie reading tests.* New York: Teachers College Press.

German, D. J. (1984). Diagnosis of word-finding disorders in children with learning disabilities. *Journal of Learning Disabilities, 17*, 353–358.

German, D. J. (1988). *Word-finding assessment and intervention for adolescents.* Paper presented at the Convention of the American Speech-Language-Hearing Association, Boston.

Gittelman, R., & Feingold, I. (1983). Children with reading disorders—I. Efficacy of reading remediation. *Journal of Child Psychology and Psychiatry, 24*, 167–191.

Gleason, J. B., & Wolf, M. (1988). Child language, aphasia and language disorder: Naming as a window on normal and atypical language processes. *Aphasiology, 2,* 189–294.

Goodglass, G. (1980). Disorders of naming following brain injury. *American Scientist, 68,* 637–655.

Goodglass, H., & Kaplan, E. (1972). *The assessment of aphasia and related disorders.* Philadelphia: Lea & Febiger.

Gough, P., & Tunmer, W. (1986). Decoding, reading and reading disability. *Remedial and Special Education, 7*(1), 6–10.

Gray, W. (1967). *Gray oral reading test.* New York: Bobbs-Merrill.

Kail, R., & Leonard, L. B. (1986). Word-finding abilities in language-impaired children. *ASHA Monographs, 25.*

Kameenui, E. J., Carnine, D. W., & Freschi, R. (1982). Effects of text construction and instructional procedures for teaching word meanings on comprehension and recall. *Reading Research Quarterly, 17,* 367–388.

Kameenui, E. J., Dixon, R. C., & Carnine, D. W. (1987). Issues in the design of vocabulary instruction. In M. G. McKeown & M. E. Curtis (Eds.), *The nature of vocabulary acquisition* (pp. 129–145). Hillsdale, NJ: Erlbaum.

Kamhi, A. G. (1988). A reconceptualization of generalization and generalization problems. *Language, Speech and Hearing Services in Schools, 19*(3), 304–313.

Kaplan, E., Goodglass, H., & Weintraub, S. (1983). *The Boston Naming Test.* Philadelphia: Lea & Febiger.

Katz, R. (1986). Phonological deficiencies in children with reading disability: Evidence from an object-naming task. *Cognition, 22,* 225–257.

Liberman, I. Y., Liberman, A. M., & Mattingly, I. G. (1980). Orthography and the beginning reader. In J. Kavanagh & R. Venezky (Eds.), *Orthography, reading, and dyslexia.* Baltimore: University Park Press.

Lovett, M. W., Benson, N. J., & Olds, J. (1988). *Individual difference predictors of treatment outcome in the remediation of specific reading disability.* Manuscript submitted for publication.

Lovett, M. W., Ransby, M. J., Hardwick, N., & Johns, M. S. (in press). Can dyslexia be treated? Treatment-specific and generalized treatment effects in dyslexic children's response to remediation. *Brain and Language.*

Lovett, M. W., Warren-Chaplin, P. M., Ransby, M. J., & Borden, S. (1987). *Training the word recognition skills of dyslexic children.* Paper presented at the 15th annual meeting of the International Neuropsychological Society, Washington, DC.

Lundberg, I., Frost, J., & Peterson, O. P. (1988). Effects of an extensive program for stimulating phonological awareness in pre-school children. *Reading Research Quarterly, 23,* 263–284.

Mattis, S., French, J. H., & Rapin, I. (1975). Dyslexia in children and adults: Three independent neuropsychological syndromes. *Developmental Medicine and Child Neurology, 119,* 121–127.

McGregor, K. K., & Leonard, L. B. (1989). Facilitating word-finding skills of language impaired children. *Journal of Speech and Hearing Disorders, 54*(2), 141–147.

McKeown, M. G., Beck, I. L., Omanson, R. C., & Perfetti, C. A. (1983). The effects of long term vocabulary instruction on reading comprehension: A replication. *Journal of Reading Behavior, 15*, 3–18.

Meltzer, L. (1984). Cognitive assessment and the diagnosis of learning problems. In M. Levine & P. Satz (Eds.), *Middle childhood: Development and dysfunction* (pp. 131–152). Baltimore: University Park Press.

Morris, R., Blashfield, R., & Satz, P. (in press). Developmental classification of reading disabled children. *Journal of Experimental and Clinical Neuropsychology.*

Morrison, F. J. (1980). *Reading disability: Toward a reconceptualization.* Paper presented at the annual meeting of The Psychonomic Society, St. Louis.

Murphy, L. A., Pollatsek, A., & Well, A. D. (1988). Developmental dyslexia and word retrieval deficits. *Brain and Language, 35*, 1–23.

Nagy, W. E., & Herman, P. A. (1987). Breadth and depth of vocabulary knowledge: Implications for acquisition and instruction. In M. G. McKeown & M. E. Curtis (Eds.), *The nature of vocabulary acquisition* (pp. 19–35). Hillsdale, NJ: Erlbaum.

Novoa, L., & Wolf, M. (1984, October). *Word retrieval and reading in bilingual children.* Paper presented at Boston University Conference on Language Development, Boston.

Oldfield, R. C., & Wingfield, A. (1966). *A series of pictures for use in object-naming* (MCR Psycholinguistic Research Unit Special Report No. PLU/65/19). Cambridge, England: Cambridge University.

Olson, R., & Wise, B. (1988). *Computer-based reading remediation with segmented speech and orthography.* Paper presented at the 29th annual meeting of The Psychonomic Society, Chicago.

Perfetti, C. A. (1985). *Reading ability.* New York: Oxford University Press.

Pressley, M., Levin, J. R., & McDaniel, M. A. (1987). Remembering versus inferring what a word means: Mnemonic and contextual approaches. In M. G. McKeown & M. E. Curtis (Eds.), *The nature of vocabulary acquisition* (pp. 107–127). Hillsdale, NJ: Erlbaum.

Roditi, B. (1988). *Automaticity, cognitive flexibility, and mathematics: A longitudinal study of children with and without learning disabilities.* Unpublished doctoral dissertation, Tufts University, Medford, MA.

Rubin, H., & Liberman, I. (1983). Exploring the oral and written language errors made by language disabled children. *Annals of Dyslexia, 33*, 111–120.

Rubin, H., Rotella, T., & Schwartz, L. (1988). *The effect of phonological analysis training on naming performance.* (Unpublished manuscript.)

Rudel, R. (1983). Definition of dyslexia: Language and motor deficits. In F. Duffy & N. Geschwind (Eds.), *Dyslexia: current status and future directions.* Boston: Little, Brown.

Segal, D. (1986a). *The development of the meaning of non-ostensive words in a group of primary school children.* Unpublished doctoral dissertation, Rhodes University, Grahamstown, South Africa.

Segal, D. (1986b). *The "grammar" of non-ostensive words in 6–12 year olds: A case study of pain.* Paper presented at the New England Child Language Association, Harvard University, Cambridge, MA.

Segal, D. (1986c). *The use of non-ostensive words in varied linguistic contexts: A study of word awareness in 6–12 year olds.* Paper presented at Boston University Conference on Language Development, Boston.

Segal, D. (1989). *Linguistic flexibility in language-impaired children.* Unpublished manuscript.

Seidenberg, M. S., Bruck, M., Fornarolo, G., & Backman, J. (1985). Word recognition processes of poor and disabled readers. Do they necessarily differ? *Applied Psycholinguistics, 6,* 161–180.

Siegel, L. S., & Ryan, E. B. (1984). Reading disability as a language disorder. *Remedial and Special Education, 5,* 28–33.

Spring, C., & Davis, J. (1988). Relations of digit naming speed with three components of reading. *Applied Psycholinguistics, 9,* 315–334.

Stacey, R. (1985). *Instructional strategies for word retrieval.* Unpublished manuscript.

Stanovich, K. E. (1986). Matthew effects in reading: Some consequences of individual differences in the acquisition of literacy. *Reading Research Quarterly, 21,* 360–407.

Stanovich, K. E. (Ed.). (1988). *Children's reading and the development of phonological awareness.* Detroit: Wayne State University Press.

Sternberg, R. J. (1987). Most vocabulary is learned from context. In M. G. McKeown & M. E. Curtis (Eds.), *The nature of vocabulary acquisition* (pp. 89–105). Hillsdale, NJ: Erlbaum.

Sternberg, R. J., & Powell, J. S. (1983). Comprehending verbal comprehension. *American Psychologist, 38,* 878–893.

Swanson, L. B. (1989). *Analyzing naming speed-reading relationships in children.* Unpublished doctoral dissertation, University of Waterloo, Waterloo, Ontario.

Thompson, C. K., Hall, H. R., & Sison, C. E. (1986). Effects of hypnosis and imagery training on naming behavior in aphasia. *Brain and Language, 28,* 141–153.

Vellutino, F. R. (1979). *Dyslexia: Theory and research.* Cambridge, MA: M. I. T. Press.

Vellutino, F. R., & Scanlon, D. M. (1987). Phonological coding, phonological awareness, and reading ability: Evidence from a longitudinal and experimental study. *Merrill-Palmer Quarterly, 33,* 321–363.

Vogel, S. A. (1985). *Syntactic abilities in normal and dyslexic children.* Baltimore: University Park Press.

Wagner, R., & Torgesen, J. (1987). The nature of phonological processing and its causal role in the acquisition of reading skills. *Psychological Bulletin, 101,* 192–212.

Wiig, E. H., & Semel, E. (1980). *Language assessment and intervention for the learning disabled.* Columbus, OH: Merrill.

Winner, E. (1988). *The point of words.* Cambridge, MA: Harvard Press.

Wolf, M. (1979). *The relationship of disorders of word-finding and reading in children and aphasics.* Unpublished doctoral dissertation, Harvard University, Cambridge, MA.

Wolf, M. (1982). The word-retrieval process and reading in children and aphasics. In K. Nelson (Ed.), *Children's Language,* (Vol. 3, pp. 437–493). Hillsdale, NJ: Erlbaum.

Wolf, M. (1985). When words fail: Insights for psychopathology from the developmental cognitive sciences. *McLean Hospital Journal, 10,* 15–36.

Wolf, M. (1986). Rapid alternating stimulus naming in the developmental dyslexias. *Brain and Language, 27,* 360–379.

Wolf, M., Bally, H., & Morris, R. (1986). Automaticity, retrieval processes, and reading: A longitudinal study in average and impaired readers. *Child Development, 57,* 988–1000.

Wolf, M., & Goodglass, H. (1986). Dyslexia, dysnomia, and lexical retrieval. *Brain and Language, 28,* 154–168.

Wolf, M., & Obregon, M. (1989). *Early naming deficits, developmental dyslexia and the specific retrieval-deficit hypothesis.* Manuscript submitted for publication.

Wolf, M., & Segal, D. (1989). *Serious child's play: The use of innovative compounds by dyslexic and average readers.* Manuscript submitted for publication.

Wolff, P., Michel, G., & Ovrut, M. (1989) *Temporal resolution and automatized naming in developmental dyslexia.* Unpublished manuscript.

6

Strategy Training for People with Language-Learning Disabilities

Elisabeth H. Wiig

This chapter focuses on communication-strategy training issues, theories, models, and procedures. The objectives of the introduction are to set the stage for understanding that mature communication requires strategic action and to relate this perspective to metalinguistic ability and maturation. A synopsis is then provided of the emergence and development of communication strategies during childhood and adolescence. A framework follows for a strategic inefficiency perspective of communication disorders and language-learning disabilities. Prerequisites for communication strategy development are delineated, and a generic framework and models for strategy training are provided. The models discussed—levels of competence, learning and reasoning approaches, and a process model for communication strategy development—are delineated and illustrated with examples from communication strategy training. Settings, traditional language intervention options, and curriculum-related language intervention formats are then introduced, compared, and contrasted.

Communication as Strategic Action

A recent text carried the enticing title *Communication: Strategic Action in Context* (Haslett, 1987). The title captures one of the current trends in speech-language pathology. The trend views the failures and delays in completing the linguistic transitions to metalinguistic maturity among students with language-learning disabilities to be the results of strategic inefficiencies (Silliman, 1987; Wiig, 1989; Wiig & Secord, 1989. This view can best be understood by considering the distinguishing features of efficient communicators.

In a longitudinal comparison of communicatively competent and incompetent speakers, Loban (1976) identified three distinguishing features. Competent and incompetent communicators differed along three continua:

1. Fluency in language production (ability to find words rapidly and consistently to express semantic intents)

2. Coherence in language production (ability to plan and organize the content of a message, before it is communicated)

3. Effectiveness and control (ability to master conventional grammar and use a variety of structures and to express higher level concepts or ideas by using conditional statements)

Mature speakers of a language are involved in both problem solving, in which the focus is on generating possible actions and responses, and decision making, which focuses on selecting the most effective action(s) and response(s). They are, in other words, involved in strategic action in context, while engaged in spoken and/or written communication.

This chapter will discuss language and communication strategy training for children and adolescents with language-learning disabilities. The discussion will take the perspective that language-learning disabilities in part reflect strategy inefficiency. The view held is that many students with diagnosed language-learning disabilities do not develop flexible and efficient cognitive-linguistic strategies to support the development and maturation of linguistic competence and metalinguistic ability.

Strategic language ability and metalinguistic ability will first be defined and compared. Processes involved in problem solving and decision making will be discussed. A short overview of stages and processes in communication strategy development will be featured next. The relationship between strategy acquisition and expertise will then be explored. The chapter will then take a closer look at the strategic inefficiency perspective in special education and broaden this perspective to language-learning disabilities.

An overview of some prerequisites for strategic language use will be provided as a background for discussing general principles for strategy training. A macro-model and a strategic process model for language intervention to foster communication strategy acquisition will then be introduced. Reasoning paradigms are also discussed as they relate to communication strategy training. Settings and format options for communication strategy training are also discussed and the need for proactive, rather than reactive training, is emphasized. The chapter conclusion explores the benefits of communication strategy training and relates the principles to the language content for reading and writing.

Strategic Language Use and Metalinguistic Ability

One of the current perspectives of school-age language problems is metalinguistic. It is represented by, among others, Menyuk (1983), Kamhi (1987), Lahey (1988), Wallach (1990), Wiig and Secord (1989), and Wiig (1989). The term *metalinguistic ability* refers to the conscious awareness of language and the ability to reflect on characteristics or aspects of language use (Cazden, 1972). Another way to view metalinguistic ability is that the speaker uses language as a tool (Menyuk, 1983). It implies that the speaker can distance herself or himself from language, view it as if it were an object, and modify and adapt it as if it were a tool.

Sometimes the term *metalinguistic ability* is tied to specific linguistic and communicative attainments such as figurative language use (Kamhi, 1987). Such specification limits the scope of application of the term and overlooks the learning processes involved. It may also lead to the erroneous assumption that the only aspect of language that needs to be developed to establish metalinguistic maturity is figurative language, or some other domain-specific ability. This may lead to practices in which developing content knowledge assumes a greater role than developing strategies (procedural knowledge). Although there is considerable overlap in the meanings and uses of "metalinguistic ability" and "strategic language use," an important difference is that strategic language use presupposes both metalinguistic and metacognitive abilities and has its basis in problem solving and decision making.

Problem Solving and Decision Making

Problem solving (generating options) for strategic language use is complicated by expectations that the mature speaker functions under a number of interactive constraints. The speaker must (a) adhere to principles and maxims for interpersonal communication, relating to quality and quantity; (b) respond to the controlling variables for communication (participants, settings, media, topic, objective); (c) respond to the conceptual and/or affective perspective of the audience; (d) follow schema or scripts for discourse or narrative; and (e) utilize acquired linguistic and pragmatic knowledge to formulate response options (speech acts) with appropriate social register, attenuation, or amplification. These, and other, constraints add to the complexity of mature communication (Allen & Brown, 1977; Austin, 1962; Grice, 1975, 1977; Labov, 1972; Searle, 1969, 1975; Stubbs, 1983; Wells, 1973, 1981).

Decision making (selecting among options) for strategic language use (strategic action) is complicated by two, if not more, factors (Gilhooly, 1988). Selecting a plan of action for communicating most often involves "risky" decision making. This is because there is always a degree of uncertainty about the outcome or effectiveness of any approach. Consider as an example that you were to apologize to a friend about an omission. In that case, you might generate and consider several options before communicating the apology. Should you use the phone? Should you write a card? Would it be most effective to be direct and candid in your apology?

Decisions in strategic language use are usually multiattribute and multistage decisions. Generally, several attributes must be weighed and integrated with information about the salient attributes to arrive at a decision. If we return to the example of apologizing to a friend, the friend's ego needs, age, social status, and expectations, to mention a few variables, must be considered, weighed, and integrated. Moreover, a sequence of decisions is involved. In the process, each choice leads to one of a number of choices. If we return again to the apology, a decision to use the telephone will lead to one set of communication options. A decision to write a note will lead to another set of options.

To communicate fluently, coherently, and effectively, the mature speaker must problem solve to generate options by (a) isolating salient dimensions of communicative tasks and contexts; (b) recognizing patterns formed by the isolated dimensions; and (c) formulating hypotheses about the significance of the patterns relative to the communicative task, context, and/or objective. He or she must make decisions by selecting and organizing a plan of action for communication from among the options generated. Last, but not least, the speaker must monitor, self-evaluate, and revise based on efficacy and outcome, among other considerations. The process is metacognitive and metalinguistic, and language is used as a tool for strategic action. The process is not necessarily hierarchical as portrayed in this breakdown.

Communication Strategy Development

It is interesting, but not unexpected, to observe that the normal progressions in cognitive and language and communication strategy acquisition follow parallel paths. In the cognitive domain, the emergence of strategy-based communication occurs around ages 5 to 7 years. It is tied to the transition to concrete operational functioning and decentration (i.e., ability to consider and integrate two or more dimensions of a task in problem solving) (Flavell, 1976; Inhelder & Piaget, 1964; Piaget, 1952, 1968, 1970).

In relation to the traditional curriculum, major changes in metacognition and strategy use can be observed in Grades 1 and 2 (ages 6 to 8), during the transition to the concrete operational stage, and Grade 6 (ages 11 to 12), during the transition to the formal operational stage. The age, grade, and cognitive stage relationship to metacognition and strategy use agrees well with the transitions to metalinguistic ability evident in the semantic-pragmatic behaviors of children in the age ranges from 7 to 8 and 12 to 13 years.

In communication strategy development, the 7- to 8-year age range is characterized by the first major transition toward strategic language use. The shift involves a change from a self-oriented to an other-oriented perspective. Listener characteristics are perceived, even though efficient linguistic adaptation to the listener's perspective is not yet in place. The transition to maturity occurs in the age range from 12 to 13 years and is characterized by affective and conceptual perspective taking (Alvy, 1973; Delia & Clark, 1977; Delia, Kline, & Burleson, 1979; Wiig, 1982). As examples, 12- to 13-year-olds adapt their messages to the listener's needs through, among other strategies, attenuation of negative content, amplification of positive aspects, statement of reasons and justifications, and anticipation of counterarguments.

In concept formation and figurative language development, we see similar transition patterns. Double-function modifiers such as *sweet* and *hard* are used primarily to describe physical attributes during the preschool years. The ages 7 to 8 years constitute a transition period when children begin to relate physical and psychological meanings. Consolidation occurs between ages 9 and 12 years, and maturity is assumed to be reached at ages 13 to 14 years (Asch & Nerlove, 1960; Nippold, Cuyler, & Braunbeck-Price, 1988).

Metaphoric ability is acquired in parallel stages. Rudimentary interpretations with reliance on preoperational abilities is in evidence between ages 4 and 7 years. Interpretation of similarity metaphors with shared attributes (e.g., "She is a sly fox"), which relies on concrete operational abilities, emerges between ages 8 and 10 years. Interpretation of proportional metaphors with analogies (e.g., "His head is an apple without a core"), which relies on formal operational abilities, occurs between ages 11 and 13 years (Billow, 1975, 1977; Nippold, Leonard, & Kail, 1984).

Strategy Use and Expertise

Before we can consider how communication strategies can be trained, we need to consider the definitions, characteristics, and processes involved. Implementing communication strategy training requires that new philosophies and perspectives are accepted and embraced. Above all, it is important to recognize the differences between traditional language intervention perspectives, which tend to be skill-based, and strategy training perspectives, which are process oriented. Let us start with definitions.

Strategy Defined

The term *strategy* will now be defined first as others have used it, and then as it is used here. *Strategy* is often used in relation to game playing. In that context, a strategy can be thought of as a method by which, given a decision point (node), a move is chosen that leads to an ultimate win, whenever a win is possible (Banerji, 1987). It should be obvious that communication is not unlike game playing and that Banerji's definition is therefore applicable in this context.

Restle (1962) provided a somewhat broader definition. A strategy is defined as a particular pattern of responses to stimuli or tasks that has been inferred by a learner over a series of trials. This definition implies that strategies are acquired as the learner plans and develops a scheme for achieving some purpose.

An even broader definition can be found in the work by the University of Kansas Institute for Research in Learning Disabilities (Lenz, Clark, Deshler, & Schumaker, 1988). They defined a strategy as "an individual's approach to a task." They further stated that "it includes how a person thinks and acts when planning, executing and evaluating performance on a task and its outcomes."

The definition for strategy used here is that it is a procedural routine or process that responds to underlying concepts, communication plans (scripts, schema), goals (objectives, intentions), and perspectives (conceptual, affective). The procedural routine or process (strategy) may be communication context specific or it may be context independent (Wiig, 1989). Inherent in this definition is the feature that efficient (strategic) communication must follow underlying plans (schema/ scripts), must move toward a goal, and must respond to the listener's knowledge and personality needs (conceptual/affective perspectives). In some instances, strategies are context specific. This is the case for strategies for interpreting metaphors. Knowledge of the four universal structures of metaphors (orientational, part-whole, structural, ontological) leads to pattern recognition, hypothesis formulation and testing, and interpretation (Lakoff & Johnson, 1980; Wiig, 1985, 1989). In some instances strategies may be relatively context independent. Pragmatic strategies for discourse, formed by integrating goals, plans, and perspectives, can be applied to written dialogue in plays, novels, and short stories and to communication in a variety of settings (e.g., academic, vocational, social) and using a variety of media (e.g., face-to-face, telephone, writing).

There is general agreement about the way strategy acquisition occurs. Strategies are acquired in goal-directed processes. The process requires active participation by the learner. It is guided by the learner's cognitive level and reasoning style. There is also agreement that the use of efficient strategies characterizes expert performance (Bruner, Oliver, & Greenfield, 1966; Flavell, 1971, 1976; Gholson, 1980; Neisser, 1967; Piaget, 1952, 1968, 1970; Schiffman, 1972; Stevenson, 1973; Swanson, 1989).

Development of Expertise

There are several views of what constitutes expertise and how it is developed. Common to all is the recognition that expertise is related to efficient use of domain-related strategies for solving problems and making decisions. Dreyfus and Dreyfus (1986) proposed a model for the progression toward expertise. The progression in any field of endeavor is described to occur in five universal stages. Each stage is described behaviorally and related to the degree to which strategies for problem solving and decision making have been acquired, integrated, and automatized. The model takes into account that a learner may be an expert at some aspects and at the same time a novice at other aspects of the same domain.

The Beginner (Stage 1) learns and applies a limited set of rules to context-free features. The learner uses a trial-and-error approach and performs in a disjointed and unpredictable manner, because the situational knowledge is inadequate. The Advanced Beginner (Stage 2) recognizes aspects of a new situation based on similarity to prototypical cases. The learner begins to recognize similarities and differences between new and "old" examples and experiences. The learner classifies and contrasts instances, but has no overall plans for following through in complex situations.

The Competent Performer (Stage 3) organizes behavior. This is done by selecting goals (e.g., communication objectives and intentions), plans (e.g., underlying concepts, schema, scripts), and perspectives (e.g., conceptual, affective) to guide what facts to consider and what rules to apply. The learner formulates hypotheses about the significance of dimensions and patterns in stimuli and tasks and about possible responses. The competent performer goes through a conscious problem-solving and decision-making process.

The Proficient Performer (Level 4) has tested different approaches and strategies that were efficient and have been automatized. The learner selects goals, plans, and perspectives holistically and automatically. However, carrying out a plan of action may still require analysis and conscious decision making. Performance at this level is relatively fluent and flexible, and revisions and repairs are required only when any task or situation becomes too complex or multidimensional.

The Expert (Level 5) understands situations and tasks holistically and intuitively. Efficient strategies, decisions, and actions are called up automatically. Performance is rapid, fluent, flexible, and coherent. Relative to language and communication, this is the level of the competent, mature speaker. It is the level of performance to which we hope to bring students with language disabilities.

Gilhooly (1988) reminded us that expertise takes a long time to develop. Research has suggested that 10 years of study and practice is required in many areas. The distinction between the novice and the expert in domains such as physics, political science, and medical diagnosis can be captured. The change from novice to expert seems characterized by a shift in strategy from working backward to reasoning forward from the givens to a solution. In medical diagnosis it appears that both novices and experts follow a hypothetico-deductive approach with few quantitative differences. However, experts develop better sets of initial hypotheses and derive more specific hypotheses earlier.

Studies of children with and without learning disabilities point to yet other features of expertise (Swanson, 1989). Expert performance among children seems to be related to strategy transformation. In this transformation, simple strategies are reworked into more efficient strategies. Information may be reduced to a rule with a constant relationship, several strategies or operations may be chunked into a single unit, and parts that are unnecessary for solving a problem may be deleted (Swanson, 1989).

Strategic Inefficiency

Special education takes the perspective that strategic inefficiencies are central problems in students with learning disabilities (Alley & Deshler, 1979; Baker, 1982; Gerber, 1983; Hallahan, 1980; Meichenbaum, 1977; Reid & Hresko, 1981; Swanson, 1989). Swanson (1989) summarized recent research findings as follows: "LD children experience difficulty with such self-regulating mechanisms as checking, planning, monitoring, revising, and evaluating during an attempt to learn or solve problems" (p. 4).

The strategic inefficiency perspective can be generalized to students with language-learning disabilities based on observations of their communicative inefficiencies (Bernstein & Seidenberg, 1988; Larson & McKinley, 1987; Mathinos, 1988; Ripich & Spinelli, 1985; Silliman, 1987; Simon, 1985; Wiig, 1984, 1985, 1989; Wiig & Becker-Caplan, 1984; Wiig & Secord, 1989). Silliman (1987) proposed that the strategic inefficiencies among students with language-learning disabilities can be related to three, if not more, factors: (a) insufficient content knowledge, (b) inefficient processing, and (c) inadequate management of available processing resources. To this may be added inefficiencies or limitations in reasoning, problem solving, and decision making.

Differential patterns in problem solving have been reported among adolescents with learning disabilities (Stone & Forman, 1988). On a formal-operational task (the bending rods task), three deficit patterns emerged. In descending order of prevalence, they were (a) a specific developmental delay in testing hypotheses and acquiring an isolation-of-variables strategy (29%); (b) poor awareness of the implicit demands of the experimental task, associated with highly general conclusions about solving the problem (26%); (c) a general conceptual deficit, affecting all aspects of problem solving (7%).

Stone and Forman (in press) also studied problem solving in 10 adolescents with language-learning disabilities, using the bending rods task. Half the group exhibited evidence of problem-solving deficits. Of the deficits, hypothesis testing difficulties were most common (30%); poor awareness of implicit task demands and general conceptual deficits were less common (10% each). These findings provide added support for strategy inefficiencies in students with language-learning disabilities.

There are other observations of the nature of strategy inefficiencies among students with learning disabilities (LD) that can be generalized to language-learning disabilities. Wansart (1990) used the Tower of Hanoi task to compare strategies used by students with LD and non-

LD age peers. The normally achieving 10- to 12-year-olds advanced to a more sophisticated level of strategy use that the children with LD. As a group they used a final representational strategy, resulting in ability to transfer the solution. In contrast, the group with LD tended to use a final procedural strategy, bound to situationally specific aspects of the problem materials. Similar procedural strategies were reported for normally achieving 7- to 8-year-olds (Blanchet, 1981).

Swanson (1989) highlighted other strategy-related differences in the performances by students with LD and normally achieving peers. He pointed to indirect and direct evidence that students with learning disabilities may use qualitatively different mental operations and processing routes from their achieving peers. Children with LD have difficulties using isolated heuristics related to problem representation and deleting irrelevant information. Nondisabled children are superior in the use of strategies for pattern extraction, feedback, evaluation, and systematic problem solving. Swanson suggested that LD "children's mental processing is more likely driven by heuristics than by algorithms" (p. 9). In other words, students with LD tend to use heuristics, that is, to make ad hoc best guesses that may be opportunistic at decision points and that do not guarantee a solution and certainly not an optimal solution. Normal achievers tend to use algorithms, that is, to use procedural routines that guarantee a solution where a solution is feasible.

Prerequisites for Strategic Language Use

When new models and perspectives are introduced, there is a tendency to abandon previous models and perspectives without considering how the new and the old relate. There is also a tendency to begin communication strategy training without attention to prerequisites and assuring that these are either in place or being developed in the process. We can identify four prerequisite areas for strategy use and expertise: content and concept knowledge, linguistic pattern recognition, organization of communicative behaviors, and automatization of communication strategy use. Each of these is discussed in this section.

Content Knowledge

Some of the important prerequisites for and transitions toward expertise can be abstracted and related to the process of acquiring strategies for communication (Table 6.1). The model for the acquisition of expertise first points out that the acquisition of linguistic skills and rules (content knowledge) is a prerequisite for moving toward strategic func-

TABLE 6.1
Overview of Transitions in the Acquisition of Strategies for
Language and Communication

Acquisition	Description
Linguistic Skills/Content Knowledge	Basic syntactic, semantic, and pragmatic skills must be adequate and available as tools.
Pattern Recognition	Patterns in semantic-syntactic-pragmatic and contextual stimuli must be recognized and assigned significance.
Organization of Communication Behaviors	Communication objectives, underlying plans, structures (schema), and perspectives to be taken must be integrated and used in planning for communication.
Automatization	Processes involved in organizing communication behaviors must be used intuitively and automatically.

tioning. For expert communication, a speaker must have access to syntactic, semantic, and pragmatic skills, rules, and repertories that constitute content knowledge. The linguistic knowledge base must be adequate and easily accessible to allow for strategic language use and communication.

Pattern Recognition

The next developmental prerequisite is to recognize patterns in semantic, syntactic, pragmatic, and contextual stimuli. Many patterns—underlying concepts, plans, scripts, and schema—must be recognized before it is possible to function strategically as a communicator. Among these patterns are underlying concepts, schema for turn taking in conversation, and underlying structural schema for situational and event scripts, goal-oriented communication, and narratives. As an example, the patterns (underlying structure) in metaphoric expressions must be recognized before the transition to figurative language use can take place (Lakoff & Johnson, 1980). Pattern recognition in linguistic, pragmatic, or contextual stimuli presupposes ability to abstract significant features, attributes, or variables and to compare them with stored prototypes. The process of pattern recognition in linguistic stimuli and communication contexts seems to progress almost magically in children with normal language and cognitive development. Children with language-learning disabilities seem inadequate to the task. The transition from functional to strategic language use may be severely delayed or blocked for many of them.

Organization of Behavior

The next prerequisite is organization of communication behaviors. The emerging organization results from conscious awareness and attention to communication objectives, controlling variables, underlying plans (structure, schema, scripts), and to the perspective to be taken during communication. Organization cannot take place if the speaker approaches the communicative interaction impulsively. The speaker must approach the communication task reflectively. In the early stages of transition to competent and integrated organization of communication behaviors, the speaker may pay attention only to the goals and objectives. Later, awareness of underlying plan (structure, schema, script) is added. Last, the perspectives to be taken vis-à-vis an audience are integrated with goals and plans in a process of organization. As integration progresses, the process becomes more and more holistic and intuitive and the next transition toward expertise can take place.

Automatization

The last transition requires that the processes involved in organizing communication behaviors become intuitive and automatic. When automaticity has been established through practice, the communicator's performance will be fluent, flexible, and efficient. The need to revise is recognized intuitively, and revisions or repairs are achieved readily. The expert communicator can, in other words, be thought of as a consummate editor. It is easy to recognize speakers who are experts at communicating. In the academic arena, they can lecture and answer questions fluently about content that has been internalized. In the vocational arena, an expert receptionist in an office or hotel can answer any questions, in person or by telephone, fluently as long as the information is internalized. If a lecturer or a receptionist were asked questions outside of his or her sphere of knowledge, the individual could no longer rely on automatized responses. He or she would have to pause, plan, and possibly revise.

Strategy Training Models and Procedures

Strategy training can be conducted within a variety of frameworks. However, communication strategy training should always be viewed as a progressive, sometimes hierarchically organized, process. Intervention models can provide a framework or structure for capturing the process as a whole as well as individual phases or stages of the process. In this section we first consider generic recommendations for effective strategy training. A macro-level model for communication strategy training is then introduced. This is followed by discussions of learning and reasoning approach options and of a micro-level process model. Finally, options for settings and formats for communication strategy training are considered.

Effective Strategy Training

Swanson (1989) listed several advantages of strategy instruction. First, strategy training "focuses on what is modifiable" and relevant. Second, "it allows for conscious and active rule creation and rule following." Third, it incorporates the notion that strategies may operate differently in students with different declarative knowledge (internal organization of prior knowledge) and procedural knowledge (knowledge about real-life performances). Fourth, "it allows the child to be actively involved in the instruction" (p. 5).

Effective strategy training appears to have common characteristics across domains of application, whether it is math, reading, writing, or oral language and communication. Among commonalities are that strategy training takes account of the learner's knowledge base. It focuses on task-specific, as well as general, aspects of problem solving and learning and on having the student plan and monitor strategies.

Effective strategy training for communication requires that task demands, rules, underlying concepts or plans, and necessary perspectives are made explicit to the learner. The role of the trainer is to structure the contents and tasks. The trainer should support the student in analyzing task demands, identifying important features (attributes), recognizing patterns in linguistic stimuli and communication contexts, and formulating options for responding. The trainer should also support the student in monitoring, evaluating, and revising for effectiveness in communicating.

In real-life communication several strategy and response options are usually available to the speaker. The trainer must support the student in recognizing what options are available. This can be done by providing linguistic models and examples of communications from which a response can be selected and evaluated for efficacy. The trainer can also provide models of strategies from which the student can select one or more options. Training to support strategy selection and monitoring is related to developing executive (higher order) processes and strategies.

The general suggestions for effective strategy training can be applied directly to language intervention. To be effective in supporting communication strategy development, training must:

1. Differentiate linguistic skill and rule acquisition from strategic language use to the degree possible

2. Support the student in perceiving, abstracting, and/or using underlying patterns in linguistic stimuli (concepts, structure, schema, scripts)

3. Assist the student in forming alternative hypotheses about the significance of the perceived patterns

4. Ask the student to (a) act on more than one alternative (e.g., make two inferences, give two interpretations, switch social register) or (b) make a deliberate choice between two or more alternatives

5. Support the student in planning and organizing communication behaviors by goals, plans, and perspectives (e.g., planning for production of sentences, paragraphs, discourse, narratives under different constraints)

A Macromodel for Training

Pressley et al. (Pressley, Symons, Snyder, Cariglia-Bull, 1989; see Chap. 13 in this volume) have delineated aspects that must be present in comprehensive strategy training. First, the trainer must understand the processes that are involved in performing a task. Translated to communication strategy training, the trainer must be able to task analyze and have knowledge of communication maxims, rules, and controlling variables, and of underlying concepts, schema, or scripts. Second, there must be a complete model of strategy training and use. Goldman (1989) and Paris and Oka (1989) have added that strategy instruction must (a) be matched to the student's knowledge base, (b) focus on content as well as process, (c) demonstrate the use of particular strategies, (d) provide for student-trainer dialogue about the strategies being trained, and (e) include instruction to promote generalization. These principles are represented in some communication training models and resources (Hoskins, 1987; Wiig, 1982, 1985, 1989).

When strategies for language interpretation and use are trained, an active and interactive learning process is involved. This process can be described in terms of specific levels of competence, which are delineated in the Levels of Competence Model (Wiig, 1989). This model is discussed briefly in Table 6.2.

TABLE 6.2
Overview of the Levels of Competence Model

Level	Objectives
Basic Training	Develop awareness of significant features and underlying patterns (scripts/schema).
Extension to Pragmatic Uses	Strengthen the awareness of features and patterns and extend the knowledge to real-life uses.
Extension to Media, Participants and Contexts	Provide opportunities for generalization of knowledge to complex tasks with more controlling variables or at a higher level of abstraction.
Self-Directed Training	Foster independent application of knowledge to establish competence.

Note. Adapted from *Steps to Language Competence: Developing Metalinguistic Strategies* by E. H. Wiig, 1989, San Antonio, TX: The Psychological Corporation.

In the Levels of Competence Model, the first level (Basic Training) provides essential training to develop knowledge of critical features, underlying concepts, or patterns (structure, schema, scripts). The focus of training will vary as a function of the linguistic domain and content for which strategies are being trained. The objectives are, however, fairly independent of context. They are to develop (a) awareness, recognition, and knowledge of significant features of linguistic stimuli (e.g., semantic features, politeness features, listener characteristics) and/or (b) recognition of underlying patterns or controlling variables (e.g., structure of metaphors, turn-taking rules, functional segments in discourse, scripts, narrative structure).

The trainer's primary task is to structure the experience to make the features (semantic/syntactic/pragmatic/contextual) and underlying patterns (structure/schema/scripts) explicit to the student. In regular classroom teaching, structure and explication are often missing, as they may not be needed. As an example, in relation to concept formation, the trainer's goal is to decontextualize word definitions so that the underlying concepts can be generalized across contexts, to problem solving, and to figurative uses (e.g., *empty* tells that the expected contents of a given container are absent). Decontextualizing word meanings for *empty* and *full* can be accomplished by introducing structured comparisons of familiar containers (e.g., glass, mug, garbage can) with expected contents (e.g., beverage, hot beverage, garbage) and relative amounts of the contents (e.g., empty, full, half-full).

As an example in relation to pragmatics for goal-directed communication, the objective is to make the underlying structure of the communication explicit. This can be accomplished by modeling, for example, complaints, and abstracting functional segments (e.g., greeting, response to greeting, statement of reason for complaint, acknowledgment, statement of desired action, acknowledgment).

The second level (Extension to Pragmatic Uses) extends the knowledge of features and/or underlying patterns to pragmatic uses in fairly simple tasks. Among objectives are to strengthen the knowledge of features and their implications and to consolidate recognition and use of underlying patterns in communication. As an example, the decontextualized meanings for "empty–full" may be extended to conversational stimuli for problem solving and making inferences (e.g., The mother said, "Shouldn't you empty the vase before putting it away?" What should the person do?). In that case, problem solving and making inferences would depend on knowledge of the underlying concepts that each container has an expected content (e.g., a vase can contain water and/or flowers).

As a second example, explicit knowledge of the functional segments for complaining could be extended to making complaints about everyday occurrences, such as getting a pencil without an eraser for an exam from a teacher. In that case, the speaker would first have to call the teacher's attention. The teacher would have to give an acknowledgment. The student would then tell what happened and either wait for the teacher's action or tell what he or she wanted to happen.

The third level (Extension to Media, Participants, and Contexts) extends the acquired knowledge to more and more complex communication tasks with more controlling variables. The focus is on generalization of acquired knowledge and strategies. The learner becomes more independent in functioning. As an example, the objective may be to extend the knowledge of semantic features of key concepts (e.g., empty–full) to figurative expressions by using learned strategies. In the case of figurative expressions with the concepts *empty* or *full* (e.g., "They are empty-headed," "John came to the birthday empty-handed," "My heart is full"), the strategy can be stated as "Look for the container (e.g., head, hands, heart); look for the expected contents based on the context or topic (e.g., thoughts, presents, feelings/love)." The semantic knowledge of the key concepts could also be extended to curriculum contexts (e.g., containers, contents, and measurements of content in physics and chemistry).

The last level (Self-Directed Training) provides assignments for the student to carry out independently. The objective is to support independent application of the acquired strategies. As an example from figurative language training, students may select tasks such as finding and reporting on figurative expressions used in newspapers and journal ads, TV commercials, cartoons and comics, plays, novels, or poetry. The last step is designed to provide opportunities for planning, organizing, self-monitoring, self-evaluating, editing, revising, and automatizing strategy use. It can be considered to establish performances related to expertise (Dreyfus & Dreyfus, 1986).

Reasoning Paradigms

Strategy training for language and communication can be implemented by using a variety of models for learning and reasoning (Bruner, Goodnow, & Austin, 1956; Chandrasekaran, 1983, 1986; Pierce, 1957; Shapiro, Eckroth, & Vallasi, 1987) (see Table 6.3).

One approach to strategy training is direct implanting of knowledge. In this approach, the learner is given and internalizes a specific approach (a tactic) by direct instruction, rote learning, and/or use of mnemonics. As an example, students could be told directly about the four underlying structures for metaphors and given the category labels *structural*, *ontological*, *synechdoche*, and *orientational* (Lakoff &

TABLE 6.3
Overview of Reasoning Paradigms for Strategy Training

Type	Characteristics
Direct implanting of knowledge	The learner acquires knowledge or tactics by direct instruction without problem solving.
Experimental learning	The learner is provided with experiences, models, or demonstrations of actions, interactions, and processes and abstracts knowledge.
Inductive learning	The learner abstracts patterns, draws inferences and conclusions from observations, given facts, examples, and models.
Deductive learning	The learner explores prior knowledge about stimuli and tasks and uses new information to arrive at deductions.
Learning by analogy	The learner adapts an already established concept or strategy to a new context.
Abductive learning	The learner uses existing facts and prior knowledge to develop a set of hypothetical assertions.

Johnson, 1980). They could be told to recall the names of the categories by a mnemonic; by saying "SOSO." The students could then identify the structure of a given metaphor be recalling the mnemonic "SOSO" as a cue. Direct implanting of knowledge can lead to rapid acquisition and rapid forgetting. It does not involve the learner actively in a problem-solving process and therefore does not qualify as executive strategy training.

In an experiential approach to strategy training, the essential component is to provide demonstration or modeling of an action, a relationship, a feature, an interaction, or a process. Students abstract knowledge about goals, plans, and perspectives from the demonstration. The acquired knowledge is applied in more complex problem-solving tasks. This approach can be used effectively for basic training of, among others, underlying concepts and structures. It allows the student to interact in a multisensory learning experience in real-life contexts. As an example, the trainer may use objects such as glasses, pencils and rulers, Scotch tape, paper pads, and pitchers and beakers of different sizes to illustrate underlying dimensions and relations described by the spatial terms big–small, long–short, wide–narrow, deep–shallow. The students abstract the dimension(s), verbalize the comparisons, and describe the consequences of dimensional changes in everyday contexts (e.g., using narrow vs. wide Scotch tape to close a package). This approach is effective in combination with learning by induction or deduction.

In inductive learning, students recognize patterns, draw inferences, and arrive at conclusions based on observations, supplied facts, examples, and/or models. The inductive learning process can be supported by asking open-ended questions (e.g., What? How? Why?) to promote divergent thinking. The inductive process leads to classification and hierarchical organization of concepts and knowledge and generates hypotheses and predictions. In other words, the process is one of discovery, in which students are active participants. In relation to the Levels of Competence Model, induction is advocated for basic training. The inductive process is also effective at higher levels of training to extend the use of concepts and knowledge to more complex and self-directed tasks.

In the deductive process, students explore their prior knowledge about linguistic and contextual stimuli and communication tasks. Students are directed to use semantic, syntactic, pragmatic, and contextual clues to arrive at deductions based on either new information or stored background knowledge. The outcome is stored for future use. In relation to the Levels of Competence Model, the deductive process is advocated for basic training and extension to pragmatic uses and across media, participants, and contexts. Students may be asked what they have seen or heard before, believe to be the case, have just learned, or already know. As an example, they might be asked how they have heard others complain in different situations or how they themselves have complained about things in the past. They may be asked to judge the effectiveness of model complaints. The students' stored knowledge and new models can then be compared for similarities, differences, and relative effectiveness.

Learning by analogy can be viewed as a combination of inductive and deductive learning. In the process, an already established concept, rule, or strategy is adapted to fit a new context. Analogous reasoning is an especially appropriate way to problem solve for the translation vocabulary from literal to figurative uses (Extension to Media, Participants, and Contexts). As an example, assume that the underlying concepts for *empty* and *full* are extended to the figurative expression, "Her compliments are only empty gestures." By analogy, compliments would be identified as the container, the expected contents as truth, and the absence (empty) would indicate lack of truth or lying. In relation to pragmatics, learning by analogy could occur by extending the discourse rules, the perspectives to be taken, and the social registers used in U.S. presidential circles to the discourse in Shakespeare's *Julius Caesar*. By analogy, students might arrive at a better understanding of who was allowed to speak to Caesar, why a person would address Caesar spontaneously, how Caesar's advisors and servants were supposed to address him, and how he would address them. The process of learning by analogy may be supported by questioning about patterns, similarities and differences, and expected outcomes.

In learning by "abduction" (Pierce, 1957), the learner makes a leap from observed facts and background knowledge to a set of hypothetical assertions. As an example, most children in my neighborhood know that we have two English mastiffs and that a family several blocks away also has a mastiff. Assume that a child on my street were to find a mastiff on the loose. Chances are, the child would reason as follows, "That's a mastiff, just like the Wiigs' dogs. Maybe it belongs to the Wiigs. If it doesn't, it probably belongs to the Joneses." Inferences in communication frequently follow an abductive reasoning path. The most likely assertion, based on probability, is accepted as a first working hypothesis. Alternative hypotheses may be formulated and kept ready, as needed. In the Levels of Competence Model, the extension of concepts, principles, and structures to pragmatic uses relies heavily on abductive reasoning.

A Micromodel for Strategy Training

Wiig (1982, 1985, 1989) also described and applied a micromodel for linguistic and communication strategy training. The Process Model for Strategy Development, in combination with the Levels of Competence Model, has been supported experimentally in a comparison of efficacy in developing constraint-seeking (yes/no) question asking in transition class children with learning disabilities (Mandelbaum, 1985). The process model, presented in an overview in Table 6.4, is not unlike the Executive Strategy training model (Ellis, Deshler, & Schumaker, 1989). That model features the following steps: (a) Focus on the problem situation, (b) identify and analyze the critical features of the problem, (c) generate a series of problem-solving steps, and (d) monitor the effectiveness of the self-generated strategy and make necessary modifications. One difference in the models is that the process model isolates and focuses more specifically on pattern recognition and hypothesis formulation and testing as steps in the strategy development process.

The Process Model for Strategy Development assumes that linguistic and communication strategy acquisition occurs in a process that can be directed. The model assumes that (a) the trainer can support strategy development by refocusing attention, providing models and cues, and rewarding problem solving, and (b) the learner must be actively involved. The model contains five major steps, each of which is essential. The process of acquisition is considered to be hierarchical, recursive, and reducible with increasing competence. This means that at any level of the process, the learner can return to a lower level and go through the process again. The learner can combine or skip steps, transform the process, and develop higher level strategies.

The first objective (Step 1) is to get the learner to actively identify features of linguistic stimuli and communication contexts that may, or may not, be significant. In other words, the objective is for the learner to identify words, phrases, or supporting contextual cues (e.g., body language, prosody, topic) that must be evaluated. Typically, students with language-learning disabilities (LLD) with strategic inefficiencies may focus conservatively. They may identify one or two, but not all, potentially important linguistic or contextual features. The student's attention can be refocused by asking what other features (words, tone of voice, facial expression, topic of discussion, title) could be important. The objective is, in other words, to foster divergent thinking.

The second objective (Step 2) is to get the learner to perceive patterns in the targeted features of linguistic stimuli and contexts. As an example, the learner might be given an unfamiliar metaphor such as, "A lion cannot hide in the grass." The learner would be asked and

TABLE 6.4
Overview of Steps in the Process Model for Strategy Development

Step	Major Objectives
	TO ESTABLISH ABILITY TO:
1	Identify features of stimuli and contexts that may (or may not) be significant in problem solving
2	Perceive patterns in targeted features of stimuli and contexts
3	Formulate and test hypotheses generated about the significance of the perceived patterns
4	Select and execute responses judged to have a high level of probability for success
5	Self-monitor and evaluate the efficacy of the selected response, and repair or revise as needed

Note. Adapted from *Steps to Language Competence: Developing Metalinguistic Strategies* by E. H. Wiig, 1989, San Antonio, TX: The Psychological Corporation.

helped to search actively for similar patterns stored in memory (e.g., "Have you heard another expression that uses the words 'in the grass'? to elicit 'a snake in the grass' "). Because students with LLD may have short- and long-term memory deficits, the search for stored patterns may be cumbersome or futile. In that case, the trainer can provide examples and models to support pattern recognition. Because linguistic stimuli and communication in context feature recurring patterns (e.g., semantic, syntactic, pragmatic patterns; discourse and narrative structure), pattern recognition is an important step in developing communication strategies.

The third objective (Step 3) is to get the learner to formulate and test hypotheses about the significance of the perceived linguistic or contextual patterns. The learner must be reinforced for coming up with and testing more than one hypothesis. Typically, students with LLD formulate and test hypotheses based on single features in "conservative focusing" (Bruner et al., 1966). As an example, given an ambiguous situation in which two boys face each other with clenched fists, but with smiles on their faces, students with LLD might focus exclusively on the fists and what they signify. They would then hypothesize that the boys were going to fight. The objective is to direct the student to formulate hypotheses based on multiple features (decentration). In the example of the boys, the students should be directed to formulate hypotheses that incorporate the feature of the fists and the feature of the faces. As a result, they should come up with alternative hypotheses such as, "Maybe they'll fight, but they smile; it's probably only a mock fight." Students should then be assisted in testing either one hypothesis at a time (successive scanning) or two or more hypotheses at the same time (simultaneous scanning).

The fourth objective (Step 4) is to get the learner to select and execute a response. It is important at this point that the learner dares to fail. The process model is not a behavior modification model, and errors are integral to learning. The trainer's role is to direct the student to come up with alternative responses. This allows the learner to compare options and evaluate the probability that an option will be effective. As a pragmatic example, the learner may be asked to come up with two or more ways to complain and to select one to try for effect.

The last objective (Step 5) is to get the learner to self-monitor and evaluate the efficacy of the selected response, and to repair or revise as needed. It is important that the trainer neither reinforces nor punishes responses. Self-monitoring and revising, as a process, must be reinforced. If the learner cannot come up with alternatives for revising a response, models and examples can be introduced for the learner to evaluate. As the student becomes increasingly competent, action plans (responses) are selected intuitively and holistically. Progress is measured by the level of organization of communication behaviors and by the level of fluency and flexibility in responding.

There is increasing evidence in the literature that communication strategies can be trained in a structured process (Mandelbaum, 1985; Simmonds, 1989). The reserach by Mandelbaum suggests that communication strategy training can be effective in developing constraint-seeking question asking with even 7- to 8-year-olds and that modeling without explicit problem solving is less effective. In contrast, Simmonds (1989), in an unrelated study of constraint-seeking question asking in 9- to 12-year-olds, found cognitive modeling to be as effective as cognitive modeling with explication of strategies. This difference may have resulted from differences in the levels of cognitive development in the two groups of children. Field-testing suggests that strategy training for social verbal communication and for figurative language can be effective with students with language-learning disabilities (Wiig, 1989). Controlled research is, however, needed for further validation.

Settings and Options

Strategy training for language and communication can occur in a variety of settings and with varying degrees of structure and preparation. The options for communication strategy training range from pullout language therapy to classroom-based interventions. Each option has distinguishing features, some of which may impose significant limitations for the efficacy of training (Wiig, 1990).

The traditional option for language intervention is pullout therapy. Training generally occurs biweekly for short periods of 20 minutes or more. The content of language therapy is usually determined by developmental sequences. Various approaches to training may be used, but training does not traditionally focus on development strategies or procedural knowledge. Because the training content is usually not determined by curriculum needs, training may lack relevance and topical and contextual applications, and opportunities for practice may not occur naturally. The limitations of pullout therapy make it inadequate as the only option, for meeting the strategy training needs of students with language-learning disabilities.

Tutoring is another traditional option for intervention in which strategy training should occur. The content in tutoring is determined by the student's failures. Strategy training would therefore occur after the fact and may lack relevance. Opportunities for practice and generalization of the strategies may not occur, because the curriculum content has changed in the meantime. If tutoring is based in reactive practices, it may have a less than desired effect on language and communication strategy development. This is because strategies would be trained after they were needed and because the curriculum may not require use of the trained strategies till a later point in time. If the practices in tutoring could be changed to be proactive, tutoring for strategy development might provide relevant, but not necessarily sufficient, training.

Strategy training for communication can occur in the classroom in the form of midactivity training. In this option, the teacher stops to train a strategy when language- and communication-related difficulties are encountered in the curriculum. Training would be unscheduled, but it would be context and use related, and applicable immediately. Lack of knowledge of the patterns and underlying schema in communication (e.g., metaphors, discourse, narrative) would be expected to limit the efficacy of training, as would lack of structure in training.

Other options are to provide communication strategy training in preteaching or minilesson formats (Atwell, 1987; Wiig, 1989). For these options, the trainer may be a classroom teacher, resource room specialist, or a speech-language pathologist. Several professionals may also interact in consultation or collaboration.

In preteaching, the strategies to be developed are determined by the content of curriculum texts, lessons, teaching units, or assignments. The rules, structures, or patterns to be taught are abstracted from the curriculum content. Preteaching activities can be planned in advance and can be structured. They may strengthen content knowledge of, for example, semantic features or networks, syntactic structures, semantic-pragmatic interfaces, underlying plans (schema/scripts), or rules. They may also be designed to develop specific strategies for language and communication. Because the acquired knowledge is applicable to the curriculum immediately, opportunities for practice and generalization are built in and training is relevant.

Minilessons are designed to train specific rules, techniques, categorization systems, or strategies. The content of training is determined by the future curriculum needs. The curriculum itself provides opportunities for practice and generalization of rules, techniques, and strategies. In the minilesson option, training is scheduled, planned, and structured. Training occurs within a relatively short period prior to application and is related to context and topic of use. A combination of the training options discussed above would seem most ideal for developing communication strategies, due to the intensity of training that could result. Communication strategy training can be expanded to specific subject areas such as sciences and social studies. In that way training could occur in different settings, with different trainers, and with different topical and contextual applications.

It is generally accepted that language-learning disabilities do not disappear with increased age. Rather, the nature of the disability changes as a function of the academic and social demands and the cognitive-linguistic transitions that are not instantiated. Communication strategy training, rather than linguistic skill training, responds to the need for supporting the linguistic transitions expected of children and adolescents in the middle and upper school years. Because best practices are relevant practices, we consider communication strategy training to be a best practice. The approach to communication strategy training described here is related to other process-oriented models for developing strategies for writing, reading, and other academic learning (Atwell, 1987; Ellis et al., 1989; Swanson, 1989). The discussions have stressed that conceptual, rule, and schema knowledge are essential for communication strategy acquisition. If this knowledge is not taught with adequate attention to structuring experiences, examples, and models; explicating concepts, rules, and schema; and involving the learner actively in problem solving, it may not be internalized by the learner. The strategies to be taught can be motivated by the content of the curriculum in, for example, reading, writing, and social sciences. It can also be motivated by everyday, social, or emotional needs. In a similar vein, the conceptual, rule, and schema knowledge and the developed strategies can be applied directly to listening, speaking, reading, and writing, because the shared content of all of these is language.

References

Allen, R. R., & Brown, K. L. (1977). *Developing communication competence in children*. Skokie, IL: National Textbook.

Alley, D., & Deshler, D. (1979). *Teaching the learning disabled adolescent: Strategies and methods*. Denver: Love.

Alvy, K. T. (1973). The development of listener adapted communications in grade-school children from different social-class backgrounds. *Genetic Psychology Monographs, 87,* 33–104.

Asch, S. E., & Nerlove, H. (1960). The development of double function terms in children. In B. Kaplan & S. Wapner (Eds.), *Perspectives in psychological theory*. New York: International Universities Press.

Atwell, N. (1987). In the middle: Writing, reading, and learning with adolescents. Portsmouth, NH: Heinemann.

Austin, T. T. (1962). *How to do things with words*. Cambridge, MA: Harvard University Press.

Baker, L. (1982). An evaluation of the role of metacognitive deficits in learning disabilities. *Topics in Learning and Language Disabilities, 2,* 27–36.

Banerji, R. (1987). Game playing. In S. C. Shapiro (Ed.), *Encyclopedia of artificial intelligence* (Vol. 1, pp. 312–318). New York: Wiley.

Bernstein, D. K., & Seidenberg, P. L. (1988). Language and cognitive processing: Issues for assessment and intervention. *Topics in Language Disorders, 8,* 1–71.

Billow, R. M. (1975). A cognitive developmental study of metaphor comprehension. *Developmental Psychology, 11,* 415–423.

Billow, R. M. (1977). Metaphor: A review of the psychological literature. *Psychological Bulletin, 84,* 81–92.

Blanchet, A. (1981). *Etude genetique des significations et des modeles utilises par l'enfant lors de resolution de problèmes*. Doctoral dissertation, University of Geneva, Switzerland.

Bruner, J. S., Goodnow, J. J., & Austin, G. A. (1956). *A study of thinking*. New York: Wiley.

Bruner, J. S., Oliver, R., & Greenfield, P. (1966). *Studies in cognitive growth*. New York: Wiley.

Cazden, C. (1972). *Child language and education*. New York: Holt, Rinehart & Winston.

Chandrasekaran, B. (1983). Towards a taxonomy of problem-solving types. *AI Magazine, 4,* 9–17.

Chandrasekaran, B. (1986, Fall). Generic tasks in knowledge-based reasoning: High-level building blocks for expert system design. *IEEE Expert,* pp. 23–30.

Delia, J., & Clark, R. A. (1977). Cognitive complexity, social perception, and the development of listener-adapted communication in six-, eight-, ten-, and twelve-year-old boys. *Communication Monographs, 4,* 326–345.

Delia, J., Kline, S., & Burleson, B. (1979). The development of persuasive communication strategies in kindergartners through twelfth-graders. *Communication Monographs, 46,* 241–256.

Dreyfus, H., & Dreyfus, S. E. (1986). *Mind over machine*. New York: Macmillan.

Ellis, E. S., Deshler, D. D., & Schumaker, J. B. (1989). Teaching adolescents with learning disabilities to generate and use task-specific strategies. *Journal of Learning Disabilities, 22*, 108–119.

Flavell, J. H. (1971). What is memory development in the development of questions? *Human Development, 14*, 272–278.

Flavell, J. H. (1976). Metacognitive aspects of problem solving. In B. L. Resnick (Ed.), *The nature of intelligence*. Hillsdale, NJ: Erlbaum.

Gerber, M. (1983). Learning disabilities and cognitive strategies: A case for training or constraining problem solving. *Journal of Learning Disabilities, 16*, 255–260.

Gholson, B. (1980). *The cognitive developmental basis of human learning: Studies in hypothesis testing*. New York: Academic Press.

Gilhooly, K. J. (1988). *Thinking: Directed, undirected and creative*. New York: Academic Press.

Goldman, S. R. (1989). Strategy instruction in mathematics. *Learning Disability Quarterly, 12*, 43–56.

Grice, H. P. (1975). Logic and conversation. In P. Cole & J. Morgan (Eds.), *Syntax and semantics* (Vol. 3, pp. 41–58). New York: Academic Press.

Grice, H. P. (1977). *William James lectures*. Unpublished manuscript, Harvard University, Cambridge, MA.

Hallahan, D. P. (1980). Teaching exceptional children to use cognitive strategies. *Exceptional Children Quarterly, 1*, 1–9.

Haslett, B. (1987). *Communication: Strategic action in context*. Hillsdale, NJ: Erlbaum.

Hoskins, B. (1987). *Conversations: Language intervention for adolescents*. Allen, TX: DLM.

Inhelder, B., & Piaget, J. (1964). *The early growth of logic in the child*. New York: Norton.

Kamhi, A. G. (1987). Metalinguistic abilities in language-impaired children. *Topics in Language Disorders, 7*, 1–12.

Labov, W. (1972). *Sociolinguistic patterns*. Philadelphia: University of Pennsylvania Press.

Lahey, M. (1988). *Language disorders and language development*. New York: Prentice-Hall.

Lakoff, G., & Johnson, M. (1980). *Metaphors we live by*. Chicago: University of Chicago Press.

Larson, V. L., & McKinley, N. L. (1987). *Communication assessment and intervention strategies for adolescents*. Eau Claire, WI: Thinking Publications.

Lenz, B. K., Clark, F. L., Deshler, D. D., & Schumaker, J. B. (1988). *The strategies instructional approach*. Lawrence: University of Kansas Institute for Research in Learning Disabilities.

Loban, W. (1976). *Language development: Kindergarten–Grade 12*. Urbana, IL: National Council of Teachers of English.

Mandelbaum, S. E. (1985). *Constraint questions: How can they be taught to children with special needs?* Unpublished doctoral dissertation, Boston University, Boston.

Mathinos, D. A. (1988). Communicative competence of children with learning disabilities. *Journal of Learning Disabilities, 21*, 437–443.

Meichenbaum, D. (1977). *Cognitive behavior modification: An integrative approach.* New York: Plenum.

Menyuk, P. (1983). Language development and reading. In T. M. Gallagher & C. A. Prutting (Eds.), *Pragmatic assessment and intervention issues in language disorders* (pp. 151–170). San Diego: College-Hill.

Neisser, U. (1967). *Cognitive psychology.* New York: Appleton-Century-Crofts.

Nippold, M. A., Cuyler, J. S., & Braunbeck-Price, R. (1988). Explanation of ambiguous advertisements: A developmental study with children and adolescents. *Journal of Speech and Hearing Research, 31*, 466–474.

Nippold, M. A., Leonard, L. B., & Kail, R. (1984). Syntactic and conceptual factors in children's understanding of metaphors. *Journal of Speech and Hearing Research, 27*, 197–205.

Paris, S. G., & Oka, E. R. (1989). Strategies for comprehending text and coping with reading difficulties. *Learning Disability Quarterly, 12*, 32–42.

Piaget, J. (1952). *The language and thought of the child.* London: Routledge & Kegan Paul.

Piaget, J. (1968). *Six psychological studies.* New York: Random House.

Piaget, J. (1970). Piaget's theory. In P. H. Mussen (Ed.), *Carmichael's manual of child psychiatry* (Vol. 1) (3rd ed.). New York: John Wiley.

Pierce, C. S. (1957). *Essays in the philosophy of science.* New York: The Liberal Arts Press.

Pressley, M., Symons, S., Snyder, B. L., & Cariglia-Bull, T. (1989). Strategy instruction research comes of age. *Learning Disability Quarterly, 12*, 16–31.

Reid, D. K., & Hresko, W. P. (1981). *A cognitive approach to learning disabilities.* New York: McGraw-Hill.

Restle, F. (1962). The selection strategies in cue learning. *Psychological Review, 69*, 329–343.

Ripich, D. N., & Spinelli, F. M. (Eds.). (1985). *School discourse problems.* San Diego: College-Hill.

Schiffman, H. R. (1972). Some components of sensation and perception for the reading process. *Reading Research Quarterly, 7*, 588–612.

Searle, J. R. (1969). *Speech acts: An essay in the philosophy of language.* Cambridge, England: Cambridge University Press.

Searle, J. R. (1975). A taxonomy of illocutionary acts. In K. Gunderson (Ed.), *Language, mind, and knowledge.* Minneapolis: University of Minnesota Press.

Shapiro, S. C., Eckroth, D., & Vallasi, G. A. (1987). *Encyclopedia of artificial intelligence.* New York: Wiley.

Silliman, E. R. (1987). Individual differences in the classroom performance of language-impaired students. *Seminars in Speech and Language, 8*, 357–375.

Simmonds, E. P. M. (1989). The effectiveness of two methods for teaching a constraint-seeking questioning strategy to students with learning disabilities. *Journal of Learning Disabilities, 23*, 229–232.

Simon, C. S. (1985). The language-learning disabled student: Description and therapy implications. In C. S. Simon (Ed.), *Communication skills and classroom success: Therapy methodologies for language-learning disabled students* (pp. 1–56). San Diego: College-Hill.

Stevenson, H. W. (1973). *Children's learning*. New York: Appleton-Century-Crofts.

Stone, C. A., & Forman, E. A. (1988). Differential patterns of approach to a complex problem-solving task among learning disabled adolescents. *The Journal of Special Education, 22*, 167–185.

Stone, C. A., & Forman, E. A. (in press). Cognitive development in language-learning-disabled adolescents: A study of problem-solving performance in an isolation-of-variable task. *Learning Disability Research*.

Stubbs, M. (1983). *Discourse analysis: The sociolinguistic analysis of natural language*. Chicago: University of Chicago Press.

Swanson, H. L. (1989). Strategy instruction: Overview of principles and procedures for effective use. *Learning Disability Quarterly, 12*, 3–15.

Wallach, G. (1990). Magic buries Celtics: Looking for broader interpretations of language learning and literacy. *Topics in Language Disorders, 10*, 63–80.

Wansart, W. L. (1990). Learning to solve a problem: A microanalysis of the solution strategies of children with learning disabilities. *Journal of Learning Disabilities, 23*, 164–170.

Wells, G. (1973). *Coding manual of the description of child speech*. Bristol, England: University of Bristol, School of Education.

Wells, G. (1981). *Learning through interaction: The study of language development*. Cambridge, England: Cambridge University Press.

Wiig, E. H. (1982). *Let's talk inventory for adolescents*. San Antonio, TX: Psychological Corp.

Wiig, E. H. (1984). Language disabilities in adolescents: A question of cognitive strategies. *Topics in Language Disorders, 4*, 51–58.

Wiig, E. H. (1985). *Words, expressions, and contexts: A figurative language program*. San Antonio, TX: Psychological Corp.

Wiig, E. H. (1989). *Steps to language competence: Developing metalinguistic strategies*. San Antonio, TX: Psychological Corp.

Wiig, E. H. (1990). The continuum of linguistic transitions: A strategic learning perspective. *Learning Disability Quarterly, 13*, 128–140.

Wiig, E. H., & Becker-Caplan, L. (1984). Linguistic retrieval strategies and word-finding difficulties among children with language disabilities. *Topics in Language Disorders, 4*, 1–8.

Wiig, E. H., & Secord, W. (1989). *Test of language competence–Expanded*. San Antonio, TX: Psychological Corp.

7

Achievement-Related Beliefs in Children with Learning Disabilities: Impact on Motivation and Strategic Learning

Barbara G. Licht

About a decade ago, a "cognitive-motivational" model was proposed to account for the motivational problems (e.g., inattention, off-task behavior) commonly shown by children with learning disabilities (Licht, 1983; Thomas, 1979; Torgesen, 1980). It was proposed that repeated school failure experienced by children with learning disabilities leads these children to believe that their intellectual abilities are very low and that their achievement efforts are useless (Licht, 1983; Thomas, 1979; Torgesen, 1977). As a consequence of these beliefs, they are not likely to try very hard (Butkowsky & Willows, 1980; Torgesen & Licht, 1983), which increases the chances of continued failure. This, in turn, reinforces the children's belief that their intellectual abilities are extremely low. Although it may be realistic for children with learning disabilities to believe some of their abilities are low, the concern of researchers and practitioners was that these children may overgeneralize this belief. Thus, children with learning disabilities may exert very little effort, even on tasks they are capable of mastering. This model is considered "cognitive-motivational" because it proposes that children's achievement-related beliefs or "cognitions" have important motivational consequences.

This chapter addresses five major aspects of children's achievement-related beliefs. First is a review of research demonstrating that children's beliefs about the utility of their efforts influence how hard they try and, consequently, influence their achievements. Two lines of research are presented in support of this. One line of research demonstrates that children who believe in the utility of their efforts show more persistence in the face of difficulty and make greater academic gains over the years than children whose initial achievements are the same, but who do not believe in the utility of their efforts. The other line of supportive research consists of treatment studies demonstrating that teaching children to attribute their difficulties to insufficient effort (as opposed to insufficient ability) improves their persistence and performance on difficult tasks. The second topic the chapter addresses concerns the achievement-related beliefs that children with learning disabilities frequently develop. As suggested by the model presented above, it is shown that children with learning disabilities are significantly more likely than their peers to believe that their abilities are low and that trying hard will not pay off. Third, discussion focuses on individual differences among children with learning disabilities in terms of their achievement-related beliefs and classroom behavior. Although children with learning disabilities frequently develop maladaptive achievement-related beliefs, some children with learning disabilities are able to maintain confidence in their abilities, and these children persist in the face of difficulty. The causes and long-term consequences of these individual differences are examined. Fourth is an exploration of research on the achievement-related beliefs of children with inattentive, hyperactive classroom behavior and children with aggressive behavior. It is important to understand the beliefs of these children because research has shown that children with learning disabilities who also show inattentive, hyperactive, and/or aggressive behaviors have the worst long-term prognosis. Finally, the chapter includes an examination of some promising treatments for children who do not believe in the utility of their achievement efforts. Particular attention is paid to more recent treatment studies that have integrated training in strategy use with techniques for altering children's achievement-related beliefs.

Impact of Children's Achievement-Related Beliefs on their Achievement Efforts

A number of cognitive-motivational theories have proposed that the beliefs students develop about their abilities and efforts influence how they behave in achievement situations. Although different theories address different belief patterns, most cognitive-motivational theories explicitly or implicitly propose that students are more likely to take an active, effortful approach to learning if they believe this effort will pay off. For example, locus of control theorists (e.g., Crandall, Katkovsky, & Crandall, 1965) discuss the importance of believing that academic successes and failures are due to "internal" factors, such as the individual's own efforts and skills, as opposed to "external" factors, such as luck or an unfair task. Attributional theorists (e.g., Dweck & Licht, 1980; Weiner, 1979) stress the importance of attributing academic difficulties to controllable factors, such as insufficient effort, rather than attributing difficulties to uncontrollable factors, such as insufficient ability. Self-efficacy theorists (e.g., Bandura, 1982; Schunk, 1989) stress the importance of believing that one has the ability to perform well. Self-efficacy is very similar conceptually to both perceived competence (Harter, 1982, 1985) and self-concept of ability (Marsh, Byrne, & Shavelson, 1988), and these terms will be used interchangeably. (See Weisz & Cameron, 1985, and Skinner, Chapman, & Baltes, 1988, for other relevant theories.)

As indicated, each of the above theories proposes that students' achievement-related beliefs are important determinants of their achievement behavior. One line of supportive research has demonstrated that children who hold different achievement-related beliefs respond differently in achievement situations. When children confront difficulty on an achievement task, children who attribute their difficulties to controllable factors, such as insufficient effort, are more likely to persist than are children who attribute their difficulties to uncontrollable factors, such as insufficient ability (Butkowsky & Willows, 1980; Diener & Dweck, 1978: Dweck & Reppucci, 1973; Licht, Kistner, Ozkaragoz, Shapiro, & Clausen, 1985).

Most of the early research on this topic has examined children's persistence on laboratory tasks. More recently, researchers have increased the ecological validity of their findings by focusing on actual achievement scores and classroom behaviors. For example, Kistner, Osborne, and LeVerrier (1988) examined the relationship between the achievement-related beliefs (assessed by questionnaires) of children with learning disabilities and the academic gains the children made over a 2-year period (assessed by standardized achievement scores). They found that the children who were most likely to attribute their difficulties to insufficient effort showed more positive academic gains over the years than did children whose initial achievements and IQs were the same, but who attributed their difficulties to insufficient ability.

Licht and Dweck (1984) also increased the ecological validity of the findings in this area by examining the relationship between children's achievement-related beliefs (assessed by questionnaires) and how they coped with confusing material in an actual classroom setting. The question of interest was whether children would get so discouraged after reading two pages of confusing material that they would fail to master five pages of *non*confusing material that was presented immediately afterward. It is important to note that the confusing and nonconfusing material covered separate topics. Thus, if reading the confusing pages had negative effects on children's mastery of the nonconfusing pages, these effects would most plausibly be *motivational* (e.g., children might stop concentrating after they read the confusing pages). As a control group, half of the children were given only nonconfusing pages to read. Licht and Dweck's (1984) findings were consistent with the earlier laboratory studies. Children who attributed their difficulties to insufficient effort were undaunted by having read the confusing material. About 70% of these children mastered the nonconfusing material, regardless of whether it was preceded by confusing material. (Mastery was defined as answering all questions correctly on a written test of the nonconfusing material.) In contrast, children who attributed their difficulties to factors that were beyond their control (e.g., insufficient ability) were strongly affected by having read the confusing material. Only 37% of these children mastered the nonconfusing material when it was preceded by confusing material. However, the poor performance of these children was *not* due to a lesser ability to learn the material, as evidenced by the fact that they performed as well as their peers when the exact same nonconfusing material was *not* preceded by confusing material (i.e., 77% mastered). This study suggests that when children confront challenging or confusing material, those who do not believe that their efforts will help them overcome their difficulties will fail to learn material they are capable of mastering.

A second line of research supporting the notion that children's achievement-related beliefs influence their achievement behaviors consists of attribution retraining studies. These studies have shown that teaching children to attribute their difficulties to insufficient effort improves their persistence and performance on difficult tasks (e.g.,

Andrews & Debus, 1978; Dweck, 1975; Fowler & Peterson, 1981; Shelton, Anastopoulos, & Linden, 1985; Thomas & Pashley, 1982). In the early attribution retraining studies, children were presented with an achievement task that assured some failure experiences, and the children were taught to attribute these failures to insufficient effort. For example, the child might be given more problems than he or she could complete in the allotted time. When this occurred, the trainer might say, "You didn't finish them all. That means you weren't trying hard enough." In some of these studies (e.g., Fowler & Peterson, 1981; Shelton et al., 1985), children's successes also were attributed to their level of effort (e.g., "That was very good. That means you tried hard"). In general, these studies demonstrated that children who received attribution retraining were more persistent than children in the control groups.

Although these early studies made important theoretical contributions, they were criticized on practical, educational grounds. It was argued that most children with learning disabilities cannot overcome their academic difficulties by simply trying harder; they also need to learn strategies for guiding their efforts (Anderson & Jennings, 1980; Borkowski, Weyhing, & Turner, 1986; Palincsar & Brown, 1984; Pearl, 1985; Torgesen & Licht, 1983). To address this concern, Borkowski, Weyhing, & Carr (1988) integrated attribution retraining with strategy training. Children with reading disabilities were taught strategies for improving reading comprehension, such as finding a topic sentence. The attribution retraining was designed to demonstrate the importance of trying hard and using the appropriate strategies. In part, this was done by discussing with the child specific instances where the child used the strategies and succeeded in addition to instances where the child did not use the strategies and made mistakes. Borkowski et al. (1988) found that when children received attribution retraining combined with strategy training, children were more likely to use the new strategies than when they were given strategy instruction alone. In fact, students who received strategy instruction without attribution retraining showed no significant increase in their use of the strategies once treatment was terminated. A similar study conducted with underachieving hyperactive children (Reid & Borkowski, 1987) also showed that students are more likely to use new strategies if they believe that an effortful application of these strategies will enhance their performance.

Children with Learning Disabilities

As suggested by the cognitive-motivational model presented earlier, repeated failure does appear to lead children to doubt their abilities and the utility of their efforts. When compared to their normally achieving peers, children with learning disabilities (both labeled and unlabeled) show lower academic self-concepts (Boersma & Chapman, 1981; Lincoln & Chazan, 1979; Rogers & Saklofske, 1985; Winne, Woodlands, & Wong, 1982) and have lower expectancies for future academic performance (Boersma & Chapman, 1981; Butkowsky & Willows, 1980; Rogers & Saklofske, 1985). Children with learning disabilities are more likely than their peers to attribute their failures to low ability and are less likely to attribute their failures to insufficient effort (Butkowsky & Willows, 1980; Licht et al., 1985; Palmer, Drummond, Tollison, & Zinkgraff, 1982; Pearl, 1982; Pearl, Bryan, & Donahue, 1980). In addition, children with learning disabilities are less likely to take credit for their successes. They are more likely than their peers to attribute their successes to luck or to an easy task (Butkowsky & Willows, 1980; Pearl, 1982; Pearl, Bryan, & Herzog, 1983).

Additional information on how failure influences children's achievement-related beliefs comes from longitudinal studies that examine how children's beliefs change over time. One might hypothesize that the self-evaluations of children with learning disabilities would get progressively lower over the years as they encounter more and more failure. On the other hand, one might predict that if these children are provided with remedial instruction, their self-evaluations would become more similar to the self-evaluations of their normally achieving peers. That is, over time, there may be less of a gap between the beliefs of children with learning disabilities and the beliefs of their peers. Remedial instruction has the potential to decrease children's failure experiences and help children recognize the importance of developing alternate strategies. Remedial instruction also may provide children with another comparison group (i.e., other children with learning disabilities), against which they would compare more favorably (Renick & Harter, 1989; Strang, Smith, & Rogers, 1978).

Two recent studies followed children longitudinally to determine what happens to their beliefs over a 2-year period. Chapman (1988) examined a group of junior high students who were not labeled and who had not received remedial help. Consistent with previous research, he found that students with learning disabilities had lower academic expectations and lower perceptions of their abilities than their normally achieving peers. When he followed these students longitudinally, he found that the differences between children with and without learning disabilities stayed constant over the 2-year period. Kistner et al. (1988) followed a group of students in Grades 3 through 8 who were identified by their schools as having learning disabilities and who all were receiving resource room instruction for parts of their school day.

Kistner et al.'s findings were consistent with Chapman's. Children with learning disabilities were more likely than their peers to attribute their failures to low ability and less likely to attribute their failures to insufficient effort; these differences remained constant over the 2-year period despite the fact that the children with learning disabilities all were receiving remedial services.

It could be argued that it is actually encouraging to find that the beliefs of children with learning disabilities do not get progressively more self-deprecating over the years. In fact, Kistner et al. (1988) found that although the gap between the beliefs of children with and without learning disabilities did not decrease over the years, both groups of children showed more adaptive attributions as they got older. Specifically, both groups increasingly attributed their failures to insufficient effort. Nonetheless, even if the self-evaluations of children with learning disabilities do not become progressively lower over the years, their self-evaluations may have more debilitating effects on their achievement in the later school years because academic tasks increase in complexity over the years. The belief that one's efforts will not pay off and the resulting tendency not to try hard should be more detrimental with advanced, complex academic material than with easier, more basic material.

Individual Differences Among Children with Learning Disabilities

Although these longitudinal data may not suggest optimistic outcomes, some optimism is suggested by research on individual differences among children with learning disabilities. Put simply, not all children with learning disabilities believe their abilities are low and their achievement efforts are useless (Licht & Kistner, 1986). Some of these children believe that by working hard, they will be able to overcome many of their problems. Further, as indicated earlier, these optimistic beliefs seem to have positive effects on the children's later achievements (Kistner et al., 1988).

Several factors may contribute to individual differences among children with learning disabilities, in addition to the overall magnitude of their learning problems. For example, research conducted in regular classrooms suggests that children with learning problems are more likely to evaluate their abilities as low when social comparison information (i.e., how a child performs relative to his or her peers) is highly visible (Ames & Archer, 1988; Stipek & Daniels, 1988). Social comparisons may be visible when evaluations of children's work are made public, for example, when only "A" papers are displayed on the bulletin board. In addition, it may be easier for children to compare themselves to their peers when everyone in the class works on the same materials at the same time than when different children are engaged in different activities (Rosenholtz & Simpson, 1984). Further, the range of abilities within the class may be important. Social comparison information does not appear to have much impact when children within the same class are relatively homogeneous with respect to their abilities (Mac Iver, 1988). In addition, as suggested by attribution retraining studies, children's beliefs may be influenced by the manner in which teacher feedback stresses the links among children's efforts and their academic successes.

Some individual differences may be related to sex differences. Some studies have found that girls with learning disabilities are more likely than boys with learning disabilities to attribute their failures to insufficient ability (Kistner, White, Haskett, & Robbins, 1985; Ryckman & Peckham, 1986). When boys with learning disabilities develop maladaptive attributions, they are more likely to attribute their failures to external factors, such as the teacher or the task (Licht et al., 1985). Blaming one's failures on external factors is not as adaptive as blaming one's own efforts. However, failure attributions to external factors are not as consistently related to poor persistence and poor academic gains as are failure attributions to insufficient ability (Dweck, Goetz, & Strauss, 1980; Kistner et al., 1988; Licht et al., 1985). Blaming external factors may allow children to maintain some optimism about their abilities.

The research on sex differences among children with learning disabilities presents an interesting paradox. As stated above, girls appear more likely than boys to attribute their difficulties to insufficient ability, which is *negatively* related to academic gains. On the other hand, some recent research has suggested that girls with learning disabilities may have more long-term academic success than boys with learning disabilities. S. A. Vogel (personal communication, 1989) found that among college students identified as having learning disabilities, females were more successful than males.

There are some plausible explanations for this paradox. Although the achievement-related beliefs of girls may put them at greater risk than boys, this may be offset by other sex differences. For example, girls with learning disabilities are less likely to exhibit behavior problems than are boys with learning disabilities. The problems that these boys are most likely to show include inattention and conduct problems such as aggression. In contrast, when the girls have behavior problems, they are more likely to show withdrawn and/or dependent behavior

(Epstein, Cullinan, & Gadow, 1986; Epstein, Cullinan, & Lloyd, 1986). Further, research by McKinney and colleagues has shown that inattention and conduct problems contribute to poorer academic gains than does withdrawn, dependent behavior or "normal" classroom behavior. More specifically, these researchers found that about 54% of children with learning disabilities are characterized by either attention deficits and/or conduct problems (e.g., aggression, lack of positive classroom behaviors), about 11% are characterized as excessively withdrawn and dependent (primarily girls), and approximately 35% are relatively free of maladaptive classroom behaviors (McKinney, 1989; Speece, McKinney, & Appelbaum, 1985). These researchers found important age-related changes, which are discussed below.

The three different subtypes of children with learning disabilities did not show different levels of academic achievement at 6 or 7 years (Speece et al., 1985). However, when they were followed longitudinally over a 3-year period, the different subtypes showed different patterns of progress (McKinney & Speece, 1986). Children who were characterized either by attention deficits or by behavior problems showed progressive declines in reading comprehension relative to their peers. That is, the distance between the achievements of these children and their normally achieving peers widened over the years. In contrast, the children with learning disabilities who exhibited no maladaptive class room behavior or who manifested withdrawn/dependent behavior did *not* show progressive declines in achievement. The discrepancy in achievement between these children and their normally achieving peers remained constant over the 3-year period. Thus, the apparent sex difference paradox may exist because the greater incidence of inattention and conduct problems among boys with learning disabilities may, in the long run, put them at greater academic risk than girls with learning disabilities, even though the achievement-related beliefs of girls may be more maladaptive than the beliefs of boys. This could be attributed, in part, to the fact that sex differences in children's classroom conduct are probably stronger than sex differences in achievement-related beliefs.

Children with Inattentive/Hyperactive Behavior and Children with Aggressive Behavior

The research just described highlights the importance of understanding the conduct and attention problems of children with learning disabilities. As discussed above, these behaviors have a negative impact on the children's long-term achievements (McKinney, 1989). Although there are many reasons for these negative effects, these effects may be mediated, in part, by children's achievement-related beliefs. That is, poor classroom conduct can lead to frequent negative interactions with teachers (Brophy & Evertson, 1981). These negative interactions can lead children to develop maladaptive achievement-related beliefs (in addition to the maladaptive beliefs they may develop as a result of their academic difficulties). These maladaptive beliefs, in turn, can contribute to further problems.

There also is reason to believe that different types of conduct problems may be related to different types of achievement-related beliefs. For example, children who are defiant and aggressive are likely to have the most negative interactions with the teacher (Brophy & Evertson, 1981). Teachers are likely to see defiant, aggressive children as causing problems *intentionally*. Consequently, teachers are likely to use punitive control techniques when dealing with them (Brophy, 1985; Brophy & Rohrkemper, 1981). This may lead aggressive children to believe (perhaps realistically) that the teacher does not like them. Thus, they may come to feel that they will not receive praise or good grades, even if they behave well and do good work. In other words, they may attribute their successes and failures to powerful others. The characterization of aggressive children as blaming others for their problems also is consistent with research by Dodge and colleagues (e.g., Dodge & Newman, 1981; Dodge & Somberg, 1987). They found that when faced with ambiguous provocations, aggressive children are more likely than their peers to attribute malicious intent to others.

Children who have problems of inattention and hyperactivity, but who are not aggressive or defiant, are more likely to be viewed as exhibiting problems that are not completely under their control (Brophy, 1985; Brophy & Rohrkemper, 1981). Although teachers often attribute these problems to carelessness, they usually do not think that these children are causing problems intentionally. Consequently, teachers are more likely to use training procedures designed to build self-control (Brophy, 1985). Thus, children with problems of hyperactivity and inattention may infer that they lack the ability to control their behavior. In other words, their perceived competence may be low. However, there is no reason to expect them to see powerful others as controlling their successes and failures.

To date, there has been very little research on the relationship between children's classroom conduct and their achievement-related beliefs. There is some evidence that children with behavior problems (nature of problems unspecified) tend to believe they do not have control over whether they succeed or fail (Linn & Hodge, 1982). In a recent study, Hartsfield, Licht, Swenson, & Thiele (1989) examined the achievement-related beliefs of children who had problems of hyperactivity and inattention and children who were defiant and aggressive. Because there has been so little research on this topic, this study is described in detail below.

Hartsfield et al. (1989) administered a series of questionnaires to 400 children from regular school classrooms in Grades 3, 4, and 5. These children represented the entire range of abilities and behavior problems. Children's perceived competence was assessed using Harter's (1985) *Self-Perception Profile for Children.* This scale yields separate perceived competence scores for five domains: scholastic, social, athletic, physical appearance, and behavioral conduct. It also assesses children's perceptions of their global self-worth (i.e., the degree to which they like themselves as persons). Connell's (1985) *Multidimensional Measure of Children's Perceptions of Control* was also administered. This scale assesses children's perceived control in four domains: cognitive, social, physical skill, and general. In addition, a behavioral conduct domain was developed for this study. For each of these domains, three separate scores were derived: (a) *Internal* reflected the degree to which children reported that their own behaviors determined their success or failure (e.g., "If somebody doesn't like me, it's usually because of something I did"); (b) *Powerful Others* reflected the degree to which they believed other people determined their success or failure (e.g., "The best way for me to get good grades is to get the teacher to like me"); and (c) *Unknown* reflected the degree to which children reported not knowing why outcomes occurred (e.g., "If I get a bad grade in school, I usually don't understand why I got it").

Children's classroom behavior was assessed with teacher rating questions that were taken from the *Conners' Teacher Rating Scale* (Conners, 1969). Based on these questions, each child received one score for inattention/overactivity and a separate score for aggression (Loney & Milich, 1982; Milich, Loney, & Landau, 1982). For brevity, inattention/overactivity is referred to here as "hyperactivity."

Overall, Hartsfield et al. (1989) found that children rated high in hyperactivity displayed low perceived competence, whereas aggressive children did not. Specifically, hyperactive children rated their *scholastic* competence lower than did children who were not hyperactive; and this occurred even when comparing children of the *same achievement level.* In contrast, aggressiveness was not related to children's perceived scholastic competence, despite the fact that aggressive children had significantly lower grades and achievement scores than nonaggressive children.

In the *behavioral conduct* domain, both hyperactive children and aggressive children rated their behavior less favorably than did their peers. However, when multiple regression analysis was used to control for the fact that hyperactivity and aggressiveness are highly correlated ($r = .67, p < .001$), the only variable that predicted low self-ratings of conduct was hyperactivity. Similarly, both hyperactivity and aggressiveness were related to lower feelings of *global self-worth*. However, after controlling for the relationship between hyperactivity and aggressiveness, only hyperactivity was related to lower feelings of self-worth. There was a tendency for both hyperactive and aggressive children to rate their *physical appearance* less favorably than did their peers. However, these were weak relationships that did not remain significant after the relationship between hyperactivity and aggressiveness was controlled. Neither hyperactive nor aggressive children showed lower self-concepts in the *athletic* domain. Interestingly, neither hyperactive nor aggressive children had lower perceived *social* competence, despite the fact that aggressive and hyperactive children tend to be disliked by their peers (Pelham & Bender, 1982; Putallaz & Gottman, 1983). This could possibly result from the fact that children do not receive regular and systematic feedback about their social status the way they receive report card grades for their scholastic performances and classroom conduct. These findings may also reflect the strong emphasis that is generally placed on academic performance.

With respect to Connell's perceived control scale, neither hyperactivity nor aggressiveness showed consistent relationships with any of the scores. However, there was some tendency for hyperactive children to report that they did not know what caused their successes and failures in the behavioral conduct and social domains. The tendency to not know what determines their successes and failures also was characteristic of younger children.

In sum, this study suggests that children who are hyperactive (i.e., inattentive and overactive), but not defiant or aggressive, are likely to suffer from low perceived competence. The fact that hyperactive children rated their scholastic competence lower than nonhyperactive children of the same achievement level suggests that their low perceived competence was more than a reflection of their lower achievements. Further, their feelings of incompetence in the scholastic and behavioral conduct domains seemed to extend to their overall feelings of self-worth. Thus, it is likely that treatments for these children will need to address these beliefs (Reid & Borkowski, 1987).

In sharp contrasts, children whose problems are primarily aggression and defiance did not appear to suffer from low perceived competence. Nor did aggressive children believe that their successes and failures were controlled by powerful others, as was predicted. However, this should not be taken as evidence that aggressive children do not hold maladaptive beliefs. The fact that aggressiveness did not contribute to lower self-ratings in *any* domain suggests that these children may have held inflated views of themselves. Further research is needed to determine whether this inflated confidence is beneficial or causes more serious problems in the long run. Future research should also examine whether the relationships that were found by Hartsfield et al. (1989) hold among children who have specifically been identified as having learning disabilities.

Treatment and Teaching Recommendations

As indicated throughout this chapter, children's beliefs about their abilities and the utility of their efforts directly influence whether they will try hard and apply the skills and strategies they have acquired. Consequently, a number of treatments have been developed for enhancing children's belief that their achievement efforts will pay off. These treatments are reviewed next.

Integrating Strategy Instruction with Attribution Retraining

As was discussed earlier, the probability that children would use specific strategies was increased significantly when attribution retraining was integrated with strategy instruction (Borkowski et al., 1988; Reid & Borkowski, 1987). Impressively, strategy use was maintained at a 10-month follow-up (Reid and Borkowski, 1987).

There are several likely reasons why the attribution retraining employed by Borkowski et al. (1988) and Reid and Borkowski (1987) was so effective. First, the trainer did not simply tell the children that trying hard and using the new strategies would facilitate performance. The trainer provided *concrete* evidence. For example, Reid and Borkowski (1987) taught children a "clustering" strategy for improving their ability to recall lists of items. During strategy instruction, children were given problems containing 15 pictures of items to be recalled. The trainer showed the children how to sort the pictures into categories (e.g., pictures of food, pictures of clothing), and then how to rehearse the items within the proper category. Although children recalled the items more accurately when they effortfully applied the strategy than when they did not use the strategy, they may not have been aware of this relationship until the trainer gave them attributional feedback. For success attributional feedback, the trainer chose correctly recalled items for which the child was observed to use the strategy. The trainer pointed out to the child how the strategy helped him or her recall those items correctly. For failure attributional feedback, the trainer picked items if they were not recalled correctly, and the child showed no evidence of strategy usage when studying those items. The trainer showed the child how those items could have been recalled more easily had they been grouped according to what they had in common (e.g., they may all have been items of clothing). In this way, the trainer concretely illustrated the important relationship between an effortful use of the strategies and children's successes.

A second likely reason for the effectiveness of this attribution retraining was the manner in which the trainer stressed the importance of trying hard. The trainer did not imply that the child was lazy nor did he or she convey an overly negative evaluation of the child's prior performances. Earlier research has shown that not all effort statements have the same impact. For example, Schunk (1982) found that responding to children's progress by saying, "You've been working hard," increased children's self-efficacy and acquisition of arithmetic skills; however, responding with, "You need to work hard," did not have any positive effects. These two effort statements convey very different messages. The effective message, "You've been working hard," not only relates the child's progress to his or her efforts, but also conveys an overall positive evaluation. In contrast, simply telling a child, "You need to work hard," may convey a negative evaluation of the child's progress and may imply that the child has been lazy.

As suggested, the attribution retraining employed by Reid and Borkowski (1987) and Borkowski et al. (1988) did not appear to convey negative messages. For example, during the early phase of attribution retraining, the trainer intentionally made a mistake while demonstrating each task; and the trainer attributed this mistake to not trying hard to use the correct strategy. Children are less likely to feel they are being accused of laziness if adults show that they too can make mistakes due to controllable factors such as insufficient effort or failure to use the proper strategy.

The concern that attributing a child's failures to insufficient effort can imply laziness has led some researchers to suggest that children should be taught to attribute their difficulties exclusively to ineffective strategies (e.g., Clifford, 1986). It has been shown that attributing one's failures to ineffective strategies produces more adaptive responses to failure than attributing one's failures to insufficient ability (Anderson & Jennings, 1980) or insufficient effort (Clifford, 1986). However, there is no evidence concerning the relative benefits of attributing one's difficulties to ineffective strategies versus attributing them to a combination of effort and strategies. It is likely that children will develop more adaptive responses to failure when taught to attribute their difficulties to a combination of effort and strategies, as exemplified by Borkowski et al. (1988) and Reid and Borkowski (1987). Two reasons can be advanced in support of this contention. First, most useful learning strategies require mental effort, sometimes for extended periods of time. Children are not likely to make progress if they believe that success is simply a matter of finding the right strategy. They must *effortfully* apply these strategies. Second, there are a number of situations where children with learning problems would show progress if they simply spent more time on task. This was demonstrated in a recent study by Gettinger (1989), who assessed children's performance on a task that involved reading short passages of factual material and answering questions about the material. Gettinger identified children who were not spending enough time on the task to master it. She found that reinforcing them for spending more time on task led to significantly better performance. Thus, although strategy instruction is crucial for children with learning disabilities, one should not lose sight of the fact that insufficient effort also is a major contributor to the poor performance of many children.

Another variable that may influence the effectiveness of attribution retraining is the amount of success and failure children experience. To ensure that children maintain optimism about the usefulness of their efforts, they must experience some success. However, research clearly argues against providing success by giving easy tasks requiring little effort (Chapin & Dyck, 1976; Dweck, 1975; Nation, Cooney, & Gartrell, 1979; Schunk, 1989). Rather, tasks should be at a level of difficulty where success is obtainable if the child tries hard and, when appropriate, applies specific strategies.

Additional Treatments

Other treatments, besides attribution retraining, have the potential to strengthen children's belief that they are capable of succeeding. For example, Bandura and Schunk (1981) found that prompting children to set specific, *proximal* goals (i.e., indicating the number of problems they would try to complete in one training session) led to higher self-efficacy and performance than setting *distal* goals (i.e., indicating how many sessions it would take to complete an entire instructional booklet). Most probably, when children met their proximal goals at the end of a session, this demonstrated to them that they were indeed making progress.

Verbalizing strategies aloud may be another procedure for increasing self-efficacy. Schunk and Cox (1986) found that when children were taught new strategies for solving subtraction problems, requiring them to verbalize the strategies aloud enhanced their feelings of self-efficacy and their task performance. It is likely that verbalizing aloud forced additional rehearsal of the subtraction rules. It also is likely that whenever children heard themselves verbalize the strategies, it concretely demonstrated to them that they did indeed know how to approach the subtraction problems.[1] (See also Asarnow & Meichenbaum, 1979; Fowler & Peterson, 1981; Hallahan, Kneedler, & Lloyd, 1983; Meichenbaum, 1977; Schunk & Rice, 1984.)

Viewing other children perform the skills and strategies being taught also has the potential to increase children's self-efficacy. These potential benefits of modeling seem to go beyond the fact that watching someone perform new skills provides additional instruction. Watching a peer solve the problems can communicate to children that they too are capable of learning how to solve the problems. This is particularly true when children perceive the model as similar to themselves. For example, Schunk, Hanson, and Cox (1987) found that, for children who had experienced difficulty with subtraction, viewing a "coping" model (i.e., a child who initially experienced difficulty with the problems, but eventually performed well) raised their self-efficacy for learning subtraction more than viewing a "mastery" model (i.e., a child who performed well from the start). Based on this study and a considerable amount of other research (Bandura, 1986), it is clear that modeling can have powerful effects. However, it is also possible that watching a peer perform a new task could highlight the fact that the model possesses skills that the viewer does not possess. This could discourage some children rather than enhance their self-efficacy. Future research is needed to determine the conditions under which such an outcome is likely to occur.

The treatments described thus far are explicitly or implicitly intended to teach children that they are capable of succeeding, that is, attaining their goals. However, more than one type of success or goal can be attained in academic achievement situations. Dweck and Elliott (1983) distinguished between two types of goals—performance goals versus learning goals. Children may strive to demonstrate high ability relative to their peers (or avoid demonstrating low ability). These are *performance goals.* They also may strive to improve or master skills. These are *learning goals.* Similar distinctions have been made by Nicholls (1984), who contrasted ego involvement versus task involvement, and by Ames and Archer (1988), who contrasted performance with mastery goals.

Children may give priority to one type of goal over the other as a result of parental influences (Ames & Archer, 1987) and/or classroom

---

[1]If verbalizing task strategies aloud enhances the acquisition of these strategies, then verbalizing attributions aloud during attribution retraining may enhance the acquisition of these attributions.

conditions (Ames & Archer, 1988; Rosenholtz & Simpson, 1984). Further, the particular goal that is given priority influences children's beliefs about their efforts (Nicholls, Patashnick, & Nolen, 1985). For example, when children are oriented toward performance goals, children with learning problems are not likely to believe that trying hard will lead to success. After all, they are unlikely to demonstrate higher ability than their peers, even if they exert considerable strategic effort. Even if children with learning problems give up the goal of demonstrating high ability and focus only on not demonstrating extremely low ability, they still may not view trying hard as an avenue for accomplishing their goals. If they try hard and still fail, this provides the clearest demonstration of low ability. Thus, children who lack confidence in their ability may believe it is easier to avoid demonstrating low ability if they do not do the work at all (Nicholls, 1984). In contrast, when children are oriented toward learning goals, even children who perform poorly relative to their peers can maintain optimism that success (i.e., improving and mastering skills) can be achieved through hard work and the application of appropriate strategies (Ames & Archer, 1988; Bandura & Dweck, 1983; Elliott & Dweck, 1988).

A number of classroom variables may influence whether children given priority to learning versus performance goals. Performance goals are more likely to predominate when grades, praise, and other rewards are determined primarily on the basis of children's performance relative to their peers (referred to as a competitive goal structure). In contrast, learning goals are more likely to predominate when rewards are contingent on mastering specific tasks and/or performing well relative to one's own prior performances (referred to as an individualistic goal structure) (Ames, 1984; Ames & Ames, 1981; Ames & Archer, 1988; Dweck & Elliott, 1983; see also Slavin, 1980).

Particular achievement goals may also be highlighted by the comments teachers make. Two types of written teacher comments have been shown to be beneficial. Subject matter comments are based on absolute standards and generally include specific information about what the student did well and what could be done differently (e.g., "You know how to solve the task—the formula is okay—but your computation is wrong in this instance"). Individually oriented comments indicate how the student's current performance compares with his or her prior performance (e.g., "In comparison with your prior performance, you have improved a lot") (examples from Krampen, 1987, p. 138). When either type of comment was regularly written on students' tests or class assignments, this enhanced students' learning goals, increased their self-perceptions of success, and led to improved performances when compared to normatively based grades or comments (i.e., those indicating how the child's performance compared with his or her peers') or to no written comments (Butler, 1987; Elawar & Corno, 1985; Krampen, 1987).

Qualifications Concerning the Treatment and Teaching Recommendations

The research reviewed above supports the importance of de-emphasizing social comparison information. It should be noted, however, that this research does not imply that educators should eliminate *all* normatively based grades and feedback. In fact, based on existing research (Ames & Archer, 1988; Jagacinski & Nicholls, 1987), it is likely that giving normatively based report card grades will have few negative consequences if the teachers' *daily* feedback stresses the subject matter and how the child is improving relative to his or her own past performance. Further, children need to be explicitly taught the importance of their efforts and strategies.

Two additional qualifications should be made concerning the treatment recommendations discussed in this chapter. First, all these motivational treatments are likely to be effective only if they are integrated with good instructional programs. In other words, these motivational treatments are not substitutes for skill or strategy instruction. Second, the treatments discussed are not likely to be effective with all types of motivational problems. These treatments probably will be most beneficial for children who believe their efforts are useless because they believe their abilities are low or for children who simply do not recognize the importance of trying hard and using effective strategies. These treatments may not be helpful for children who believe their efforts will not pay off because the whims of powerful others determine who gets rewards or punishments. Demonstrating that the effortful use of strategies leads to good academic performance is unlikely to motivate children who believe that the quality of their academic performance does not determine whether they receive praise and good grades. Although there is little literature from which to draw suggestions, one may speculate that these children might profit from an elaboration of the specific classroom behaviors (both conduct and academic performances) that lead to rewards (praise, good grades, extra privileges) and punishments (criticism, bad grades), with concrete examples of instances when they were rewarded for performing well. To the extent possible, it also may be helpful to provide consistent rewards (e.g., praise) for good behavior and work and consistent negative consequences (e.g., removal of privileges) for bad conduct. Over time, this may make it clear to children that the rewards and punishments they receive are related to their behavior and not to the whims of powerful others or to unknown forces (Grolnick & Ryan, 1989).

Conclusion

This chapter has emphasized the important role that children's achievement-related beliefs play in determining how much effort children will exert toward learning and applying new skills and strategies. It also has been shown that children with learning disabilities frequently believe that their achievement efforts are useless. However, there are important individual differences in the achievement-related beliefs of children with learning disabilities. That is, some of these children have confidence in their abilities; and this leads to greater persistence, which, in turn, contributes positively to their academic achievements. Researchers have just begun to address some of the factors (e.g., social comparison information, range of abilities within classroom) that contribute to individual differences in the achievement-related beliefs of children with learning disabilities. Identifying the variables that contribute to these individual differences should be a major focus of future research. By understanding the factors that lead some children with learning disabilities to maintain adaptive beliefs, researchers and teachers will be better able to develop learning environments that foster adaptive beliefs for all children. The research on children with behavior problems suggests that some of the individual differences may be related to certain kinds of teacher-student interactions. That is, certain types of behavior problems may elicit certain types of teacher feedback, which, in turn, can foster particular maladaptive beliefs. Thus, it would be fruitful for future research to examine the relationships among different types of conduct and attentional problems, teacher-student interactions, and children's achievement-related beliefs. Finally, some effective teaching and treatment procedures for promoting adaptive achievement-related beliefs, were examined in the chapter. Future research should continue the recent trend of examining actual academic tasks (as opposed to laboratory tasks). In addition, the children's actual teachers should implement the treatment procedures whenever possible. The most ecologically valid research findings are likely to emerge through collaborations between researchers and teachers.

Throughout this chapter, it has been emphasized that children must believe that an *effortful* use of strategies can help them overcome the challenges they face. This same message needs to be recognized by teachers faced with the challenges of motivating children who are not working at the levels of which they are capable. That is, if effortfully applied, many of the treatment and teaching recommendations made in this chapter can help teachers promote more adaptive achievement-related beliefs in their students. It should be noted that the treatment recommendations in this chapter are clearly more difficult to apply in the classroom than in the research settings described here. Further, not all children respond to these treatments in the same way. Thus, different treatments may need to be used with different children. Finally, it is likely that long-term benefits will derive only when treatments are applied in varied situations and over relatively long periods of time (Kendall & Braswell, 1982; Meichenbaum & Asarnow, 1979). Nonetheless, the research reviewed in this chapter suggests that if teachers *effortfully* apply these motivational treatments (e.g., attribution retraining, goal setting, comments and rewards focusing on intra-individual comparisons), they may be better able to motivate many children who are not performing at the levels of which they are capable.

References

Ames, C. (1984). Achievement attributions and self-instructions under competitive and individualistic goal structures. *Journal of Educational Psychology, 76*, 478–487.

Ames, C., & Ames, R. (1981). Competitive versus individualistic goal structures: The salience of past performance information for causal attributions and affect. *Journal of Educational Psychology, 73*, 411–418.

Ames, C., & Archer, J. (1987). Mothers' beliefs about the role of ability and effort in school learning. *Journal of Educational Psychology, 79*, 409–414.

Ames, C., & Archer, J. (1988). Achievement goals in the classroom: Students' learning strategies and motivation processes. *Journal of Educational Psychology, 80*, 260–267.

Anderson, C. A., & Jennings, D. L. (1980). When experiences of failure promote expectations of success: The impact of attributing failure to ineffective strategies. *Journal of Personality, 48*, 393–407.

Andrews, G. R., & Debus, R. L. (1978). Persistence and the causal perception of failure: Modifying cognitive attributions. *Journal of Educational Psychology, 70*, 154–166.

Asarnow, J. R., & Meichenbaum, D. (1979). Verbal rehearsal and serial recall: The mediational training of kindergarten children. *Child Development, 50*, 1173–1177.

Bandura, A. (1982). Self-efficacy mechanism in human agency. *American Psychologist, 37*, 122–147.

Bandura, A. (1986). *Social foundations of thought and action.* Englewood Cliffs, NJ: Prentice-Hall.

Bandura, A., & Schunk, D. H. (1981). Cultivating competence, self-efficacy, and intrinsic interest through proximal self-motivation. *Journal of Personality and Social Psychology, 41,* 586–598.

Bandura, M., & Dweck, C. (1983). *Self-conceptions and motivation: Conceptions of intelligence, choice of achievement goals, and patterns of cognition, affect, and behavior.* Unpublished manuscript, Pennsylvania State University, Altoona, PA.

Boersma, F. J., & Chapman, J. W. (1981). Academic self-concept, achievement expectations, and locus of control in elementary learning-disabled children. *Canadian Journal of Behavioural Science, 13,* 349–358.

Borkowski, J. G., Weyhing, R. S., & Carr, M. (1988). Effects of attributional retraining on strategy-based reading comprehension in learning-disabled students. *Journal of Educational Psychology, 80,* 46–53.

Borkowski, J. G., Weyhing, R. S., & Turner, L. A. (1986). Attributional retraining and the teaching of strategies. *Exceptional Children, 53,* 130–137.

Brophy, J. (1985). Teachers' expectations, motives, and goals for working with problem students. In C. Ames & R. Ames (Eds.), *Research on motivation in education, Vol. 2: The classroom milieu* (pp. 175–214). Orlando, FL: Academic Press.

Brophy, J. E., & Evertson, C. M. (1981). *Student characteristics and teaching.* New York: Longman.

Brophy, J. E., & Rohrkemper, M. M. (1981). The influence of problem ownership on teachers' perceptions of and strategies for coping with problem students. *Journal of Educational Psychology, 73,* 295–311.

Butkowsky, I. S., & Willows, D. M. (1980). Cognitive-motivational characteristics of children varying in reading ability: Evidence for learned helplessness in poor readers. *Journal of Educational Psychology, 72,* 408–422.

Butler, R. (1987). Task-involving and ego-involving properties of evaluation: Effects of different feedback conditions on motivational perceptions, interest, and performance. *Journal of Educational Psychology, 79,* 474–482.

Chapin, M., & Dyck, D. G. (1976). Persistence in children's reading behavior as a function of N length and attribution retraining. *Journal of Abnormal Psychology, 85,* 511–515.

Chapman, J. W. (1988). Cognitive-motivational characteristics and academic achievement of learning disabled children: A longitudinal study. *Journal of Educational Psychology, 80,* 357–365.

Clifford, M. M. (1986). The effects of ability, strategy, and effort attributions for educational, business, and athletic failure. *British Journal of Educational Psychology, 56,* 169–179.

Connell, J. P. (1985). A new multidimensional measure of children's perceptions of control. *Child Development, 56,* 1018–1041.

Conners, C. K. (1969). A teacher rating scale for use in drug studies with children. *American Journal of Psychiatry, 126,* 152–156.

Crandall, V. C., Katkovsky, W., & Crandall, V. J. (1965). Children's beliefs in their own control of reinforcements in intellectual-academic achievement situations. *Child Development, 36,* 91–109.

Diener, C. I., & Dweck, C. S. (1978). An analysis of learned helplessness: Continuous changes in performance, strategy, and achievement cognitions following failure. *Journal of Personality and Social Psychology, 36,* 451–462.

Dodge, K. A., & Newman, J. P. (1981). Biased decision-making processes in aggressive boys. *Journal of Abnormal Psychology, 90,* 375–379.

Dodge, K. A., & Somberg, D. R. (1987). Hostile attributional biases among aggressive boys are exacerbated under conditions of threats to the self. *Child Development, 58,* 213–224.

Dweck, C. S. (1975). The role of expectations and attributions in the alleviation of learned helplessness. *Journal of Personality and Social Psychology, 31,* 674–685.

Dweck, C. S., & Elliott, E. S. (1983). Achievement motivation. In E. M. Hetherington (volume editor) & P. H. Mussen (editor), *Handbook of child psychology* (Vol. IV, pp. 643–691). New York: Wiley.

Dweck, C. S., Goetz, T. E., & Strauss, N. L. (1980). Sex differences in learned helplessness: IV. An experimental and naturalistic study of failure generalization and its mediators. *Journal of Personality and Social Psychology, 38,* 441–452.

Dweck, C. S., & Licht, B. G. (1980). Learned helplessness and intellectual achievement. In J. Garber & M. E. P. Seligman (Eds.), *Human helplessness: Theory and applications* (pp. 197–221). New York: Academic Press.

Dweck, C. S., & Reppucci, N. D. (1973). Learned helplessness and reinforcement responsibility in children. *Journal of Personality and Social Psychology, 25,* 109–116.

Elawar, M. C., & Corno, L. (1985). A factorial experiment in teachers' written feedback on student homework: Changing teacher behavior a little rather than a lot. *Journal of Educational Psychology, 77,* 162–173.

Elliott, E. S., & Dweck, C. S. (1988). Goals: An approach to motivation and achievement. *Journal of Personality and Social Psychology, 54,* 5–12.

Epstein, M. H., Cullinan, D., & Gadow, K. D. (1986). Teacher ratings of hyperactivity in learning-disabled, emotionally disturbed, and mentally retarded children. *The Journal of Special Education, 20,* 219–229.

Epstein, M. H., Cullinan, D., & Lloyd, J. W. (1986). Behavior-problem patterns among the learning disabled: III. Replication across age and sex. *Learning Disability Quarterly, 9,* 43–54.

Fowler, J. W., & Peterson, P. L. (1981). Increasing reading persistence and altering attributional style of learned helpless children. *Journal of Educational Psychology, 73,* 251–260.

Gettinger, M. (1989). Effects of maximizing time spent and minimizing time needed for learning on pupil achievement. *American Educational Research Journal, 26,* 73–91.

Grolnick, W. S., & Ryan, R. M. (1989). Parent styles associated with children's self-regulation and competence in school. *Journal of Educational Psychology, 81,* 143–154.

Hallahan, D. P., Kneedler, R. D., & Lloyd, J. W. (1983). Cognitive behavior modification techniques for learning disabled children: Self-instruction and self-monitoring. In J. D. McKinney & L. Feagans (Eds.), *Current topics in learning disabilities* (Vol. I, pp. 207–244). Norwood, NJ: Ablex.

Harter, S. (1982). The perceived competence scale for children. *Child Development, 53,* 87–97.

Harter, S. (1985). *Manual for the self-perception profile for children.* Denver: University of Denver.

Hartsfield, F., Licht, B., Swenson, C., & Thiele, C. (August, 1989). *Control beliefs and behavior problems of elementary school children.* Paper presented at the meeting of the American Psychological Association, New Orleans.

Jagacinski, C. M., & Nicholls, J. G. (1987). Competence and affect in task involvement and ego involvement: The impact of social comparison information. *Journal of Educational Psychology, 79,* 107–114.

Kendall, P. C., & Braswell, L. (1982). Cognitive-behavioral self-control therapy for children: A components analysis. *Journal of Consulting and Clinical Psychology, 50,* 672–689.

Kistner, J. A., Osborne, M., & LeVerrier, L. (1988). Causal attributions of learning-disabled children: Developmental patterns and relation to academic progress. *Journal of Educational Psychology, 80,* 82–89.

Kistner, J., White, K., Haskett, & Robbins, F. (1985). Development of learning-disabled and normally achieving children's causal attributions. *Journal of Abnormal Child Psychology, 13,* 639–647.

Krampen, G. (1987). Differential effects of teacher comments. *Journal of Educational Psychology, 79,* 137–146.

Licht, B. G. (1983). Cognitive-motivational factors that contribute to the achievement of learning-disabled children. *Journal of Learning Disabilities, 16,* 483–490.

Licht, B. G., & Dweck, C. S. (1984). Determinants of academic achievement: The interaction of children's achievement orientations with skill area. *Developmental Psychology, 20,* 628–636.

Licht, B. G., & Kistner, J. A. (1986). Motivational problems of learning-disabled children: Individual differences and their implications for treatment. In J. K. Torgesen & B. Y. L. Wong (Eds.), *Psychological and educational perspectives on learning disabilities* (pp. 225–255). Orlando, FL: Academic Press.

Licht, B. G., Kistner, J. A., Ozkaragoz, T., Shapiro, S., & Clausen, L. (1985). Causal attributions of learning disabled children: Individual differences and their implications for persistence. *Journal of Educational Psychology, 77,* 208–216.

Lincoln, A., & Chazan, S. (1979). Perceived competence and intrinsic motivation in learning disability children. *Journal of Clinical Child Psychology, 8,* 213–216.

Linn, R. T., & Hodge, G. K. (1982). Locus of control in childhood hyperactivity. *Journal of Consulting and Clinical Psychology, 50,* 592–593.

Loney, J., & Milich, R. (1982). Hyperactivity, inattention, and aggression in clinical practice. In M. Wolraich & D. K. Routh (Eds.), *Advances in developmental and behavioral pediatrics* (Vol. 3, pp. 113–147). Greenwich, CT: JAI Press.

Mac Iver, D. (1988). Classroom environments and the stratification of pupils' ability perceptions. *Journal of Educational Psychology, 80,* 495–505.

Marsh, H. W., Byrne, B. M., & Shavelson, R. J. (1988). A multifaceted academic self-concept: Its hierarchical structure and its relation to academic achievement. *Journal of Educational Psychology, 80*, 366–380.

McKinney, J. D. (1989). Longitudinal research on the behavioral characteristics of children with learning disabilities. *Journal of Learning Disabilities, 22*, 141–150.

McKinney, J. D., & Speece, D. L. (1986). Academic consequences and longitudinal stability of behavioral subtypes of learning disabled children. *Journal of Educational Psychology, 78*, 365–372.

Meichenbaum, D. (1977). *Cognitive behavior modification: An intergrative approach.* New York: Plenum Press.

Meichenbaum, D., & Asarnow, J. (1979). Cognitive-behavioral modification and metacognitive development: Implications for the classroom. In P. C. Kendall & S. D. Hollon (Eds.), *Cognitive-behavioral interventions: Theory, research, and procedures* (pp. 11–35). New York: Academic Press.

Milich, R., Loney, J., & Landau, S. (1982). Independent dimensions of hyperactivity and aggression: Validation with playroom observation data. *Journal of Abnormal Psychology, 91*, 183–198.

Nation, J. R., Cooney, J. B., & Gartrell, K. E. (1979). Durability and generalizability of persistence training. *Journal of Abnormal Psychology, 88*, 121–136.

Nicholls, J. G. (1984). Achievement motivation: Conceptions of ability, subjective, experience, task choice, and performance. *Psychological Review, 91*, 328–346.

Nicholls, J. G., Patashnick, M., & Nolen, S. B. (1985). Adolescent's theories of education. *Journal of Educational Psychology, 77*, 683–692.

Palincsar, A. S., & Brown, A. L. (1984). Reciprocal teaching of comprehension-fostering and comprehension-monitoring activities. *Cognition and Instruction, 1*, 117–175.

Palmer, D. J., Drummond, F., Tollison, P., & Zinkgraff, S. (1982). An attributional investigation of performance outcomes for learning-disabled and normal-achieving pupils. *The Journal of Special Education, 16*, 207–219.

Pearl, R. A. (1982). LD children's attributions for success and failure: A replication with a labeled learning disabled sample. *Learning Disability Quarterly, 5*, 173–176.

Pearl, R. (1985). Cognitive-behavioral interventions for increasing motivation. *Journal of Abnormal Child Psychology, 13*, 443–454.

Pearl, R. A., Bryan, T., & Donahue, M. (1980). Learning disabled children's attributions for success and failure. *Learning Disability Quarterly, 3*, 3–9.

Pearl, R., Bryan, T., & Herzog, A. (1983). Learning disabled and nondisabled children's strategy analyses under high and low success conditions. *Learning Disability Quarterly, 6*, 67–74.

Pelham, W. E., & Bender, M. E. (1982). Peer relationships in hyperactive children: Description and treatment. In K. Gadow & I. Bialer (Eds.), *Advances in learning and behavioral disabilities* (Vol. I, pp. 365–436). Greenwich, CT: JAI Press.

Putallaz, M., & Gottman, J. (1983). Social relationship problems in children: An approach to intervention. In B. Lahey & A. Kazdin (Eds.), *Advances in clinical child psychology* (Vol. 6, pp. 1–43). New York: Plenum Press.

Reid, M. K., & Borkowski, J. G. (1987). Causal attributions of hyperactive children: Implications for teaching strategies and self-control. *Journal of Educational Psychology, 79,* 296–307.

Renick, M. J., & Harter, S. (1989). Impact of social comparisons on the developing self-perceptions of learning disabled students. *Journal of Educational Psychology, 81,* 631–638.

Rogers, H., & Saklofske, D. H. (1985). Self-concepts, locus of control and performance expectations of learning disabled children. *Journal of Learning Disabilities, 18,* 273–278.

Rosenholtz, S. J., & Simpson, C. (1984). The formation of ability conceptions: Developmental trend or social construction? *Review of Educational Research, 54,* 31–63.

Ryckman, D. B., & Peckham, P. D. (1986). Gender differences on attribution patterns in academic areas for learning disabled students. *Learning Disabilities Research, 2,* 83–89.

Schunk, D. H. (1982). Effects of effort attributional feedback on children's perceived self-efficacy and achievement. *Journal of Educational Psychology, 74,* 548–556.

Schunk, D. H. (1989). Self-efficacy and cognitive achievement: Implications for students with learning problems. *Journal of Learning Disabilities, 22,* 14–22.

Schunk, D. H., & Cox, P. D. (1986). Strategy training and attributional feedback with learning disabled students. *Journal of Educational Psychology, 78,* 201–209.

Schunk, D. H., Hanson, A. R., & Cox, P. D. (1987). Peer-model attributes and children's achievement behaviors. *Journal of Educational Psychology, 79,* 54–61.

Schunk, D. H., & Rice, J. M. (1984). Strategy self-verbalization during remedial listening comprehension instruction. *Journal of Experimental Education, 53,* 49–54.

Shelton, T. L., Anastopoulos, A. D., & Linden, J. D. (1985). An attribution training program with learning disabled children. *Journal of Learning Disabilities, 18,* 261–265.

Skinner, E. A., Chapman, M., & Baltes, P. B. (1988). Control, means-ends, and agency beliefs: A new conceptualization and its measurement during childhood. *Journal of Personality and Social Psychology, 54,* 117–133.

Slavin, R. E. (1980). Effects of individual learning expectations on student achievement. *Journal of Educational Psychology, 72,* 520–524.

Speece, D. L., McKinney, J. D., & Appelbaum, M. I. (1985). Classification and validation of behavioral subtypes of learning disabled children. *Journal of Educational Psychology, 77,* 67–77.

Stipek, D. J., & Daniels, D. H. (1988). Declining perceptions of competence: A consequence of changes in the child or in the educational environment. *Journal of Educational Psychology, 80,* 352–356.

Strang, L., Smith, M. D., & Rogers, C. M. (1978). Social comparison, multiple reference groups, and the self-concepts of academically handicapped children before and after mainstreaming. *Journal of Educational Psychology, 70,* 487–497.

Thomas, A. (1979). Learned helplessness and expectancy factors: Implications for research in learning disabilities. *Review of Educational Research, 49,* 208–221.

Thomas, A., & Pashley, B. (1982). Effects of classroom training on LD students' task persistence and attributions. *Learning Disability Quarterly, 5,* 133–144.

Torgesen, J. K. (1977). The role of non-specific factors in the task performance of learning disabled children: A theoretical assessment. *Journal of Learning Disabilities, 10,* 27–35.

Torgesen, J. K. (1980). Conceptual and educational implications of the use of efficient task strategies by learning disabled children. *Journal of Learning Disabilities, 13,* 364–371.

Torgesen, J. K., & Licht, B. (1983). The learning disabled child as an inactive learner: Retrospect and prospects. In J. D. McKinney & L. Feagans (eds.), *Current topics in learning disabilities* (Vol. I, pp. 3–31). Norwood, NJ: Ablex.

Weiner, B. (1979). A theory of motivation for some classroom experiences. *Journal of Educational Psychology, 71,* 3–25.

Weisz, J. R., & Cameron, A. M. (1985). Individual differences in the student's sense of control. In C. Ames & R. Ames (Eds.), *Motivation in education: Vol. 2. The classroom milieu* (pp. 93–140). London: Academic Press.

Winne, P. H., Woodlands, M. J., & Wong, B. Y. L. (1982). Comparability of self-concept among learning disabled, normal, and gifted students. *Journal of Learning Disabilities, 15,* 470–475.

8

Learning Disabilities and Attention Deficits in the School Setting

Sally E. Shaywitz
Bennett A. Shaywitz

Attention deficit disorder (ADD) is now recognized as the most common neurobehavioral disorder in children, affecting an estimated 10% to 20% of the school-age population (Shaywitz & Shaywitz, 1988). Furthermore, based on studies examining the prevalence of stimulant medication usage in children, it appears that the disorder is being diagnosed more frequently now than a decade ago (Safer & Krager, 1988). Despite the increased importance that ADD now plays in pediatrics and child neurology, investigators and clinicians continue to debate even such fundamental questions as whether ADD can be distinguished from learning disabilities and whether those behaviors characterized as conduct disorder and oppositional disorder (C/O)[1] (Shaywitz & Shaywitz, 1988) are part of the ADD spectrum or

Supported in part by Grants No. PO1 HD21888 and 1P50 HD25802 from NICHD.

Note. This chapter is adapted from "Co-morbidity: A critical issue in attention deficit disorder" by B. A. Shaywitz and S. E. Shaywitz, 1991, *Journal of Child Neurology, 6,* pp. S-13–S-22. Adapted by permission.
[1]For purposes of this review, conduct disorder and oppositional disorder are considered together as conduct/oppositional disorder (C/O).

co-occur with ADD. Such questions are of considerably more than just intellectual interest. Good evidence indicates that those children who have been identified either by their parents or by their school as exhibiting symptoms consonant with ADD are also very likely to be diagnosed as having a learning disability (LD) and often of having C/O as well. Furthermore, the prognosis in children with ADD and C/O may be considerably different from those with ADD alone.

It is our purpose to examine the interrelationships among ADD, LD, and C/O. We indicate that at the present investigators from a number of disciplines (child neurology, behavioral pediatrics, psychology, and child psychiatry) believe that it is reasonable to consider ADD as a distinct entity, frequently co-occurring with LD on the one hand, and C/O on the other. Such a conceptualization, we believe, will provide the framework for the diagnositician and educator to better comprehend the rapidly proliferating literature that sometimes confounds and obscures these interrelationships. It will also be valuable to investigators who must clarify these interrelationships to select the most homogeneous groups of children for their research studies.

We first review the interrelationships between ADD and LD, beginning with critical issues of definition, issues that are central to all other considerations. We then trace the historical antecedents of ADD and LD, indicating how these disorders emerged from similar roots, and examine the prevalence of ADD and LD. We conclude this section by focusing on newer studies designed to differentiate cognitive from attentional mechanisms in children with ADD, LD, or both ADD and LD. We next review the evidence linking ADD with C/O. We show how referral bias in some earlier investigations confounded this distinction and how more recent investigations have accounted for this bias. We conclude this section with a review of studies suggesting that the antecedents, clinical characteristics, and prognosis may differ in children with ADD alone when compared to ADD occurring in association with C/O.

More comprehensive reviews covering other issues in ADD are readily available (Barkley, 1990; Garfinkel & Wender, 1989; Shaywitz & Shaywitz, 1988, 1989; Whalen, 1989), and the interested reader may want to refer to these.

Attention Disorder and Learning Disability

Definitional Issues

Definitional issues represent perhaps the most fundamental considerations in efforts to examine the interrelationships between ADD and

LD. The diagnosis of ADD is established on the basis of a history of symptoms representing the cardinal constructs of ADD—inattention, impulsivity, and sometimes hyperactivity. Most North American investigators would diagnose ADD on the basis of a history obtained from the parents, reflecting behavior in a particular situation (situational ADD). In contrast, some British investigators (Taylor, 1986) would insist that the symptoms be noted as well by the child's teachers; that is, the symptoms should be observed in many situations (pervasive ADD). This controversy over situational versus pervasive symptomatology clearly reflects fundamental conceptualizations of how ADD is defined in North America compared to Great Britain. Though this controversy has not been resolved to everyone's satisfaction, the major American diagnostic formulations, *Diagnostic and Statistical Manual of Mental Disorders, Third Edition* (DSM-III) (American Psychiatric Association, 1980), *Diagnostic and Statistical Manual for Mental Disorders, Third Edition–Revised* (DSM-III-R) (APA, 1987), and *Diagnostic and Statistical Manual of Mental Disorders, Fourth Edition* (DSM-IV) (APA, in preparation), indicate that a history of symptoms of ADD obtained from the parents is sufficient for the diagnosis of ADD. If the teacher or other observers note the same symptoms, all well and good, but not necessary. A more detailed discussion of definitional issues in ADD is presented elsewhere (Shaywitz & Shaywitz, 1988).

In contrast to the diagnosis of ADD that depends solely on history, the diagnosis of learning disability is established on the basis of performance on tests of ability and achievement. Historically, LD has been conceptualized as an inability to learn in children of otherwise normal or above normal intelligence. Guidelines (provided as an attempt at the operationalization of Public Law 94-142 (1975) of a severe discrepancy between achievement and intellectual ability (U.S. Office of Education, 1977) offer the most generally accepted criteria throughout the English-speaking world (Cone & Wilson, 1981; Reynolds, 1984; Rutter, 1970; Thorndike, 1963). What the guidelines do not provide are clearly stated rules that would allow the examiner to precisely diagnose a child as having learning disabilities. For example, how are achievement and intellectual ability to be determined? Most diagnosticians recognize that these must be individually administered measures. Tests are available that measure intellectual ability; the *Wechsler Intelligence Scale for Children–Revised* (WISC-R) (Wechsler, 1974) is most often used, but which component of the scale—the Verbal (VIQ), the Performance (PIQ), or the Full Scale measure—is to be used? In both our research and clinical work we use either VIQ or PIQ, whichever provides the greatest discrepancy. The achievement measure employed must provide scores in the same metric as the WISC-R so that the scores may be compared and a discrepancy calculated. The *Woodcock-Johnson Psycho-Educational Battery* (Woodcock & Johnson, 1977) offers such a metric and provides for the determination of letter and word identification (Subtest 13), word attack (nonsense words, Subtest 14), reading comprehension (Subtest 15), calculations (Subtest 16), and mathematical concepts (Subtest 17). But which of these scales should be compared to which of the ability measures to calculate a discrepancy? Should *age-* or *grade-* standardized scores be used for comparison? We routinely use *age-* standardized scores of the combined scores of Subtests 13 and 14 to provide a measure of decoding skill, the age-standardized reading cluster score (combined scores of Subtests 13, 14, and 15) to provide a measure of overall reading and the calculation score to provide a measure of arithmetic skill.

How should the discrepancy be calculated? Assuming that the standard deviation of the IQ and achievement measures is 15 points, some investigators use a difference of approximately 22 points between the IQ and achievement scores, approximating a difference of 1.5 standard deviations. Different state laws specify how the definition of LD is to be established, and although a difference between ability and achievement of 1.5 standard deviations represents the law in Connecticut, other states specify different formulas. Whichever cutoff is decided on, the clinician must consider the phenomenon of regression to the mean effect; it is far superior to employ a regression equation to calculate this discrepancy (Cone & Wilson, 1981; Reynolds, 1984). Failure to recognize the regression to the mean effect will result in overidentification of children with high IQ and underidentification of children with low IQ. However, the regression approach requires the availability of a population that would provide the norm-based data to calculate such a regression, and such a population is not generally available to most diagnosticians.

Most cases of LD represent difficulties in reading, and the terms LD and reading disability (or dyslexia) are frequently used interchangeably. Within the last two decades, the work of Isabelle Liberman and her colleagues (Liberman & Shankweiler, 1985; Mann, Cowin, & Schoeheimer, 1989) and Frank Vellutino and his associates (Vellutino, 1978, 1979; Vellutino & Scanlon, 1987), as well as other investigators, has supported the belief that reading disability represents difficulties with language and words—their use, significance, meaning, pronunciation, and spelling and the problems generated by this lexical difficulty. Thus, children with speech and language difficulties are far more likely to exhibit deficits in reading than children without early language problems. Furthermore, poor readers consistently perform less well than good readers on tasks involving language. Both observations support the position that emphasizes the centrality of language in the genesis of reading disability.

Recognition that reading disability reflects a disturbance in language is of critical importance to the diagnostician, particularly when dealing with older children and young adults suspected of having LD. Investigators are increasingly aware of very bright students with learning disabilities, some of whom have matriculated to our most selective institutions (Aaron & Phillips, 1986; Shaywitz, 1989; Shaywitz & Shaw, 1988). The diagnosis of these students must recognize the centrality of reading and language disturbances, and should not necessarily follow an ability achievement discrepancy formula that is far more appropriate for younger, school-age children. A recent report described the characteristics of college students with learning disabilities:

> They do well until they enter high school. Here, if they are attending a large public high school and have reasonable social skills they may go unnoticed. If they are in a more competitive setting *and* if accommodations are not provided, they may begin to experience difficulties. Records of these students attest to their hard work, use of intellect to compensate, and high level of success that they often attain. The disability is chronic, it neither suddenly emerges nor does it suddenly remit. Like any other chronic disability, constant effort at a tremendous cost to the student is required so that the disability does not become a handicap. Although these students can compensate and master the material, the lingering remnants of their language disability cause them to work slowly. Simple accommodations such as allowing extra time for tests and completion of assignments minimizes the possibility that the reading disabled college student will be overly penalized by his/her disability.
>
> Testing data confirms the lingering residua of a language based disability. Rather than performing extremely poorly on language related measures; these intellectually gifted students may only exhibit evidence of their disability under conditions that stress their capacity to compensate—for example, timed tests, poor teaching or attempting to learn a foreign language. . . . Performance on untimed measures may be in the top percentiles, while that on timed measures average, or at times, slightly above or below average. The comments of the students are illuminating: "I manage"; "I feel it is remarkable that I have done as well as I have. I can read and write well if I have the time. I also have a great desire to succeed and reach my goals"; and "The problem is more easily overcome if it is understood by those around me." (Shaywitz, 1989)

As increasing numbers of school-age students with learning disabilities reach college age, those professionals called on to evaluate and manage children with learning and attention disorders will have to adjust their perspective to incorporate these very bright individuals.

Historical Perspective

Historically, the antecedents of the current controversies surrounding the relationship between ADD and LD can be traced to the late 19–early 20th century. In a remarkably prescient report, Still (1902) described children with what he termed "morbid defects in moral control." In that same era other physicians were linking the description of similar behaviors to disorders causing brain damage: traumatic brain injury (Goldstein, 1936; Meyer, 1904); the sequelae of von Economo's encephalitis (Hohman, 1922); or a variety of other childhood central nervous system infections (Bender, 1942). In a series of influential reports, Strauss and his associates (Strauss & Lehtinen, 1947; Werner & Strauss, 1941) extrapolated the notion of brain damage to include children with behaviors similar to those observed after known brain injuries. According to Strauss, the conceptual entity of the "brain-injured [damaged] child" depended only on the child's behavior; a history consistent with brain damage was not necessary for diagnosis.

By the 1950s, investigators had become disillusioned by these notions, and the concept of brain "dysfunction" rather than brain "damage" began to emerge. According to Laufer and Denhoff (1957), the hyperkinetic behavior disorder was caused by an underlying "injury to or dysfunction of the diencephalon" (p. 467). Even more influential, however, was Clements and Peters' (1962) elaboration of the notion of minimal brain dysfunction (MBD). In their view, minimal brain dysfunction could be inferred from the presence of a cluster of symptoms including specific learning deficits, hyperkinesis, impulsivity, and short attention span and confirmed by findings on examination of "equivocal" neurological signs and a borderline abnormal or a definitely abnormal EEG.

At the time, the notion of MBD was viewed as a real advance in incorporating the diverse manifestations thought to reflect the syndrome while not emphasizing a particular interpretation of the nature of the brain insult. However, this loose conglomeration of behavioral and learning symptomatology created confusion as well. Almost immediately, a schism developed in the way the medical and the educational communities viewed the disorder. The medical literature accepted the term *minimal brain dysfunction* and incorporated the entity into a medical model. In contrast, the educational literature focused more on the findings of a learning difficulty and preferred to describe affected children as having a specific learning disability. Despite attempts at operationalization of MBD (Bax & MacKeith, 1962), two decades of research have led to the recognition that MBD is meaningless, and the term has been abandoned by most investigators. However, its legacy lives on in the current confusion between ADD and LD that can be traced directly to the confounding of learning difficulties and behavioral disturbances in MBD.

Publication of DSM-III in 1980 marked a watershed in the evolution of ADD and in diagnosticians' ability to distinguish ADD from LD and from C/O. For the first time, specific exclusion and inclusion criteria were established for ADD; LD was not considered a specific criterion, though school failure was noted as a common complication. Despite clear criteria for ADD, in retrospect the seeds of some of the current difficulties in differentiating ADD and LD could be discerned in DSM-III, which differentiated two subtypes of ADD based on the presence or absence of symptoms of hyperactivity: attention deficit disorder with hyperactivity (ADDH) and attention deficit disorder without hyperactivity (ADDnoH). DSM-III was unclear whether "they are two forms of a single disorder or represent two distinct disorders" (American Psychiatric Association, 1980; p. 41). Publication of DSM-III-R in 1987 represented a distinct change and unfortunately added considerable confusion to the differentiation of LD and ADD. In contrast to DSM-III, DSM-III-R blurred the distinction between attention disorder with and without hyperactivity by focusing primarily on ADDH, now termed attention deficit–hyperactivity disorder (ADHD), and relegating ADDnoH to a category now termed undifferentiated attention disorder (U-ADD). The reasons for the decision to demote ADDnoH were described by Barkley, Spitzer, and Costello (1990) and related primarily to the belief by some of the committee members that ADDnoH might actually "represent a type of inattention believed to accompany the non-verbal learning disabilities (Rourke, 1989) and so might be a new subtype of the existing category of Specific Developmental Disorders." In the opinion of many investigators and thoughtful clinicians, this decision was, indeed, a retrogressive step, again confounding ADD with LD, rather than attempting to disentangle the two.

Subtypes of ADD

Good evidence supports this differentiation between subtypes of attention disorder, demonstrating that although ADDH and ADDnoH do not differ on independent measures of attention (Edelbrock, Costello, & Kessler, 1984; King & Young, 1982; Lahey & Carlson, 1991; Lahey, Schaughency, Hynd, et al., 1987). Children with ADDH and ADDnoH demonstrate significantly different behavioral, academic, and social patterns (Edelbrock et al., 1984). Of particular interest, Lahey et al. (1987) indicated that boys with ADDnoH are rated by their teachers as manifesting a poorer school performance compared to boys with ADDH, a finding supported by the high rate of retention (71.5%), high even in relation to boys with ADDH (16.7%). More recently, Lahey, Pelham and Schaughency (1988) investigated a clinic sample of 41 children with ADDH and 22 children with ADDnoH as well as a large school sample. They found that symptoms clustered into two domains: inattention-disorganized (ADDnoH) and hyperactive-impulsive (ADDH), providing still further support for the construct of ADD without hyperactivity.

Studies indicating that children manifesting inattention but not hyperactivity may represent a high-risk group for school failure mandate that the occurrence of such an attentional subtype be investigated and, if validated, definitional rules for its diagnosis provided. This takes on a particular urgency in view of findings of a strong correlation between externalizing behaviors and identification for special education services (Sandoval & Lambert, 1984–1985). These data and those of Berry et al. (1985), indicating that girls with ADD are less likely to be hyperactive and also less likely to receive special education services although they demonstrate significant attentional, cognitive, and language deficits, suggest that current school identification procedures rely heavily on the presence of hyperactivity or other externalizing behaviors. The implication is that children, particularly girls, who may be inattentive and experiencing academic difficulties but who are not hyperactive may not be identified for special services. Thus, children with ADDnoH may represent an underidentified and, as a consequence, underserved group of children who are at significant risk for long-term academic, social, and emotional difficulties.

Recognizing that many children with ADD exhibit symptoms that are less disturbing to those around them, the symptoms characterizing C/O, DSM-IV will in all likelihood consider ADD a separate category, distinct from other disruptive disorders of childhood. Furthermore, based on the data just reviewed, DSM-IV tentatively suggested that ADDnoH be considered as a separate entity within the ADD classification.

Prevalence of ADD and LD

Evidence from a number of investigative groups suggests a substantial overlap between attention disorder and learning disabilities. The prevalence of LD in children with ADD is estimated to be 9% to 10% in hyperactive boys (Halperin, Gittelman, Klein, & Rudel, 1984) and 11% in an epidemiologic sample of 8-year-old Connecticut school children (Shaywitz, 1986). Conversely, the prevalence of hyperactivity in populations with learning disabilities has varied from 41% (Holborow & Berry, 1986) to 80% (Safer & Allen, 1976), with a prevalence of 33% reported in an epidemiological sample (Shaywitz, 1986). Studies examining the academic achievement of children with hyperactivity compared to control children have supported the notion that significantly more children with ADDH experience academic achievement problems. They are more likely to perform below expectations in reading and arithmetic and, compared to controls, are behind both in their academic subjects and in more academic subjects (Cantwell, 1978). Holborow and Berry (1986) found seven times as many children rated as hyperactive were described as experiencing "very much" difficulty in all academic areas compared to their nonhyperactive classmates.

More recent evidence indicates that children with ADDnoH comprise a significant subset of those diagnosed as having ADD. Thus, Anderson, Williams, McGee, and Silva (1987) administered structured clinical interviews to 11-year-olds and questionnaires to their parents, the subjects representing a subset of a sample of New Zealand schoolchildren followed since age 3 years. Forty-five children were identified as having ADDH and 8 as having ADDnoH. Costello, Costello, Edelbrock, et al., (1988) administered structured interviews to 300 children and their parents seen in a general pediatric clinic of a large health maintenance organization. They found 11 cases of ADDH and 2 with ADDnoH.

Nature of Association Between ADD and LD

Given the substantial overlap between ADD and LD, it is not surprising that investigators have begun to explore the mechanisms underlying this association. Utilizing factor-analytic studies, Lahey et al. (1978, 1988) have identified separate LD and hyperactivity factors (Lahey et al., 1988; Lahey, Stempniak, Robinson, & Tyroler, 1978). Other investigators have employed what Share & Schwartz (1988) referred to as a "multiple comparison" approach. Felton, Wood, Brown, et al. (1987) examined children with ADD alone compared to children with reading disability. Children with reading disability exhibited difficulty with tasks involving confrontation naming and rapid automatized naming; children with ADD had most trouble with word-list learning and recall. Though these findings have generated considerable controversy (see contrasting views by Share & Schwartz, 1988, and Wood, Felton, & Brown, 1988), they suggest that naming and linguistic fluency deficits reflect reading disability, whereas verbal learning and memory deficits are linked to attention disorder. It should be noted that it has been and continues to be extremely difficult to disentangle attentional from memory deficits. With this in mind, it may be that on these tests of memory, attentional rather than memory difficulties, per se, account for the difficulties. More recently, August and Garfinkel (1989) examined 50 students with ADHD, 11 of whom also exhibited reading disability defined as a discrepancy between ability and reading achievement (referred to as cognitive). Children in this group exhibited deficits in lexical decoding and rapid word naming. Such findings support a language-based deficit for reading disability in these children with ADD.

In contrast, other studies (Ackerman, Anhald, Dykman, & Holcomb, 1986; Halperin et al., 1984) comparing hyperactive and mixed hyperactive–reading disability groups have found very few measures on which the two groups differed, results contrary to the notion that the two are discrete subgroups. In a recent report, McGee, Williams, Moffitt, and Anderson, (1989) compared groups of 13-year-olds selected from their ongoing study of New Zealand schoolchildren. A battery of tasks including copying, delayed recall, pegboard, mazes, Wisconsin card sort, and word association was administered to four subject groups: (a) ADD without reading disability, (b) ADD with reading disability, (c) reading disability without ADD, and (d) control group without ADD or reading disability. No specific cognitive deficit was demonstrated for ADD alone, although ADD with reading disability and reading disability alone both exhibited verbal deficits. The authors concluded that their findings failed to support "a unique set of cognitive impairments" (p. 50) in ADD. However, criteria for selection of the group with reading disability were far different from those used in most studies, indexing as having reading disability all children whose reading performance was below the median of reading in the ADD group. Most investigators employ an ability-achievement discrepancy or reading achievement below the 25% percentile. McGee et al.'s (1989) use of less-impaired readers may have biased the findings of their study, producing results inconsistent with those of Felton et al. (1987).

Most recently, van der Meere, van Baal, and Sergeant (1989) proposed a novel strategy to differentiate the slow and inaccurate task performance, primarily prolonged reaction time, of children with ADD and LD. By combining the additive factor method of Sternberg (1969, 1975) and the selective attention model of Schneider and Shiffrin (1977), they found children with LD to be impaired in memory search and decision processes, whereas children with ADD exhibited deficits in motor decision processes. Although the selection criteria for ADD and LD are problematic, van der Meere et al.'s strategy and novel approach to a difficult issue represent a real conceptual advance.

Although these approaches are interesting, they emphasize the relative paucity of research studies utilizing well-defined, non–system-identified children with learning disabilities where the diagnoses of both ADD and LD were made on the basis of rigorous criteria. Studies now in progress should provide a clearer understanding of (a) the prevalence of the co-occurrence of ADD and LD and (b) their mechanisms of interaction including the expression and course of one on the other. The ultimate aim, of course, is to provide rational approaches to intervention in children with both disorders.

Attention Disorder and Oppositional/Conduct Disorder

The nature of the relationship (co-morbidity) between attention disorder and those behavioral disturbances characterized as oppositional/conduct disorders represents a significant problem that continues to plague both clinicians and investigators. Loney (1983) identified three central possibilities regarding the relationship between attention disorder and oppositional/conduct disorder: (a) The disorders are interchangeable, (b) they are intertwined, or (c) they are independent. Proponents of the intertwined position view the disorders as overlapping, whereas those who believe the disorders are independent (the view of DSM-III and DSM-III-R) regard them as separate with distinct diagnostic features, etiology, treatment, and prognosis.

Difficulty in resolving the relationship between ADD and C/O may reflect the consequences of selective referral patterns that ensure that significant biases are built into any study of ADD primarily employing children referred to a mental health clinic. Thus, Loney and Milich (1982) compared children with ADD selected from schools ("nonreferred") to a group of children with ADD referred to a mental health clinic ("referred"). In the nonreferred sample, the proportion of boys with ADD who also exhibited C/O was only 18%, a decline from 71% in the referred group.

Loney and her colleagues have succeeded in developing, through employment of convergent and divergent validation strategies, the Divergent and Convergent Interview (DACI) (Loney, 1987) with distinct Inattention and Aggression factors.[2] Based on chart ratings (Loney et al., 1978; Milich et al., 1982; Loney, 1987) Loney, Langhorne, and Paternite (1978) posited that there were three clinical groups: purely inattentive, purely aggressive, and a mixed inattentive-aggressive group. This view that there are both distinct groups of inattentive and aggressive children and also a mixed group was supported by the results of Trites's large-scale study as well (Trites & LaPrade, 1983). These investigators were also able to identify subgroups of pure Hyperactivity, pure Conduct problem, and a mixed Hyperactivity-Conduct problem group. The differentiation of ADD from C/O has been supported as well by a

---

[2]Aggression represents the dimensional approach to the categorical diagnoses of C/O utilized in DSM-III-R.

number of recent studies including reports by Taylor (Taylor, Everitt, Thorley, et al., 1986; Taylor, Schachar, Thorley, & Wieselberg, 1986), which corrects an earlier report (Sandberg, Rutter, & Taylor, 1978) and clearly demonstrates that ADD is distinct from C/O. Recent epidemiologic studies have reached similar conclusions (Anderson et al., 1987; Bird, Canino, Rubio-Stipec, et al., 1988; Costello, Costello, Edelbrock, et al., 1988; Werry, Reeves, & Elkind, 1987; Reeves, Werry, Elkind, & Zametkin, 1987). Thus, it seems reasonable to postulate that both ADD and C/O can occur independently, but that they also co-occur in many instances.

Such studies have important implications and consequences for the diagnosis of children with attention disorder. Perhaps the most important of these is that because of the often biased nature of the subjects referred to mental health clinics, nonrepresentative associations may emerge that are not typical of most children with attention disorder. Any generalizations from studies utilizing solely mental health clinic subjects may not be appropriate. Rather than being regarded as prototypical of all children with attention disorder, children referred to mental health facilities may represent simply an extreme of the continuum. This potential bias may be magnified still further by the tendency of some investigators to identify as having attention disorder only children with severe and pervasive hyperactivity, a group who often also exhibit oppositional/conduct problems as well (Sandberg et al., 1978; Schachar, Rutter, & Smith, 1981). Such children, however, because they are so extreme may not be representative of children with attention disorder but rather represent a population with multiple disturbances and disabilities that is contaminated by a variety of confounding influences (Shaywitz & Shaywitz, 1987, 1988).

Such findings are of more than academic interest. The influence of referral bias represents a significant factor in the way both educators and health care providers view children with ADD. For example, if the definition of ADD is established on the basis of the symptomatology of children referred to mental health centers, then it is likely that C/O problems will be prominent. This will have the effect of encouraging educators to identify ADD on the basis of C/O behavioral problems, adding considerable confusion to an already complicated area.

In order (a) to examine the full spectrum of children who may be diagnosed and labeled as ADD and (b) to determine whether children diagnosed as ADD in mental health settings represent a different group from those diagnosed by pediatricians or child neurologists, we recently compared diagnoses in children referred from four sources: child neurology clinic, in-patient child psychiatry service, community pediatricians, and a community psychologist (Epstein, Shaywitz, Shaywitz, & Woolston, 1991). Our data suggest that referral bias does exist and that different children are diagnosed as having ADD by different disciplines or practitioners. The children referred to child neurologists have similar complaints to those referred to pediatricians and psychologists; and child neurologists make similar diagnoses to those of pediatricians and psychologists. From the perspective of the educator, children referred to pediatricians, psychologists, and child neurologists appear to represent a more representative group than those referred to child psychiatrists, who tend to see a different and more disturbed population exhibiting more behavioral and psychiatric problems.

Our findings are similar to those observed by other investigators. Thus, in a study cited earlier, Loney and Milich (1982) noted that between 63% and 71% of the children in a clinic sample displayed both aggressive and hyperactive symptoms contrasted with 18% in a classroom control sample. Similar findings were noted by McGee, Williams, & Silva, 1984, with the referral rate in boys who had both hyperactivity and aggression six times that for boys who had simply hyperactivity. Moreover, the boys with both hyperactivity and aggression demonstrated more associated problems including poorer cognitive skills.

Two more recent studies addressed the issue of co-occurrence of ADD and C/O. Utilizing data derived from the Ontario Child Health Study, Szatmari, Boyle, and Offord (1989) found 86 children with pure ADD, 84 with pure C/O, and 64 children with mixed ADD + C/O. Children with ADD tended to be younger and exhibited more developmental problems but fewer psychosocial difficulties than those children with C/O. These distinctions were much clearer in boys than in girls. Biederman and his associates (Biederman, Faraone, Keenan, & Tsuang, 1989; Faraone, Biederman, Keenan, & Tsuang, in press) have recently exploited the strategy of family genetic studies to provide external validation of the distinction between ADD and C/O and to clarify the nature of this association. Their findings indicate that mixed ADD + C/O appears to be a genetic variant of ADD, perhaps a more virulent form.

Another potential strategy to differentiate ADD from C/O involves the differential response to stimulant medications. Klorman et al. (1988) examined the effect of methylphenidate (MPH) on parent and teacher ratings and performance on a continuous performance test of children with ADD with and without aggression (Safer & Krager, 1988). Barkley et al. (1990) employed similar measures to examine the effects of MPH administered over 7 to 10 days to aggressive and nonaggressive children with ADD. Both investigative groups found that MPH significantly improved performance in both groups of children with ADD. Although such findings do not help to clarify distinctions between ADD and C/O, they do offer some optimism for therapy in aggressive children with ADD. Previous studies (Hinshaw, Henker, & Whalen, 1984) had suggested that MPH did not improve aggression and self-control in children with ADD. The studies of Klorman and Barkley together with the most recent study by Hinshaw, Buhrmester, and Heller (1989) have documented that MPH may indeed prove beneficial in controlling anger in children with ADD.

Summary

This review has examined the interrelationships between ADD and two related conditions, LD on the one hand and C/O on the other. Current evidence suggests that, conceptually, ADD should be considered as a distinct entity, often co-occurring with these two other disorders.

The interface between ADD and LD has roots that extend back almost 80 years, but it is only recently that investigators have begun to clarify these interrelationships. ADD is defined on the basis of inclusion and exclusion criteria, which are established by history and reflect behavioral concerns. LD (primarily reading disability) is defined as a discrepancy between ability (as measured by a test of IQ, e.g., WISC-R) and performance on achievement tests (as measured, for example, by the Woodcock-Johnson reading achievement test). Good evidence suggests a relationship between reading disability and anatomical disturbances in the language-related areas of brain, primarily in the left temporal lobe.

The relationship between ADD and C/O has begun to receive increasing attention in recent years. Both ADD and C/O are defined by inclusion and exclusion criteria. Accummulating evidence now supports the belief that ADD and C/O are distinct disorders that may co-occur in a significant number of children. Some investigators have found that ADD occurs in younger children with more developmental problems. In contrast, C/O seems to occur in older children with psychosocial disadvantage. Some investigators have suggested that the combination of ADD + C/O represents a more virulent disorder than the pure form of either ADD or C/O.

Studies employing newer classification strategies designed to better differentiate ADD from LD and from C/O are currently in progress. Rather than academic exercises, such a classification is fundamental "to exploring the causes of relationships and similarities among organisms. Classifications are theories about the basis of natural order, not dull catalogues compiled only to avoid chaos" (Gould, p. 118, 1989). Furthermore, "the work of placing . . . in categories, carefully weighing similarities and differences and occasionally discarding an old category and inventing a new one leads, inexorably, to a new view" (Gleick,

p. 41, 1989). By better defining ADD, LD, C/O and their interrelationships, investigators believe they will be able to provide more specific and effective interventions for children with these disabling conditions.

Currently, children with ADD and children with LD, as well as children in whom the disorders co-occur, are being treated similarly. The major thrust of our own investigations, as well as that of other studies under way, is to develop a nosology for the broad range of problems currently grouped within attention and learning disorders. A major impetus for this work is that more precise interventions are dependent on the delineation of homogeneous subgroups of both attention disorder and learning disability. Once these groups have been identified and characterized, specific and more effective interventions can be developed to address the learning characteristics of children within each subgroup. At this time, it is important to be aware that (a) LD and ADD are separate disorders and that (b) they can co-occur. Therefore, any child being evaluated for either of these conditions should be assessed for the possibility of both a learning disability and an attentional disorder. The role of, for example, stimulant medication in the treatment of LD is beginning to be evaluated. Early indicators suggest that stimulant medication is as helpful in treating children with ADD and reading disability as it is in treating children with only ADD (Dyckman & Ackerman, in press). Similarly, Abikoff (in press) indicated that stimulants are as, or more, effective than cognitive training in treating children with ADD. The difficulty in clarifying which treatment is best for which child reflects the fact that until very recently most samples of children with reading disability had mixtures of both reading disability and ADD, and not pure reading disability. As investigators appreciate the importance of disentangling ADD from LD, samples will be purer, and the emerging information more helpful in determining which therapies are most effective in each disorder.

References

Aaron, P. G., & Phillips, S. (1986). A decade of research with dyslexia college students: A survey of findings. *Annals of Dyslexia, 36,* 44–65.

Abikoff, H. (in press). Cognitive training in ADHD children: Less to it than meets the eye. *Journal of Learning Disabilities.*

Ackerman, P. T., Anhald, J. M., Dykman, R. A., & Holcomb, P. J. (1986). Effortful processing in children with reading and/or attention disorders. *Brain and Cognition, 5,* 22–40.

American Psychiatric Association. (1980). *Diagnostic and statistical manual of mental disorders, third edition* (DSM III). Washington, DC: Author.

American Psychiatric Association. (1987). *Diagnostic and statistical manual of mental disorders, third edition, revised* (DSM III-R). Washington, DC: Author.

American Psychiatric Association (in preparation). *DSM-IV options book: Work in progress. Task force on DSM-IV.* Washington, DC: Author.

Anderson, J. C., Williams, S., McGee, R., & Silva, P. A. (1987). DSM-III disorders in preadolescent children. *Archives of General Psychiatry, 44,* 69–76.

August, G. J., & Garfinkel, B. D. (1989). Behavioral and cognitive subtypes of ADHD. *Journal of the American Academy of Child and Adolescent Psychiatry, 28,* 739–748.

Barkley, R. A. (1990). *Attention deficit disorder—A handbook of diagnosis and treatment.* New York: Guilford Press.

Barkley, R. A., McMurray, M. B., Edelbrock, C. S., & Robbins, K. (1989). The response of aggressive and nonaggressive ADHD children to two doses of methylphenidate. *Journal of the American Academy of Child and Adolescent Psychiatry, 6,* 873–881.

Barkley, R. A., Spitzer, R., & Costello, A. (1990). *The development of the DSM-III-R criteria for the disruptive behavior disorders.* Woosher, MA: University of Massachusetts Medical Center.

Bax, U., & MacKeith, R. C. (1963). "Minimal brain damage"—A concept dysfunction. In R. C. MacKeith & M. Bax (Eds.), *Minimal cerebral dysfunction* (Foreword). London: SIMP with Heinemann.

Bender, L. (1992). Post encephalitic behavior disorders in childhood. In L. Bender (Ed.), *Encephalitis: A clinical study* (pp. 363–384). New York: Grune & Stratton.

Berry, C. A., Shaywitz, S. E., & Shaywitz, B. A. Girls with attention deficit disorder: A silent minority? A report on behavioral and cognitive characteristics. *Pediatrics, 76,* 801–809.

Biederman, J., Faraone, A., Keenan, K., & Tsuang, M. (1989). Family genetic and psychosocial risk factors in attention deficit disorder [Abstract]. *Biological Psychiatry, 25,* 145A (Supple.).

Bird, H. R., Canino, G., Rubio-Stipec, M., et al. (1988). Estimates of the prevalence of childhood maladjustment in a community survey in Puerto Rico. *Archives of General Psychiatry, 45,* 1120–1126.

Cantwell, D. P. (1978). Hyperactivity and antisocial behavior. *American Academy of Child Psychiatry, 17,* 252–262.

Clements, S. D. (1966). *Minimal brain dysfunction in children* (Public Health Service Publication No. 1415). Washington, DC: U.S. Dept. of Health, Education and Welfare.

Clements, S. D., & Peters, J. E. (1962). Minimal brain dysfunctions in the school-aged child. *Archives of General Psychiatry, 6,* 185–187.

Cone, T. E., & Wilson, L. R. (1981). Quantifying a severe discrepancy: A critical analysis. *Learning Disability Quarterly, 4,* 359–371.

Costello, E. J., Costello, A. J., Edelbrock, C., et al. (1988). Psychiatric disorders in pediatric primary care. *Archives of General Psychiatry, 45,* 1107–1116.

Dykman, R. A., and Ackerman, P. T. (in press). Attention deficit disorder and specific reading disability: Separate but often overlapping disorders. *Journal of Learning Disabilities.*

Edelbrock, C., Costello, A. J., & Kessler, M. D. (1984). Empirical corroboration of attention deficit disorder. *Journal of the American Academy of Child Psychiatry, 23,* 285–290.

Epstein, M. A., Shaywitz, S. E., Shaywitz, B. A., & Woolston, J. L. (1991). The boundaries of attention deficit disorder. *Journal of Learning Disabilities, 24,* 78–86.

Faraone, S. V., Biederman, J., Keenan, K., Tsuang, M. T. (in press). Attention deficit disorder with associated antisocial disorders as a distinct subtype: Evidence from family-genetic data. *Biological Psychiatry.*

Felton, R. H., Wood, F. B., Brown, I. S., et al. (1987). Separate verbal memory and naming deficits in attention deficit disorder and reading disability. *Brain and Language, 31,* 171–184.

Garfinkel, B. D., & Wender, P. (1989). Attention deficit hyperactivity disorder. In H. Kaplin, B. Sadock (Eds.), *Comprehensive textbook of psychiatry* (pp. 1828–1837). Baltimore: Williams & Wilkins.

Gleick, J. (1989, October 22). Book review: Reviewing Stephan Jay Gould's "Wonderful Life." *New York Times,* pp. 1, 40, 41.

Goldstein, K. (1936). Modification of behavior consequent to cerebral lesion. *Psychiatric Quarterly, 10,* 539–610.

Gould, S. J. (1989). *Wonderful life: The burgess shale and the nature of history.* New York: Norton.

Halperin, J. M., Gittelman, R., Klein, D. F., & Rudel, R. G. (1984). Reading disabled hyperactive children: A distinct subgroup of attention deficit disorder with hyperactivity? *Journal of Abnormal Child Psychology, 12,* 1–14.

Hinshaw, S. P., Buhrmester, D., & Heller, T. (1989). Anger control in response to verbal provocation: Effects of stimulant medication for boys with ADHD. *Journal of Abnormal Child Psychology, 17,* 393–407.

Hinshaw, S. P., Henker, B., & Whalen, C. K. (1984). Self-control in hyperactive boys in anger-inducing situations: Effects of cognitive-behavioral training and of methylphenidate. *Journal of Abnormal Child Psychology, 12,* 55–77.

Hohman, L. B. (1922). Post encephalitic behavior disorders in children. *Johns Hopkins Hospital Bulletin, 380,* 372–375.

Holborow, P., & Berry, P. A. (1986). Multinational, cross-cultural perspective on hyperactivity. *American Journal of Orthopsychiatry, 56,* 320–322.

King, C., & Young, D. (1982). Attentional deficits with and without hyperactivity: Teacher and peer perceptions. *Journal of Abnormal Child Psychology, 10,* 483–496.

Klorman, R., Brumaghim, J. T., Salzman, L. F., et al. (1988). Effects of methylphenidate on attention-deficit hyperactivity disorder with and without aggressive/noncompliant features. *Journal of Abnormal Psychology, 97,* 413–422.

Lahey, B. B., & Carlson, K. (1991). Validity of a diagnostic category of attention deficit disorder without hyperactivity: A review of the literature. *Journal of Learning Disabilities, 24,* 110–120.

Lahey, B. B., Pelham, W. E., Schaughency, E. A., et al. (1988). Dimensions and types of attention deficit disorder. *Journal of the American Academy of Child and Adolescent Psychiatry, 27,* 330–335.

Lahey, B. B., Schaughency, E. A., Hynd, G. W., et al. (1987). Attention deficit disorder with and without hyperactivity: Comparison of behavioral characteristics of clinic-referred children. *Journal of the American Academy of Child and Adolescent Psychiatry, 26,* 718–723.

Lahey, B. B., Stempniak, M., Robinson, E. J., & Tyroler, M. J. (1978). Hyperactivity and learning disabilities as independent dimensions of child behavior problems. *Journal of Abnormal Psychology, 87,* 333–340.

Laufer, M., & Denhoff, E. (1957). Hyperkinetic behavior syndrome in children. *Journal of Pediatrics, 50,* 463–474.

Liberman, I. Y., & Shankweiler, D. (1985). Phonology and the problems of learning to read and write. *Remedial and Special Education, 6,* 8–17.

Loney, J. (1983). Research diagnostic criteria for childhood hyperactivity. In S. B. Guze, F. J. Earls, & J. E. Barrett (Eds.), *Childhood psychopathology and development* (pp. 109–115). New York: Raven Press.

Loney, J. (1987). Hyperactivity and aggression in the diagnosis of attention deficit disorder. In B. B. Lahey & A. E. Kazdin (Eds.), *Advances in clinical child psychology* (Vol. 10, pp. 99–135). New York: Plenum Press.

Loney, J., Langhorne, J. E., & Paternite, C. E. (1978). An empirical basis for subgrouping the hyperkinetic/MBD syndrome. *Journal of Abnormal Psychology, 87,* 431–441.

Loney, J., & Milich, R. (1982). Hyperactivity, inattention, and aggression in clinical practice. *Advances in Development and Behavioral Pediatrics, 3,* 113–147.

Mann, V. A., Cowin, E., & Schoeheimer, J. (1989). Phonological processing, language comprehension, and reading ability. *Journal of Learning Disabilities, 22,* 76–89.

McGee, R., Williams, S., Moffitt, T., & Anderson, J. (1989). A comparison of 13-year-old boys with attention deficit and/or reading disorder on neuropsychological measures. *Journal of Abnormal Child Psychology, 17,* 37–53.

McGee, R., Williams, S., & Silva, P. (1984). Behavioral and developmental characteristics of aggressive, hyperactive and aggressive-hyperactive boys. *Journal of the American Academy of Child Psychiatry, 23,* 270–279.

Meyer, A. (1904). The anatomical facts and clinical varieties of traumatic insanity. *American Journal of Insanity, 60,* 373–441.

Milich, R., Loney, J., & Landau, S. (1982). Independent dimensions of hyperactivity and aggression: A validation with playroom observation data. *Journal of Abnormal Psychology, 91,* 183–198.

Public Law 94-142. Education for All Handicapped Children Act, S.6, 94th Congress [Sec. 613(a) (4)] 1st Session, June, 1975, Report No. 94–168.

Reeves, J. C., Werry, J. S., Elkind, G. S., & Zametkin, A. (1987). Attention deficit, conduct, oppositional, and anxiety disorders in children: II. Clinical characteristics. *Journal of the American Academy of Child and Adolescent Psychiatry, 26,* 144–155.

Reynolds, C. R. (1984). Critical measurement issues in learning disabilities. *The Journal of Special Education, 18,* 451–476.

Rourke, B. P. (1989). *Nonverbal learning disabilities: The syndrome and the model.* New York: Guilford Press.

Rutter, M. (1970). Psychological development-predictions from infancy. *Journal of Child Psychology and Psychiatry, 11,* 49–62.

Safer, D. J., & Allen, R. D. (1976). *Hyperactive children: Diagnosis and management.* Baltimore: University Park Press.

Safer, D. J., & Krager, J. M. (1988). A survey of medication treatment for hyperactive/inattentive students. *Journal of the American Medical Association, 260,* 2256–2258.

Sandberg, S. T., Rutter, M., & Taylor, E. (1978). Hyperkinetic disorder in psychiatric clinic attenders. *Developmental Medicine and Child Neurology, 20,* 279–299.

Sandoval, J., & Lambert, N. M. (1984–1985). Hyperactive and learning disabled children: Who gets help? *The Journal of Special Education, 18,* 495–503.

Schachar, R., Rutter, M., & Smith, A. (1981). The characteristics of situationally and pervasively hyperactive children: Implications for syndrome definition. *Journal of Child Psychology and Psychiatry, 22,* 375–392.

Schneider, W., & Shiffrin, R. M. (1977). Controlled and automatic human information processing: I. Detection, search and attention. *Psychological Review, 84,* 1–66.

Share, D. L., & Schwartz, S. (1988). A note on the distinction between attention deficit disorder and reading disability: Are there group-specific cognitive deficits? *Brain and Language, 34,* 350–352.

Shaywitz, S. E. (1986). Early recognition of vulnerability—EREV (Technical report to Connecticut State Department of Education). New Haven, CT: Yale University.

Shaywitz, S. E. (1989). A rational basis for the identification of learning disabled students at selective institutions. In R. Crooks (Ed.), *The next step: An invitational symposium on learning disabilities in selective colleges. Proceedings.*

Shaywitz, S. E., Escobar, M. D., Shaywitz, B. A., & Fletcher, J. M. (in press). Evidence that dyslexia may represent the lower tail of a normal distribution of reading ability. *New England Journal of Medicine, 326,* 145–150.

Shaywitz, S. E., & Shaw, R. (1988). The admissions process: An approach to selecting learning disabled students at the most selective colleges. *Learning Disabilities Focus, 3,* 81–86.

Shaywitz, S. E., & Shaywitz, B. A. (1987). *Hyperactivity/attention deficit disorder in learning disabilities: A report to the U.S. Congress prepared for the Interagency Committee on Learning Disabilities.* Washington, DC: U.S. Government Printing Office.

Shaywitz, S. E., & Shaywitz, B. A. (1988). Increased medication use in attention-deficit hyperactivity disorder: Regressive or appropriate? *Journal of the American Medical Association, 260,* 2270–2272.

Shaywitz, B. A. & Shaywitz, S. E. (1989). Learning disabilities and attention disorders. In K. F. Swaiman (Ed.), *Pediatric neurology* (Vol. II, pp. 857–894). St. Louis: Mosby.

Sternberg, S. (1969). Discovery of processing stages: Extensions of Donders' method. In W. G. Koster (Ed.), *Attention and performance* (Vol. 2, pp. 276–315). Amsterdam: North-Holland.

Sternberg, S. (1975). Memory scanning: New findings and current controversies. *Quarterly Journal of Exp. Psychology, 27,* 1–32.

Still, G. F. (1902). The Coulstonian lectures on some abnormal physical conditions in children. *Lancet, 1,* 1008–1012, 1077–1082, 1163–1168.

Strauss, A. A., & Lehtinen, L. E. (1947). *Psychopathology and education in the brain-injured child.* New York: Grune & Stratton.

Szatmari, P., Boyle, M., & Offord, D. R. (1989). ADDH and conduct disorder: Degree of diagnostic overlap and differences among correlates, *Journal of the American Academy of Child and Adolescent Psychiatry, 28,* 865–872.

Taylor, E. A. (1986). Attention deficit. In E. A. Taylor (Ed.), *The overactive child* (pp. 73–106). Philadelphia: Lippincott.

Taylor, E., Everitt, B., Thorley, G., et al. (1986). Conduct disorder and hyperactivity: II. A cluster analytic approach to the identification of a behavioural syndrome. *British Journal of Psychiatry, 149,* 768–777.

Taylor, E., Schachar, R., Thorley, G., & Wieselberg, M. (1986). Conduct disorder and hyperactivity: I. Separation of hyperactivity and antisocial conduct in British child psychiatric patients. *British Journal of Psychiatry, 149,* 760–767.

Thorndike, R. L. (1963). *The concepts over- and under-achievement.* New York: Bureau of Publications, Teachers College, Columbia University.

Trites, R. L., & LaPrade, K. (1983). Evidence for an independent syndrome of hyperactivity. *Journal of Child Psychology and Psychiatry, 24,* 573–586.

U.S. Office of Education, Assistance to states for education for handicapped children: Procedures for evaluating specific learning disabilities. Federal Register 1977; 42:62082-62085.

van der Meere, J., van Baal, M., & Sergeant, J. (1989). The additive factor method: A differential diagnostic tool in hyperactivity and learning disability. *Journal of Abnormal Child Psychology, 17,* 409–422.

Vellutino, F. R. (1978). Toward an understanding of dyslexia: Psychological factors in specific reading disability. In A. L. Benton & D. Pearl (Eds.), *Dyslexia: An appraisal of current knowledge,* (pp. 61–111). New York: Oxford University Press.

Vellutino, F. R. (1979). *Dyslexia: Theory and research.* Cambridge, MA: MIT Press.

Vellutino, F. R., & Scanlon, D. (1987). Phonological coding and phonological awareness and reading ability: Evidence from a longitudinal and experimental study. *Merrill-Palmer Quarterly, 33,* 321–363.

Wechsler, D. (1974). *Wechsler intelligence scale for children–Revised*. New York: Psychological Corp.

Werner, H., & Strauss, A. A. (1941). Pathology of the figure-background relation in the child. *Journal of Abnormal Social Psychology, 36*, 236–248.

Werry, J. S., Reeves, J. C., & Elkind, G. S. (1987). Attention deficit, conduct, oppositional and anxiety disorders in children: I. A review of research on differentiating characteristics. *Journal of the American Academy of Child and Adolescent Psychiatry, 26*, 133–143.

Whalen, C. K. (1989). Attention deficit and hyperactivity disorders. In T. H. Ollendick & M. Hersen (Eds.), *Handbook of child psychopathology*, (2nd ed., pp. 131–169). New York: Plenum Press.

Wood, F. B., Felton, R. H., & Brown, I. S. (1988). The dissociation of attention deficit disorder from reading disability: A reply to Share and Schwartz. *Brain and Language, 34*, 353–358.

Woodcock, R. W., & Johnson, M. B. (1977). *Woodcock-Johnson psycho-educational battery*. Hingham, MA: Teaching Resources.

PART 3

Academic Competencies and Strategy Instruction

"Reeling and Writhing, of course, to begin with," the Mock Turtle replied; and then the different branches of Arithmetic—Ambition, Distraction, Uglification, and Derision.

(*Lewis Carroll,* Alice in Wonderland)

S trategic learning is not free of context and frequently occurs in relation to the academic areas of reading, writing, and mathematics. Over the years, most work has focused on language and reading disorders, and a large body of literature has been amassed concerning different theories of reading disabilities. In contrast, writing and mathematics have received less attention, and there has been limited exploration of the interactions among automatic memory, mechanical skills, and strategic learning in these academic areas. The chapters in this section address such issues in a comprehensive manner and will hopefully stimulate more research of relevance to these topics.

In Chapter 9, Annemarie Palincsar, Judith Winn, Yvonne David, Barbara Snyder, and Dannelle Stevens review six strategy instruction systems for improving reading ability. They summarize an exploratory study that compares three of these models, and their findings demonstrate that students with learning disabilities benefit as much from structured systems as they do from holistic reading approaches. In contrast, good readers flourish when holistic methods of instruction are used.

In Chapter 10, Steve Graham and Karen Harris emphasize the importance of addressing cognitive, behavioral, and affective processes when strategy instruction occurs in the various academic areas, particularly written output. They also address an issue that is of critical importance for strategy instruction—namely, transfer and generalizability—and they emphasize that students and teachers must all value the strategies taught. They recommend more in-classroom research to ensure ecological validity, as little information is available currently regarding which student characteristics reliably predict who will benefit from which strategies.

In Chapter 11, Bethany Roditi discusses the importance of an applied developmental approach for the understanding, identification, and teaching of students with learning disabilities. Mathematics deficits are discussed within the broad framework of language, automatic memory, and problem-solving approaches, and data are presented that demonstrate the combined influence of these processes on mathematics performance. To emphasize the important links between theory and practice, a case study is detailed and specific assessment and teaching approaches are discussed.

The chapters in this section highlight the importance of ongoing research that is classroom based, ecologically valid, and addresses the critical issue of strategy generalizability and transfer. All chapters emphasize the need to broaden existing teaching models to account for the cognitive, motivational, behavioral, and social components of learning as they impact on the acquisition of reading, writing, and mathematics skills. When learning and strategy instruction are considered within such a multidimensional framework, transfer and generalizability of specific teaching methods can occur.

9

Approaches to Strategic Reading Instruction Reflecting Different Assumptions Regarding Teaching and Learning

*Annemarie Sullivan Palincsar,
Judith Winn, Yvonne David,
Barbara Snyder, Dannelle Stevens*

With each decade the instructional agenda attending the teaching of reading is redefined to include increasingly lofty goals. As Resnick and Resnick (1977) reminded us, it was not until the 1920s that the emphasis on reading for the purpose of deriving meaning from text emerged as a goal for reading instruction. In previous years, reading was valued principally for mastery of a very lim-

The research reported in this chapter was supported, in part, by OSE Grant No. G008400648 from the Department of Education. The authors are grateful to the third-grade teachers, Ms. Jury and Ms. Graven, for their cooperation in the completion of this research. Please send correspondence regarding this chapter to A. Palincsar, 1360F SEB, University of Michigan, 610 East University, Ann Arbor, MI 48109.

ited set of prescribed, religious texts. Today, discussions of the goals of reading instruction turn to "high literacy" or the pursuit of learning that is beyond that of adapting to the goals of the prevailing culture (Bereiter & Scardamalia, 1987) and "critical literacy" or the ability to use reading and writing to go beyond the demands associated with minimum competency (McGinley & Tierney, 1989). Integral to the dialogue regarding the goals of literacy instruction is the tenet that every child has the right to this level of literacy, not simply "bright children," "normally achieving children," or the children of majority culture or middle-class families.

Essential to the attainment of high or critical literacy is the ability to engage in intentional self-regulated learning with an awareness of the variables that influence learning and an ability to take control of one's activity as a learner (Palincsar & Brown, 1989). In the field of learning disabilities, strategy instruction has assumed prominence as the means by which we can help children experiencing difficulty to become self-regulatory in their learning activities. Within the reading domain, the purpose of strategy instruction is to provide students with methods for organizing and transforming information in a range of reading situations (Stone, 1989).

Although few professionals contest the goals of strategy instruction, the methods for achieving these goals are more controversial. For example, Poplin (1988), in her critique of diagnostic and instructional procedures employed in the area of learning disabilities, has decried the overapplication of reductionist thinking with its underlying tenet that human learning can be broken into component parts. Stone (1989) has urged that prolepsis, or teaching in anticipation of competence, assume a more significant role in instruction. Common to many of these criticisms are the assumed and ascribed roles of learners and teachers in instruction. This chapter reports on an exploratory study (Palincsar, David, Winn, & Stevens, 1989) in which teaching and learning were represented along a continuum with teacher control at one end of the continuum and student control at the other. The purpose of the study was to evaluate the implementation process as well as the differential effects of using three approaches for instructing heterogeneous groups of third-grade students to be strategic in their reading activity.

Before discussing this study, background information is provided regarding self-regulation in reading, the characteristics of children experiencing reading difficulty, the instructional match between the goals of strategy instruction and the needs of poor readers, and finally, an overview of traditional approaches to strategy instruction in reading.

Self-Regulation in Reading

Self-regulated readers are able to use three principal types of knowledge in a flexible manner: (a) knowledge of strategies for accomplishing learning tasks efficiently; (b) metacognitive knowledge of one's own learner characteristics and the task demands, which enables the reader to select, employ, monitor, and evaluate strategy use; and (c) real-world knowledge (Brown, Campione, & Day, 1981; Pressley, Borkowski, & Schneider, 1987). In addition, the self-regulated learner demonstrates the motivation to employ this knowledge effectively (Paris & Oka, 1986).

A sizable literature, employing interview, self-report, and measures of on-line processing of text, documents the failure of students with reading difficulties to display the knowledge, beliefs, and behaviors that characterize self-regulated learners. For example, Paris and Jacobs (1984), obtained significant correlations between metacognitive knowledge and reading achievement among third and fifth graders. Students with higher metacognitive awareness also had higher scores on comprehension measures. Good and poor reader differences have been found with regard to sensitivity to a variety of text features. Good readers, when compared with poor readers, are able to discriminate among idea units in text in terms of their relative importance; they are sensitive to the level of difficulty of text and the organization of text (Bransford, Stein, Shelton, & Owings, 1980; Brown & Smiley, 1977). Garner (1980) and August, Flavell, and Clift (1984) have documented significant good and poor reader differences in the detection of inconsistencies in text due to the failure of the poor readers to monitor for comprehension. A number of studies reported by Garner and her colleagues (e.g., Garner & Reis, 1981; Garner, Wagoner, & Smith, 1983) have suggested differences in good and poor readers' knowledge and effective use of strategies while reading.

Although these metacognitive and strategy deficits cannot be identified as the cause of all reading problems (Swanson, 1989; Wong, 1986), there is substantial evidence that many poor readers, in comparison with more capable readers, are not as aware of the variables that interact in reading and do not engage in the strategic activity that enhances reaching.

Given these differences among good and less capable readers, it is important to consider the instruction provided poor readers. To what extent does their instruction focus on self-regulation in reading activity?

The Nature of Instruction Provided for Poor Readers

Research investigating the nature of reading instruction provided for poor readers has indicated a general lack of attention to the knowledge, beliefs, and learning activities associated with self-regulation. In fact, the observational research in this area has suggested the possibility of differential instructional effects (Brown, Palincsar, & Purcell, 1985). For example, Allington and McGill-Franzen (1989), have reported differences in the opportunities good and poor readers have to engage in sustained reading as well as differences in the manner in which teachers interact with good and poor readers during reading instruction. For example, teachers are more likely to interrupt poor readers during oral reading, even when their errors are semantically appropriate. Although teachers were observed to encourage good readers to use semantic and syntactic analysis to decode words, poor readers were prompted to focus on graphophonemic cues. The questions teachers asked of good readers promoted inferential thinking on the part of the students, whereas poor readers were asked questions requiring recall of factual information.

Analyzing the discourse occurring among third-grade reading groups, Collins (1982) observed that the discussions were less collaborative in the low than in the high reading groups. Teachers incorporated fewer of the lower students' responses into subsequent questions, thus reducing the likelihood of dialogue. Although the discussions among high reading groups fostered the conceptualization of reading as problem solving and provided opportunities for students to become actively engaged in problem-solving activity while reading, there were few occasions for this to occur among the poor readers.

A particularly alarming finding emerges from studies of the reading instruction occurring in special education settings where it has been observed that little reading instruction even takes place. Leinhart, Zigmond, and Cooley (1981) examined reading instruction in primary self-contained learning disabilities classrooms. Although there was variability, on the average, students were involved in reading activities for only 10% of their days, averaging 16 minutes of reading a day.

Replicating the study by Leinhart et al. (1981), Haynes and Jenkins (1986) examined the reading instruction provided fourth through sixth graders in resource room programs. Although students were involved in reading activities for 44% of the time they were scheduled for resource room instruction, the majority of this activity took place in the form of independent seatwork. Ysseldke, Thurlow, O'Sullivan, and Christensen (1989) confirmed that special education students spend significantly more time engaged in independent seatwork (14.7% to 25.8% of the time) than in teacher-led activities (4.0% to 10.0% of their time).

In a comparison of the opportunities to read and write in special education and Chapter One elementary and middle school programs, Allington and McGill-Franzen (1989) determined that special education students received fewer minutes of reading instruction than did Chapter One students as a consequence of the reading time special education students missed in the general education classroom. The special education teachers engaged in the smallest proportion of active teaching and provided the largest proportion of seatwork activities. In both special education and Chapter One settings, seatwork activities were judged to be undifferentiated, not designed to meet individual needs.

In a study designed to investigate the amount of time teachers, who had been prepared in their teacher education programs to conduct strategy instruction, actually engaged in strategy instruction, Swanson (1984) determined that the mean percentage of time spent in strategy instruction was less than 10%. Less than 3% of teacher-student interaction addressed metacognitive variables such as the nature of the task the children were engaged in, the relationship between the task and strategies that would promote success with that task, and self-monitoring. These findings were particularly striking given that the teachers observed in this study were unanimous in rating strategy instruction as very important for their students.

In summary, despite the evidence suggesting that students with reading difficulty need to be taught the knowledge and activity that facilitate self-regulation in reading, this instruction is not occurring in general or special education settings. Juxtaposed with this body of observational research regarding the dearth of strategy instruction, is a significant body of intervention research indicating that special education students do indeed respond to strategy instruction. In the next portion of this chapter, we examine several approaches to strategy instruction that have been investigated in the reading domain.

Models of Strategy Instruction

The approaches to strategy instruction that will be considered include (a) direct instruction, (b) cognitive behavior modification, (c) the strategies intervention model, (d) direct explanation, (e) informed strategies for learning, and (f) reciprocal teaching. An overview of each approach will be presented as well as a summary of investigations of each approach.

Direct Instruction

In direct instruction, the steps of the strategies targeted for instruction are presented in a sequential fashion, generally determined through a task analysis. The teacher, typically using scripts for initial presentation and systematic error correction procedures, defines each step of the strategy and models its use. Students practice these steps as the teacher provides, and eventually fades, prompts. Each step of the strategy is practiced until the students attain mastery before attempting the next step. Evaluation of performance is based on whether or not the students are following the identified steps. Evaluation is conducted by the teacher who corrects errors immediately, principally by referring to the rules or heuristics used in the initial presentation of the procedures. A hallmark of direct instruction is the active and directive role assumed by the teacher.

> The teacher, in a face-to-face, reasonably formal manner, tells, shows, models, demonstrates, *teaches* the skill to be learned. The key word here is *teacher*, for it is the teacher who is in command of the learning situation and leads the lesson, as opposed to having instruction "direct" by a worksheet, kit, learning center, or workbook. (Baumann, 1988, p. 714)

The effects of direct instruction have been investigated with general and special education students learning an array of comprehension strategies such as identifying the main idea (Baumann, 1984), understanding anaphoric relationships (Baumann, 1986), critical reading (Darch & Kaneenui, 1987; Patching, Kaneenui, Carnine, Gersten, & Colvin, 1983), and study skills (Adams, Carnine, & Gersten, 1982). Typically, the comparative condition in these studies has been a form of traditional instruction as represented by commercial language arts curricula. The results of these studies indicate that direct instruction is an effective means of teaching the targeted comprehension skills. Both normally achieving and below average readers have mastered the skills presented. What is less clear from these studies is what the students have gained beyond learning the targeted strategies; that is, the extent to which their ability to understand and recall text has been enhanced as a consequence of the direct instruction of particular strategies. In part, the results are inconclusive as a function of the measures included. Those direct instruction studies that have included measures of generalization beyond the targeted strategies (Adams et al., 1982) suggest that improvement is typically limited to the targeted strategies; that is, students who have demonstrated mastery of the targeted strategies have not concurrently indicated enhanced comprehension and recall of text, nor have they displayed the flexibility necessary to use the targeted strategies in novel contexts.

Cognitive Behavior Modification

Like direct instruction, cognitive behavior modification (CBM), has become a widely encompassing term, used by some (e.g., Ryan, Weed, & Short, 1986) to refer to all self-instruction programs. Traditionally, a cognitive behavior modification approach is one in which students come to regulate their performance by means of internalizing a prescribed set of monitoring statements (once again determined through task analysis) before, during, and after performing a task.

The procedural steps of cognitive behavior modification, as identified by Meichenbaum (1985), include: (a) An adult model performs the task while thinking aloud; (b) the child performs the same task with external guidance from the adult; (c) the child performs the task, instructing herself or himself aloud while doing so; (d) the child performs the task while whispering instructions to herself or himself; and (e) the child performs the task using private, inner speech.

The development of cognitive behavior modification was influenced by several theoretical perspectives on learning (Meichenbaum, 1985; Meichenbaum & Asarnow, 1979). Social learning theory emphasized the importance of students' cognitions in facilitating self-control, drawing researchers' attention from overt behaviors to the ways in which students were mediating these behaviors. The research on verbal mediation pointed to the importance of teaching for production and use of mediators as well as task comprehension. A third influence was the focus of the Soviet psychologists Vygotsky (1978) and Luria (1976) on the shift of psychological functions from the interpersonal to intrapersonal levels. Luria proposed that this shift occurred in three phases. First, the adult's speech controls the child's behavior. Second, the child is directed by his or her own overt speech. Finally, this speech, and thus the control, becomes internalized.

Cognitive behavior modification has been implemented in the instruction of study skills (Dansereau et al., 1979) and error detection (Miller, 1985; Miller, Giovenco, & Rentiers, 1987). For example, in the error detection task (Miller, 1985), children were taught to internalize five statements designed to (a) define the problem; (b) identify an approach to the problem—"As I read I will ask myself if there is anything wrong with this story"; (c) evaluate the approach; (d) engage in self-reinforcement; and (e) evaluate task completion. Characteristically, instruction proceeded from experimenter modeling and oral description of the steps to joint oral labeling of the steps to, finally, subvocalized identification of the steps. The results of investigations of cognitive behavior modification indicate that it is an effective means of strategy instruction, particularly when used with above average learners. The CBM research has not addressed issues related to flexibility of strategy use, generalized use of instructed strategies, nor changes in reading awareness and attitudes following instruction. These are particularly important considerations given the inefficient and inflexible strategy use frequently indicated by students identified as having learning disabilities (Meltzer, Solomon, Fenton, & Levine, 1989).

The Strategies Intervention Model

The strategies intervention model, developed at the University of Kansas Institute for Research in Learning Disabilities (Deshler & Lenz, 1989; Deshler & Schumaker, 1986), has emerged from an extensive research program focused on the academic performance of students identified as having learning disabilities and low achievement. The model addresses both academic and social goals: (a) to foster independent learning by teaching specific learning strategies; (b) to promote skill in specific social strategies by teaching strategies appropriate to social interaction; (c) to empower students to earn high school diplomas; and (d) to enable students to be successful in the transition from high school to postsecondary life (Deshler & Schumaker, 1986).

In the academic domain, the specific reading strategies that have been taught include word identification, visual imagery, paraphrasing, interpreting visual aids, and learning from text. As in direct instruction and cognitive behavior modification, the strategies are taught as a series of sequenced steps. As with cognitive behavior modification, self-evaluation is embedded within the steps. Unlike direct instruction and CBM, the strategies intervention model comprises two phases of instruction. In the first, or acquisition phase, the focus is on teaching students the knowledge to apply the strategy in a supported setting, outside of the general classroom. In the second, or generalization phase, students learn to apply the strategy in the general education setting. The strategies intervention model is also distinguished by the fact that instruction is preceded by assessment regarding the students' current approach to a particular activity. The remaining steps in the instruction of the strategies are comparable to those employed in direct instruction and CBM, including the use of description of the strategy, modeling its use, verbal rehearsal of the steps, and guided practice and feedback with materials controlled for complexity, length, and difficulty. Similar to direct instruction, mastery criteria are used to determine when the student can proceed to more difficult materials. In keeping with the interest that the Kansas research team has regarding generalized use of instructed strategies, their dependent measures have included assessments not only of strategy acquisition, but also of the effects of strategy acquisition on the learning of both ability-level and grade-level text. Results of their investigations indicate that this sustained instruction is successful in improving strategy use as well as content learning (see Deshler, Chap. 12 of this volume).

Direct Explanation

Direct explanation (Duffy et al., 1986; Duffy et al., 1987) is distinguished from the other models of strategy instruction presented in this section in several respects. It is an approach suggesting that any skill can be recast as a strategy. To do so, the teacher must explicitly provide declarative knowledge (i.e., inform the students about the name of the strategy, the purpose for which it would be useful, steps to deploying the strategy), procedural knowledge (i.e., teach the students how to use the strategy), and conditional knowledge (i.e., inform the students about when the strategy would be appropriately used). To teach the skills as strategies, the teachers "talk aloud" about the mental processes they use when they are experiencing difficulty understanding text, how application of the skill can increase comprehension, and what mental steps should be taken to use the skills strategically. This process occurs in five steps: (a) The teacher introduces the focus of the lesson, providing declarative and conditional information about the strategy to be presented; (b) the teacher models the use of the strategy, emphasizing the reasoning involved in applying it to a comprehension problem; (c) the teacher provides guided practice, correcting students who are having difficulty by again returning to the thought processes helpful in using the strategy; finally, (d) the students receive independent practice and (e) opportunities to apply the strategy.

The following passage illustrates how the teacher models the thinking involved in using a strategy, specifically the strategy of using context clues to determine the meaning of a word.

> I want to show you what I do when I come to a word I don't know the meaning of. I'll talk out loud to show you how I figure it out. [Teacher reads] "The cocoa steamed fragrantly." [Teacher says] "Hmmm, I've heard that word 'fragrantly' before, but I don't really know what it means here. I know one of the words right before it though, 'steamed.' I watched a pot of boiling water once and there was steam coming from it. The water was hot, this must have something to do with the cocoa being hot. Okay, the pan of hot cocoa is steaming on the stove. That means steam is coming up

and out, but that still doesn't explain what 'fragrantly' means. Let me think about the hot cocoa on the stove and try to use what I know about cocoa as a clue. Hot cocoa bubbles, steams, and smells! Hot cocoa smells good! [Teacher rereads] 'The cocoa steamed fragrantly.' That means it smelled good!" (Duffy & Roehler, 1987, p. 517)

Direct explanation has been investigated with third- and fifth-grade teachers working with their lowest groups of readers. Students in the experimental groups showed significantly greater procedural and conditional knowledge regarding strategies. In addition, their scores were significantly higher than control students' on a concept interview that assessed their awareness of the strategic nature of reading. Finally, measures of reading achievement were somewhat mixed, with experimental students scoring significantly higher on the word study subtest of a reading achievement test (the Gates-MacGinitie) but not the comprehension subtest of this measure.

Direct explanation attends to the instruction of strategies in a more holistic fashion than the other models reviewed thus far. In addition, emphasis is placed on the thinking processes, rather than the steps or procedures alone.

Informed Strategies for Learning

Informed strategies for learning (ISL) represents a curricular approach to strategy instruction (Paris, 1986; Paris, Cross, & Lipson, 1984). Specifically, ISL consists of 20 modules addressing four comprehension processes: planning for reading, identifying meaning, reasoning while reading, and monitoring comprehension. Each module highlights a different strategy (e.g., finding the main idea), and each strategy is taught in three lessons. The lessons inform students about the value of the strategy, provide metaphors that will assist the children to understand the strategy, offer guided practice in strategy use, and provide the occasion for applying the strategy in science and social studies content.

What distinguishes ISL from the previous methods of strategy instruction are group dialogues in which the teachers and students discuss their thoughts and feelings about the strategies and their use, emphasizing personal aspects of strategy use. Although investigations of ISL support its effectiveness in increasing children's awareness of strategies and strategy use, the results regarding reading achievement have been less encouraging.

Reciprocal Teaching

Reciprocal teaching (Brown & Palincsar, 1989; Palincsar & Brown, 1984) focuses on the instruction of four strategies that are taught and practiced as a set of complementary activities to be used flexibly as the text, the needs of the reader, and the demands of the text suggest. In contrast to direct explanation, reciprocal teaching places less emphasis on teacher explanation and greater emphasis on teachers and students collaborating to bring meaning to text.

In reciprocal teaching, teachers and students take turns leading a dialogue about the meaning of the text with which they are working. The discussion focuses on generating questions from the text, summarizing the text, clarifying portions of the text that impair understanding, and predicting upcoming content based on clues that are provided by the content and structure of the text.

Before beginning the dialogues, five lessons introduce the students to the "language" of reciprocal teaching by providing direct instruction in each strategy. When the dialogues begin, the teacher assumes principal responsibility for leading and sustaining the discussion, modeling skilled use of the strategies for the purpose of understanding the content. However, even from the first day of instruction, the children are encouraged to participate in the discussions; for example, by commenting on the teacher's summaries or suggesting additional predictions. The teacher supports each student's participation in the dialogue through the use of specific feedback, additional modeling, and explanation.

Investigations of reciprocal teaching have been conducted with at-risk students in the primary grades (as a listening activity) as well as remedial readers in middle school. Reciprocal teaching, at both levels, has resulted in significant increases in the students' ability to use the targeted strategies as well as improved comprehension scores on both standardized and criterion-referenced measures. These gains have been demonstrated to maintain over time and to generalize to settings beyond the experimental setting.

Summary

In this portion of the chapter, six models of strategy instruction were presented. Research on each of these models supports, at least to some degree, the benefits of strategy instruction with poor as well as normally achieving readers. What is not yet possible is a comparison of the relative effectiveness of these various approaches. Student outcome measures have been quite different across these studies. For example, not all studies have examined metacognitive knowledge. Even when metacognitive measures have been included across the studies, they have been conducted in disparate fashion. For example, open-ended questions were used to assess metacognitive knowledge in direct explanation research; multiple-choice questions were used in informed strategies for learning research. Although reciprocal teaching and strategies intervention research has included direct measures of strategy use, other procedures have not examined strategy use. Likewise, the array of procedures used to assess comprehension renders comparisons across the studies difficult.

The investigations have also differed in terms of the contexts in which the interventions were conducted. Although most of the procedures have been investigated in small group instruction, ISL takes place with entire classrooms of children. Although CBM and direct instruction studies have generally been conducted over several lessons, other procedures have been investigated over several months.

Although the present status of strategy instruction research does not permit empirical comparisons across the various models, this would seem an important endeavor, particularly given the low incidence of strategy instruction currently taking place in both general and special education settings. Each of the six models represents a different conception of teaching and learning, suggesting different goals of instruction and significantly different roles for teachers and students. Comparative research could inform the literature regarding the critical features of strategy instruction in addition to aiding educators to select a model or model(s) of strategy instruction most compatible with their own conceptions of teaching and learning. The final portion of this chapter presents an exploratory study that was conducted to compare the differential effects of three models of strategy instruction.

An Exploratory Study: A Comparison of Three Models of Strategy Instruction

In this investigation teaching and learning were represented along a continuum with teacher control at one end of the continuum and student control at the other end. Another way of characterizing the continuum is to suggest that reductionism prevailed at one end of the continuum and a holistic/constructivist perspective informed the other end of the continuum. Reductionism refers, in this case, to the practice of segmenting the process of learning into smaller pieces, which are practiced in an isolated manner, as in the sequential steps of teaching a strategy. The holistic/constructivist perspective represents learning as the construction of knowledge through transformation and self-regulation (Poplin, 1988) maintaining the integrity of the process to be learned. Three instructional conditions were designed to represent three locations along the continuum: (a) directed learning at the teacher-controlled/reductionist end; (b) reciprocal teaching approaching the middle of the continuum; and (c) collaborative problem solving representing student controlled/holistic/constructivist instruction.

Constant across the three instructional conditions were (a) instructional time, (b) the text with which the children were working, (c) the information regarding the purpose of the instruction, and (d) for the most part, the specific strategies in which the children were engaged. The targeted strategies included summarizing, question generating, predicting, and clarifying.

The Instructional Procedures

The first condition was directed learning. In this condition, each strategy was presented in a series of sequenced steps. The teacher provided crafted explanations and demonstrations regarding each step and guided the children's practice with each step. For example, students were taught summarizing via four steps derived from the work of Kintch and VanDijk (1978). They practiced each step with explicit as well as implicit main idea text. The teacher instructed by verbalizing the steps that were guiding her activity; for example, "The first thing I need to do is figure out the topic of this paragraph."

This condition has its theoretical roots in behaviorism as well as cognitive psychology. It typifies the reductionist approach that Poplin criticized. Emphasized in this condition is the role of the teacher as informer and the role of student as information recipient (Anderson, 1990). The support or scaffolding provided the students was a function of sequencing the instruction from easy to hard and moving on in the sequence only as the children indicated mastery with each step. Finally, this condition can best be described as activity driven; the text and the context of the reading situation did little to inform the course of instruction (cf. Poplin, 1988). The very explicit agenda was learning the strategies.

The second procedure was reciprocal teaching (Brown & Palincsar, 1989; Palincsar & Brown, 1984). Reciprocal teaching takes place in a cooperative learning group that features guided practice in applying concrete strategies to the task of text comprehension. As described earlier in this chapter, the teacher and group of students take turns leading a discussion on the content of a section of text that they are jointly attempting to understand and remember. The discussions are somewhat free-ranging but are constrained by the requirement that four strategic activities are employed in the course of the discussion: questioning, summarizing, clarifying, and predicting. The goal of the dialogues is the joint construction of meaning. The strategies provide concrete heuristics for getting the procedure going; the reciprocal nature of the procedure promotes student engagement; and the teacher modeling provides examples of expert performance. Reciprocal teaching has its roots in cognitive psychology as well as social constructivist theory, emphasizing the active role of the learner as well as the critical role played by social interactions in learning.

The third procedure is called collaborative problem solving (CPS). In collaborative problem solving, the goals of instruction were to have the students identify strategies they thought would be useful to understand and test their understanding of text. In addition to generating the strategies, the students would evaluate the effectiveness of the strategies as well as the criteria for determining their success in implementing the identified strategies.

This procedure began by providing opportunities for the students to work collaboratively and establish a participation structure that would promote collaboration. Prior to introducing text to the group, there were 2 days of the following activities. On Day 1, the children in this condition were asked to collaborate in the creation of a new animal. When the group concurred that the creature was finished, they described each feature and explained how these features would influence the animal's behavior, suggest its habitat, means of defense, and so on. The second activity involved the completion of a cloze task. Given ambiguous paragraphs with words deleted, the students were encouraged, as a group, to suggest possible solutions to the missing segments of text. As a group, the children determined whether a particular solution was reasonable and whether one solution might be more appropriate than others.

Following each of these activities, the teacher led a discussion regarding the process of working as a collaborative group and the role of individual contributions to the group effort. In addition, the teacher described the activities as problem solving and illustrated how there was often more than one satisfactory solution to each problem. Finally, the teacher introduced the concept of reading as problem solving and encouraged the students to identify the kinds of problems they might encounter as they read text and how they might solve these problems.

The students were next given descriptions of various purposes for reading (e.g., reading a story to learn more about the games children in other countries play). They were also told about two children's approaches to achieving the goal of the reading activity; for example, one child looked up all the hard words in the story, whereas another child thought about how the games were alike and different when compared to games he knew how to play. The teacher used the word *strategy* to describe the plans the children developed to reach their reading goals. The students were asked to evaluate each child's strategy by voting for the child they thought would do better. The group discussed why they voted as they did (Why might this be a helpful strategy? What is the other child doing that might not be so helpful?). Disagreements among the group members were discussed, and, following the discussion, the group was encouraged to reach consensus and to label each hypothetical child's strategy. These strategies were listed on the poster board.

In a separate lesson, to elicit additional strategies from the students, they were introduced to a robot who could read all the words, but nevertheless had no understanding of what it read. The teacher asked, "If we could program the robot to be a good reader, what would we teach the robot to do to help it to understand what it read?" The children then identified a list of strategies. The list generated by the students was combined with the list of strategies generated during the vignettes.[1] After these 3 days, the children were given the same texts that were being used in the directed learning and reciprocal teaching groups. The children discussed purposes for reading and decided which strategy they would like to implement with each segment of text. They tested out the strategy, discussed how they used the strategy, what the outcomes were, and whether or not this was an effective strategy. There was no modeling on the part of the teacher; rather, the teacher's instruction was in response to the attempts that the children made as they discussed the text. The Collaborative Problem Solving condition was informed by holistic as well as social constructivist theories of learning.

Methodology

Two classes of third-grade students from two different schools, with decoding and comprehension skills ranging from first grade through fifth grade (as measured by the *Metropolitan Reading Achievement Test*, Nurss & McGauvran, 1986), were administered an array of pretests assessing comprehension of expository text, metacognitive knowledge of reading, and strategy use. The students within each class

---

[1]The list of strategies generated by the students included memorizing, clarifying, picturing, summarizing what you already know, using punctuation, questioning (before, during, and after reading), summarizing, predicting, and using context clues.

were then placed in triads according to the results of the pretest measures, and one child from each triad was then randomly assigned to one of the three instructional conditions. This resulted in two groups of six or seven heterogeneous third graders experiencing each instructional condition.

Instruction occurred for 30 to 40 minutes a day, 3 days a week, for a total of 25 sessions. Teaching was done by the investigators assigned such that each condition was taught by more than one investigator. The text with which the children were working across the three conditions was expository passages written at the third-grade level about an array of topics that were science-like in content (e.g., "Living Lights," "Life in an Ant Nest"). In each condition, reading was conducted as a read-along to accommodate the varying decoding levels of the participants (for details, see Palincsar et al., 1989).

Issues of Implementation

Throughout this study the investigators/teachers maintained field notes regarding the instruction. In addition, all instruction was audiotaped, several lessons were videotaped, and the investigators met frequently (often daily) to discuss issues of implementation. Several issues have been selected for discussion in this chapter: ease of implementation, the participation structure, assessment of response to instruction, and group heterogeneity.

Ease of Implementation.   Researchers such as Shavelson and Stern (1981) have written about the role of uncertainty in teaching. Carrying out preselected activities, monitoring student participation, and managing student transitions constitute a full agenda for many teachers. It is difficult for teachers to simultaneously think about what children are trying to say, build upon their responses, and tailor assistance as opportunities and the need arises. Our experiences have indicated that as teachers abdicated control of the instruction and worked toward establishing intersubjectivity with the students (cf. Rommetveit, 1974), the instruction became increasingly difficult. This was particularly true of the CPS condition. A solid knowledge of the text did not ensure preparation to teach in this condition. Literally, throughout the study, the teachers had to resist the urge to plan the direction the lessons should take. Of major importance for teaching was renewing the teaching goals; vis-à-vis student generation of strategies, student identification of the heuristics for strategy implementation, student evaluation of their own success with the strategies, and student evaluation of the merits of the strategies selected. Teacher attention was focused on alternative means of assisting students to achieve these outcomes. Children's participation in determining these techniques was also solicited. For example, midway through instruction in the CPS condition, the children suggested that they work in pairs, each pair using a different strategy to compare the outcomes and evaluate the differential effectiveness of the selected strategies.

The Participation Structure. Sociolinguists and others who study classroom interactions have noted the powerful role of participation structures in classroom settings. Cazden (1986) defined the participation structure as "the rights and obligations of participants with respect to who can say what, when, and to whom" (p. 437). In this study, the directed learning condition represented a traditional participation structure; consequently, it was easily understood by all. The semistructured nature of the reciprocal teaching dialogues assisted the teachers and students in establishing the participation structure in this condition. The undefined nature of the participation structure in the CPS condition meant that it was continually evolving. The children's conceptions of this condition also differed from the teachers'. To illustrate, when one group of children in the CPS condition determined that they would summarize the text together, one child offered to write the first sentence and then passed the paper onto the next child: a case of serial collaboration. In another instance, when the children elected to generate questions in small groups within the CPS group, they were indignant when their peers had generated the same questions and accused one another of cheating. The teacher used this as an occasion to discuss why the children's questions were similar and the criteria they had used to determine these questions.

Assessment of Response to Instruction. There were striking differences across the three conditions in terms of the role that assessment of student progress played. Assessment is a critical issue to the extent that the teacher needs to be aware of each individual's response to instruction; what has each child learned about strategic activity in comprehension; with what is each child experiencing success and difficulty; what is each child internalizing in the group activity and using in his or her individual comprehension efforts (see Meltzer, Chap. 4 of this volume)?

In the directed learning condition, the teacher was aware of who was experiencing difficulty and with what. In the reciprocal teaching condition, assessment is somewhat more difficult but is eased by the children's turn taking leading the discussion. However, in CPS assessment and diagnosis of individual participants learning was much more unwieldy. However, what was open to assessment was much broader in CPS. For example, in neither of the other conditions were the naive conceptions children held about reading so available to the teacher. For example, in the CPS condition, the children's initial strategy list included: (a) Memorize every word, and (b) picture it all in your head. As the children attempted to implement these strategies, they quickly realized their shortcomings. As one child stated (regarding picturing), "We all came up with different pictures. This could be good but maybe not." They then discussed the role that the text as well as the purposes for reading played in determining whether "picturing" was a good strategy.

The Issue of Heterogeneity.   As was indicated earlier, the children were grouped heterogeneously. The reciprocal teaching and collaborative problem solving groups more easily accommodated this diversity. In fact, the multiple opportunities for children to participate at various levels were a particular advantage for lower achieving students. In the directed learning condition, teaching to mastery meant that certain children were given unnecessary instruction and practice.

There are numerous other dimensions for contrasting these three instructional conditions, including ease of motivating the children across the three conditions. Actually, this evolved as an issue peculiar to each instructional group as opposed to instructional condition. In addition, there was the tension between strategy instruction and content instruction. This tension was particularly keen in the collaborative problem solving condition where it was often difficult to maintain a balance between discussion of the content and discussion of the strategies useful to learning about the content.

The issues raised during implementation suggest that although there was something to recommend each of the instructional conditions, it is also the case that each instructional condition had its own set of problems. The costs associated with each condition increase the value of determining the outcomes of each condition.

Results

In addition to ascertaining the children's decoding ability on a pretest, there were four measures administered on a pretest and posttest basis, including (a) criterion-referenced measures of comprehension, in which the children read 450-word expository passages written at an instructional level as determined through decoding rates; (b) a two-part metacognitive interview in which the children responded to questions concerning awareness of self as a reader, awareness of strategies, sensitivity to task, and sensitivity to text features; (c) a think-aloud while reading ambiguous text that was scored for monitoring or awareness of ambiguity, paraphrasing of text, elaborations, indications of reasoning about the text, and engaging in fix-up activity during the reading of the text; and, finally, (d) strategy measures in which the children were asked to read extended text and generate predictions, questions, a summary, and issues for clarification.

All scoring was conducted blind to the child, instructional condition, and time of administration. Interrater reliability was obtained by working through specimen sets as a group before scoring independently. All measures were scored by two independent raters, and differences were resolved through further discussion.

The results indicate that there were no significant differences across the six groups on any of pretest measures. Instruction had a significant positive effect for the criterion-referenced, metacognitive, strategy, and standardized measures but not for the think-aloud, across the three instructional conditions. Further analyses examining whether one of the three instructional conditions was more effective than the other two indicated that only one measure was sensitive to differential outcomes. For these heterogeneous groups of students, the collaborative problem solving condition was the most effective, as determined by changes on the criterion-referenced measure. When inquiring about differential effects according to the entering achievement levels of the students, the analyses indicated that, overall, lower achieving students showed greater gains from instruction than higher achieving students on all but the metacognitive measure, regardless of the instructional condition. Finally, when asking about main effects for instructional condition when the sample is divided into lowest and highest achieving thirds, the analyses indicated that, for the strategy measure alone, direct instruction was not as effective as reciprocal teaching nor collaborative problem solving for high-achieving students. There were no significant differences among the instructional conditions for low-achieving students.

In this study different visions of what it means to nudge students from one level of competence to another within their own zones of proximal development were explored. Each vision constituted a different definition of what it means to teach children to be strategic readers. In addition, each vision depicted a significantly different role in instruction for the teacher, peer group, and learner. What was learned? First, as important as collecting outcome data was the systematic collection of implementation data. Second, the complexity of the outcomes (only hinted at in this chapter) serves as a reminder that conclusions from this type of research cannot be drawn summarily. Furthermore, although this research will require replication, the trends suggest that the most taxing (vis-à-vis the teachers) of the instructional conditions was the most productive for these heterogeneous groups of learners.

Conclusion

The literature regarding the reading profiles of children who are experiencing difficulty with comprehension activity suggests that there is an important place for teaching these children to engage in self-regulatory activity. There are numerous models in the research literature for teaching children to be strategic readers. Each of these models has garnered some degree of empirical support. Unfortunately, classroom observational studies suggest that strategy instruction is not yet prominent in special education and remedial settings.

The exploratory study reported in this chapter suggests that teachers actually have several options to pursue when engaging in strategy instruction. The choice teachers make among various models of strategy instruction needs to be informed by a number of factors. One such factor is the match between the model and the teacher's beliefs about how children learn and the role the teacher perceives for himself or herself in this instruction. Although special education teachers may be more familiar with reductionistic teaching methods (due to the longstanding influence that behaviorism has had in special education), the work reported in this chapter suggests that lower achieving students were as responsive to more holistic and constructivist models of instruction as they were to a reductionist model. Furthermore, for heterogeneous groups of students, the holistic/constructivist model had the edge over the reductionist model, as indicated by the comprehension assessment that most closely parallels the way in which teachers evaluate reading comprehension. The heterogeneity issue is an important one, to the extent that, with the decreased emphasis on "pullout" models, there is increased interest in service delivery models that would result in more heterogeneously grouped students.

The challenge for teachers and researchers is the design of instructional interventions that incorporate the most positive features of strategy instruction. Ideally, instruction should include opportunities to (a) examine children's conceptions of the activity in which they are engaged; (b) provide opportunities for flexible and opportunistic practice of strategic reading; and (c) solicit students' partnerships in learning.

References

Adams, A., Carnine, D., & Gersten, R. (1982). Instructional strategies for studying content area texts in the middle grades. *Reading Research Quarterly, 18*(1), 27–55.

Allington, R. (1980). Teacher interruption behavior during primary-grade oral reading. *Journal of Educational Psychology, 72,*(3), 371–377.

Allington, R. L., & McGill-Franzen, A. (1989). School response to reading failure: Instruction for Chapter 1 and special education students in Grades two, four, and eight. *Elementary School Journal, 89*(5), 529–542.

Anderson, L. M. (1990). Implementing instructional programs to promote meaningful, self-regulated learning. In J. Brophy (Ed.), *Advances in research on teaching: Vol. 1. Teaching for meaningful learning and self-regulation.* Greenwich, CT: JAI Press.

August, D. L., Flavell, J. H., & Clift, R. (1984). Comparison of comprehension monitoring of skilled and less skilled readers. *Reading Research Quarterly, 20*(1), 39–53.

Baumann, J. F. (1984). The effectiveness of a direct instruction paradigm for teaching main idea comprehension. *Reading Research Quarterly, 2*(1), 93–115.

Baumann, J. F. (1986). Teaching third-grade students to comprehend anaphoric relationships: The application of a direct instruction model. *Reading Research Quarterly, 21*(1), 70–90.

Baumann, J. F. (1988). Direct instruction reconsidered. *Journal of Reading Behavior, 31*(8), 712–718.

Bereiter, C., & Scardamalia, M. (1987). An attainable version of high literacy: Approaches to teaching higher-order skills in reading and writing. *Curriculum Inquiry, 17,*(1), 9–30.

Bransford, J. D., Stein, B. S., Shelton, T. S., & Owings, R. A. (1980). Cognition and adaptation: The importance of learning to learn. In J. Harvey (Ed.), *Cognition, social behavior, and the environment* (pp. 13–25). Hillsdale, NJ: Erlbaum.

Brown, A. L., Campione, J. C., & Day, J. D. (1981). Learning to learn: On training students to learn from texts. *Educational Researcher, 10,* 14–22.

Brown, A. L., & Palincsar, A. S. (1989). Guided cooperative learning and individual knowledge acquisition. In L. Resnick (Ed.), *Knowing and learning: Issues for a cognitive psychology of learning. Essays in honor of Robert Glaser.* Hillsdale, NJ: Erlbaum.

Brown, A. L., Palincsar, A. S., & Purcell, L. (1985). Poor readers: Teach, don't label. In V. Neisser (Ed.) *The academic performance of minority children: New perspectives* (pp. 105–143). Hillsdale, NJ: Erlbaum.

Brown, A. L., & Smiley, S. S. (1977). Rating the importance of structural units of prose passages: A problem of metacognitive development. *Child Development, 48,* 1–8.

Cazden, C. (1986). Classroom discourse. In M. Wittrock (Ed.), *Handbook of research on teaching* (pp. 432–463). New York: Macmillan.

Collins, J. (1982). Discourse style, classroom interaction and differential treatment. *Journal of Reading Behavior, 14*(4), 429–437.

Dansereau, D. F., Collins, K. W., McDonald, B. A., Holley, C. D., Garland, J., Diekkoff, G., & Evans, S. H. (1979). Development and evaluation of a learning strategy training program. *Journal of Educational Psychology, 71*(1), 64–73.

Darch, C., & Kaneenui, E. J. (1987). Teaching LD students critical reading skills: A systematic replication. *Learning Disability Quarterly, 10,* 82–91.

Deshler, D. D., & Lenz, B. K. (1989). *The strategies instructional approach.* Unpublished manuscript, University of Kansas, Lawrence.

Deshler, D. D., & Schumaker, J. B. (1986). Learning strategies: An instructional alternative for low-achieving adolescents. *Exceptional Children, 52*(6), 583–590.

Duffy, G. G., & Roehler, L. R. (1987). Teaching skills as strategies. *The Reading Teacher, 40,* 514–521.

Duffy, G. G., Roehler, L. R., Meloth, M. S., Vavrus, I. G., Book, C., Putnam, J., & Wesselman, R. (1986). The relationship between explicit verbal explanations during reading skill instruction and student awareness and achievement: A study of reading teacher effects. *Reading Research Quarterly, 21*(3), 237–252.

Duffy, G. G., Roehler, L. R., Sivan, E., Rackliffe, G., Book, C., Meloth, M. S., Vavrus, I. G., Wesselman, R., Putnam, J., & Bassiri, D. (1987). Effects of explaining the reasoning associated with using reading strategies. *Reading Research Quarterly, 22*(3), 347–368.

Garner, R. (1980). Monitoring of understanding: An investigation of good and poor readers' awareness of induced miscomprehension of text. *Journal of Reading Behavior, 12*(1), 55–63.

Garner, R., & Reis, R. (1981). Monitoring and resolving comprehension obstacles: An investigation of spontaneous lookbacks among upper-grade good and poor comprehenders. *Reading Research Quarterly, 16*(4), 569–582.

Garner, R., Wagoner, S., & Smith, T. (1983). Externalizing question-answering strategies of good and poor comprehenders. *Reading Research Quarterly, 18*(4), 439–447.

Haynes, M. C., & Jenkins, J. R. (1986). Reading instruction in special education resource rooms. *American Educational Research Journal, 23,* 161–190.

Kintch, W., & VanDijk, T. A. (1978). Toward a model of text comprehension and production. *Psychological Review, 85,* 363–394.

Leinhart, G., Zigmond, N., & Cooley, W. (1981). Reading instruction and its effects. *American Educational Research Journal, 18,* 343–361.

Luria, A. R. (1976). *Cognitive development: Its cultural and social foundations.* Cambridge, MA: Harvard University Press.

McGinley, W., & Tierney, R. J. (1989). Traversing the topical landscape. *Written Communication, 6*(3), 243–269.

Meichenbaum, D. (1985). Teaching thinking: A cognitive-behavioral perspective. In S. F. Chipman, J. W. Segal, & R. Glaser (Eds.), *Thinking and learning skills. Vol. 2: Research and open questions.* Hillsdale, NJ: Erlbaum.

Meichenbaum, D., & Asarnow, J. (1979). Cognitive behavior modification and metacognitive development: Implications for the classroom. In P. C. Kendall & S. D. Hollan (Eds.), *Cognitive-behavioral interventions: Theory, research, and practice* (pp. 11–35). New York: Academic Press.

Meltzer, L. J., Solomon, B., Fenton, R., & Levine, M. D. (1989). A developmental study of problem-solving strategies in children with and without learning difficulties. *Journal of Applied Developmental Psychology, 10,* 171–193.

Miller, G. E. (1985). The effects of general and specific self-instruction training on children's comprehension monitoring performances during reading. *Reading Research Quarterly, 20*(5), 616–628.

Miller, G. E., Giovenco, A., & Rentiers, K. A. (1987). Fostering comprehension monitoring in below average readers through self-instruction training. *Journal of Reading Behavior, 19*(4), 379–393.

Nurss, J. R., & McGauvran, M. E. (1986). *Metropolitan tests.* Orlando, FL: Harcourt Brace Jovanovich.

Palincsar, A. S., & Brown, A. L. (1984). Reciprocal teaching of comprehension-fostering and comprehension-monitoring activities. *Cognition and Instruction, 1*(2), 117–175.

Palincsar, A. S., & Brown, A. L. (1989). Instruction for self-regulated reading. In L. B. Resnick & L. E. Klopfer (Eds.), *Toward the thinking curriculum: Current cognitive research* (pp. 19–39). Alexandria, VA: Association for Supervision and Curriculum Development.

Palincsar, A. S., David, Y. M., Winn, J. A., & Stevens, D. D. (1989, November). *Examining the differential effects of teacher- versus student-controlled activity in comprehension instruction.* A paper presented at the annual meeting of the American Educational Research Association, Boston.

Paris, S. G. (1986). Teaching children to guide their reading and learning. In T. Raphael (Ed.), *Contexts of literacy* (pp. 115–130). New York: Longman.

Paris, S. G., Cross, D. R., & Lipson, M. Y. (1984). Informed strategies for learning: A program to improve children's reading awareness and comprehension. *Journal of Educational Psychology, 76*(6), 1239–1252.

Paris, S. G., & Jacobs, J. E. (1984). The benefits of informed instruction for children's reading awareness and comprehension skills. *Child Development, 55,* 2083–2093.

Paris, S. G., & Oka, E. R. (1986). Self-regulated learning among exceptional children. *Exceptional Children, 53*(2), 103–108.

Patching, W., Kaneenui, E., Carnine, D., Gersten, R., & Colvin, G. (1983). Direct instruction in critical reading skills. *Reading Research Quarterly, 18*(4), 406–418.

Poplin, M. S. (1988). The reductionistic fallacy in learning disabilities: Replicating the past by reducing the present. *Journal of Learning Disabilities, 21*(7), 389–400.

Pressley, M., Borkowski, J. G., & Schneider, W. (1987). Cognitive strategies: Good strategy users coordinate metacognition and knowledge. In R. Vasta & G. Whitehurst (Eds.), *Annals of Child Development* (Vol. 5, pp. 89–129). Greenwich, CT: JAI Press.

Resnick, D. P., & Resnick, L. B. (1977). The nature of literacy: An historical exploration. *Harvard Educational Review, 47*(3), 370–385.

Rommetveit, R. (1974). *On message structure: A framework for the study of language and communication.* New York: Wiley.

Ryan, E. B., Weed, K. A., & Short, J. (1986). Cognitive behavior modification: Promoting active, self-regulatory learning styles. In J. Torgeson & B. Wong (Eds.), *Psychological and educational perspectives on learning disabilities* (pp. 42–60). New York: Academic Press.

Shavelson, R. J., & Stern, P. (1981). *Research on teachers' pedagogical thoughts, judgments, decisions, and behavior. Review of Educational Research, 51,* 455–498.

Stone, C. A. (1989). Improving the effectiveness of strategy training for learning disabled students: The role of communication dynamics. *Remedial and Special Education, 10*(1), 35–42.

Swanson, H. L. (1984). Does theory guide teaching practice? *Remedial and Special Education, 5*(5), 7–16.

Swanson, H. L. (1989). Strategy instructions: Overview of principles and procedures for effective use. *Learning Disability Quarterly, 12,* 3–14.

Vygotsky, L. S. (1978). *Mind in society: The development of higher psychological processes.* Cambridge, MA: Harvard University Press.

Wong, B. (1986). Metacognition and learning disabilities: A review of a view. *The Journal of Special Education, 20*(1), 9–29.

Ysseldyke, J. E., Thurlow, M. L., O'Sullivan, R., & Christensen, S. L. (1989). Teaching structures and tasks in reading instruction for students with mild handicaps. *Learning Disabilities Research, 4*(2), 78–86.

10

Teaching Writing Strategies to Students with Learning Disabilities: Issues and Recommendations

Steve Graham
Karen R. Harris

T he purpose of this chapter is to examine issues that need to be considered when teaching writing strategies to students who have difficulty with learning. Specifically, issues related to strategy selection, instruction, evaluation, and application in school-based settings are examined. Although these same issues are pertinent to strategy instruction in other academic areas, in this chapter we concentrate directly on how they affect research and instructional efforts in teaching composition strategies for planning, producing, and revising text. To better illustrate certain issues, procedures and findings from our own research are used whenever appropriate. Special attention is also directed at drafting recommendations designed to promote effective instruction as well as advance research efforts in this area.

We begin this chapter by establishing a rationale for teaching composition strategies to students with learning disabilities (LD). This is followed by a brief overview of the major programs of writing strategy research. The remainder and bulk of the chapter concentrates on issues central to the advancement of theory, research, and instruction in this area.

Why Should Writing Strategies Be Taught to Students with LD?

During the last decade, a cognitive revolution has occurred among researchers investigating educational phenomena. The cognitive science approach has been especially useful in studying complex mental processes "which all sides agree are of central concern in writing" (Scardamalia & Bereiter, 1986, p. 780). As a result, several models of writing have been put forth that emphasize the processes involved in composing (cf. Augustine, 1981; Beaugrande, 1984; Flower & Hayes, 1980). For instance, one popular conceptualization of composing is that writing is a problem-solving activity (Flower & Hayes, 1977). In developing a particular paper, for example, a writer might first develop an internal representation of the problem (i.e., write a paper that is clear and informative), including the determination of specific goals as well as ways of achieving these goals. During writing or on completion of a section or draft of the paper, success in achieving the selected goals then would be evaluated; based on this assessment, goals would be restructured as necessary. These types of mental processes occur not only during writing, but when people try to solve a wide range of problems (Flower & Hayes, 1980).

Perhaps the most influential and explicit description of the mental processes underlying the act of writing was provided by Flower and Hayes (1980). They indicated that writing is goal directed, goals are hierarchically organized, and writers use the cognitive processes of planning, translating, and revising to accomplish their goals. Planning involves various mental operations including the generation of information to write about, culling and organizing information to be included, establishing criteria for judging the text, and developing en route tactics for completing the paper. Translation involves transforming the writing plan into acceptable written English; for example, this could include putting nonverbal ideas into written form or carrying out specific goals or plans such as writing an introduction. Revising includes the writer's attempt to improve the text, ranging from editing for simple violations of written conventions to the reformulation of the structure of the whole text. The cognitive processes identified by Flower and Hayes are overlapping and recursive—planning can occur before, during, or after writing, for instance. In addition, the writer must be able to effectively manage and orchestrate these cognitive processes so that attention can be switched among these functions as well as a host of mechanical and substantive issues (Scardamalia & Bereiter, 1986).

As can be seen from these descriptions, writing is a complex and difficult task. Although even many "normally" achieving students have considerable difficulty mastering the intricacies of written language (Scardamalia & Bereiter, 1986), learning to write clearly and effectively has proven to be especially problematic for students with learning difficulties. To illustrate, most students classified as learning disabled have writing problems severe enough to impede effective communication, and these problems usually persist into adulthood (Graham & Harris, in press; Graham & MacArthur, 1987). Graham and Harris (1989a, 1990; Wong, Harris, & Graham, in press) have suggested that the writing problems of students with LD are in large part due to the following three factors.

One impediment to the writing of students with LD relates to their proficiency in text production skills. Their papers are replete with spelling, capitalization, and punctuation errors (cf. Poteet, 1979), and the quality of their penmanship is generally poor (cf. Graham, Boyer-Schick, & Tippets, 1989). Having to consciously attend to the lower level skills of producing written language can interfere with higher order cognitive processes such as planning and content generation. For example, Graham (1989b) and MacArthur and Graham (1987) found that the papers written by students with LD improved when the mechanical demands of writing were removed via dictation.

Second, students with LD further appear to lack knowledge central to the process of writing and/or have difficulties gaining access to the knowledge that they do possess. For instance, they may not know enough about the subjects they are asked to write about as illustrated by their inordinately short compositions (cf. Deno, Marston, & Mirkin, 1982) and/or they may have difficulties retrieving what they do know. Similarly, they may not have developed adequate knowledge of the characteristics of different types of writing genres (e.g., conventions, purpose, types of content, etc.) as demonstrated by their development of papers that fail to meet the basic structural requirements for common narrative and expository writing tasks (Englert & Thomas, 1988; Graham & Harris, 1989b), and/or they may be unable to gain conscious access to this knowledge. In addition, several studies have shown that students with LD have difficulties assessing their own capabilities and being able to recognize what strategies are needed and how to regulate their use (Englert, Raphael, Fear, & Anderson, 1988; Graham, Schwartz,

& MacArthur, 1990). Not surprisingly, a lack of pertinent knowledge or difficulty in accessing it can result in texts that are impoverished, incomplete, and/or inconsiderate to the needs of the reader (Graham & Harris, 1990).

It also appears that students with LD employ ineffective cognitive moves or strategies when planning or revising text. MacArthur and Graham (1987) found that these students spent very little time planning their compositions in advance of writing. Furthermore, Graham (1989b) and Thomas, Englert, and Gregg (1987) have indicated that the planning of students with LD can best be described as converting the writing task into simply telling whatever one knows. In terms of revising, their basic outlook and approach is to detect and correct mechanical and stylistic errors, and the revisions that are made have little impact on improving either the surface features or the substantive aspects of their text (Mac-Arthur & Graham, 1987; MacArthur, Graham, & Schwartz, 1989).

In this chapter we advance the proposition that how students with LD go about the process of composing and what they write can be improved by teaching them to use appropriate strategies and self-management routines independently. Effective writing involves the use and coordination of a variety of cognitive moves and processes, many of which appear to be problematic for students with LD. Moreover, writing necessitates active task involvement on the part of the author, and, unfortunately, students with LD are often characterized by a lack of active task engagement (Harris, 1982). Strategy instruction provides a good match to the task under consideration and the characteristics of these students; it provides mechanisms for promoting active task involvement on the part of poor writers and can be used to advance the development of mental processes central to effective writing.

What Writing Strategies Have Been Field-Tested with Students with LD?

At least three major programs of research have examined the effectiveness of teaching specific writing strategies to students with LD (for more detail on each see Englert & Raphael, 1988; Graham & Harris, 1989a; Schumaker, Deshler, Alley, & Warner, 1983). The strategies tested by these researchers have been designed to affect a variety of cognitive processes in writing, including self-monitoring of productivity and text appearance, content generation, framing and planning of text, text production, and editing and revising.

Several studies have examined the use of self-regulation procedures as a means for increasing the writing output and active task involvement of students with LD. Interestingly, well-known authors such as Hemingway have regulated their literary output by establishing production goals, monitoring daily output, and rewarding or punishing themselves dependent on performance (Wallace & Pear, 1977). In a study by Seabaugh and Schumaker (1981), behavioral contracting, self-recording, self-evaluation, and self-reinforcement were used to increase the number of writing lessons completed by adolescents with learning disabilities. Similarly, Harris and McElroy (1989) found that having students with LD monitor their written productivity resulted in both longer papers and higher levels of on-task behavior.

Self-regulation procedures have also been used as a mechanism for improving the overall appearance of the writing produced by students with learning disorders (cf. Anderson-Inman, Paine, & Deutchman, 1984). Blandford and Lloyd (1987), for example, reported that the neatness of the journal writing of students with LD was improved via a self-instructional procedure students used to direct and evaluate the formation and spacing of the letters in their writing as well as their posture as they wrote.

Other text production skills that have been taught via strategy instruction include sentence and paragraph production. Schumaker and Sheldon (1985) developed a strategy to guide sentence production that includes 14 different sentence formulas and mastery of a host of grammatical structures relevant to common sentence types. Questions have been raised, however, related to the utility and cost-effectiveness of this strategy (cf. Graham & Harris, 1989a). Moran, Schumaker, and Vetter (1981) developed a paragraph-writing strategy that appears to provide a relatively simple and effective means for generating different types of expository paragraphs.

The area that has been investigated most thoroughly is the use of strategies designed to promote the deployment and development of processes central to the planning of text. Planning strategies that have been successful in field tests with students with LD have included self-directed routines for generating individual words in advance and during writing that are relevant to the paper and genre under consideration (Harris & Graham, 1985), generating and organizing ideas in advance and during writing using prefabricated frames that involve prompts related to the basic elements or components included in the genre in question (Englert & Raphael, 1988; Graham & Harris, 1989b, 1989c; Graves, Montague, & Wong, 1989), and setting product goals for what the target paper would accomplish as well as articulating process goals for how the desired accomplishments would be achieved (Graham, MacArthur, Schwartz, & Voth, 1989).

Finally, several strategies have been designed to affect the editing and revising behavior of students with learning disabilities. Schumaker, et al. (1982) found that adolescents with LD improved their skills for detecting and correcting mechanical errors following instruction in an editing strategy that focused attention on capitalization, punctuation, spelling, and appearance of the paper. Graham and MacArthur (1988) reported that the quality of the essays produced by students with LD was improved by using a strategy that included self-directed prompts for improving the clarity and cohesiveness of the writer's argument, adding relevant textual material, and detecting and correcting mechanical errors. Stoddard and MacArthur (1989) found that the written products of adolescents with LD could be improved by teaching them two strategies: one for initially editing a peer's paper in terms of content, and a second (follow-up strategy) for editing the same paper for mechanics and grammar.

This brief review and other more extensive examinations of the literature (Graham & Harris, 1989a; Harris, Graham, & Pressley, in press; Wong, Harris, & Graham, in press) suggest that carefully planned strategy instruction can have a positive effect on the writing of students classified as learning disabled. However, there are still a number of issues that remain unresolved or require further examination. These are discussed next.

Teaching Writing Strategies: Issues and Recommendations

Strategy Selection

One problem that hampers classroom teachers in deciding what strategies should be taught is that the list of writing strategies that have been evaluated (using scientific methods) with students with LD is quite short. As a result, there is considerable need for researchers to locate and test additional writing strategies with these students. This should include testing the effectiveness of (a) writing strategies used by capable students that have not yet been examined scientifically; (b) writing strategies that have been shown to improve the performance of other student populations (for instance, Graham, 1989a, is presently examining the use of the Compare–Diagnose–Operate revision strategy developed by Scardamalia & Bereiter, 1983, that has been used with normally achieving students); and (c) strategies that are based on a careful analysis of the writing task, the target students, and the cognitive moves used by good writers as they negotiate the selected task.

Teachers' selection of writing strategies is further restricted because most of the strategies that have been used with students with LD have been designed to promote planning in advance of writing or revision once a first draft has been generated; relatively little effort has been aimed at helping students direct their attention to planning and revising processes while they write. Because good writers use planning, translation, and revising processes recursively (Flower & Hayes, 1980), strategies that promote switching into and out of different writing processes at appropriate times need to be investigated.

An important consideration in deciding if a particular strategy should be taught concerns the amount and quality of the evidence available to support its effectiveness. With this in mind, it should be noted that a critical aspect in establishing scientific support is replication. Unfortunately, replication studies have not been especially common in the field of learning disabilities or in terms of validating writing strategies. We are only aware of two studies that have attempted to replicate, at least in part, results obtained from previous writing strategy studies conducted with students with LD: Reynolds, Hill, Swassing, and Ward (1988) replicated the positive results obtained by Schumaker et al. (1982) when using an error-monitoring strategy with adolescents with LD; and Sawyer, Graham, and Harris (1989) replicated and extended the positive findings obtained by Graham and Harris (1989b) when using a planning strategy involving the use of a story grammar frame for generating content. Thus, although strategy instruction can have a positive impact on the writing performance of students with LD, evidence to support the selection or use of specific, individual strategies is quite limited. More attention must be given to including replication as an integral part of the process of evaluating strategy effectiveness.

Another issue that classroom teachers must confront when deciding what strategies to teach concerns how widely the strategies of interest can be applied. Pressley and his colleagues (Pressley, Goodchild, Fleet, Zajchowski, & Evans, 1989) have indicated that some strategies are *task-limited* and can be used only in very specific situations in particular domains (e.g., remembering the notes on the treble staff by using the sentence, <u>E</u>very <u>G</u>ood <u>B</u>oy <u>D</u>oes <u>F</u>ine), whereas other strategies cut across domains. These latter strategies generally include *goal-limited strategies* and *general strategies*. Goal-limited strategies are used to accomplish specific goals such as writing an entertaining story. Many of the strategies used to accomplish this goal, however, could also be used to write a term paper in history; both forms of writing, for instance, would benefit from the use of prewriting organizational strategies. General strategies such as setting goals or checking performance, on the other hand, can be applied across a wide variety of domains and can be used in conjunction with goal-limited strategies.

As these labels imply, some strategies can be applied more broadly than others. It is tempting to suggest that students with LD be taught a universal strategy for writing such as making writing goals explicit and cycling through a planning, writing, and revising sequence a number of times. A recursive strategy of this nature, however, would not be useful for the majority of the writing tasks that students encounter in school (Pressley et al., 1989). Applebee (1986) indicated that most school writing assignments are a page or less, are completed in class or taken home to finish, and usually serve an examination purpose. Even for writing assignments where there is ample time for planning and revising, a general strategy would have to be flexible enough to be responsive to the purpose, conventions, and types of content germane to the genre under consideration. Applebee's reaction to this situation is that students should be taught different strategies for different writing purposes.

Although Applebee's (1986) suggestion is basically sound, some clarification is needed before implementing this recommendation in school settings. First, instead of teaching a different strategy for each different writing task, it would appear to be more profitable to teach goal-limited strategies that can be applied with a variety of content or that cut across domains (Pressley et al., 1989). Several examples from our own research illustrate writing strategies that meet these requirements. In a study by Graham and Harris (1989b), students with LD were taught a strategy for generating and organizing notes in advance of writing by responding to a series of sequential questions related to the basic components included in common short stories (e.g., "Where does the story take place?"). A modified version of this strategy has been used to produce meaningful gains in reading comprehension among poor readers (Bednarczyk & Harris, 1989; Short & Ryan, 1984); thus, students can use this strategy to both write and read stories. In a subsequent experiment (Graham & Harris, 1989c), this task-specific strategy was incorporated as an interchangeable part of a more global executive routine that could be applied to a variety of writing tasks. The initial step of the strategy was a cue to remind the student to consider who would read the text and the purpose for doing the assignment. The next step directed the student to plan the composition in advance by selecting and using a structural frame (like the one noted above) for the genre under consideration. The final step was a cue to continue the planning process while writing by adding ideas and details. Clearly, a strategy of this nature has strong generality, but at the same time can be used to meet very specific goals.

Second, it is also suggested that researchers and practitioners use general strategies in conjunction with the goal-limited strategies that students are taught. Harris and Graham (1985), for instance, taught students with learning disabilities how to use a goal-limited strategy for generating specific types of words to use in their compositions. This involved having students use brainstorming to generate, in advance of writing, possible words to use in their composition. In addition, students were taught more general strategies designed to promote strategy self-regulation. These included setting goals (number of words to be included in the paper), self-monitoring and self-evaluation of success in attaining the target goals, and self-delivered reinforcement contingent on performance. By promoting the interactive use of goal-limited with general strategies, practitioners should be able to help students with LD become better strategy users.

Components, Characteristics, and Procedures

Strategy instruction is an emerging approach, and one that is continuously being revised in the light of new data and new understandings (Harris & Pressley, in press). Harris (1985) and Wong et al. (1991) identified five interrelated assumptions underlying the use of strategy interventions (particularly cognitive-behavioral based approaches) with children with LD. These assumptions are directly related to the components, characteristics, and procedures involved in effective strategy instruction in written language. They include, but are not necessarily limited to the following assumptions: (a) Affect, behavior, and cognition are transactionally related; (b) children are active participants in the learning process; (c) developmental progressions among affective, behavioral, and cognitive dimensions are critical in the design of interventions; (d) ecological variables, including the situational, cultural, and systems network of which the individual is a part, are also critical concerns; and (e) a purposeful, integrated intervention approach that combines affective, behavioral, and cognitive intervention components within developmental and ecological parameters is necessary when children face significant and debilitating difficulties.

The assumptions that underlie strategy instructional approaches point to the importance of analyzing both the writing task and the learner in terms of affective, behavioral, and cognitive characteristics; promoting active learning; individualization; and enthusiastic and responsive teaching (Harris, 1982). Good strategy instruction is not rote and entails far more than memorization and execution of task strategies (Harris & Pressley, in press). Sound strategy instruction actively involves students in the construction, evaluation, and modification of strategies. The good strategy instructor models, discusses, explains, and re-explains strategies and strategy acquisition procedures to help students develop an awareness of the purpose of strategies, how and why they work, and when and where they can be used. Extensive practice with strategic procedures is provided in the context of ongoing school instruction, allowing students to develop personalized mastery of the process.

The overall objective of strategy-based instruction is the development of self-regulated learners. It is frequently suggested by theorists and researchers that to meet this goal, strategy instruction in academic domains should include three major components: strategies, knowledge about the use and significance of those strategies (metastrategy information), and self-regulation of strategic performance (Brown, Campione, & Day, 1981; Graham & Harris, 1989b). Variations in the combination and operationalization of the components and characteristics of strategy instruction have led to the development of several strategy instruction models that can be applied in school-based settings (cf. Deshler & Schumaker, 1986; Graham & Harris, 1989a; Palincsar, 1986). It is becoming increasingly apparent, however, that even sound strategy acquisition procedures incorporating these components may not be enough to ensure that well-taught and well-learned strategies will be used regularly and effectively (Garner & Alexander, 1989). Aspects of motivation are becoming well recognized as critical in strategy instruction; goal orientations and attitudinal dispositions may profoundly affect the use of learning strategies. Although metacognitive information about strategies can perform both an attributional-training and goal-setting function (Harris, 1988), teachers may find it necessary to provide explicit attributional retraining and to develop a mastery orientation among students to obtain meaningful, lasting strategies performance (Garner & Alexander, 1989; Harris, Graham, & Pressley, in press).

Components Analyses

Multicomponent strategy interventions (which typically combine instruction of the target strategy, knowledge about the use and significance of the strategy, and self-regulation of strategic performance) have been successful in improving the written language skills of students with LD (cf. Graham & Harris, 1989b; Harris & Graham, 1985). Furthermore, each of the components in multicomponent strategy interventions has a theoretical base (cf. Brown et al., 1981; Graham & Harris, 1988; Harris, 1982). Nonetheless, major issues in strategy instruction research include determining the relative contributions of each of these components as well as identifying the variable responsible for change in students' cognitions, affect, or behaviors (Harris, 1986, in press). Confirmation of the mediational effects of differing components is needed in conjunction with and determination of the active, necessary, and sufficient components with particular learners engaged in particular tasks. These issues have been addressed in only a handful of studies (Harris, in press). Cost-benefit relationships among components must also be determined.

Components analyses research in the teaching of writing to students with LD can be illustrated with two studies conducted by Graham, Harris, and their colleagues. The first study involved fifth- and sixth-grade students with LD who were taught a prewriting story grammar strategy (Graham & Harris, 1989b). In this study Graham and Harris investigated the theoretically proposed incremental effects of explicit self-regulation procedures (including proximal goal setting, self-assessment, and self-recording) over and above strategy instruction that included instruction in the use of the strategy and the significance of the strategy. Explicit self-regulation has been theorized not only to result in incremental treatment effects but to be critical to effective strategy deployment, production of new metastrategy information, independent strategy use, and maintenance and generalization of effects (Graham & Harris, 1989b; Pressley & Levin, 1986). In this first study, groups of two or three students participated in 15-minute self-instructional strategy training sessions 2 to 3 days a week, for 2 to 3 weeks. Instruction was criterion-based; that is, students were required to master each lesson before proceeding to the next. The total number of instructional sessions required ranged from five to seven. This training produced meaningful and lasting effects on several composition measures and on a self-report of self-efficacy, but the addition of explicit self-regulation did not produce incremental effects on any of the measures. A second study replicated and extended the results of the first study (Sawyer, Graham, & Harris, 1989). In this study, the students with LD who received strategy training and explicit self-regulation training performed significantly better than both a writing practice control group and a direct instruction group on both posttest and generalization measure. Differences between the self-instructional strategy training only group and the group that also received explicit self-regulation training were nonsignificant, thus replicating the results of the previous study. Only the combination of self-instructional and explicit self-regulation training, however, resulted in nonsignificant differences between the students with learning disabilities and a group of normally achieving peers on story quality ratings. Thus, this second study provides some evidence for the theoretically proposed importance of explicit self-regulation.

Graham and Harris (1989b) pointed out that the situation might be even more complex than previously realized; characteristics of strategy instruction might need to be considered as well as components (task strategy, knowledge of the strategy's importance, and self-regulation of the strategy) of the intervention. Characteristics of instruction noteworthy in their studies were the use of a meaningful academic task, interactivie learning with the student acting as collaborator, instruction by preservice teachers in the students' schools, and criterion-based rather than time-based teaching. Any or all of these characteristics may interact with various components of training. The multifaceted nature of strategy instruction and the need to collect reciprocal influence data present particular challenges to research models and procedures. Bandura (1983) noted that although such a task may appear overwhelming, it is profitable to study different segments of reciprocality without having to study every possible interactant at one time. Multiple research methodologies, including qualitative interview and case study type approaches, may be helpful in improving our understanding of the procedures, processes, and outcomes of strategy instruction.

Harris (1988, in press; Harris, Graham, & Pressley, in press) introduced the concept of intervention integrity to expand on and subsume the concept of treatment integrity in ways particularly relevant to multicomponent interventions. Intervention integrity first requires that each and every component of a strategy intervention is both delivered and carried out as intended and recommended based on available empirical literature; this requirement parallels the treatment integrity concept. Unfortunately, this aspect of intervention integrity has not been clearly established in some studies or, for that matter, in classroom applications. Simplistic, naive conceptualization and construction of strategy interventions, as well as inadequate learner and task analyses, has led to ineffective interventions in some cases (Harris & Pressley, in press). In addition to paralleling treatment integrity, intervention integrity expands on this concept by requiring *assessment of the processes of change as related to both intentions and outcomes.* Specification and assessment of intervention processes and the mechanisms of change (i.e., establishing intervention integrity) is necessary to determine whether strategy interventions work for the reasons they are hypothesized to work. Thus, we can both test and expand the strategy instruction model/theoretical base by establishing intervention integrity.

Evaluation of Writing Strategies

An adequate evaluation of a particular writing strategy necessitates the collection of multiple sources of data ranging from evidence that students use the strategy to confirmation that the strategy effects a change in what and how students write. Previously, we discussed the importance of components analyses in terms of understanding the process of change; here we focus on the need for multiple outcome measures. The use of multiple assessment techniques to evaluate the effects of a target strategy and its corresponding training procedures should be undertaken by not only researchers but teachers as well (Harris, 1985). In conducting strategy instruction in classroom settings, teachers need to carefully assess their efforts to determine when and how instruction needs to be modified. In this section, several recommendations for the types of assessments that will yield useful information in evaluating strategy effectiveness are provided. The collection of social validity data, an important ingredient in the evaluation process, is covered in a subsequent section of the chapter.

Cognitive, behavioral, and affective measures. It is reasonable for researchers and teachers to expect that strategy instruction will have multiple effects. Most of the writing strategies described in previous sections were designed not only to affect some aspect of how students write (e.g., increased time in advanced planning), but also to improve their written products in some meaningful way. Similarly, as students become more adept at using a strategy to successfully complete writing assignments, it is not unrealistic to expect that their confidence in their writing skills and their attitudes toward writing would improve as well. Effective strategy interventions commonly include some combination of behavioral (e.g., modeling, successive approximation, prompts, feedback, and social reinforcement), cognitive (e.g., self-efficacy statements, cognitive and metacognitive strategies), and affective components (e.g., self-instructions for coping with failure). Thus, cognitive components of training may produce cognitive change as well as non-specific behavioral and affective change, and so on (Harris, 1985). Consequently, an evaluation that concentrates on only behavioral changes in writing performance, for instance, may provide a very truncated picture of strategy effectiveness.

The multiple effects of strategy training on students with LD can be demonstrated by examining a recently completed study. Graham, MacArthur, et al. (1989) taught fifth- and sixth-grade students with LD who were poor writers a strategy that was structured around a means-ends analysis; students set product goals for what the paper would accomplish and articulated process goals for how this would be done. The writing task was broken down further into several realted sub-problems: Develop goals, generate notes, organize notes, write and continue planning, and evaluate success in obtaining the goals. In addition to the anticipated behavioral changes in students' writing following strategy instruction (including papers that were more structurally complete, longer, and judged to be of better quality), their approach to writing changed as well; prior to learning the strategy students did all of their planning as they wrote, whereas after training they planned both before and during writing. Moreover, students also became more accurate in their perceptions of their writing competence (self-efficacy), their knowledge of writing strategies increased, and their perceptions of what good writers do shifted from a concentration on writing mechanics to substantive concerns including planning and content generation. Contrary to expectations, instruction in the strategy had little impact on students' attitudes toward writing; the students participating in the study generally had positive attitudes to begin with. Although this latter finding appears to be counterintuitive, the results from a subsequent study showed that students with LD were, in general, positive about writing (Graham et al., 1990).

The determination of which affective, behavioral, and/or cognitive indices should be a researcher's or teacher's focus of interest depends on the components incorporated into the strategy and the corresponding training regime. All of the measures used in the Graham, Mac-Arthur, et al. (1989) investigation were selected on the basis of specific predictions. For instance, it was anticipated that students would expend more effort (write longer) and form more accurate perceptions of their writing competence because goal setting has a motivational function and provides information that facilitates self-evaluation.

Evidence on how students use a strategy.   It is also recommended that researchers and teachers collect evidence on students' use and modification of the target strategy. One benefit for teachers of collecting such data is that it provides evidence on whether the instructional program resulted in students' acquisition of the strategy. Furthermore, confirmation that students use the strategy provides supportive evidence that the strategy mediates changes in students' writing behaviors. Just as important, such information provides considerable insight into what students internalize as a result of strategy instruction and how they modify or corrupt a strategy over time.

A study by Graham and MacArthur (1988) provides an example of how evidence on strategy usage can be collected. In this study, students with LD were taught the following six-step strategy for revising assigned opinion essays composed on a computer: (1) Read the essay; (2) Is the sentence that tells what you believe clear?; (3) Add two reasons why you believe it; (4) SCAN each sentence (does it make *sense?;* Is it *connected* to your belief?; Can you *add* more?; *note* errors.); (5) Make changes on the computer; and (6) Re-read the essay and make final changes. Two types of evidence on students' use of the strategy were collected: One, examiners kept a written record of their observations of strategy use including any modifications made by students; and, two, student revisions were classified according to purpose (each purpose corresponded to a step in the strategy). The observations revealed that students ignored the first and last steps in the strategy, and examination of the classification of revisions by purpose showed that some of the strategy steps were more salient to students than others: Students frequently made changes to correct mechanical errors, add reasons, and make individual sentences clearer, whereas other types of revisions (e.g., make statement of belief clearer) were not made because the students' papers were not deficient in these areas.

Sensitivity to individual differences. As Pressley et al. (1989) noted, considerable instructional resources may be needed to teach some strategies to certain students. Further, some students benefit more from a particular strategy than others. It is important in both research studies and the classroom setting, therefore, to monitor students' progress in acquiring a specific strategy so that modifications in the instructional regime can be made for individual students when necessary. It is equally important to examine possible interactions between student characteristics and the result of strategy instruction. Graham and Harris (1989a), for example, found that all but two of the students with LD participating in their study made writing gains on a measure of story structure following instruction in using a prewriting strategy involving a story grammar frame. Instruction in this particular strategy may have had little or no impact on these two students, because they were already successful in writing stories that contained the basic story parts; their pretraining stories were similar to those written by normally achieving students. The collection of data of this nature by researchers would be especially valuable, because there is presently very little information available about which student characteristics reliably predict who will benefit from which strategies (Harris, 1985; Pressley et al., 1989).

Researchers and teachers should also be sensitive to the different ways that strategy instruction will influence different students. For example, in the revision study by Graham and MacArthur (1988) noted above, two of the subjects' first drafts became longer after instruction in the revision strategy, whereas the other subject wrote shorter first drafts (when asked why his papers became shorter, he indicated that he could add more when he revised).

Maintenance and generalization.   One of the key challenges in strategy instruction has revolved around issues concerning maintenance and generalization. As Harris and Pressley (in press) indicated, strategy maintenance and generalization do not occur in all studies with all students, although evidence for both is increasing. It is necessary, therefore, to monitor if students can use a target strategy flexibly and continue to use it once instructional supports are no longer in effect. Information of this nature is invaluable to both researchers and teachers in judging the adequacy of the strategy and its corresponding instructional regime. Furthermore, if teachers monitor students' maintenance and generalization of a strategy, the need for additional instructional support can be determined and booster sessions can be provided as needed. Harris and Graham (1985), for instance, reported that students with LD maintained strategy training effects for up to 6 weeks following instruction. Nonetheless, at the start of a new school year, about 4 months after instruction, training effects had dissipated. The students still remembered the steps to the strategy they had been taught, however. Because the problem at this point appeared to be one of rusty application, an experimenter or teacher could probably have returned performance rates to their initial posttreatment level by using a booster session.

Knowledge about how to promote maintenance and generalization has increased in the past decade, however, and evidence available to date indicates that generalization and maintenance can be obtained using cognitive strategy instructional approaches (Elliott-Faust & Pressley, 1986; Reeve & Brown, 1985; Wong, 1985). When maintenance and generalization are not obtained, researchers have pointed to numerous problems including the following: short-term training, lack of long-term follow-up, need for informed learners, narrow content of instruction, questionable relevance of the training tasks, and the need to consider ecological, systems, and agent variables (Harris, 1985; Harris, Graham, & Pressley, in press; Wong, 1985). We suggest, in addition, that researchers have failed to attend to a critical element: the developmental nature and constraints of the abilities required to generalize and maintain performance of strategic behaviors.

Without descriptive, developmental studies of the breadth, depth, and course of the development of maintenance and generalization capabilities in children, we have little but intuition to guide us in setting reasonable criteria and evaluating outcomes in our research (Harris,

1985, 1988). The limited research that is available indicates that even adults evidence difficulties with transfer, that metacognitive abilities that develop with age are critically involved in transfer, and that older normally achieving children need less-explicit instruction to promote durable strategy instruction than do younger children (Brown & Kane, 1988; Elliott-Faust & Pressley, 1986; Harris & Pressley, in press; Harris, Graham, & Pressley, in press). Developmental studies of both maintenance and generalization capabilities among exceptional and normally achieving children will meaningfully inform cognitive strategy instructional approaches for teaching writing. Such research will assist in determining developmentally and situationally appropriate expectations and criterion levels, provide insight regarding the acquisition of maintenance and generalization capabilities, and suggest functional relationships that may improve intervention efficacy in terms of transfer and maintenance. Thus, research of this nature could meaningfully inform both curriculum development and classroom instruction.

Implications for Teaching: Applications in School-Based Settings

There is presently very little evidence of school-based strategy instruction in the area of writing (Applebee, 1986). In fact, most of the research reviewed in this chapter has been conducted by researchers and their staff, not by actual teachers. Although some of this research did occur in school-based settings, it is not clear if teachers would actually use these strategies in their own classrooms, or if their use of these procedures would result in student gains comparable to those obtained in the experimental investigations. Because a critical criteria in judging the effectiveness of strategy training lies in the breadth and success of its application in school settings, more attention needs to be devoted to both these issues.

Social validity. Students are unlikely to use, adapt, or maintain writing strategies, or other strategies for that matter, if they do not view them as being efficient, effective, useful, and reasonably easy to use. As a result, assessment of consumer satisfaction or social validity should be an integral part of strategy instruction. Researchers and teachers should make it a common practice to interview students concerning their perceptions of the effectiveness of the target strategy and the corresponding teaching procedures and to solicit recommendations and feedback concerning what they liked and did not like about the strategy and instructional procedures. The implementation and efficacy of strategy instruction also depend on its acceptability to classroom teachers. Teachers are unlikely to teach writing strategies, even those that have been validated, if they do not believe they are appropriate, fair, or reasonable for their students (Kazdin, 1980). Although there is some evidence to indicate that special education teachers do view strategy instruction as an acceptable treatment (Harris, Preller, & Graham, in press), more research is needed to determine if teachers view writing strategy instruction in a similar way.

Finally, it has been recommended elsewhere (Graham & Harris, 1989a) that writing strategy instruction for students with LD should not supplant the traditional writing program. Rather, it should be incorporated as an integral part of the instructional regime. This recommendation is based on the assumption that teaching students pertinent writing strategies has an augmental effect on their compositions and composing behavior over and above that accounted for by recommended writing programs such as the process approach to writing. This recommendation, however, needs to be validated by empirical research. In addition, researchers need to study the problems that teachers encounter in implementing strategy instruction in their writing programs, and investigate social-contextual variables that may serve to promote or hinder the use of writing strategy instruction by students and teachers.

Concluding Comments

The available evidence suggests that strategy instruction can make a difference in the way students with LD write. The challenge that teachers face is to make writing strategy instruction work in their classrooms. Although there are a number of obstacles to implementing new innovations in school settings, strategy instruction can work if teachers take a "small is beautiful" approach (at least at first); start by implementing a few powerful strategies using effective teaching procedures (Pressley et al., 1989). It should be noted, however, that teachers' efforts in teaching writing strategies will have little impact if students are not involved in frequent and meaningful writing activities (Graham & Harris, 1988). Although strategy instruction in writing provides a viable mechanism for changing what and how students write, it can have no meaningful effect if students write infrequently or do not write at all.

References

Anderson-Inman, L., Paine, S., & Deutchman, L. (1984). Neatness counts: Effects of direct instruction and self-monitoring on the transfer of neat-paper skills to nontraining settings. *Analysis and Intervention in Developmental Disabilities, 4,* 137–155.

Applebee, A. (1986). Problems in process approaches: Toward a reconceptualization of process instruction. In A. Petrosky, D. Bartholomae, & K. Rehage (Eds.), *The teaching of writing: Eighty-fifth yearbook of the National Society for the Study of Education* (pp. 95–113). Chicago: University of Chicago Press.

Augustine, D. (1981). Geometries and words: Linguistics and philosophy: A model of the composing process. *College English, 43,* 221–231.

Bandura, A. (1983). Temporal dynamics and decomposition of reciprocal determinism: A reply to Phillips and Orton. *Psychological Review, 90,* 166–170.

Beaugrande, R. de (1984). *Text production: Toward a science of composition.* Norwood, NJ: Ablex.

Bednarczyk, A. M., & Harris, K. R. (1989). [Story grammar instruction to improve reading comprehension]. Unpublished raw data.

Blandford, B., & Lloyd, J. (1987). Effects of a self-instructional procedure on handwriting. *Journal of Learning Disabilities, 20,* 342–346.

Brown, A. L., Campione, J. C., & Day, J. D. (1981). Learning to learn: On training students to learn from texts. *Educational Researcher, 10,* 14–21.

Brown, A. L., & Kane, M. J. (1988). Preschool children can learn to transfer: Learning to learn and learning from example. *Cognitive Psychology, 20,* 493–523.

Deno, S., Marston, D., & Mirkin, P. (1982). Valid measurement procedures for continuous evaluation of written expression. *Exceptional Children, 48,* 368–371.

Deshler, D. D., & Schumaker, J. B. (1986). Learning strategies: An instructional alternative for low-achieving adolescents. *Exceptional Children, 52,* 583–590.

Elliott-Faust, D. J., & Pressley, M. (1986). How to teach comparison processing to increase children's short- and long-term comprehension monitoring. *Journal of Educational Psychology, 78,* 27–33.

Englert, C., & Raphael, T. (1988). Constructing well-formed prose: Process, structure and metacognition in the instruction of expository writing. *Exceptional Children, 54,* 513–520.

Englert, C., Raphael, T., Fear, K., & Anderson, L. (1988). Students' metacognitive knowledge about how to write informational text. *Learning Disability Quarterly, 11,* 18–46.

Englert, C., & Thomas, C. (1988). Sensitivity to text structure in reading and writing: A comparison of learning disabled and non-learning disabled students. *Learning Disability Quarterly, 11,* 18–46.

Flower, L., & Hayes, J. (1977). Problem-solving strategies and the writing process. *College English, 39,* 449–461.

Flower, L., & Hayes, J. (1980). The dynamics of composing: Making plans and juggling constraints. In L. Gregg & E. Steinberg (Eds.), *Cognitive processes in writing* (pp. 31–50). Hillsdale, NJ: Erlbaum.

Garner, R., & Alexander, P. A. (1989). Metacognition: Answered and unanswered questions. *Educational Psychologist, 24,* 143–158.

Graham, S. (1989a). [Procedural facilitation: The effectiveness of the compare-diagnosis, and operate revision procedure with students with learning disabilities]. Unpublished raw data.

Graham, S. (1989b, April). *The role of production factors in learning disabled students' compositions.* Paper presented at Annual Meeting of the American Educational Research Association, San Francisco.

Graham, S., Boyer-Schick, K., & Tippets, E. (1989). The validity of the handwriting scale from the Test of Written Language. *Journal of Educational Research, 82,* 166–171.

Graham, S., & Harris, K. R. (1988). Instructional recommendations for teaching writing to exceptional students. *Exceptional Children, 54,* 506–512.

Graham, S., & Harris, K. R. (1989a). Cognitive training: Implications for written language. In J. Hughes & R. Hall (Eds.), *Cognitive behavioral psychology in the schools: A comprehensive handbook* (pp. 247–279). New York: Guilford.

Graham, S., & Harris, K. R. (1989b). A components analysis of cognitive strategy instruction: Effects on learning disabled students' compositions and self-efficacy. *Journal of Educational Psychology, 81,* 353–361.

Graham, S., & Harris, K. R. (1989c). Improving learning disabled students' skills at composing essays: Self-instructional strategy training. *Exceptional Children, 56,* 201–216.

Graham, S., & Harris, K. R. (1990). *Cognitive strategy instruction in written language for learning disabled students.* Unpublished manuscript.

Graham, S., & MacArthur, C. (1987). Written language of the handicapped. In C. Reynolds & L. Mann (Eds.), *Encyclopedia of special education* (pp. 1678–1681). New York: Wiley.

Graham, S., & MacArthur, C. (1988). Improving learning disabled students' skills at revising essays produced on a word processor: Self-instructional strategy training. *The Journal of Special Education, 22,* 133–152.

Graham, S., MacArthur, C., Schwartz, S., & Voth, T. (1989, April). *Improving LD students' compositions using a strategy involving product and process goal-setting.* Paper presented at Annual Meeting of the American Educational Research Association, San Francisco.

Graham, S., Schwartz, S., & MacArthur, C. (1990). [Learning disabled and normally achieving students' knowledge of the writing process]. Unpublished raw data.

Graves, A., Montague, M., & Wong, Y. (1989, April). *The effects of procedural facilitation on story composition of learning disabled students.* Paper presented at the Annual Meeting of the American Educational Research Association, San Francisco.

Harris, K. R. (1982). Cognitive-behavior modification: Application with exceptional students. *Focus on Exceptional Children, 15,* 1–16.

Harris, K. R. (1985). Conceptual, methodological, and clinical issues in cognitive behavioral assessment. *Journal of Abnormal Child Psychology, 13,* 373–390.

Harris, K. R. (1986). The effects of cognitive-behavior modification on private speech and task performance during problem solving among learning disabled and normally achieving children. *Journal of Abnormal Child Psychology, 14,* 63–67.

Harris, K. R. (April, 1988). *What's wrong with strategy intervention research: Intervention integrity.* Paper presented at the Annual Meeting of the American Educational Research Association, New Orleans.

Harris, K. R. (in press). Developing self-regulated learners: The role of private speech and self-instructions. *Educational Psychologist.*

Harris, K. R., & Graham, S. (1985). Improving learning disabled students' composition skills: Self-control strategy training. *Learning Disability Quarterly, 8,* 27–36.

Harris, K. R., Graham, S., & Pressley, M. (in press). Cognitive strategies in reading and written language. In N. Singh & I. Beale (Eds.), *Current perspectives in learning disabilities: Nature, theory, and treatment.* New York: Springer-Verlag.

Harris, K. R., & McElroy, K. (1989). [A comparison of self-monitoring of attention and self-monitoring of productivity on the writing of students with LD]. Unpublished raw data.

Harris, K. R., Preller, D., & Graham, S. (in press). Acceptability of cognitive-behavioral and behavioral interventions among teachers. *Cognitive Therapy and Research.*

Harris, K. R., & Pressley, M. (in press). The nature of cognitive strategy instruction: Interactive strategy construction. *Exceptional Children.*

Kazdin, A. (1980). Acceptability of alternative treatments for deviant child behavior. *Journal of Applied Behavior Analysis, 13,* 259–273.

MacArthur, C., & Graham, S. (1987). Learning disabled students' composing with three methods: Handwriting, dictation, and word processing. *The Journal of Special Education, 21,* 22–42.

MacArthur, C., Graham, S., & Schwartz, S. (1989). *Knowledge of revision and revising behavior among learning disabled students.* Manuscript submitted for publication.

Moran, M., Schumaker, J., & Vetter, A. (1981). *Teaching a paragraph organization strategy to learning disabled adolescents* (Research Rep. No. 54). Lawrence: University of Kansas Institute for Research in Learning Disabilities.

Palincsar, A. S. (1986). The role of dialogue in providing scaffolded instruction. *Educational Psychologist, 21* (1&2), 73–98.

Poteet, J. (1979). Characteristics of written expression of learning disabled and non-learning disabled elementary school students. *Diagnostique, 4,* 60–74.

Pressley, M., Goodchild, F., Fleet, J., Zajchowski, R., & Evans, E. (1989). The challenges of classroom strategy instruction. *Elementary School Journal, 89,* 301–342.

Pressley, M., & Levin, J. R. (1986). Elaborative learning strategies for the inefficient learner. In S. J. Ceci (Ed.), *Handbook of cognitive, social, and neuropsychological aspects of learning disabilities* (pp. 175–211). Hillsdale, NJ: Erlbaum.

Reeve, R. A., & Brown, A. L. (1985). Metacognition reconsidered: Implications for intervention research. *Journal of Abnormal Child Psychology, 13,* 343–357.

Reynolds, C., Hill, D., Swassing, R., & Ward, M. (1988). The effects of revision strategy instruction on the writing performance of students with learning disabilities. *Journal of Learning Disabilities, 21,* 540–545.

Sawyer, R., Graham, S., & Harris, K. R. (1989). [Improving learning disabled students' composition skills with story grammar strategy training: A further components analysis of self-instructional strategy training]. Unpublished raw data.

Scardamalia, M., & Bereiter, C. (1983). The development of evaluative, diagnostic and remedial capabilities in children's composing. In M. Martlew (Ed.), *The psychology of written language: Developmental and educational perspectives* (pp. 67–95). London: John Wiley.

Scardamalia, M., & Bereiter, C. (1986). Written composition. In M. Wittrock (Ed.), *Handbook of research on teaching* (3rd ed., pp. 778–803). New York: Macmillan.

Schumaker, J., Deshler, D., Alley, G., & Warner, M. (1983). Toward the development of an intervention model for learning disabled adolescents. The University of Kansas Institute. *Exceptional Education Quarterly, 4,* 45–74.

Schumaker, J., Deshler, D., Alley, G., Warner, M., Clark, F., & Nolan, S. (1982). Error monitoring: A learning strategy for improving adolescent performance. In W. M. Cruickshank & J. Lerner (Eds.), *Best of ACLD* (Vol. 3, pp. 170–183). Syracuse, NY: Syracuse University Press.

Schumaker, J., & Sheldon, J. (1985). *The sentence writing strategy.* Lawrence: University of Kansas.

Seabaugh, G., & Schumaker, J. (1981). *The effects of self-regulation training on the academic productivity of LD and NLD adolescents* (Research Rep. No. 37). Lawrence: University of Kansas Institute for Research in Learning Disabilities.

Short, E. J., & Ryan, E. B. (1984). Metacognitive differences between skilled and less skilled readers: Remediating deficits through story grammar and attribution training. *Journal of Educational Psychology, 75,* 225–235.

Stoddard, B., & MacArthur, C. (1989). [Teaching LD students to revise their writing: A word processing and peer editing strategy training approach]. Unpublished raw data.

Thomas, C., Englert, C., & Gregg, S. (1987). An analysis of errors and strategies in the expository writing of learning disabled students. *Remedial and Special Education, 8,* 21–30.

Wallace, L., & Pear, J. (1977). Self-control techniques of famous novelists. *Journal of Applied Behavioral Analysis, 10,* 515–525.

Wong, B. Y. L. (1985). Issues in cognitive-behavioral interventions in academic skill areas. *Journal of Abnormal Child Psychology, 13,* 425–442.

Wong, B. Y. L., Harris, K. R., & Graham, S. (1991). Cognitive-behavioral procedures: Academic applications with students with learning disabilities. In P. C. Kendall (Ed.), *Child and adolescent therapy: Cognitive-behavioral procedures* (pp. 245–275). N.Y.: Guilford.

11

Mathematics Assessment and Strategy Instruction: An Applied Developmental Approach

Bethany Roditi

S ince the early 1980s, it has become increasingly evident that psychologists and educators share a responsibility to identify and to teach students with learning problems in mathematics. The present chapter examines an interdisciplinary approach to math disabilities within the framework of a newly emerging discipline, applied developmental psychology, Goldstein et al., 1983 (Morrison, Lord, & Keating, 1984; Scholnick, 1983; Scott, 1983; Sigel, 1983; Wertlieb, 1983). An applied developmental perspective on math learning disabilities incorporates theories and research from numerous fields such as developmental dyslexia, cognitive psychology, developmental psychology, neuropsychology, educational psychology, as well as cognitive science, mathematics, and mathematics education. This applied developmental

I would like to thank my associate and friend, Lynn Meltzer, PhD, for giving me the opportunity to participate in the preparation of this book, for her encouraging words, and for helpful suggestions on multiple drafts of this chapter. I would also like to thank my students, who have taught me so much over the years.

approach to mathematics assessment and strategy instruction is guided by research and theory about the development of children in classrooms, in resource rooms, at home, and at play. The challenge is to examine current multidisciplinary theory and research and to apply newly acquired knowledge and strategies to enhance our teaching methods. The cycle continues from theory to research to practice and back. This applied developmental approach unites psychological and educational research models, provides a balance between pure and applied research, and integrates research findings through multidisciplinary collaboration among psychologists, educators, and special educators.

This chapter focuses on a model of mathematics assessment and instruction developed within an applied developmental framework, the Assessment for Teaching (AFT) model (Meltzer & Roditi, 1989). An alternate form of math assessment is described that focuses on the underlying psychological factors and instructional variables that enhance or interfere with smooth mathematical processing. Assessment findings yield rich descriptions of students' cognitive and learning profiles and result in the development of instructional goals for promoting the acquisition of skills as well as strategies. Guided by this process-based assessment, decisions can be made regarding *what* teaching techniques and materials to use and *how* to use them most effectively. Instructional methods are suggested to enhance strategy use, build automaticity, develop a number sense, and solve math word problems.

Learning Problems in Mathematics: Current Issues

The past decade has witnessed an increasing number of studies of developmental disorders in childhood, such as reading disabilities and other largely language-based disorders. Only recently, students with learning problems in mathematics have received increasing attention. This renewed interest in the dyscalculias—learning disabilities in mathematics—has coincided with recommendations from the National Council of Teachers of Mathematics (NCTM) (1989) to reevaluate mathematics education. Findings indicate that students who have been drilled on arithmetic computational skills cannot apply these lower level skills to solve higher level problems (Fennema, 1981; NCTM, 1984–1985). In response, the nation's primary goal for mathematics in the 1980s and 1990s has been to shift the focus of instruction from rote computation to meaningful problem solving.

The proliferation of calculators and computers in our society has also challenged prior expectations that schoolchildren must learn to automatize basic number facts and arithmetic skills (e.g., number identification, regrouping in addition, multidigit division algorithm) before they encounter complex problems that they are required to solve. Whether these lower level arithmetic skills, typically difficult for students with learning problems in mathematics (Ackerman, Anhalt, & Dykman, 1986; Garnett & Fleischner, 1983), are necessary precursors to higher levels of mathematical thinking and problem solving remains an open question.

Nevertheless, as we enter the 1990s, students and teachers are caught in a transition within math education. The curriculum goals and teaching methods of the industrial age are changing; new goals and teaching techniques are emerging to meet the cultural needs of the information age of today. As a basis for change, the National Council of Teachers of Mathematics (1989) has published the curriculum and evaluation standards for North American schools (kindergarten through 12th grade). These criteria aim to guide future curriculum reform, development, and evaluation in school mathematics for the next decade. New goals for students include:

1. To learn to value mathematics

2. To increase their confidence in mathematics

3. To become mathematical problem solvers

4. To learn how to communicate mathematically

5. To learn to reason mathematically

These goals represent a major shift from rote computation to meaningful problem solving. Some features are embodied within the standards that aim to facilitate achievement of these goals. First, emphasis is on *doing* rather than *knowing* mathematics. That is, math students of tomorrow are viewed as active learners who construct knowledge by engaging in purposeful activity rather than math students of today who have been master memorizers of fundamental concepts and procedures. This constructivist view is aligned with what developmental and educational psychologists have been proposing for years (Dewey, 1916; Piaget, 1952; Polya, 1957; Schoenfeld, 1987; Vygotsky, 1978). Further, because technology is significantly changing mathematics and its applications, the standards cite that:

• Students should have access to calculators at all times

• Teachers should have access to a computer in the classroom for instructional purposes

- Students should have computers available for individual and group work

- Students should learn how to use calculators and computers as tools for thinking about and solving problems

The 1990s have heralded the new standards in mathematics and, along with them, a new curriculum that emphasizes real-world problems to solve. Students with learning disabilities are now required to learn how to solve math problems whether they have or have not automatized basic arithmetic facts and procedures. They must learn both lower level and higher level mathematics skills simultaneously. They need a *balance* of rote drill and meaningful instruction. Strategy instruction can assist them to automatize processes and to establish a number sense. Students need to learn how to make decisions about which tool to use in the process of solving math problems: mental computation, calculators, computers, software. Further, they have to learn to plan and to formulate effective problem-solving strategies.

Teachers, well aware of the realities of such an enormous task, need a systematic approach that allows them to make informed instructional decisions to teach effectively in a given amount of time. An applied developmental approach to mathematics assessment and instruction can assist them in understanding how each student's cognitive and linguistic skills and strategies manifest in the math domain. With this diagnostic information, classroom teachers are able to pinpoint *what* math skills to teach and *how* to teach them to their students with diverse learning profiles.

Conceptual Perspectives and Math Disabilities

New forms of math assessment need to account for the psychological and educational variables that affect the development of mathematical thinking and academic performance in children with learning disabilities. The implied goal of math education is the development of skills and reasoning—quantitative and spatial—that will allow children to identify and to solve problems encountered in daily life. For all children, but particularly for children with learning disabilities, achievement of this goal may depend partially on the smooth development of cognitive and linguistic skills. Automaticity and language processes need to be examined in the context of math deficits and abilities. The following discussion focuses on current theories and research on cognition and language in relation to math disabilities. Although cognitive developmental, linguistic, and neuropsychological perspectives are discussed individually, they can be linked under the broad framework of applied developmental psychology.

Cognitive and Developmental Perspectives

Cognitive researchers have varied widely in their perspectives on the development of mathematical thinking and problem solving. Several researchers have shown that arithmetic failure may be partially explained by a lack of automaticity (Ackerman et al., 1986; Garnett & Fleischner, 1983; Meltzer et al., 1984; Resnick & Ford, 1981; Roditi, 1988). Other researchers have focused on the development of quantitative thinking with no specific consideration for an underlying automaticity factor (Gelman & Gallistel, 1978; Ginsburg, 1983; Russell & Ginsburg, 1981). Russell and Ginsburg (1981) identified math-delayed (MD) children who experienced difficulties with the recall of number facts. Although no reason was cited, a memory disorder was hypothesized. Meltzer (1984) examined the relationships between automaticity and problem solving in the context of educational tasks and developed a problem-solving paradigm that is particularly germane to the study of math disabilities because of its emphasis on the interaction between automaticity and strategy use in children with learning disabilities. Research has shown that these children typically experience difficulties in utilizing effective cognitive strategies for the purpose of reading comprehension (Meltzer, 1984; Stone & Michals, 1986; Swanson, 1989). These strategy deficits include weaknesses in planning, identifying salient details, recognizing and analyzing linguistic and visual-spatial patterns, organizing information, self-monitoring, and self-correcting. Other researchers have studied mathematical problem solving in the context of strategy theory (Goldman, 1989; Pressley, 1986).

Linguistic Perspectives

Research in the areas of language, reading, automaticity, and word retrieval are relevant to investigations of mathematics performance. Receptive and expressive language skills are involved in learning mathematical concepts, math symbols, and rules of operations. Lerner (1976) stated that "arithmetic is a symbolic language that enables human beings to think about, record, and communicate ideas concerning the elements and the relationships of quantity" (p. 292). In particular, the study of the word-retrieval process, with its naming methodology, appears critical for differentiating linguistically based subgroups of mathematics disabilities. In their review of the dyscalculia literature,

Benson and Denckla (1969) identified frequent word-finding difficulties in clinical cases. They concluded that even subtle or latent aphasic symptoms often interfere with successful mathematics computation and that verbal paraphasias may often mask intact knowledge of computational processes. Rudel et al. (1980) cited "naming deficits" as the most important symptom of children referred for reading problems, and she hypothesized that word-retrieval skills differentiate subgroups of dyslexics. Harold Goodglass & Kaplan (1972) designed a naming methodology for the evaluation of brain-language relationships in alexic and aphasic patients. In cross-sectional and longitudinal research, Wolf (1984a) demonstrated that systematic investigation of naming processes offered a unique understanding of the "developing linguistic system of the child." Results from Wolf's 5-year longitudinal study of children with linguistically based reading problems indicated that neurolinguistic assessment of specific aspects of the naming process in young children predicted linguistically based reading disorders and differentiated subgroups of developmental dyslexics (Wolf, 1982).

Such studies of developmental reading disorders can guide research on students with math disabilities. As a group, these students exhibit many observable symptoms similar to those of students with reading deficits (Johnson & Myklebust, 1967; Kosc, 1974; Reid & Hresko, 1981). These symptoms include problems in the areas of visual spatial perception, visual motor integration, sensory and perceptual weaknesses, sequencing, attention, memory, and verbal expression. Many children with learning problems in mathematics are known to experience language problems (Levine, Brooks, & Shonkoff, 1980). When students find it difficult to articulate mathematical terms and relations (e.g., identifying numbers of objects, digits, operational symbols, and mathematical operations), they may be classified as verbally dyscalculic (Kosc, 1981). This type of math learning problem is qualitatively different from the problems of students classified as lexically dyscalculic. These students find it difficult to read the mathematical symbols and struggle with lower level mathematics processes that involve lexical retrieval (e.g., number word or digit naming, recall of basic math facts, and naming the sequence of steps in algorithms). It should be noted that language issues impact the math learning process in many different ways ranging from the ability to recall arithmetic math facts to the ability to read and to understand math word problems.

Neuropsychological Perspectives

Math disabilities have also been studied within the framework of neuropsychological theories and research. Early studies of acalculia, acquired mathematics disorders, have emerged from aphasia research and have focused on adults (Gerstmann, 1924; Head, 1926; Henschen, 1991, cited in Reid & Hresko, 1981; Singer & Low, 1933). Later researchers described neurological dysfunction based on mathematical difficulties linked to poor spatial organization, poor visual discrimination of numbers and operational signs, and poor visual motor integration (Goldstein, 1948; Luria, 1966). Cohn (1961) analyzed case studies of patients with brain injury with dyscalculia or developmental mathematics disorders. These individuals manifest partial disturbances in arithmetic ability as opposed to a complete loss of this ability. Cohn's findings, based on error analyses of written computation tests, indicate that memory and sequencing are the two major processes necessary for accurate numerical computation. Researchers have continued to debate brain localization of mathematical activities (Luria, 1966, 1969, 1973) and have suggested that complex functional systems of the brain are responsible for specific behaviors related to mathematical performance.

Based on this theory, researchers have studied specific relationships between mathematical disorders and neurological dysfunction (Cohn, 1971; Kosc, 1974, 1981; Weinstein, 1978). Cohn's research has focused on the possible linguistic bases for mathematical learning disabilities. Kosc defined developmental dyscalculia as a

> structural disorder of mathematical abilities which had its origin in a genetic or congenital disorder of those parts (functional systems) of the brain that were the direct anatomico-physiological substrate of the maturation of the mathematical abilities adequate to age, without a simultaneous disorder of general functions. (1974, p. 47)

He offered a classification of various types of developmental dyscalculias. Weinstein has examined the possible link between mathematical learning problems and a developmental lag in certain left hemisphere processes.

Ginsburg (1983) refuted this line of research on several grounds. First, he pointed out that Cohn's (1971) and Kosc's (1974) studies are not based on a sound theory of children's mathematical behavior. Second, these studies have overemphasized the importance of neurological soft signs as accurate indices of neurological function. Third, correlations have been drawn that have not necessarily confirmed a causal relationship. He agreed with the premise that severe brain damage may result in mathematical disorders, yet he argued that the converse is not necessarily true. That is, all math learning problems are not necessarily due to minimal brain damage.

Although research in developmental neuropsychology has broadened the scope of existing assessment methods and procedures, diagnosticians and teachers have recognized the importance of going beyond the level of identifying which area of the brain is responsible for which type of mathematics disorder. Psychological and educational evaluations, holistic and dynamic in nature, are much more useful to teachers and students because they yield rich descriptions of students' learning profiles and account for the effects of developmental changes. This process-oriented form of math assessment helps teachers to understand *why* their students have or have not learned specific math skills. Further, this diagnostic information leads to the identification of instructional goals and the selection of teaching methods that match student profiles. To conclude, an applied developmental approach to math assessment and instruction must account for typical neurodevelopmental, cognitive, and linguistic factors that underlie learning disabilities in mathematics.

Toward an Applied Developmental Approach to Math Assessment

An applied developmental approach to math assessment must be student-centered as well as content-oriented. It must account for typical developmental, cognitive, and linguistic factors that underlie mathematics disorders. Students with learning disabilities in mathematics have been found to lack automaticity in terms of rapid, accurate recall of basic number facts (Ackerman et al., 1986; Garnett & Fleischner, 1983). Some have word-finding difficulties, whereas others have difficulties sequencing linguistic and/or geometric patterns. Some students may be good conceptualizers and categorizers of verbal information but may lack a number sense. Others may utilize inefficient problem-solving strategies and may lack self-monitoring and self-regulation skills. Some students with math learning disabilities have difficulty completing applied problems within a time limit and need more time to process information, whereas others have difficulty shifting mental sets easily and effectively.

Traditionally, math assessment has provided valuable information about math skills that a student has or has not learned, but has failed to give us insight into the underlying cognitive and linguistic skills and strategies that a student employs while solving verbal problems. Further, math test results have not indicated how efficiently students use certain strategies and whether they have an adequate number sense.

Number sense refers to the student's ability to conceptualize the relevant quantitative information in relation to the problem. At the number level, students must recognize, identify, and understand math symbols and the quantity that they represent. At the algorithm level, students must integrate the concepts underlying the symbols for arithmetic operations, rules, and procedures necessary to operate on the numbers (addition, subtraction, multiplication, and division). At the application level, students must be able to integrate number sense established at lower levels with higher level problem-solving processes. Students with good number sense understand what the numbers represent in the problems and are able to use this number sense to self-monitor and self-correct.

Several researchers and theoreticians have provided an organizational framework for understanding the cognitive processes relevant to specific phases of the math problem-solving process (Garofalo & Lester, 1985; Goldman, 1989; Polya, 1957): (a) Define the unknown; (b) plan and organize; (c) calculate; and (d) verify. Some students with math learning problems may not be able to read and/or conceptualize the word problem to take the first step: Define the unknown. Students with a good number sense and effective math problem-solving strategies are able to:

- Conceptualize the problem and organize details (identify relevant from irrelevant information)
- Plan (brainstorm strategies for solving the problem)
- Transfer (translate the problem from one representation to another)
- Execute (calculate)
- Verify (check for the reasonableness of the solution)

Problem-solving models for students with math learning problems must emphasize an initial conceptualization phase to ensure that students understand the problem. Teaching techniques, educational materials, and software tools are needed that represent numbers in multiple forms, (e.g., diagrams, concrete manipulatives, computer simulations, and/or verbal summarization). Math problems may be reframed in ways that minimize the demands on language and reading and ease the cognitive shift from one symbol system to another. Number sense may be instilled by formulating problems based on students' personal experiences and by concretizing quantitative concepts. In the math problem-solving process, automaticity, language, cognitive strategy use, and number sense interlink.

Rather than examining these cognitive, linguistic and neurodevelopmental processes that underlie the students' learning difficulties, most math diagnostic tests that are available assess gaps in learning arithmetic computation and concepts, and in solving word problems. Currently, several tests are available (e.g., *Test of Mathematical Abilities* [TOMA; Brown & McEntire, 1984]; *Diagnostic Test of Arithmetic Strategies* [DTAS; Ginsburg & Mathews, 1984]; *Sequential Assessment of Mathematics Inventories* [SAMI; Reisman & Hutchinson, 1985]) that address error patterns in several arithmetic areas. Some commonly used math tests are listed in Table 11.1. The majority of these math tests or subtests are content-oriented and focus primarily on math achievement and identification of a general mathematics disability. They are largely based on a traditional hierarchy of mathematical skills and concepts (e.g., addition, subtraction, multiplication, division, fractions, decimals, and percents). Similarly, when the arithmetic subtests of the

TABLE 11.1*
Math Subtests

Tests/Math subtests	Grade Range
Brigance Diagnostic Comprehensive Inventory of Basic Skills	K–9
Brigance Diagnostic Inventory of Essential Skills	4–12
California Achievement Tests	K–12
Diagnostic Mathematics Inventory/Mathematics Systems	1–12
Diagnostic Tests and Self-Helps in Arithmetic	3–8
Enright Diagnostic Inventory of Basic Arithmetic Skills	
Iowa Tests of Basic Skills	P–3
Kaufman Tests of Educational Achievement	1–12
Key Math–Revised	K–6
Metropolitan Achievement Tests	
Peabody Individual Achievement Text–Revised (PIAT-R)	K–12
Sequential Assessment of Mathematics Inventories (SAMI)	K–8
Test of Computational Processes	
Standard Diagnostic Mathematics Test	K–12
Survey of Problem-Solving and Educational Skills (SPES)	4–8
Test of Mathematical Abilities (TOMA)	3–12
Wechsler Individual Intelligence Tests–Revised (Arithmetic subtest)	
Wide Range Achievement Test–Revised (WRAT–R)	K–12
Woodcock-Johnson Psycho-Educational Battery Tests of Achievement–Revised	P–12
Woodcock-Johnson Psycho-Educational Battery Tests of Cognitive Ability	3–Adult

*adapted from Lerner, 1989

Wechsler Intelligence Scale for Children–Revised (WISC-R; Wechsler, 1974) and the Wide Range Achievement Test (WRAT; Jastak & Wilkinson, 1984) are used to diagnose math disabilities, they indicate a math problem and an achievement level (which was known before the testing); the results do not easily guide the selection of teaching methods and materials. A valuable extension to traditional math assessment is evident in the TOMA, which includes vocabulary and attitude scales to examine language and social-emotional areas that may impact on math performance. Though recent tests go beyond the product to examine error types, the focus remains, for the most part, on subject matter rather than on the child's information processing and development.

New math assessment approaches and measures are needed to supplement the many math subject–based tasks. These new assessment methods need to focus on the child's information processing within the math domain and must also account for developmental changes. Further, they can address the underlying cognitive and linguistic strategies that a student employs in the process of solving math problems. It is important to determine which diagnostic tasks are effective measures of these variables. Math assessment results must link directly to teaching. Applied developmental research can provide a methodology for achieving these objectives and for improving math assessment approaches and diagnostic tasks. Within the applied developmental framework, a study was designed to investigate the specific cognitive and linguistic variables that affect the development of mathematical problem solving in children with and without learning disabilities (Roditi, 1988).

Assessment of Automaticity, Language, and Cognitive Strategies in the Math Domain

A longitudinal and cross-sectional investigation examined the links among early automatic retrieval processes, early set-shifting, and later mathematical problem solving (Roditi, 1988). The naming methodology was examined for its potential value in the detection of learning disabilities in mathematics. The sample consisted of 70 sixth and seventh graders (12 to 13 years) from the public school in Waltham, Massachusetts. These children constituted a large subgroup of the original sample of a major longitudinal study of reading and language development and disorders (Wolf, 1982) where the children had been tested from kindergarten through Grade 4. In this math study, the same subjects received a diagnostic battery that included language measures (continuous naming tests and a confrontation naming task), three general problem-solving tasks (Survey of Problem-Solving Skills subtests; Meltzer, 1987), and three mathematics-specified measures (Survey of Educational Skills math subtests; Meltzer, 1987) (see Table 11.2). Data from the longitudinal study were analyzed using multiple regression analyses. Findings indicate that continuous naming speed measured by the Rapid Automatized Naming Test (RAN; Denckla & Rudel, 1976) and the Rapid Alternating Stimulus Test (RAS; Wolf, 1986) in first grade was an important predictor of both seventh grade math-fact retrieval and higher levels of mathematical problem solving. In addition, set-switching in first grade (as measured by the RAS, was found to be a better predictor of seventh-grade mathematical problem solving and sequential reasoning than of cognitive flexibility (as measured by the subtests of the SPES). These results indicate that a broad range of set-switching tasks are needed to examine cognitive flexibility at critical points in development.

Findings from the cross-sectional study indicate that specific Surveys of Problem Solving and Educational Skills (SPES) subtests, continuous-naming tests (e.g., RAN and RAS) and the *Boston Naming Test* (BNT; Kaplan, Goodglass, & Weintraub, 1983) may constitute a powerful diagnostic battery for differentiating average-to-able from severely impaired math problem solvers and for explaining delayed performance (see Table 11.3 for summary data). Findings from regression analy-

TABLE 11.2
Alternative Diagnostic Battery: Waltham Math Study

	Reference
Language Measures	
Rapid Automatic 3rd Naming Tests (R.A.N.)	Denckla & Rudel (1976)
Rapid Alternating Stimulus (R.A.S.)	Wolf (1986)
Boston Naming Test (BNT)	Kaplan et al. (1983)
Boston Naming Test: Children's version-multiple choice component	Wolf & Goodglass (1986)
Cognitive Measures	
Surveys of Problem-Solving Skills (SPES)	Meltzer (1987)
Series Completion Task	
Category Shift Task	
Sequential Reasoning Task	
Mathematics Measures	
SPES Math Inventory	Meltzer (1987)
SEDS Math Automaticity Task (FAF)	
SPES Math Automaticity Task–Written version	Roditi (1988)

ses also supported the use of the RAS in first grade as a sensitive screen for the early detection of potential math problems. Analysis of children's performance on the various automaticity and problem-solving tasks indicate that the means of the impaired math problem-solving group differed significantly from the means of the average group of math problem-solvers.

TABLE 11.3
Summary Statistics for Grade 7:
Average (to Able) and Severely Impaired Math Problem Solvers

	Mean	(Standard Deviation)
Age:		
Average	12.9	(.30)
Impaired	12.9	(.30)
Sex:		
Average	18 girls; 22 boys	
Impaired	7 girls; 9 boys	
Peabody Picture Vocabulary Test IQ (kindergarten)		
Average	109.1	(12.2)
Impaired	106.0	(20.1)
Math Computation		
Average	3.4	(.7)***
Impaired	.7	(.7)
Math Word Problems		
Average	2.8	(.9)***
Impaired	.5	(.5)
Automatic Retrieval Rate–Numbers (total seconds)		
Average	19.2	(2.9)**
Impaired	21.8	(4.5)
Automatic Retrieval Rate–Letters (total seconds)		
Average	19.0	(3.1)**
Impaired	21.9	(5.2)
Automatic Retrieval Rate–Set-switching Letters, Numbers, Colors (total seconds)		
Average	25.5	(4.0)**
Impaired	29.0	(5.9)
Math Fact Retrieval–Verbal (number correct in 45 seconds)		
Average	15.5	(2.2)***
Impaired	10.6	(3.4)

(continued)

	Mean	(Standard Deviation)
Math Fact Retrieval–Written (time in seconds)		
Average	37.5	(10.4)***
Impaired	54.9	(8.7)
Mathematics Problem Solving (number correct)		
Average	6.3	(.9)***
Impaired	1.2	(.8)
(time in seconds)		
Average	369.5	(93.8)**
Impaired	447.5	(118.5)
Series Completion–Answers		
Average	5.1	(.8)***
Impaired	3.8	(1.3)
Series Completion–Explanations		
Average	8.9	(1.6)***
Impaired	7.1	(1.9)
Sequential Reasoning–Answers		
Average	4.4	(1.3)***
Impaired	2.3	(1.3)
Cognitive Flexibility–Answers		
Average	4.2	(1.3)**
Impaired	3.3	(1.3)
Cognitive Flexibility–Explanations		
Average	15.1	(3.3)**
Impaired	11.3	(2.7)
Boston Naming Test		
Average	48.9	(4.9)***
Impaired	43.2	(5.1)
BNT Multiple Choice Supplement		
Average	7.2	(3.9)***
Impaired	10.8	(3.1)

Note. The average-to-able group scored ≥ 5 on the Math Inventory; the severly impaired group ≤ 2 on the Math Inventory. Significance Levels for 1-tailed probability estimates: * $p \leq .05$; ** $p \leq .01$; *** $p \leq .001$.

In conclusion, this preliminary study suggests an alternate form of math assessment that is both child-centered and math content–oriented. Specifically, a math diagnostic battery that includes continuous naming speed tasks combined with cognitive strategy and language measures can assist in the detection and description of learning abilities and disabilities in mathematics.

Math Strategy Instruction

From Assessment to Teaching

Moving from research back to practice, new math assessment techniques that broaden the range of tasks can be used to describe each student's learning profile. These assessment approaches can also provide a better understanding of problem-solving strategies and how they impact on math learning and performance. Math assessment, then, takes account of the student's cognitive and learning profile and developmental status, as well as the specific math task demands within the context of the classroom. Assessment and teaching are linked during the process of defining instructional goals and teaching methods that (a) match the student's learning profile and (b) aim to develop strategies that assist in the acquisition of both declarative and procedural knowledge in the math domain. This form of math assessment often occurs in the context of a global evaluation that examines all vectors of a student's development including social-emotional, linguistic, and cognitive areas. This applied developmental approach to math assessment yields test findings that help psychologists, child developmentalists, special educators, and classroom teachers to make decisions about *what* to teach as well as how and *when* to teach.

To implement the assessment for teaching (AFT) model in mathematics, teachers need an appropriate forum for reviewing and discussing the assessment results. A case conference can provide such an opportunity when it is used appropriately; this team approach offers a structured time for teachers to exchange views about each child's performance in academic domains and in social contexts. Teachers can brainstorm methods for capitalizing on a child's strengths, for improving weak areas, and for defining instructional goals within all academic areas that involve mathematics (e.g., science). These goals must address both the *what* (the domain-specific skills) and the *how* (the strategies that assist in learning math skills and concepts).

Case Summary: Maxie

This section demonstrates how math assessment can go beyond traditional IQ testing and math achievement tests to yield a holistic view of the student's educational needs. Two evaluations are compared: First, findings of an evaluation are based mostly on scores from IQ and achievement tests. The results indicate a math disability but do not suggest instructional goals and teaching methods. The second evaluation, based on the AFT model, yields a rich description of the student's learning and problem-solving profiles and guides the selection of instructional goals, objectives, and teaching strategies. Using this diagnostic information, the teacher, educational therapist, and resource room teacher can create an appropriate learning environment by matching the student's learning profile with specific teaching methods and materials that address students' strengths and weaknesses.

Maxie is a 17-year-old girl who had almost completed her junior year in high school at the time of referral. She was recently tested by a psychologist who diagnosed a mathematics disability based on scores on the WAIS-R and the WRAT. At the time of the math evaluation, she was receiving special education support services in a school resource room. She was failing algebra and was becoming increasingly school phobic. She was absent so often that her teacher had lost interest in her. Maxie did not feel comfortable asking her teacher for extra help; instead, she received academic support from the resource room teacher and her father.

The test results from the initial evaluation indicated a math disability; math tutoring and counseling were recommended. Test results were as follows. WAIS-R: Verbal IQ = 112; Performance IQ = 119; Full Scale IQ = 116.

Verbal		Performance	
Information	12	Picture Completion	12
Digit Span	10	Picture Arrangement	16
Vocabulary	17	Block Design	12
Arithmetic	6	Object Assembly	12
Comprehension	16	Digit Assembly	10
Similarities	11		

Bender Test of Visual Motor Integration: Within normal limits
Spache Reading: Satisfactory
WRAT: Word Recognition = 81st %ile; Spelling = 66th %ile;
   Arithmetic = 10th %ile
Writing Sample: Satisfactory, some handwriting difficulties due to arthritis

Maxie was referred for a second math evaluation because several questions remained unanswered:

1. Should Maxie continue to study algebra?

2. What should be the main focus of educational therapy/tutoring?

3. What should be the goals of math instruction?

4. What skills and strategies does Maxie need to learn?

5. At what level should the educational specialist begin teaching?

6. What teaching techniques best match her learning profile?

7. How does Maxie's social-emotional status affect her math learning?

With a new math assessment approach based on the Assessment for Teaching model and the new math standards for the 1990s as a guide, it is possible to answer some of the above questions. Teaching methods can be identified for students like Maxie so that they can develop more effective and efficient strategies for solving math problems.

Selected Results from the Second Math Assessment

Tests Administered

The alternate math diagnostic battery was administered along with informal math activities, a learned helplessness scale, and supplemental projective tests. Selected subtests and results are provided in Table 11.4.

Behavioral Observations

On cognitive strategy measures, Maxie initially planned a strategy, but when faced with an obstacle, she impulsively shifted strategies. She often implemented new approaches and subsequently became lost in details. She also had difficulty explaining her strategies. On math tasks she was unsure of her answers, and she needed reassurance to continue using a specific strategy. She was a slow processor who needed much discussion as well as continual help with refocusing.

Maxie's arithmetic performance was best when tasks consisted of meaningful, concrete, real-life examples. She also performed well when given a visual model or a checklist to help her organize a sequence of steps for solving a problem. This step-by-step model followed by in-context examples and much practice provided her with the structure that she needed to solve math word problems.

TABLE 11.4
Results of Alternative Math Assessment: Summary

	Strengths	Weaknesses
Language measures		
RAN		*
RAS		*
BNT and multiple choice	*	
Math tasks		
SPES math automaticity task		*
SPES math inventory		*
Informal math activities		
Cognitive strategy measures: SPES		
Pattern analysis and memory cluster:		
Series Completion (NL/nonlinguistic)		
Accuracy		*
Explanations		*
Sequential Reasoning (L/linguistic)		*
Matrix Completion (NL)		*
Conceptual/thematic flexibility cluster		
Categorization (NL)	*	
Category Shift (L)	*	
Classification (L)	*	
SEDS Educational Profile		
Reading		
Sight vocabulary	*	
Decoding isolated words	*	
Decoding text	*	
Comprehension: (free recall/reformulation)		*
Comprehension: structured questions	*	
Writing		*
Illegible handwriting; excellent ideas and adequate language usage		
Spelling		
Recognition	*	
Retrieval (dictated words)		*
In context spelling		*
Mathematics		
Automatized operations		*
Computation		*
Concepts		*
Applications		*

Note. Additional measures of informal math tasks included (work samples, estimation, calculators, concrete aids; money). Math Anxiety Scale; IAR Learned Helplessness Scale; Memory Cluster/Stanford Binet: Visual Memory (107); Auditory Memory (128); Parent and Student Interview; Teacher Questionnaires.

Formulation *(excerpts related to math learning)*

Results of math assessment indicated a broad-based learning disability that affected a number of academic areas besides math—namely, spelling and writing. Areas of weakness included her ability to automatize math facts and operations, a lack of number sense, and use of effective, systematic approaches for solving math word problems. She displayed tremendous anxiety and lack of confidence on all mathematical tasks. Attentional drifts and subtle language difficulties were also evident, especially on pattern analysis and memory tasks.

On the SPES measures, Maxie demonstrated strong conceptual reasoning and effective problem-solving strategies. Her performance indicated strengths in categorizing and memorizing meaningful verbal information in vocabulary and verbal expression. On a number of measures of categorization, organization, and cognitive flexibility, she was able to identify global themes but often became lost in details. As she struggled to focus on relevant details, she impulsively switched approaches. Weaknesses were also evident on tasks that measured automaticity, sequential analysis, and active working memory.

On the RAN and RAS, *linguistic* measures of continuous naming speed, her performance indicated that she still had not acquired automatic recall for letters and numbers. She also experienced difficulties with set-switching. On the BNT, a confrontational naming task that attempts to differentiate vocabulary deficits from word-finding problems, her performance was adequate. However, word-finding difficulties were evident on other tasks when she was asked to explain her problem-solving process.

On an oral measure of automatized *math* operations, Maxie was able to recall only nine math facts out of a possible 20 facts in the 45-second time limit, and long latencies marked her performance. She switched from counting strategies to revisualization techniques in her struggle to retrieve math facts. Basic math facts in addition, subtraction, multiplication, and division were not automatized. These deficits in automatic memory for arithmetic facts correlated with her automatic recall difficulties on the RAN and RAS continuous-naming tasks.

On the SPES computational tasks, Maxie demonstrated a solid knowledge of basic operations, time concepts, and algorithmic rules of computation including regrouping in +, -, ×. In general, Maxie's performance indicated that she needed further instruction in the relationships among fractions, decimals, and percents. As calculations became more complex, she could no longer retrieve math facts rapidly or accurately. Mental calculations were time-consuming, inefficient, and distracted her from the main problem-solving process. Lack of automaticity and a lack of number sense in conjunction with the above-mentioned gaps in her arithmetic knowledge base interfered with her performance on word problems. She was not able to select the correct operations, to complete word problems, or to mentally compute efficiently, and she needed to write down all computational details. Despite these difficulties, she tried alternative strategies and attended to operational signs and details. However, she switched strategies too often and did not complete the problem-solving process independently, despite unlimited time.

In summary, Maxie's math ability was associated with her weaknesses in automatic retrieval, sequential analysis, organizational difficulties, gaps in her arithmetic knowledge base, and slight difficulties revisualizing information. Her difficulties attending to and organizing relevant visual details in combination with her impulsivity and her impersistence had interfered with learning math in the regular classroom. It is important to note that Maxie's cognitive and learning profiles were not well matched with the teaching method that had been used with its emphasis on rote learning, math fact drills, and computational worksheets. Instead, she needed strategy- and context-based instruction in mathematics to develop automaticity and an enhanced number sense for solving real-life math problems.

Selected Recommendations

1. One-to-one educational therapy in the area of mathematics was strongly recommended with the following primary instructional goals:

   a. To learn strategies for remembering math facts

   b. To build automaticity for math facts

   c. To learn how to use math as a tool for solving real-life math problems

   d. To build a number sense using contextually based curriculum

   e. To build self-confidence in the math area

2. Based on the assessment information, the following math instructional goals were defined:

   a. Number Sense

- To take an accounting course that emphasizes real-life situations

- To learn how to use a checkbook and to manage her money

b. Automaticity

- To learn strategies for accurate math fact recall

- To gradually increase speed in recalling math facts

c. Math Problem-Solving

- To learn how to use tables, graphs, and charts for organizing information

- To learn how to use a calculator

- To learn how to self-monitor and to self-check

3. It was recommended that Maxie focus her math education on reviewing her basic skills in an applied area such as business or in an area directly related to a vocation of her choice.

Instructional goals and teaching methods such as those suggested for Maxie are guided by applied developmental theory and research. Research-based techniques for building math automaticity and for solving math word problems can be selected that best match the student's unique cognitive and learning profile. The following section provides a summary of the research findings relevant to cognitive strategy use and number sense; these approaches can be used to develop automaticity for math facts and problem-solving procedures.

Automaticity and Math Strategy Instruction

Hasselbring, T., Goin, L., and Bransford, J. (1988) described instructional steps that help students like Maxie to move from effortful and inaccurate computation to automatic retrieval of basic math facts. In the past, math facts have been drilled using flash cards, work sheets, timed tests, and drill-and-practice software. They proposed a systematic procedure recommending that direct strategy instruction precede drill and practice. First, the current level of automaticity must be assessed in detail. This analysis separates math facts into three distinct subgroups: those that are (a) automatized, (b) strategically computed, and (c) completely unknown. Math fact grids, either teacher-made or purchased, are excellent visual aids for highlighting those facts that are already known. By reducing the number of facts to learn, the task becomes less overwhelming and minimizes the working memory load. Second, students are encouraged to develop strategies that build on their prior knowledge of math facts. Third, students should focus on only two or three math facts and their reciprocals. Practice in remembering and using the strategies is guided and untimed at the strategy-building phase. Finally, timed practices or "challenge times" are used to gradually increase recall rate.

To enhance automaticity further, "shell" software programs can be used that allow the teachers or students to program those math facts under consideration into the computer-based activity. The repertoire of "strategically computed" facts gradually increases to the point that timed practices may begin. In addition, shell programs (e.g., Robomath by Mindplay) allow students to bypass their handwriting or visual-spatial difficulties. By using computer software in a systematic, planful way, students build math fact accuracy and speed within a learning environment that is enjoyable and success-oriented.

Math Word Problems and Strategy Instruction

Math word problems, or verbal problem-solving, refer here to the story problems that are presented in math textbooks. Math word problems present a tremendous challenge for students with learning disabilities, because so many cognitive processes and skills are used simultaneously. Students are often overwhelmed by math word problems when they cannot read accurately; cannot hold information in working memory; struggle to conceptualize, sequence, and understand complex syntax; or a combination of these factors. Students, like Maxie, approach word problems impulsively and operate on whatever numbers they see, whether or not they understand the problem.

Various problem-solving strategies for approaching different types of math word problems have been incorporated into math curricula and materials that are currently available commercially. Greenes et al. (1985) and Coburn, Hoogeboom, & Goodnow (1989) have developed interesting and meaningful mathematics problems that can be used for teaching various strategies. Further, these materials can be used to teach students how to use a calculator as a tool for solving math problems. Students with learning problems benefit from direct math strategy instruction, but they also need further assistance to summarize and to organize step-by-step routines for following through on various strategies. Also new math curricula focus on teaching statistical concepts and skills of data collection, organization, and formulating and testing hypotheses. In this area, some students with learning problems may benefit because the emphasis is on learning by doing rather than on learning by lecture and memorization. However, the nature of educational assistance will likely change its form from skill remediation to strategy development and organization. Future research must evaluate the impact of the new math curricula on students who have learning problems.

Currently, few studies on verbal problem solving are available in the literature on learning disabilities as most of the research focuses on normal achievers. Greeno (1987) and Riley, Greeno, and Heller (1983) examined semantic factors; Carpenter and Moser (1982) studied various approaches to problem solutions; and Ballew and Cunningham (1982) studied the interrelationships among reading, computation, and problem solving. Cawley (1985) recognized that the general literature on learning disabilities fails to address verbal problem solving. He believes that research in this area must attend to the following limitations: (a) lack of sufficient comparisons across age levels and concurrent lack of longitudinal data; (b) limited research relative to diverse mathematics topics; and (c) limited research relative to specific cognitive attributes. The longitudinal and cross-sectional math study discussed earlier (Roditi, 1988) is an attempt to address some of these issues and to present a new methodology that can be useful to the development of an alternative approach to math evaluation based on the Assessment for Teaching model.

Conclusion

An applied developmental approach to math assessment and instruction is critical. To identify and teach students with learning problems in mathematics, psychological and educational researchers must examine the cognitive, linguistic, social-emotional, and developmental factors underlying mathematics learning disabilities. Paradigms such as the Assessment for Teaching model, AFT, (Meltzer, 1991; Meltzer & Roditi, 1989) in mathematics can provide teachers with a flexible set of diagnostic tools and approaches for understanding how their students learn best. Teaching methods can be selected that foster students' strengths, remediate weaknesses, and encourage the use of effective compensatory strategies. With direct strategy instruction, students can be taught which math strategies to use when, why and how. Student progress toward instructional goals can be continually reevaluated in relation to developmental changes, varying task demands, and the changing context of the classroom. Instructional goals and teaching methods can be reviewed and modified to account for changes and to advance student progress.

Advances in mathematics education research and practice have been substantial (Silver, 1987) and have resulted in new trends in math curricula for the 1990s. Contextually based curricula such as Used Numbers (Russell & Corwin, 1989) and interactive math projects link mathematical concepts to everyday problem solving and emphasize a balance between rote memory for basic math facts and effective problem-solving strategies for higher level math applications. The trends in math software development are also extremely promising. Computer tools are becoming available that encourage students to represent and to manipulate numbers in various ways (Kaput & Pattison-Gordon, 1987). This new software concretizes the abstract and is flexible enough to address the needs of students with diverse cognitive and learning profiles. Further, an integrated system that links descriptive math assessment information with new math curricula and teaching techniques can be developed. This bank of teaching techniques can be used to access math strategies and materials that assist in teaching specific math skills to students with learning problems and that are simultaneously beneficial to all students in the classroom.

The Assessment for Teaching model (AFT) in mathematics, then, can help students learn to solve real-life math problems, to feel more confident in their math abilities, and to value mathematics as a tool for solving many of life's everyday problems. A unified approach from researchers and teachers in psychology and education is critical for advancing our techniques for mathematics assessment and strategy instruction. In this combined effort, applied developmental models and methodologies can be further developed and tested. Joint collaboration within an applied developmental framework will ultimately improve the art and science of mathematics assessment and strategy instruction.

References

Ackerman, P., Anhalt, J., Dykman, R. (1986). Arithmetic automatization failure in children with attention and reading disorders: Associations and sequela. *Journal of Learning Disabilities, 19*(4), 222–231.

Ballew, H., & Cunningham, J. (1982). Diagnosing strengths and weaknesses of sixth-grade students in solving word problems. *Journal for Research in Mathematics Education, 13*, 202–210.

Benson, F., & Denckla, M. (1969). Verbal paraphasia as source of calculation disturbance. *Archives of Neurology, 21*, pp. 96–102.

Brown, V., & McEntire, E. (1984). *Test of mathematical abilities.* Austin, TX: PRO-ED.

Carpenter, T., & Moser, J. (1982). The development of addition and subtraction problem solving skills. In T. P. Carpenter, J. M. Moser, & T. A. Romberg

(Eds.), Addition and subtraction: A cognitive perspective (pp. 9–24). Hillsdale, NJ: Lawrence Erlbaum Associates, Inc.

Carpenter, T., & Peterson, P. (1988). Learning through instruction: The study of students' thinking during instruction in mathematics. *Educational Psychologist, 23*(2), 79–85.

Cawley, J. F. (Ed.). (1985). *Cognitive strategies and mathematics for the learning disabled.* Rockville, MD: Aspen.

Coburn, T., Hoogeboom, S., & Goodnow, J. (1989). *The problem solver with calculators,* Palo Alto: Creative Publications.

Cohn, R. (1961). Dyscalculia. *Archives of Neurology, 4,* 301–307.

Cohn, R. (1971). Arithmetic and learning disabilities. In H. R. Myklebust (Ed.), *Progress in learning disabilities* Vol. 2, (p. 2). New York: Grune & Stratton.

Denckla, M. B., & Rudel, R. (1976). Rapid "automatized" naming (R.A.N.): Dyslexia differentiated from other learning disabilities. *Neuropsychologia, 14,* 471–479.

Dewey, J. (1916). *Democracy and education.* New York: Macmillan.

Fennema, E. (Ed.). (1981). *Mathematics education research: Implications for the 80's.* Alexandria, VA: Association for Supervision and Curriculum Development.

Garofalo, J., & Lester, F. J. (1985). Metacognition, cognitive monitoring, and mathematical performance. *Journal for Research in Mathematics Education, 16,* 163–176.

Garnett, K., & Fleischner, J. (1983). Automatization and basic fact performance of normal and learning disabled children. *Learning Disability Quarterly, 6,* 223–230.

Gelman, R., & Gallistel, C. R. (1978). *The child's understanding of number.* Cambridge, MA: Harvard University Press, 1978.

Gerstmann, J. (1924) Fingeragnosie: Eine umschriebene Storung der Orientierung am eigenen Korper. *Wein.klin.Wschr, 37,* 1010–1012.

Ginsburg, H., & Mathews, S. (1984). *Diagnostic test of arithmetic strategies.* Austin, TX: PRO-ED.

Ginsburg, H. (Ed.). (1983). *The development of mathematical thinking,* New York: Academic Press.

Goldstein, D., Wilson, S., & Gerstein, A. (1983). Applied developmental psychology: Problems and prospects for an emerging discussion. *Journal of Applied Developmental Psychology, 6,* 341–348.

Goldstein, K. (1948). *Language and language disturbances.* New York: Grune & Stratton.

Goldman, S. (1989). Strategy instruction in mathematics. *Learning Disability Quarterly, 12,* 43–55.

Goodglass, H. (1980). Disorders of naming following brain injury. *American Scientist, 68,* 647–655.

Goodglass, H., & Kaplan, E. (1972). *The assessment of aphasia and related disorders.* Philadelphia: Lea & Febiger.

Greenes, C., Immerzeel, G., Ockenga, E., Schulman, L., & Spungin, R. (1985). *TOPS beginning problem solving.* Palo Alto, CA: Dale Seymour.

Greeno, J. (1987). Instructional representations based on research about understanding. In A. Schoenfeld, *Cognitive science and mathematics education* (pp. 61–88). Hillsdale, NJ: Erlbaum.

Hasselbring, T., Goin, L., & Bransford, J. (1988). Developing math automaticity in learning handicapped children: The role of computerized drill and practice. *Teaching Exceptional Children, 20*(6), 3–7.

Head, H. (1926). *Aphasia and kindred disorders of speech.* New York: Macmillan.

Hiebert, J., & Wearne, D. (1987). Instruction and cognitive change in mathematics. *Educational Psychologist, 23*(2), 105–117.

Jastak, S., & Wilkinson, G. (1984). *Wide range achievement test–Revised.* Wilmington, DE: Jastab Assoc.

Johnson, D., & Myklebust, H. (1967). *Learning disabilities: educational principles and practices.* New York: Grune & Stratton.

Kaplan, E., Goodglass, H., & Weintraub, S. (1983). *Boston naming test.* Philadelphia: Lea & Febiger.

Kaput, J., & Pattison-Gordon, L. (1987). A concrete-to-abstract software ramp: Environments for learning multiplication, division, and intensive quantity. Technical (Report No. 400-83-0041). Cambridge, MA: Educational Technology Center. (ERIC Document Reproduction Service No. ED 294 713).

Kosc, L. (1974). Developmental dyscalculia. *Journal of Learning Disabilities, 7,* 164–177.

Kosc, L. (1981). Neuropsychological implications of diagnosis and treatment of mathematical learning disabilities. *Topics in Learning & Learning Disabilities, 1*(3), 19–30.

Lerner, J. (1976). *Children with learning disabilities* (2nd ed.). Boston: Houghton Mifflin.

Lerner, J. W. (1989). *Learning disabilities: Theories, diagnosis, and teaching strategies* (5th ed.). Boston: Houghton Mifflin.

Levine, M., Brooks, R., & Shonkoff, J. (1980). *A pediatric approach to learning disorders.* New York: Wiley.

Luria, A. (1966). *Higher cortical functions in man.* New York: Basic Books.

Luria, A. R. (1973). Towards the mechanisms of naming disturbance. *Neuropsychologia, 11,* 417–426.

Meltzer, L. J. (1984). Cognitive assessment and the diagnosis of learning problems. In M. D. Levine & P. Satz (Eds.), *Middle childhood: Development and dysfunction.* (pp. 131–152). Baltimore: University Park Press.

Meltzer, L. J. (1987). *Surveys of problem-solving and educational skills.* Cambridge, MA: Educational Publishing Services.

Meltzer, L. J. (1991). Problem-solving strategies and academic performance in learning-disabled students: Do subtypes exist? In L. Feagans, E. Short, & L. Meltzer (Eds.), *Subtypes of learning disabilities. Theoretical perspectives and research.* (pp. 163–188). Hillsdale, NJ: Erlbaum.

Meltzer, L., Fenton, T., & Solomon, B. (1984). *Automatization and abstract problem-solving as predictors of achievement.* Paper presented at 92nd

Annual Convention of the American Psychological Association at Toronto, Ontario, Canada.

Meltzer, L. J., & Roditi, B. N. (1989). *Assessment for teaching: An alternative approach to the diagnosis of learning disabilities.* Manuscript in preparation.

Mindplay (1980). *Robomath.* Tucson, AZ: Methods & Solutions, Inc.

Morrison, F., Lord, C., & Keating, D. (1984). *Applied developmental psychology.* (Vol. 2). Orlando, FL: Academic Press.

National Council of Teachers in Mathematics (1984–1985). The impact of computing technology on school mathematics: Report of an NCTM conference. *Journal of Computers in Mathematics and Science Teaching.* Winter, 19–22.

National Council of Teachers in Mathematics (1989). *Curriculum and evaluation standards for school mathematics.* Reston, VA: Author.

Piaget, J. (1952). *The child's conception of number.* New York: W. W. Norton.

Polya, G. (1957). *How to solve it* (2nd ed.). New York: Doubleday.

Pressley, M. (1986). The relevance of the good strategy user model to the teaching of mathematics. *Educational Psychologist, 21*(1 & 2), 139–161.

Reid, D., & Hresko, W. (1981). *A cognitive approach to learning disabilities.* New York: McGraw Hill.

Reisman, F., & Hutchinson, T. (1985). *Sequential assessment of mathematics inventories.* Columbus, OH: Merrill.

Resnick, L., & Ford, W. (1981). *The psychology of mathematics for instruction.* Hillsdale, NJ: Erlbaum.

Riley, M., Greeno, J., & Heller, J. (1983). Development of children's problem-solving ability in arithmetic. In H. P. Ginsburg (Ed.), *The development of mathematical thinking* (pp. 153–196). N.Y.: Academic.

Roditi, B. (1988) Automaticity, cognitive flexibility, mathematical problem-solving: A longitudinal study of children with and without learning disabilities (Doctoral dissertation, Tufts University). *Dissertation Abstracts International, 49,* 2396B.

Rudel, R., Denckla, M., Broman, M., et al. (1980). Word-finding as a function stimulus context: Children compared with aphasic adults. *Brain and Language, 10,* 111–119.

Russell, S. J., & Corwin, R. B. (1989) *Statistics: The shape of the data.* Palo Alto, CA: Dale Seymour.

Russell, R. L., & Ginsburg, H. P. (1981). Cognitive analysis of children's mathematics difficulties. *Cognition and Instruction, 1*(2), 217–244.

Schoenfeld, A. (1987). *Cognitive science and mathematics education.* Hillsdale, NJ: Erlbaum.

Scholnick, E. (1983). Scrutinizing application: An agenda for Applied Developmental Psychology. *Journal of Applied Developmental Psychology,* (4), 329–339.

Scott, K. (1983). ADP symposium article: Applied developmental psychology. *Journal of Applied Developmental Psychology,* (4), 319–327.

Sigel, I. (1983). Introduction: Applied developmental psychology symposium. *Journal of Applied Developmental Psychology,* (4), 117–119.

Silver, E. (1987). Foundations of cognitive theory and research for mathematics problem-solving. In A. Schoenfeld (Ed.), *Cognitive science and mathematics education*. (pp. 33–60). Hillsdale, NJ: Erlbaum.

Singer, H. D., & Low, A. A. (1933). Acalculia. *Archives of Neurology and Psychiatry, 29*, 467–498.

Spring, C., & Davis, J. (1988). Relations of digit naming speed with three components of reading. *Applied Psycholinguistics, 9*, 315–334.

Sternberg, R. J., & Wagner, M. S. (1982). Automatization failure in learning disabilities. *Topics in Learning and Learning Disabilities, 2*, 1–11.

Stone, A., & Michals, D. (1986). Problem-solving skills in learning disabled children. In S. J. Ceci (Ed.), *Handbook of cognitive, social, and neuropsychological aspects of learning disabilities*, pp. 291–315. Hillsdale, NJ: Erlbaum.

Swanson, H. L. (1989). Strategy instruction: Overview of principles and procedures for effective use. *Learning Disability Quarterly, 2*(1), 3–14.

Torgeson, J. K., & Wong, B. L. (1986). *Psychological and educational perspectives on learning disabilities*. Orlando, FL: Academic Press.

Vygotsky, L. S. (1978). *Mind in society*. Cambridge, MA: Harvard Press.

Wechsler, D. (1974). *The Wechsler intelligence scale for children*. New York: The Psychological Corp.

Weinstein, M. L. (1978). Dyscalculia:*A psychological and neurological approach to learning disabilities in school children*. Philadelphia: Unpublished Doctoral dissertation, University of Pennsylvania.

Wertlieb, D. (1983). Some foundations and directions for applied developmental psychology. *Journal of Applied Developmental Psychology*, 4(4), 349–358.

Wolf, M. (1982). The word-retrieval process and reading in children and aphasics. In K. E. Nelson (Ed.), *Children's language*, (pp. 437–493). Hillsdale, NJ: Erlbaum.

Wolf, M. (1984). Naming, reading, and the dyslexias: A longitudinal overview. *Annals of Dyslexia, 34*, 87–115.

Wolf, M. (1986). Rapid alternating stimulus (R.A.S.) naming: A longitudinal study in average and impaired readers. *Brain and Language, 27*, 360–379.

Wolf, M., Bally, H., & Morris, R. (1986). Automaticity, retrieval processes, and reading: A longitudinal study in average and impaired readers. *Child Development, 57*, 988–1000.

Wolf, M., & Goodglass, H. (1986). Dyslexia, dysnomia, and lexical retrieval. *Brain and Language, 28*, 154–169.

Wong, B. (1985). Issues in cognitive behavioral interventions in academic skill areas. Special issue: Cognitive-behavior modification with children: A critical review of the state-of-the-art. *Journal of Abnormal Child Psychology, 13*(3), 425–442.

PART 4

Strategy Instruction and Classroom Demands

L earning difficulties frequently manifest when there is a mismatch between the individual's specific developmental and learning profile and the demands of the curriculum and/or the social setting. As has been emphasized throughout this volume, the often-changing relationships among these processes, subskills, and environmental demands either allow the child to cope effectively or result in the manifestation of a learning disability that may have been previously dormant. Transition times in the curriculum are particularly problematic for these students because of the increasing requirements to coordinate multiple skills and strategies. The final section of this volume focuses on the implications of the academic setting for the identification and teaching of students with learning disabilities.

In Chapter 12, Lewis Putnam, Donald Deshler, and Jean Schumaker discuss the performance gap that occurs when students with learning disabilities are faced with curriculum requirements that are too demanding for their skills and background knowledge. They attribute the failure of many of these students to the discrepancy between their learning skills and rates on the one hand, and the difficulty of the instructional objectives on the other hand. They discuss the learning strategies and instructional methods developed by Deshler and his colleagues over the past decade, and they attribute their most successful techniques to the match with the curriculum demands. They argue for the importance of evaluating the classroom setting as well as the specific individual characteristics, and they present an alternative assessment approach for identifying these critical setting demands.

In the final chapter, Michael Pressley, John Borkowski, Donna Forrest-Pressley, Irene Gaskins, and Debra Wile provide closing thoughts on the assessment and treatment of learning disabilities within the context of a strategic learning perspective. They reiterate the major theme of the volume—namely, that learning disabilities are multifaceted and "there is no one thing wrong with the child with learning disabilities and there is no one thing to 'fix'." Their chapter summarizes the major differences between students with learning disabilities and good information processors as well as the critical components of effective assessment and intervention techniques. The link with the classroom setting is discussed in the context of the importance of training professionals who can assess and teach in ways that promote effective information processing.

This entire volume emphasizes the multifaceted nature of learning disabilities and the importance of considering multiple interactions among cognitive, affective, behavioral, and social factors as they impact on identification and intervention. The challenge of assessment and teaching is immense, as it is not currently possible to determine the exact etiology of a particular child's problems. Each child's specific neurologic/biological vulnerabilities interact with particular curricular and environmental variables to create consonance or dissonance and to either mask or uncover the learning problem. These issues combine to make assessment and teaching of this population both a science and an art and to create an exciting and challenging future for those professionals who continue to attempt to "crack the code" of these reading and learning problems.

12

The Investigation of Setting Demands: A Missing Link in Learning Strategy Instruction

M. Lewis Putnam, Donald D. Deshler, Jean B. Schumaker

Many students with learning disabilities, in spite of significant intervention efforts on their behalf, are not successful in public school settings. Often, this lack of success has been attributed to factors within the students themselves. Alternative explanations for the failure of students with learning problems disabilities in public schools may be found by examining an important element of the school setting: the school's curriculum.

Indeed, the very nature of the school's curriculum has created some very significant problems for students with learning disabilties. Curriculum materials tend to be developmental in nature, with later skills and knowledge building on previously learned skills and knowledge. Thus, as students get older, the curriculum places increased demands on the students who have not mastered the necessary skills and knowledge to comprehend and keep pace with the new content that is being delivered in the regular classroom. These increased demands are particularly evident as students move into the secondary grades where both the amount and complexity of the curriculum increase dramatically. In effect, a significant "performance gap" is created when the curriculum demands outstrip the skills and background knowledge that students possess to comprehend and acquire the new content (Deshler & Schumaker, 1988). For students who fall behind, the size of this performance gap increases as students progress through school and as the amount of work required and the complexity of the curriculum increase across grade levels (Warner, Schumaker, Alley, & Deshler, 1980).

In essence, the curriculum of any school is designed to meet the needs of the average student at each grade level. The student's degree of mastery or lack of mastery of the curriculum represents the main method by which schools measure the success or failure of individual students. Gickling and Thompson (1985) concluded that, for this one reason, the curriculum, even more than the classroom teacher, is the key variable that consistently controls a student's success or failure, thus creating what these researchers call "curriculum casualties" (p. 207). These curriculum casualties, be they low-achieving students or students with specific learning disabilities, are singled out because of their inability to keep pace with the developmental nature of the curriculum.

Many students, especially in the secondary grades, therefore, need modifications and/or special educational services because the curriculum is presented in such a way that a discrepancy is created between the difficulty of the instructional objectives and the skills and learning rates of the students (Gickling & Havertape, 1982). The emergence of learning strategy instruction as a viable instructional approach over the past decade has, in part, been aimed directly at the challenge of reducing the size of the performance gap encountered by many students with low achievement and learning disabilities. Learning strategies have been defined as sets of behaviors or routines aimed at acquiring, storing, and expressing information (Deshler & Lenz, in press). The purpose of learning strategy instruction is to teach students to use these routines in an effective and efficient manner so that they can independently keep pace with the curriculum.

The purpose of this chapter is fivefold: (a) to describe the instructional goals associated with strategies instruction and how the most effective strategies instruction is that which is designed *in light of the curriculum demands* that students must meet; (b) to present rationales for including the setting as well as the student in educational assessment and planning; (c) to describe currently available assessment methodologies for assessing setting demands; (d) to describe an alternative method for analyzing setting demands; (e) to provide an example data set from a study of setting demands in seventh- and 10th-grade classrooms derived through the application of this alternative method; and (f) to describe how a task-specific learning strategy can be designed to enable students to respond to a specific set of setting demands.

Goals Associated with Strategies Instruction

Several strategy-related instructional efforts have been developed in recent years (e.g., Borkowski, Estrada, Milstead, & Hale, 1989; Deshler & Schumaker, 1988; Palincsar & Brown, 1989; Pressley, Symons, Snyder, & Cariglia-Bull, 1989). Although there is diversity among these various approaches relative to what or how to teach certain strategies to students, they share several important factors. For example, a key assumption underlying these various strategies approaches is that, within the educational experience, the learning process should be emphasized as much as specific domains of content information. In other words, many aspects of the instructional process should focus on teaching students how to learn and how to perform. A direct way of accomplishing this focus is to teach students strategies related to how to successfully apply skills and use knowledge to meet the demands of various in-school and out-of-school situations. In short, a strategies instructional approach is seen as a way by which teachers select, deliver, and organize the curriculum such that learning is facilitated. By carefully modeling the processes of selecting, delivering, and organizing, teachers can show students how to manipulate and control content information. Over time, students master the skills involved in manipulating and controlling content information, and they become more independent in the learning process.

A major research emphasis of the University of Kansas Institute for Research in Learning Disabilities (KU-IRLD) for the past decade has been to develop a strategies instructional program for application with adolescents and young adults who evidence a learning disability or other problems associated with low achievement. As defined by the KU-IRLD staff, a strategy is an individual's approach to a task. It includes how a student thinks and acts when planning, executing, and evaluating one's performance on the task and its outcomes (Lenz, Clark, Deshler, & Schumaker, 1988). In other words, a strategy is seen as a "tool" that can be used by learners to facilitate their analysis of the demands of a given problem or setting, to help them make decisions regarding the best way(s) to address the problem, and to guide their completion of the task while carefully monitoring the effectiveness of the process along the way.

Thus, for teachers to be successful in teaching students how to be strategic in analyzing the demands associated with a task and in completing the task, they must be aware of curriculum and other setting demands. In short, they need to view the instructional decision-making process not only in light of the learning deficiencies students bring to an instructional situation, but, equally as important, in light of the setting demands with which students are expected to cope in their school environment. Furthermore, for students to become strategic learners, teachers must also take an active role in carefully orchestrating strategic instruction and learning experiences. Strategies instruction must be extensive as well as intensive. That is, a series of strategies that are matched with the curriculum and other setting demands must be deliberately taught on a daily basis over as sustained period of time (Deshler & Schumaker, 1986). Such matchups must reflect not only the setting demands that students are expected to address immediately, but also the demands they will be encountering in the near and far future. An example of an immediate setting demand is the identification and memorization of pertinent information for tests in a science course in which the student is currently enrolled; future demands might include being able to write themes in an upcoming English course or to work as a member of a team or regularly check completed work in actual on-the-job situations. Clearly, strategy instruction that is geared to address both the short- and long-term needs of students will be most effective in helping them be successful on a consistent and sustained basis (Ellis, Lenz, & Sabornie, 1987).

Rationales for Assessing Setting Demands as Well as Learner Characteristics

Thus, to be successful, learning strategy teachers need to plan and implement their instruction after considering the short- and long-term demands that their students will face. Nevertheless, as Schumaker and Deshler (1984) argued, remedial interventions for students with mild handicaps have traditionally focused solely on the specific learning characteristics manifested by the students. These students' difficulties have most frequently been measured with psychometric tests for the purpose of revealing specific areas of strengths and weaknesses in different academic areas (e.g., written expression, reading) or areas assumed to be correlated with school achievement (e.g., visual or auditory memory, picture completion).

Unfortunately, instructional interventions that have been designed according to a model that focuses solely on an analysis of student deficiencies have several limitations. First, most psychometric test instruments used to assess the characteristics of students with learning disabilities do not measure the students' performance on the wide array of skills needed to cope successfully with the curriculum and other demands that students encounter in public school settings. For example, skills such as note taking, critical listening, memorizing content information, and test taking are seldom assessed. Interventions based on limited findings may, in turn, be limited in scope and appropriateness. Second, the technical adequacy of many of the psychometric assessment instruments commonly used to assess the learning characteristics of students is questionable (Thurlow & Ysseldyke, 1982). Third, the shortcomings of assessment practices that emphasize the analysis of student deficiencies alone have been underscored by the limited amount of functional data generated through the analysis of the learner that is germane to instructional planning. This is particularly evident when attempts are made to generate individually tailored programs from standardized test data collected through group administrations (Ysseldyke & Thurlow, 1984).

Fourth, the academic failure experienced by students with learning disabilities might be best understood by analyzing a comprehensive array of factors such as teacher behaviors, curriculum expectations, response requirements, and social expectations as well as the strengths and weaknesses of an individual as a learner. Schlick, Gall, and Riegel (1981), for example, showed how basic curriculum requirements vary greatly across grade levels and subject areas and posited this variance as a major reason for analyzing factors beyond student variables. For instance, during the early years of school, teachers rely heavily on informal observation and oral responses from students to measure students' comprehension of material; however, as students move into the upper grades, the most popular procedure of measuring a student's competence is through tests. Hence, the demand for students to demonstrate their knowledge through different response modalities and through the application of different strategies across the grade levels is very apparent. Likewise, there are different demands placed on students in different subject areas within the same grade level. Wong (1985) argued, for example, that the outcome objectives for social studies and geography instruction are markedly different than the outcome objectives for science instruction. Specifically, the major goals associated with social studies/geography instruction are comprehension and retention of content knowledge, whereas the major goals associated with science instruction are the acquisition and transfer (i.e., application) of content knowledge. Thus, the variance in nonstudent factors across grade levels and subject areas underscores the importance of considering the demands of the setting as much as the deficits of the student in making instructional decisions. The probability of designing interventions that enable students with learning disabilities to cope with curriculum and other setting demands is increased only to the extent that assessment practices measure both student and nonstudent variables.

The inclusion of nonstudent variables in educational models is not a new concept. Brown, Campione, and Day (1981), for example, proposed the use of a tetrahedral model as an organizational framework for exploring questions about why learning may or may not occur. Brown suggested that a variety of factors be considered when designing an instructional plan: (a) the nature of the materials from which information is to be learned (e.g., text structure, logic of content, and available cues); (b) the critical tasks or the end point for which the learner is preparing (e.g., generalized rule use, verbatim recall vs. gist); (c) activities in which students must engage to make learning an effective process (e.g., determining whether to use strategies, rules, or procedures); and (d) general characteristics of the learner (prior experience, background knowledge, abilities, and interests). Thus, this model includes student attributes as only one of several components in a model that is to be used to explain why learning difficulties may exist.

Another model related to the learning process that includes factors outside the individual was presented as early as 1935, in Lewin's (1935) model, $[B = f(P \times E)]$, where B = behavior, P = person, and E = environment. That is, he viewed behavior as a function of the person's interaction with the environment. Researchers at the KU-IRLD have adapted this model and view the behavior of students with learning difficulties as a function of the interaction between learner variables and environmental variables. Lewin's model has been used by KU-IRLD researchers to illustrate how strategies instruction might be conceptualized and used to increase the effectiveness and efficiency of a student's performance (or behavior). In the formula $B = f(P \times E)$, an individual's behavior (B) is seen as resulting from an interaction between the demands of the school environment (E) and the characteristics of the person (P). The behavior is judged as acceptable if the demands placed on the individual are met effectively and efficiently. The goal associated with the intervention process, then, is to enable individuals to approach tasks more effectively and efficiently in the context of the situations and demands encountered across settings. In the case of KU-IRLD intervention work, the goal associated with strategies instruction is to promote effective and efficient behavior by prompting strategic learning and performance supported by the creation of strategic environments.

Research conducted at the KU-IRLD (e.g., Alley, Schumaker, Deshler, Warner, & Clark, 1983; Deshler, Schumaker, Alley, Warner, & Clark, 1982; Schumaker, Deshler, Alley, & Warner, 1983) has indicated that students with learning disabilities and other low-achieving students have deficits related to the demands of the settings in which they are required to participate and be successful. Therefore, based on what is known about setting demands and student characteristics, there is a significant mismatch between the two factors of the equation, P and E. Without effective intervention, the interaction between the environment and the individual is likely to lead to ineffective and/or inefficient behavior (Deshler & Lenz, in press).

In summary, there are numerous reasons why setting demands as well as learner characteristics should be determined when planning interventions that will be sufficiently powerful to enable learners to become independently efficient and effective in meeting those demands. Psychometric testing, as the sole method of assessment, is limited due to its often poor relationship to the demands that must be met, its technical inadequacy, and its restricted usefulness in aiding the generation of individual educational programs. Assessment systems that also take into account environmental variables are invaluable tools for helping teachers establish a meaningful link between the assessment process and instruction. Such systems are consistent with Howell's (1986) observations about the interactive process of learning:

> If the purpose of evaluation is to affect the quality of this interaction, then evaluation must address each of these elements. To focus only on one element is to avoid the interactive nature of the learning process. . . . Additionally, if the ultimate goal of evaluation is to alter current instructional practice, not merely to describe or make predictions about it, the greatest amount of attention should be directed toward variables that have the most impact on the interaction and are easiest to alter. Frequently these "alterable variables" . . . are not student variables. (p. 325)

In short, the conceptual framework being argued for is one that relies heavily on collecting and understanding data from those settings in which the student is expected to succeed (e.g., the regular classroom). By more fully understanding these factors, educators will not only be able to better grasp the dynamics contributing to a student's failure but, more important, be in a position to make sound instructional decisions regarding which strategies to teach to the student.

Available Methods for Determining Setting Demands

A major challenge confronting the classroom teachers or school psychologist who wants to help a low-achieving student or a student with learning disabilities is to collect relevant data and, in turn, transform those data into appropriate educational interventions. Significant progress has been made in recent years in the design and validation of methods that enable individuals to gather data on factors affecting a student's learning and performance. Most of these procedures are based on the assumption that a complex array of factors affects the degree of success a student encounters in school. Particularly emphasized by these instruments are environmental and instructional factors. Some of the more commonly used measures in this area are descibed below:

The Instructional Environment Scale (TIES)

TIES (Ysseldyke & Christenson, 1987) enables individuals to make qualitative judgments about the instruction within a classroom. Its two major purposes are (a) to systematically describe the degree to which a student's academic or behavior problems are a result of instructional factors within the student's environment and (b) to specify starting points in developing appropriate instructional interventions for the student. Information is gathered through observation of the student in a classroom setting and through interviews with both the student and his or her teacher. Data obtained through these methods are entered on recording forms and then rated to determine the extent to which each of 12 components (each component is considered to be a principle of effective instruction) is characteristic of instruction within the student's classroom. The following is a list of components and examples of the type of information that is evaluated: (a) instructional presentation—instruction is presented in an understandable fashion; (b) classroom environment—behavior within the classroom is systematically controlled; (c) teacher expectation—expectations are high but realistically set for the amount and accuracy of completed work; (d) cognitive emphasis—thinking skills required for successful work completion are explicitly communicated to the student; (e) motivational strategies—the student's interest and effort are heightened through the use of effective motivational strategies; (f) relevant practice—sufficient and appropriate practice is provided to the student; (g) academic engaged time—the student actively participates in completing assignments; (h) informed feedback—immediate and specific feedback is provided to the student on his or her behavior or performance; (i) adaptive instruction—the curriculum is adapted to meet the individual needs of the student; (j) progress evaluation—the student's progress toward meeting instructional objectives is directly and frequently measured; (k) instructional planning—appropriate instruction is provided based on the individual student's needs; and (l) student understanding—teacher directions and expectations are clearly communicated to the student.

The Social Behavior Survival Program (SBS)

SBS (Walker, 1983) is both an assessment system and an intervention package. Its purposes are (a) to enable the identification of appropriate regular classroom placements; (b) to provide identification of the adaptive behavioral skills required for successful integration into the regular classroom; and (c) to prepare the student to meet the teacher's minimal behavioral expectations and demands and assist the student in his or her adjustment in the regular classroom. The assessment component of this program, *Assessments for Integration into Mainstream Settings* (AIMS) (Walker, 1986), is designed for use in identifying those adaptive skills needed for successful performance within the mainstream setting and those maladaptive social behaviors deemed unacceptable by the regular classroom teacher. AIMS relies on teacher ratings of adaptive and maladaptive dimensions of a student's behavior. Teachers in mainstream classes rate item descriptions of a student's adaptive behavior in terms of whether they are *Critical, Desirable*, or *Unimportant* to a student's ability to respond to the demands for successful adjustment in the regular classroom. The outcomes of these measures are used to tailor an instructional program for students in areas of targeted student weakness or high setting demand.

The School Survival Skills (SSS) Program

The SSS (Kerr, Nelson, & Lambert, 1987) is both an assessment instrument and an intervention program designed to address the skills needed by secondary students with learning and behavioral problems to be successful within the mainstream setting. The overall goal associated with the SSS is to help students to determine the requirements for success in their mainstream classes. A series of checklists and questionnaires are used to develop a profile of the skills required by students to respond to the demands of the mainstream setting. For example, The School Survival Skill Questionnaire, completed by the classroom teacher, is used to determine the various skills that the teacher considers to be important for the target student to possess to respond successfully to the demands and expectations of that class (e.g., whether students need to turn work in on time, keep busy while waiting for the teacher's help, and raise their hands to get the teacher's attention). A checklist entitled The Study Skills Inventory is designed to be completed by the student to determine, in light of the demands of a given class, which skills are needed to be successful. A similar checklist is available for the regular class teacher to complete to determine discrepancies between the student's perceptions and the teacher's perceptions of required student skills in relation to specific setting demands.

An Alternative Method for Determining Setting Demands

Thus, several methods currently are available for determining setting demands as they relate to student characteristics. Unfortunately, although these methods focus on setting demands and can be effectively used for a variety of purposes, their focus often is not specific enough to the problem of the development and implementation of learning strategy instruction with adolescents in secondary school settings. Learning strategies, as defined by the KU-IRLD, are task specific; that is, they relate to specific tasks that students must perform (e.g., gaining information from a textbook chapter, memorizing items for a test). Without the necessary information (e.g., the readability and complexity of the textbook, the complexity of the items to be memorized), the development of meaningful interventions cannot be accomplished. An alternative method, which allows the needed analysis for learning strategy instruction, is a four-step process for assessing setting demands called the setting demand hierarchy system (Putnam, 1988). The first step in this process is the *specification of domains* that may be critical in helping teachers better understand the performance of students with learning disabilities or low achievement. In the example provided in Figure 12.1, "Tests" has been specified as the domain or demand cluster; this is listed in the top box of the figure. The second step in the Setting Demand Hierarchy System involves the *specification of performance areas* that a student must address to effectively deal or cope with the domain cluster. Because three of the necessary performance areas for responding to the demands associated with tests are preparing for tests and answering questions on a test, following directions during a testing situation, these areas appear in the set of boxes directly below the domain, "Tests." The third step in the process involves the *specification and measurement of demand elements* related to each of the performance areas. For example, one variable related to the performance area of following directions is the sentence structure of the written directions. If a sentence has many clauses, it could be more difficult to read and comprehend than a sentence having only one clause. Each of the demand elements related to a performance area must be specified and, in turn, measured. The measurement of a given demand element provides valuable information regarding the nature and magnitude of the specific setting demand as well as an indication of the type and intensity of learning strategies required to enable students to successfully address the setting demand. These setting demand elements appear in the third row of boxes in the hierarchy depicted in Figure 12.1. The final step of the process is the *specification of learning strategies* that a student should acquire to successfully respond to or cope with the presenting setting demand. Two basic sources of such strategies are depicted in the fourth row of boxes in Figure 12.1. First, teachers can select an already-designed strategy to teach a student. Several examples of ones developed by the KU-IRLD staff are listed in Figure 12.1. For example, to enable a student to successfully prepare for a test that will require the recall of several factual items and details from a chapter, students can be taught *The FIRST-Letter Mnemonic Strategy* (Nagel, Schumaker, & Deshler, 1986). This strategy has been shown to enable students to successfully identify and memorize important information in a textbook chapter. Second, if an already-designed strategy does not meet the specific requirements of a given setting demand, teachers can design a strategy to match a set of demand parameters. The work of Ellis, Lenz, and Clark (in press) provides step-by-step procedures for teachers to follow in designing strategies to meet specific setting demands. As an alternative to a strategy, it may be most appropriate to specify instructional accommodations that the regular classroom teacher can make to facilitate the learning process for at-risk students in their classrooms. For example, a classroom accommodation for teachers to use during the preparation phase would be to conduct a thorough review session that focuses students' attention on important concepts and facts and on designing mnemonic devices to aid recall.

Putnam (1988) has developed setting demand hierarchies for the class participation, textbook, teacher presentation, student work assignment, and social/behavioral domains. Figures 12.2 and 12.3 present these setting demand hierarchies for the student work assignment and social/behavioral domains. He used a variety of methodologies to collect data about these different demand domains, including tape-recording teacher lectures, analyzing teacher- and publisher-made tests, analyzing textbooks and other student-use materials, and interviewing students and teachers. A major advantage of Putnam's approach to setting demands assessment is that a setting demand hierarchy can be flexibly

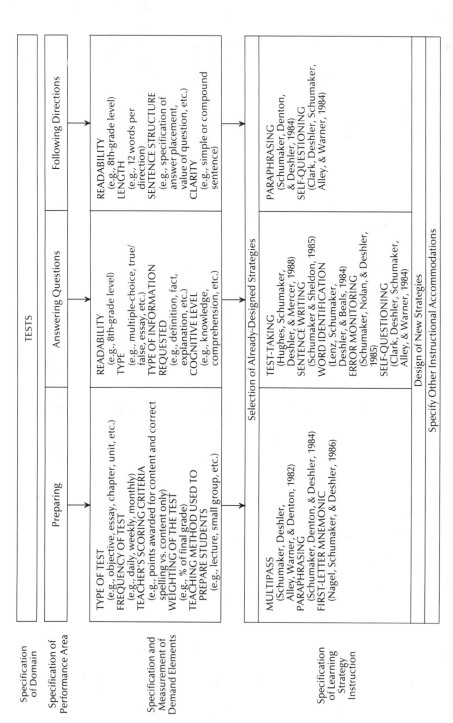

FIGURE 12.1. Setting Demands of Hierarchy System.

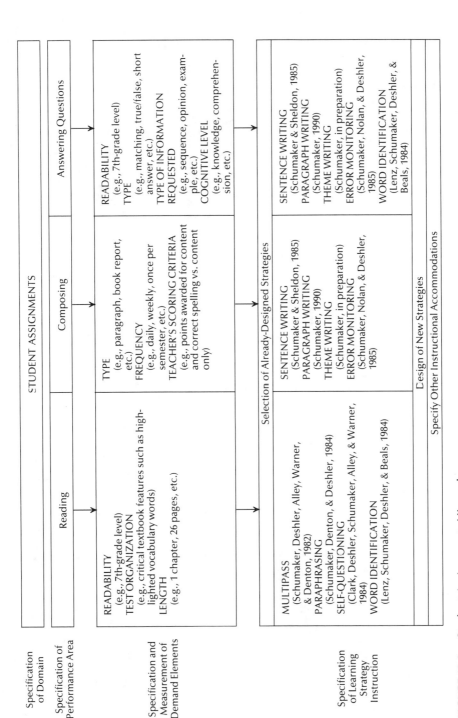

FIGURE 12.2. Student Assignments Hierarchy.

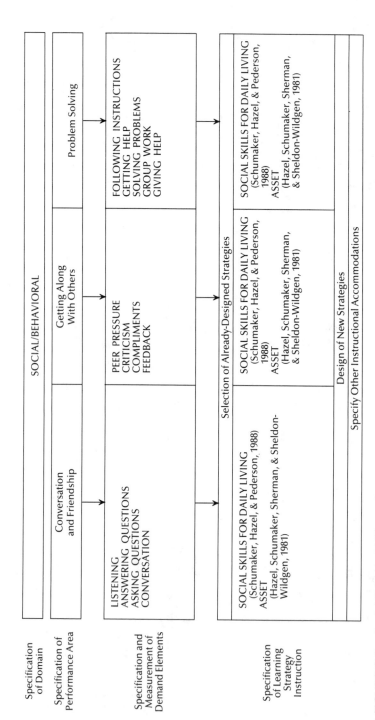

FIGURE 12.3. Social Behavioral Hierarchy.

created by anyone (including students themselves) to do a functional analysis of a setting and, in turn, to facilitate the instructional planning process including the tailoring of learning strategy instruction to meet the unique needs of an individual student or a group of students. To illustrate how a setting demand hierarchy can be used to facilitate the development of an instructional program, the data gathered in conjunction with the setting demand hierarchy in Figure 12.1 will be presented along with its resulting programmatic outcomes in the next two sections.

An Example Data Set from a Study of Seventh- and 10th-Grade Setting Demands

As shown in Figure 12.1, a number of setting demand variables (e.g., readability of test questions, type of questions) were identified as relevant to the demand domain "Tests." For educators to instruct students in such a way that they can be successful in coping with the demands within this domain, specific information is needed about each of these variables. The data presented in this section regarding the setting demands that seventh- and 10th-grade students are expected to meet relative to taking teacher- and publisher-made tests in the regular classroom will help to underscore the value of these kinds of data in making decisions on strategies instruction. These are part of a larger data set gathered to examine a broad array of setting demands in secondary schools (e.g., textbook characteristics, student work assignments, teacher presentation practices and styles). The overall goal was to create a data base on regular classroom setting demands that could provide a basis for instructional decision making and program development.

Selection of Settings and Teachers

One hundred and twenty teachers from eight school districts in the states of Kansas, Indiana, and Florida were the main data source for this study. Sixty of the teachers taught at the seventh-grade level, and 60 taught 10th-grade students. Within each grade level, the teachers were evenly divided among four subject areas (i.e., English, science, social studies, and mathematics). Twenty-six schools were represented by these teachers. Two of the districts served lower class students; four served middle class students; and two served upper class students. Two of the districts were rural, five were suburban, and one was urban. The student enrollment in the districts ranged from 832 students to 128,290 students.

Information Sources

Two sources of information provided data on the test-taking demands in seventh- and 10th-grade settings. First, each teacher was individually interviewed on 45 open-ended questions about one of the courses he or she taught at the specified grade level. These questions dealt with a broad range of topics related to how teachers constructed, prepared students for, administered, and graded tests as well as how they determined quarterly grades. Second, each of the teachers was asked to provide three different tests that he or she used to evaluate student learning in the targeted course. Thus, 360 tests were collected and analyzed. These tests covered either a chapter or a unit and were tests that were regularly administered in the targeted course.

Major Findings

Data collected from the teacher interviews and the 360 classroom tests have produced information that has value for guiding the design and instruction of strategy-based interventions. Results reported below address four major issues: general testing and grading practices, test organization, test directions, and test questions.

General Testing and Grading Practices.   A major finding of this research was the importance that secondary content teachers assign to student's performance on classroom tests. Figure 12.4 shows how a student's quarterly grade was determined by the participating English, science, social studies, and math teachers in the seventh and 10th grades. The data indicate that almost half (45.9%) of a student's grades for a 9-week grading period is based on his or her test scores. This is true at both the seventh- and 10th-grade levels and across subject areas. Another major finding was that students take an average of 11 tests per quarterly grading period per class. Typically, these tests are either teacher-made (49.6%) or publisher-made (41.6%) tests.

According to the teachers, their lectures were the major source of information on which test questions were based. Figure 12.5 shows that the teachers at both grade levels in this study were devoting an average of 47.8% of each class period to teacher lecture. This finding is consistent with other research on secondary classroom demands (Moran, 1980; Schumaker, Sheldon-Wildgen, & Sherman, 1980) and underscores Goodlad's 1984 observation about the limited range of pedagogical procedures used by secondary teachers versus a much broader array of instructional approaches used by elementary classroom teachers. The other instructional procedure used with relatively high frequency by the teachers in this study was seatwork, whereas

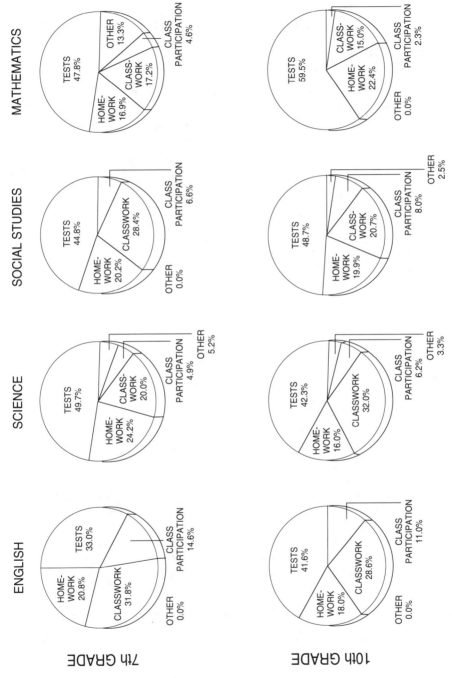

FIGURE 12.4. Determination of Grade for Grading Period.

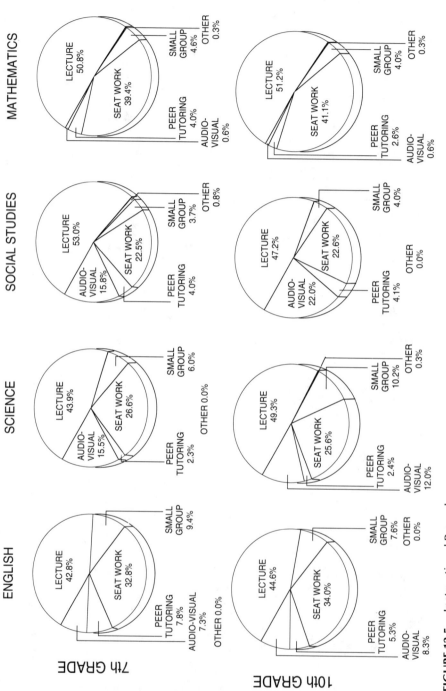

FIGURE 12.5. Instructional Procedures.

peer tutoring and small-group activites were used very infrequently. Each of these findings raises particular concerns given what is known about the characteristics of students with learning disabilities. Specifically, the large percentage of student grades determined by classroom tests as well as the large number of tests given to students during a grading period may be especially troublesome to students with LD because of their well-documented difficulties in reading and general information processing (e.g., McKinney, 1988; Warner, Schumaker, Alley, & Deshler, 1989). Similarly, students with LD have been shown to evidence deficits in listening and note-taking skills (Deshler et al., 1982) as well as on-task behavior (Hallahan, Lloyd, Kneedler, & Marshall, 1982), thus the heavy reliance on lectures and seatwork may be particularly troublesome to students with learning disabilities.

Test Organization.   When the tests were carefully inspected for organizational characteristics, the data indicated that the typical test at the secondary level was divided into an average of 3.9 sections, and the tests were organized according to the different types of questions included within them (e.g., there was a section with multiple-choice questions, a section with true-false questions, etc.). Varying point values were assigned to different sections. Data were also gathered on the number of "sectional cues" in a test. A sectional cue was defined as any signal that denotes a change in the test (i.e., through directions, lines, Roman numerals, etc.). There was a close one-to-one correspondence between the number of sections and the number of sectional cues found per test, with the exception of seventh-grade mathematics tests which were found to contain some sections devoid of sectional cues. Another test-organization measure was the number of times the question type changed per test. Results indicated that question type changed an average of 4.9 times per test, ranging from 1.8 times on seventh-grade English tests to 7.6 times on 10th-grade science tests. Thus, these data on the manner in which secondary tests are organized clearly suggest that students are expected to respond to a broad array of formats and question types when taking written examinations, and they are expected to shift flexibly from one format to another several times while taking the same test. These findings may present special challenges to students with learning disabilities, given the difficulties some of them have demonstrated relative to being flexible in learning situations (Deshler, Warner, Schumaker, & Alley, 1983) and in demonstrating their competence in variety of formats (Schumaker & Deshler, 1984).

Test Directions.   The typical test in the secondary content classroom was found to place major reading demands on students, especially in reading and following test directions. Data showed that tests contained an average of four separate directions written at an average 7.6 grade level for the seventh- grade tests and 8.4 grade level for the 10th-grade tests (based on an average of the Dale-Chall Readability Formula [Dale & Chall, 1948], the FOG Index [Klare, 1963], and the Flesch Index [Flesch, 1948]). Each direction contained an average of 3.2 sentences, and few, if any, of the five components of an adequate direction (i.e., question type—refers to whether the question type, e.g., multiple-choice, is stated in the direction; question thought—refers to whether the thought process needed to answer a question is stated in the direction; question action—refers to whether the action required to answer the question is stated in the direction; question placement—refers to whether the test direction(s) clearly specifies where students should record their response; and question value—refers to whether the point value of an answer or set of answers is stated within the directions). Specifically, only 10% of the directions stated the question type, question thought, and question value; only 20% explained where the answer was to be placed; and only 50% stated the question action. The predominant sentence structure of the typical direction was either simple or complicated-simple (i.e., a simple sentence with one or more prepositional phrases). Thus, although the structure of the directions was relatively simple, the content of the directions was not particularly helpful, and the readability of the directions was substantially difficult for low-achieving secondary students who are typically reading at or below the fourth-grade level (Warner et al., 1980).

Test Questions.   The average test was found to consist of an average of 32 questions requiring an average of 40 responses. Thus, students having 50-minute test sessions made about 1.3 responses per minute. The largest percentage of test questions (x = 27.6%) required the student to recall specific facts at the knowledge level of Bloom's (1956) Taxonomy of Educational Objectives. Almost half of the questions (x = 50.5%) were basic "recognition questions" (i.e., ones that simply required students to pick the correct answer from those provided). Examples of recognition-type questions are multiple-choice, matching, and true-false. "Recall questions" (i.e., ones that require the student to retrieve from memory the correct answer and write it in a brief form) were found to make up 9.8% of the questions on tests. These questions consisted of fill-in-the-blank items, listing items, and labeling items. "Production questions" (i.e., ones that require the student to demonstrate the correct answer in an extended written form) made up 39.5% of the test questions. These questions consisted of word problems, essay questions, short-answer questions, computation problems, and construction questions.

The data derived from the teacher interviews revealed few instances in which they provided testing accommodations for students or instruction in test-taking strategies that students could use to facilitate their test performance. When it did occur, strategy instruction was reported to be offered on a sporadic basis. The most widely taught strategy/skill was answering the easy questions first (reported by 1.18% of teachers).

Finally, when the data were examined across subject areas, they revealed that many demands are common to English, social studies, science, and mathematics tests at the secondary level. When differences did occur across the subject areas, the majority occurred between mathematics and the three other subject areas.

Designing Strategy Instruction in Light of Setting-Demand Data: An Example

The data presented above in combination with data gathered on learner characteristics (Alley et. al., 1983; Deshler et al., 1982; Warner et al., 1980) indicate that students with learning disabilities and other students with low achievement will have significant difficulties coping with these demands. They need to be taught strategies that enable them to do well on tests given in mainstream settings. One example of a learning strategy that has been designed to provide students with an effective and efficient way to improve their performance on classroom tests is the *Test-Taking Strategy* (Hughes, Schumaker, Deshler, & Mercer, 1988). This strategy has been developed to help students (a) allocate time for and prioritize the sections of a test (this is important in light of Putnam's, 1988, finding that typical tests consist of several sections with numerous questions that must be answered in a short period of time, thus requiring careful time usage); (b) carefully read and focus on important elements in test instructions (this is important in light of Putnam's finding that test instructions contain few of the elements of an adequate test instruction—question type, question thought, question action, question placement, or question value—thus students need to be cued to focus on the elements that are present); (c) utilize other learning strategies like *The FIRST-Letter Mnemonic Strategy* (Nagel, et al., 1986) in conjunction with this strategy to recall important information (this is important in light of the magnitude of the curriculum demands secondary students are expected to meet and the observed phenomenon that an intervention program in which several strategies are taught and coordinated over a sustained period of time has a greater chance of impacting at-risk learners [Deshler & Schumaker, 1988]); (d) systematically and quickly progress through the test by selectively answering or abandoning questions (this is important in light of Putnam's finding that tests consist of large number of questions with varying point values and the notion that a student's performance can be enhanced by focusing on those items that are known best and have the highest point values); (e) make well-informed guesses (this is important in light of the large number of tests that Putnam found the typical secondary student must take during an academic year and the low probability that at-risk students will be fully prepared for each test); and (f) take control of the testing situation through regular use of positive self-talk (this is important in light of Putnam's finding that approximately 50% of a student's grade in secondary classes is determined by her or his performance on classroom tests; thus, the constant demand to show their competence on the basis of tests necessitates students being empowered through such strategies as self-talk to take control of their performance independently and effectively).

Therefore, the *Test-Taking Strategy* (Hughes et al., 1988) provides students with a comprehensive routine that can be used in a variety of situations that require students to meet the parameters of setting demands similar to those described by Putnam (1988). The remembering system designed to help students recall each of the steps of this strategy is "PIRATES"; each of the letters of the acronym can be used by students to prompt themselves to perform critical behaviors in the course of taking a test in the regular classroom. The first step is "Prepare to succeed" and comprises the activities that students should complete before beginning work on the test. The specific behaviors that this step cues students to perform are: (a) Put your name and "PIRATES" on the test; (b) allot time and order to the test sections; (c) say affirmations (i.e., positive statements that enable students to connect their performance with strategy use—"I will be able to perform well on this test because I'm going to use the test-taking strategy I've learned"); and (d) start within 2 minutes. The second step is "Inspect the instructions." Specifically, students are taught to (a) carefully read the instructions; (b) underline what to do (e.g., "Circle the letter next to the most appropriate choice") and where to respond (e.g., "Put your answer in the blank in front of the question"); and (c) note any special requirements (e.g., "Mark the answer that is *not* correct"). The third step is "Read, remember, reduce." This step guides the student's behavior in dealing with the questions in the various sections on the test. The components of this step are: (a) Read the whole question—by doing so students can avoid careless errors such as missing key information in the test question or one of the multiple-choice options; (b) remember what you studied—students are prompted to reflect back on the information they studied for the test and recall specific items they committed to memory through the use of a visual image or other mnemonic device (e.g., the FIRST-Letter device); and (c) reduce choices as you read them—this prompts students to first try to eliminate obviously wrong options in multiple-choice questions. The fourth step of this strategy is "Answer or abandon." If students are certain of the answer for a question, they are to mark it on their answer sheet in the proper manner. If, however, they are unsure, they are to put a mark by the question and go on to items on the test for which they do know the answer. At a later point in the testing period, they are to return to these abandoned items.

The fifth step of the strategy is "Turn back." This step is performed after all the test questions have been answered or abandoned and simply requires students to review the entire test for the purpose of identifying and answering any questions that have been abandoned. Once an abandoned item is found, students are to use the sixth step of the strategy, "Estimate." Here, students take their best guess at answering questions that have been abandoned by using one of three "ACE Guessing Techniques": (a) Avoid absolutes—that is, avoid answer options that include such words as *never* and *always;* (b) Choose the longest and most detailed choice—that is, choose the answer that provides the greatest amount of detail; and (c) Eliminate similar choices—because there can only be one correct answer, this technique involves looking for and eliminating options that are similar. The final step of the strategy is "Survey." In this step, students carefully survey the entire test for the purpose of ensuring that all questions have been answered, that all stray marks that might be misunderstood by the teacher (or a scantron) as an item answer are erased, and that all items have been marked correctly.

Two factors are central to the success of instruction in this strategy: (a) Students must be taught to assume an active rather than a passive role during a testing situation; and (b) practice materials must be designed to mirror the demands that students will face in the mainstream. Students are taught that there is a direct correlation between their use of this strategy and their performance on classroom tests and, thus, their ability to respond to a major setting demand in secondary schools. They learn to use the strategy at mastery levels on tests specially designed to be similar to the tests they will encounter (e.g., the tests include several sections, each containing a set of directions and items similar to those they will face). Mastery not only involves use of the strategy steps but fluent completion of tests so that students can meet the demand of answering 1.3 questions per minute. Research on the effects of instruction in this strategy (Hughes & Schumaker, 1991) has indicated that students can learn the strategy and generalize their use of it to mainstream tests in such a way as to improve their quarterly grades in mainstream classes.

Therefore, this strategy is particularly useful for low-achieving students for several reasons. First, they often have difficulty passing required courses. Because a major portion of students' course grades in middle and secondary school are a function of how well they perform on classroom tests, teaching them how to pass their tests often enables them to pass their courses. Second, low achievers tend to be passive when faced with taking a test; they believe they can do little or nothing to alter their performance on a test. The routines built into this strategy have been shown to markedly alter the degree of active participation of the student in the test-taking process. The research on this strategy has indicated that relatively quick and significant gains in the classroom performance of low-achieving students can be achieved through systematic and intensive instruction in the strategy.

Finally, it is important to consider the degree to which the PIRATES strategy is unique to the learning and performance needs of students with learning disabilities as opposed to representing good instruction that will be beneficial for all students. The initial design considerations for this strategy specified that that strategy had to be sufficiently powerful to impact the performance of students with learning disabilities in the regular classroom. The data have shown this to be the case. Data are also available to suggest that the strategy can be readily learned and effectively applied by nondisabled learners. Yet to be addressed, however, is the issue of whether this strategy is more effective for certain subgroups of students with learning disabilities than others.

Conclusion

The major premise on which this chapter has been based is that instruction in learning strategy interventions can be most effectively implemented if those responsible for instructional planning consider *both* the characteristics of the learner and the demands of the setting in which the student is expected to perform. The setting that should be considered when determining setting demands is the "criterion environment," that setting(s) in which the student must perform if he or she is to successfully compete with normally achieving peers. If students are to feel good about themselves in relation to normally achieving peers, the criterion environment is the mainstream classroom or the workplace—certainly not the special education or remedial classroom. Historically, the thrust of special and remedial education has been to measure the success of intervention efforts with regard to the student's performance in the special class or remedial setting. Unfortunately, this approach falls far short of creating a match between a student's performance and the demands of the criterion setting. It also falls far short of enabling students to feel good about themselves with regard to the learning tasks they face on a daily basis. For example, if a 10th-grade student is determined to be reading at the fourth-grade reading level, and a goal is set in the remedial classroom for the student to make a 2-year gain over the course of a year in reading, such a goal and association instruction will not enable the student to meet the demands associated with obtaining information from his or her current government textbook that is written at the 12th-grade level, nor will it enable the student to feel good about his or her performance in the required government class. Such errors in instructional planning have perhaps been made because student-based assessment data can be readily collected and monitored in the special class setting without any attention being given to the student's performance in nonspecial class settings. This chapter has shown how the determination of setting demands can be successfully used to guide the design and implementation of learning strategy instruction that enables students to independently achieve success in the mainstream. Data derived after constructing a setting demand hierarchy were presented, and an example learning strategy was described to illustrate how strategy instruction can be tailored to prepare students to meet the specific demands that they may encounter in a criterion environment.

To conclude, the work in the area of setting demands as they relate to learning strategy instruction is clearly in its infancy. One obvious next step will be to design a set of instruments/procedures that can be widely used by school psychologists, regular classroom teachers, the special education teacher, and the student to identify demands and to design and plan strategy instruction. The focus of such instruments must be to determine setting demands in key domains in a given school setting. This team approach would enable key parties to understand the demands in a given domain as well as to choose the learning strategies that should be taught to enable students to more effectively and efficiently cope with the identified setting demands. By making this process highly participatory, communication will be facilitated among all parties, and special education instruction will be more closely tied to the overall educational mission of the school. This will ensure that students who are at risk for failure have a good change of succeeding and of feeling good about their participation in the mainstream.

References

Alley, G. R., Schumaker, J. B., Deshler, D. D., Warner, M. M., & Clark, F. L. (1983). Learning disabilities in adolescents and young adult populations: Research implications (Part II). *Focus on Exceptional Children, 15*(9), 1–14.

Bloom, B. L. (1956). *Taxonomy of educational objectives.* New York: McKay.

Borkowski, J. G., Estrada, M. T., Milstead, M., & Hale, C. A. (1989). General problem-solving skills: Relations between metacognition and strategic processing. *Learning Disability Quarterly, 12*(1), 57–70.

Brown, A. L., Campione, J. C., & Day, J. D. (1981). On training students to learn from texts. *Educational Researcher, 10*(2), 14–21.

Clark, F. L., Deshler, D. D., Schumaker, J. B., Alley, G. R., & Warner, M. M. (1984). Visual imagery and self-questioning: Strategies to improve comprehension of written material. *Journal of Learning Disabilities, 17,* 145–149.

Dale, E., & Chall, J. (1948). Formula for predicting readability. *Educational Research Bulletin, 27,* 11–20, 37–54.

Deshler, D. D., & Lenz, B. K. (in press). The strategies instructional approach. *International Journal of Development, Disability, and Education.*

Deshler, D. D., & Schumaker, J. B. (1986). Learning strategies: An instructional alternative for low-achieving adolescents. *Exceptional Children, 52*(6), 583–590.

Deshler, D. D., & Schumaker, J. B. (1988). An instructional model for teaching students how to learn. In J. L. Graden, J. E. Zins, & M. J. Curtis (Eds.), *Alternative educational delivery systems: Enhancing instructional options for all students* (pp. 391–411). Washington, DC: National Association of School Psychologists.

Deshler, D. D., Schumaker, J. B., Alley, G. R., Warner, M. M., & Clark, F. L. (1982). Learning disabilities in adolescents and young adult populations: Research implications (Part II). *Focus on Exceptional Children, 15*(1), 1–12.

Deshler, D. D., Warner, M. M., Schumaker, J. B., & Alley, G. R. (1983). The learning strategies intervention model: Key components and current status. In J. D. McKinney & L. Feagans (Eds.), *Current topics in learning disabilities* (Vol. 1). Norwood, NJ: Ablex.

Ellis, E., Lenz, B. K., & Clark, F. L. (in press). *TACTIC: Developing strategy interventions.* Lawrence, KS: University of Kansas Institute for Research in Learning Disabilities.

Ellis, E. S., Lenz, B. K., & Sabornie, E. J. (1987). Generalization and adaptation of learning strategies to natural environments: Part I: Critical agents. *Remedial and Special Education, 8*(1), 6–20.

Flesch, R. (1948). New readability yardstick. *Journal of Applied Psychology, 32,* 221–223.

Gickling, E. E., & Havertape, J. F. (1982). Curriculum-based assessment. In J. A. Tucker (Ed.), *Non-test based assessment.* Minneapolis: The National School Psychology Inservice Network, University of Minnesota.

Gickling, E. E., & Thompson, V. P. (1985). A personal view of curriculum-based assessment. *Exceptional Children, 52,* 205–218.

Goodlad, J. (1984). *A place called school: Prospects for the future.* New York: McGraw-Hill.

Hallahan, D. P., Lloyd, J. W., Kneedler, R. D., & Marshall, K. J. (1982). A comparison of the effects of self-versus teacher assessment of on-task behavior. *Behavior Therapy, 13,* 715–723.

Hazel, J. S., Schumaker, J. B., Sherman, J. A., & Sheldon-Wildgen, J. (1981). *ASSET: A Social Skills Program for Adolescents.* Champaign, IL: Research Press.

Howell, K. W. (1986). Direct assessment of academic performance. *School Psychology Review, 15*(3), 324–335.

Hughes, C. A., & Schumaker, J. B. (1991). Test-taking strategy instruction for adolescents with learning disabilities. *Exceptionality, 2,* 205–221.

Hughes, C. A., Schumaker, J. B., Deshler, D. D., & Mercer, C. (1988). *The Test-Taking Strategy: The instructor's manual.* Lawrence, KS: Edge Enterprises.

Kerr, M. M., Nelson, C. M., & Lambert, D. L. (1987). *Helping adolescents with learning and behavior problems.* Columbus, OH: Merrill.

Klare, G. R. (1963). *The measurement of readability.* Ames: Iowa State University Press.

Lenz, B. K., Clark, F. L., Deshler, D. D., & Schumaker, J. B. (1988). *The strategies instructional approach (Preservice training package).* Lawrence: University of Kansas Institute for Research in Learning Disabilities.

Lenz, B. K. Schumaker, J. B., Deshler, D. D., & Beals, V. L. (1984). *The Word Identification Strategy: The instructor's manual.* Lawrence: The University of Kansas Institute for Research in Learning Disabilities.

Lewin, K. (1935). *A dynamic theory of personality: Selected papers.* [Donald K. Adams & Karl E. Zener, Trans.]. New York: McGraw-Hill.

McKinney, J. D. (1988). Conceptually and empirically derived subtypes of specific learning disabilities. In M. C. Wang, M. C. Reynolds, & H. J. Walberg (Eds.), *Handbook of special education: Research and practice* (Vol. 2). New York: Pergamon Press.

Moran, M. R. (1980). *An investigation of the demands on oral language skills of learning disabled students in secondary classrooms* (Research Rep. No. 1). Lawrence: University of Kansas Institute for Research in Learning Disabilities.

Nagel, D., Schumaker, J. B., & Deshler, D. D. (1986). *The FIRST-Letter Mnemonic Strategy: Instructor's manual.* Lawrence, KS: Edge Enterprises.

Palincsar, A. S., & Brown, A. L. (1989). Instruction in self-regulated reading. In L. B. Resnick & L. E. Klopfer (Eds.), *Toward the thinking curriculum: Current cognitive research: 1989 Yearbook of the Association for Supervision and Curriculum Development* (pp. 19–39). Washington, DC: Association for Supervision and Curriculum Development.

Pressley, M., Symons, S., Snyder, B. L., & Cariglia-Bull, T. (1989). Strategy instruction research comes of age. *Learning Disability Quarterly, 12*(1), 16–31.

Putnam, M. L. (1988). *An investigation of the curricular demands in secondary mainstream classrooms containing students with mild handicaps.* Unpublished dissertation, University of Kansas, Lawrence.

Schlick, A. R., Gall, M., & Riegel, R. H. (1981). Modifying study guides, practice and tests for students with learning difficulties at the secondary level. In T. Shaw (Ed.), *Teaching handicapped students in social studies* (pp. 72–83). Washington, DC: National Education Association.

Schumaker, J. B. (1990). *The Paragraph Writing Strategy: Instructor's manual.* Lawrence: University of Kansas Institute for Research in Learning Disabilities.

Schumaker, J. B., Denton, P. H., & Deshler, D. D. (1984). *The Paraphrasing Strategy: Instructor's manual.* Lawrence: The University of Kansas Institute for Research in Learning Disabilities.

Schumaker, J. B., & Deshler, D. D. (1984). Setting demand variables: A major factor in program planning for learning disabled adolescents. *Topics in Learning Disorders, 4,* 22–44.

Schumaker, J. B., Deshler, D. D., Alley, G. R., & Warner, M. M. (1983). Toward the development of an intervention model for learning disabled adolescents. *Exceptional Education Quarterly, 3*(4), 45–74.

Schumaker, J. B., Deshler, D. D., Alley, G. R., Warner, M. M., & Denton, P. H. (1982). Multipass: A learning strategy for improving reading comprehension. *Learning Disability Quarterly, 5,* 295–304.

Schumaker, J. B., Hazel, J. S., & Pederson, C. S. (1988). *Social skills for daily living.* Circle Pines, MN: American Guidance Service.

Schumaker, J. B., Nolan, S. M., & Deshler, D. D. (1985). *The Error Monitoring Strategy: Instructor's manual.* Lawrence: The University of Kansas Institute for Research in Learning Disabilities.

Schumaker, J. B., & Sheldon, J. (1985). *The Sentence Writing Stragegy: Instructor's manual.* Lawrence: The University of Kansas Institute for Research in Learning Disabilities.

Schumaker, J. B., Sheldon-Wildgen, J., & Sherman, J. A., (1980). *An observational study of the academic and social behaviors of learning disabled adolescents in the regular classroom* (Research Rep. No. 22). Lawrence: University of Kansas Institute for Research in Learning Disabilities.

Thurlow, M. L., & Ysseldyke, J. E. (1982). Instructional planning: Information collected by school psychologists vs. information considered useful by teachers. *Journal of School Psychology, 20,* 3–10.

Walker, H. M. (1986). The assessment for integration into mainstream settings (AIMS) assessment system: Rationale, instruments, procedures, and outcomes. *Journal of Clinical Child Psychology, 15*(1), 55–63.

Walker, H. M. (1983). The SBS Program (Social Behavior Survival): A systematic approach to the integration of handicapped children into less restrictive settings. *Education and Treatment of Children, 6,* 421–441.

Warner, M. M., Schumaker, J. B., Alley, G. R., & Deshler, D. D. (1980). Learning disabled adolescents in the public schools: Are they different from other low-achievers? *Exceptional Children Quarterly, 1*(2), 47–56.

Warner, M. M., Schumaker, J. B., Alley, G. R., & Deshler, D. D. (1989). The role of executive control: An epidemiological study of school-defined LD and low-achieving adolescents on a serial recall task. *Learning Disability Research, 4*(2).

Wong, B. Y. L. (1985). Potential means of enhancing content skills acquisition in learning disabled adolescents. *Focus on Exceptional Children, 17*(5), 1–8.

Ysseldyke, J. E., & Christenson, S. L. (1987). Evaluating students' instructional environments. *Remedial and Special Education, 8,* 17–24.

Ysseldyke, J. E., & Thurlow, M. L. (1984). Assessment practices in special education: Adequacy and appropriateness. *Educational Psychologist, 3,* 123–136.

13

Closing Thoughts on Strategy Instruction for Individuals with Learning Disabilities: The Good Information-Processing Perspective

Michael Pressley, John G. Borkowski, Donna Forrest-Pressley, Irene W. Gaskins, Debra Wile

The two overarching concerns of this volume, assessment and treatment of learning disabilities, continue to present formidable challenges to the professional educator and educational research communities. Assessment of learning disabilities is a complex process, with this complexity mandated by the interaction of factors that determine academic outcomes. In turn, effective treatment is usually multifaceted. That is, there is no one thing wrong with the child with learning disabilities, and there is no one thing to "fix." Rather, a number of factors can combine to produce skilled performance. If any one of them is awry, a number of components of the system may be affected negatively. Thus, if a child does not possess efficient learning strategies, knowledge of the world will be diminished. Motivation to attempt academic work might also be reduced, because many academic tasks require much more effort in the absence of effective strategies.

This situation poses a diagnostic dilemma. Even if there were a single cause of a particular child's learning disability, it could not be identified. A diagnostician might be able to recognize lack of strategies, lack of world knowledge, and low motivation. Nonetheless, he or she usually would not be able to determine unambiguously that lack of strategies was the originating cause, because low motivation could reduce the likelihood that efficient strategies would be acquired or used and because many strategies can only operate (or only operate efficiently) given extensive world knowledge.

Our perspective is that all components covered in this volume are important to consider as part of the assessment and treatment of learning disabilities. The diverse factors reviewed by the various authors are like pieces of a puzzle that fit together to produce an overall picture of learning disabilities, consistent with our perspective about the nature of good information processing. After a brief introduction to good information processing and how students with learning disabilities differ from prototypical good information processors, assessment and intervention that is consistent with the good information processing is taken up, as is the development of professionals who can assess and teach in ways that promote good information processing.

Good Information Processing

There are various starting points for describing human cognition. Developmental psychologists have traditionally focused on issues of basic competence rather than performance, one aim being to determine the earliest age at which particular cognitive abilities, tendencies, behaviors, or strategies appear. Much is made of fundamental capabilities. Can the child manifest an ability, tendency, strategy, or behavior under any circumstances? In contrast, our approach is to focus on more generally competent performance: What would cognition be like if it were as good as it could be, in a decidedly mature and competent organism? The good information processor does well in a number of situations and tasks. A major reason for developing this model of competent performance was that the defining characteristics of immature thinking could be identified if mature cognitive functioning were better understood.

Mature Thinking

Our conception of thinking (Borkowski, 1990; Borkowski, Carr, Rellinger, & Pressley, 1990; Pressley, Borkowski, & Schneider, 1987, 1989) centers around a student's knowledge of strategic processes that can mediate important academic tasks (e.g., reading, writing, memorizing, communicating). Our approach has been referred to previously as the Good Strategy User model, because strategies were emphasized much more than other components in the earliest versions of the model. Although the model has always included metacognitive, motivational, personality, and nonstrategic knowledge components, those determinants of performance have increased in prominence in recent reformulations. Thus, the current version is dubbed the Good Information Processor model.

Whether the strategies known by a student are used appropriately depends in large part on one aspect of metacognition: knowledge about when and where particular strategies can be applied and why they are useful (O'Sullivan & Pressley, 1984; Pressley, Borkowski, & O'Sullivan, 1984, 1985). Chi and Bassok (1989) also provided an analysis that highlights these aspects of metacognition as critical in determining skilled deployment of strategies.

Whether a child uses particular strategies also depends on motivation to do so. Motivation is determined, in part, by students' understanding that the strategies they possess can improve performance, and that when they perform well on tasks, it is often because they use strategies permitting efficient performance (Clifford, 1984; also Licht, Chap. 7 of this volume). If students use task-appropriate strategies when they read, study, and problem solve, their knowledge of the world will almost certainly increase. For instance, efficient reading can be produced by use of comprehension strategies, resulting in greater absorption of information. Repeated episodes of high comprehension should sum to a well-developed knowledge base.

The state of an individual's knowledge base determines whether many specific strategies can be carried out so that they mediate performance. For example, one class of strategies used extensively by good information processors is appropriate activation and use of prior knowledge, which is an effective strategy only when there is relevant prior knowledge to activate. If relevant prior knowledge is used appropriately, it becomes more automatically accessible on occasions when it is related to new knowledge encountered in the world. The more accessible relevant old knowledge, the more likely new knowledge will be associated with it and learned. In short, use of knowledge activation strategies results in higher comprehension in the short term and a better developed knowledge base in the long term. Use of these strategies is guided by knowledge of when and where to use such strategies and fueled by appropriate beliefs (e.g., realizing that activating relevant prior knowledge improves comprehension). The better developed the knowledge base, the more likely future thinking and learning can be mediated by relating to the knowledge base. Hence, future performance is more likely to be skilled. Finally, the more skilled the performance, the more likely that the student will possess high academic self-esteem and appropriate motivational beliefs (e.g., the belief that one's cognitive efforts can facilitate performance; e.g., Weiner, 1979; also see Licht, Chap. 7 of this volume).

And so the circle continues with strategy knowledge accompanied by appropriate metacognitive knowledge and motivational beliefs resulting in greater nonstrategic knowledge of the world, which in turn makes it more likely that the students will be prepared to tackle new situations. But even this complex chain is not the complete story. Among other things, good information processors tend to be generally planful—monitoring their performances, attending appropriately to task-related information, and reflecting before acting. Table 13.1 summarizes some of the more critical factors interacting to produce good information processing.

Cognitive researchers have had little difficulty producing evidence that, as a group, students with learning disabilities are deficient in most aspects of good information processing. (See chapters by Swanson and Reid in this volume.) These students are less strategic than normally functioning students, less aware of critical metacognitive processes, less knowledgeable about the world in general, possess motivational beliefs that undermine strategic efforts (e.g., I am dumb) rather than support them, and have low academic self-esteem. Moreover, they are often too quick to respond and are generally not planful. Some are impulsive to a clinically significant degree; many others are anxious about academic pursuits. Borkowski, Schneider, and Pressley (1989) in particular reviewed the evidence that learners with learning disabilities and normal learners differ on most of the dimensions included in Table 13.1.

It must be emphasized, however, that this claim of general differences between the population with learning disabilities and normal populations is not very helpful in understanding the thinking, learning, and performance of particular students with learning disabilities. Each student with learning disabilities has specific deficiencies in information processing; just which deficiencies any one student may have compared to normals can be determined only through detailed, comprehensive assessment. (See chapters by Meltzer and Roditi in this volume.)

TABLE 13.1
Some Components of Good Information Processing

Intact Neurology

Information Stored in Long-Term Memory
    Conceptual knowledge
    Procedural knowledge
    Metacognition about strategies (e.g., knowing where and when to
        apply a procedure)
    Supportive motivational beliefs

General Cognitive Tendencies, Attitude, Styles of Students
    Planful
    Monitor performance
    Appropriately self-confident
    Selectively attentive to important task elements
    Ignore distractions
    Reflective
    Not anxious
    Habitually relate new information to what is already known
    Practice academic skills
    Aspire to improve
    Elect themselves into situations that will enrich their knowledge
        and encourage growth of their information capabilities

Assessment

Our perspective is that assessment of children with learning disabilities should focus on the abilities, strategies, tendencies, and behaviors that interact to produce good information processing. There is a need both for the development of formal assessments and for the encouragement of teacher-based informal assessments based on the components of good information processing.

Formal Assessment

Formal assessment consistent with the good information processing model would contrast with more global, psychometrically driven measurements (e.g., ones involving demonstration of discrepancies between the general intelligence of a student with learning disabilities and his or her functioning in some academic area). Formal assessment from our perspective is similar to the learning disability subtyping approach (e.g.,

Hooper & Willis, 1988), in that fine-grained measurement of cognitive strengths and weaknesses would be documented as part of assessment.

Our view differs from the subtyping perspective in three important ways: First, assessment within a subtyping model involves little more than simple decomposition of traditional psychometric measures (e.g., breaking a total intelligence test into visual perceptual, attention, and memory components). We recommend much more extensive and specific diagnoses. Thus, rather than measures of memory performance, with process inferred from these performances, our view is that more direct measures (i.e., observations, think-alouds) of rehearsal, clustering, elaboration, and other reorganization processes would be more revealing. Admittedly, this is easier said than done. For instance, it is all too easy for students to "think aloud" by saying what they know they should be doing rather than what they are actually doing. Some children's rehearsals are overt and obvious, whereas other children's are more covert, with the real dilemma that the latter, which are harder to observe, are more mature (see Schneider & Pressley, 1989, Chap. 3). Nonetheless, coping with potential ambiguities in the design of assessments that might directly reveal cognitive process seems a better way to go than to continue to rely completely on inference of cognitive processes from outcome data like that provided in psychometric subtest summaries. (See Chap. 4 by Meltzer in this volume.)

Second, we also advocate measurement of features of thinking ignored by subtyping theorists. For instance, whether students believe they can do well on academic tasks is an important motivational belief held by good information processors, as is the understanding that good performance is tied to appropriate use of strategies and prior knowledge. These critically important beliefs and knowledge states should be measured as part of the assessment process.

Most of the controllable components in Table 13.1 should be measured as part of comprehensive formal assessment; many are not captured very well by psychometric approaches routinely used by the subtyping research community, however. Again, this is easier said than done, for there is nothing even close to a standard assessment of some dimensions listed in the table, such as planfulness, habitually relating new information to what is already known, and electing situations that enrich the knowledge base in preference to other situations. Our belief is that it is high time to begin developing assessments that capture the many components making up competent information processing.

Third, the subtyping perspective is tied more to neuropsychological models of functioning than is the good information processing perspective. Our point of view is that focusing on neuropsychological deficits is unlikely to be productive with respect to the development of interventions that might ameliorate low functioning; hence, our relative disregard of neurophysiology. That is, a child's neurophysiology cannot be modified given the repertoire of interventions available to educators. On the other hand, there is good reason to believe that knowledge and use of strategies, metacognitive knowledge about strategies, motivational beliefs and self-esteem, and nonstrategic knowledge can all be affected by instruction and other environmental interventions. The good information processor model highlights controllable rather than uncontrollable factors, and thus we believe it can be empowering for educators—it is about capacities and skills that educators can affect.

No one yet has devised a formal assessment that captures the many dimensions of good information processing. There are some important advances in assessment, however, that are consistent with what we believe would be an appropriate approach to educational measurement. (For a review, see Pressley et al., 1990.) Meltzer (e.g., 1987, 1990; Meltzer, Solomon, Fenton, & Levine, 1989; Chap. 4 in this volume) in particular has provided assessment tools that tap the type of processing we believe should be measured as part of assessment. Her *Surveys of Problem Solving & Educational Skills* (SPES) permit mapping of the information-processing strengths and weaknesses of 9- to 14-year-olds on a variety of academically relevant tasks, such as verbal and nonverbal problem solving, reading, spelling, composition, and math. Single-student administration affords detailed observations of process. Strategies used by students are scored; so is student awareness and correction of errors (i.e., monitoring). There is measurement of whether students are aware of the strategies they are using and whether they can explain them. When this information about processing is combined with performance data that are collected, a great deal of information is gained about student thinking. As Meltzer reviewed in her chapter in this volume, this assessment differentiates between students with learning disabilities and normal students.

Meltzer's work is a good start in that it can provide information about a student's knowledge of strategies and metacognition about strategies as well as important general intellectual tendencies (e.g., the propensity to monitor performance). This approach needs to be extended. For instance, motivational beliefs need to be evaluated in conjunction with the testing of nonstrategic prior knowledge. A more comprehensive formal assessment device is important that extends the approach developed in the SPES. Anyone considering the design of such an instrument should consult Meltzer's work for a worthwhile perspective on how to devise assessments that tap information processing activities that transpire during academic learning.

Before departing the topic of formal assessment, we would be remiss not to point out that there is even great potential for traditional assessment devices that are currently available. One of the biggest difficulties with formal assessment is a political one. Most school systems demand a formal test (sometimes even a specific one, such as the WISC-R) when diagnosing a child as learning disabled. Because the law demands nothing more, school officials often are concerned only with obtaining a final global score. Given heavy caseloads, the school psychologist may be pressured to assess so quickly that little attention is given to qualitative data that could be gathered during the assessment. For example, observation of responding on the WISC-R can provide information about whether a child is monitoring and capable of self-correction, gets frustrated easily and underperforms, uses simple strategies such as repetition for short-term memory tasks, or guesses without reflection. Analyzing the errors the child makes while taking the test may provide additional insights. After formal testing is completed, the examiner can repeat selected test items and have a child think aloud as he or she attempts items. The examiner can also do diagnostic teaching with items the child misses, generating estimates of whether an item is in the child's zone of proximal development or far beyond it (Vygotsky, 1978). In short, a skilled clinician can gauge quite a bit about a child's information processing using existing assessment tools. Paradoxically, even though tests like the WISC-R are used almost universally to assess children with learning disabilities, they are extremely underused resources at present.

Informal Assessment

Although greater attention has been given to the design of formal assessment as an aid to developing instructional programs for children with learning disabilities than to methods of informal assessment, the day-to-day informal assessments of students by their teachers probably have more impact in program delivery (e.g., Johns, 1982, especially his discussion of the inner-ocular approach). That is, teachers often size up how their students are doing, using such informal evaluations to decide what to teach next and how to do it. Thus, a good way to encourage teaching that is consistent with good information processing may be to sensitize teachers to attend to elements of good information processing as part of daily instruction and evaluation of student performances. Teachers should be attuned to whether their students know and use efficient strategies for accomplishing the academic demands that are placed on them. Students' attributions about their performances are important to assess (e.g., a teacher should be aware if a student holds the belief that there is nothing that could be done to improve his or her performance). Such awareness by teachers is critical if they are to teach in a fashion that encourages good information processing—teaching strategies that students have not yet mastered, accompanied by information about when and where particular strategies should be used as well as information about why strategies increase performance.

Teaching

The good information processing theory implies a teaching model, one that is sufficiently complex to capture almost all of the instructional recommendations made in this volume. Although children will incidentally acquire or discover a great deal of conceptual knowledge, procedural knowledge, information about when and where to use academic procedures, and beliefs about their abilities, a great deal of important conceptual, procedural, metacognitive, and self-knowledge must be conveyed via instruction if it is to be acquired at all or at least efficiently. Instruction can do much to promote a generally planful, non-anxious approach to academic tasks. Appropriate selective attention, monitoring, and habitual association of new information to old can also be promoted via sound instruction.

In recent years, research attention has been given to the teaching of strategies as a means of promoting good information processing. More often than not, task-specific strategies have been taught, with major programs of research directed at instruction of mathematical problem solving (see Pressley, 1986, for a review), reading comprehension (for a review, see Pressley, Johnson, Symons, McGoldrick, & Kurita, 1989), and writing (see Chap. 10 by Graham & Harris in this volume). Moreover, there have been a number of important theoretical analyses and studies of how to conduct strategy instruction with grade-school children who are experiencing academic difficulties (e.g., Duffy et al., 1987; Lysynchuk, Pressley, & Vye, 1990; Palincsar & Brown, 1984; Putnam, Deshler, & Schumaker, Chap. 12 of this volume). Although there is room for debate about specific details of how strategy instruction should occur, it is possible to come to some consensus about effective methods of teaching strategies to special education students (especially students with learning disabilities) from the extant literature.

First of all, a large repertoire of strategies can be developed only over an extended period of time and only a few new strategies can be introduced effectively during an academic year. Instruction of a new strategy begins with extensive teacher modeling and explanation of a strategy and its benefits. Such modeling and explanation on an as-needed basis continues throughout instruction, but control of the strategy is gradually ceded to the student. Thus, the student is at first directed to apply the strategies to easy tasks, with substantial teacher assistance provided on an as-needed basis. Throughout the instructional process, the teacher sizes up how the student is doing and provides feedback, hints, and guidance when the student experiences difficulties. In addition, the teacher does everything possible to inform the student about when and where the strategy can be applied. This includes explicit tuition about application of the strategy and opportunities for the student to discover that a strategy can be applied to a new task. The good teacher provides gentle hints if the student does not recognize the applicability of the procedure to a new situation. (See Pressley, Goodchild, Fleet, Zajchowski, & Evans, 1989, for an elaboration of these points.)

The best strategy instruction occurs throughout the school day in the context of real academic tasks that the child is expected to perform. Thus, Pressley, Gaskins, and their colleagues (Pressley, Gaskins, Wile, Cunicelli, & Sheridan, 1991) recently completed an in-depth case study of a teacher at Benchmark School (see also Gaskins & Elliot, 1991; Pressley, Gaskins, Wile, et al., 1991), Debra Wile, who has been teaching her 10-year-old students to use text analysis and semantic mapping strategies as they read and write. Instruction occurred in writing class, during reading instruction, and as part of social studies. Students were also coached to use mapping strategies in science, although no direct instruction occurred in that class. The students applied variations of the main text analysis and semantic mapping strategies to a variety of text types. They generated a number of different types of essays by first constructing semantic maps from notes and then translating the maps into text. Instruction emphasized the manner in which these strategies could be used in coordination with other strategies. Thus, during a typical reading class, students applied strategies for prior knowledge activation, prediction, imaginal representational, clarification, and summarization. When it was appropriate to do so, students were also cued (and instructed how, if necessary) to use semantic mapping strategies. Thus, semantic mapping was not taught as an isolated activity, but rather was an approach that is part of active processing in general, one stragegy in the context of strategically mediated functioning. Instruction focused on where and when to use the semantic mapping strategies as well as information about why they worked. These explanations emphasized how mapping strategies focus attention on important information; how they force reorganization of material into more logical and, hence, more easily memorizable forms; and how they capture relationships that are often conveyed in prose and other forms of discourse (e.g., cause and effect).

Ms. Wile's informal assessments of her students guided her instructional methods, providing gentle prompts when students need them to apply or complete use of a strategy on a particular task. She pushed them to be as independent as possible, while still providing support when she perceived it was needed. Two points about Ms. Wile's teaching receive elaboration in the subsections that follow: She (a) taught for strategy transfer and (b) showed students how to use strategies flexibly.

Teaching for Generalization

How does a student move from functioning in a supportive environment, like Ms. Wile's class where strategies are prompted continuously, to classrooms and other environments where strategic instruction is not explicitly cued. Simply teaching students, especially students with learning disabilities, how to carry out a procedure rarely produces transfer of the procedure in question. Initially, researchers searched for a secret ingredient that might produce transfer (e.g., O'Sullivan & Pressley's, 1984, manipulation of whether information was or was not provided about when and where to use an imagery mnemonic strategy). Some progress was made in understanding transfer using this approach (see Pressley, Forrest-Pressley, & Elliot-Faust, 1988), especially in identifying components that had at least some impact on transfer in some situations, although the results were never as dramatic as had been anticipated at the outset of this type of inquiry.

Others took a different approach, one less analytical, one that was definitely more fruitful. Their tactic was to embellish instruction with multiple components that might facilitate transfer. As Deshler and Schumaker related it in a recent conversation (May 11, 1990; see also Putnam, et al., Chap. 12 in this volume), the approach at Kansas is to begin teaching for transfer even before the onset of formal instruction. A few of the components aimed at promoting transfer are the following: Students develop contracts with their teachers to apply what they are learning as part of strategy instruction in the resource room to their general coursework. The willingness to attempt transfer is heightened because students have a role in determining which strategies and academic goals they intend to improve. Practice is provided in flexibly adapting instructed procedures to tasks that are different from the original training tasks. Students are taught to instruct themselves to use strategies consistently, and reward themselves when they do so. Information about when and where to use instructed procedures is provided from early in the instructional process. Reinforcement is provided for transfer activities. The assistance of classroom teachers in promoting transfer to the classroom is solicited by the resource room personnel who do the original strategy training. There is long-term follow-up, including "booster shots" of instruction. This multiple-component approach has been tested both formally and informally and has proven successful in producing strategy transfer (Deshler & Lenz, in press; Deshler & Schumaker, 1988; Putnam et al., Chap. 12 of this volume; Schmidt, Deshler, Schumaker, & Alley, 1989).

Flexible Sequencing and Use of Strategies

Many strategy sequences have been recommended to students over the years. For instance, one of the better known is the SQ3R approach, requiring students to survey a text before reading it; generate questions based on the survey of pictures and headings; read the text; recite it; and review it. There are only two problems with this approach: (a) There is little evidence that it promotes comprehension and memory of text (see Forrest-Pressley & Gilles, 1983), and (b) it bears little resemblance to the study behaviors of good readers when they are reading text to learn content.

Pressley and his colleagues at Maryland have asked experts in various areas of the social sciences to read texts that are of great interest to them. These experts have been asked to report aloud what they are doing as they go through text, to provide a "window" on their use of comprehension strategies and text processing. Nothing resembling the SQ3R method has been observed in even one expert. This is despite the fact that they are extremely strategic as they read. They differentially process highly informative parts of text, spending disproportionate amounts of time on abstracts, figures, tables, and critical results. They clarify when there is confusion. They habitually relate new information to prior knowledge. All of this is done in a very flexible manner. In general, the readers begin at the beginning of the text and read forward. When there is need to be strategic, such as when particularly critical or confusing content is encountered, appropriate strategies are activated. Strategies are sequenced to meet task demands—much like they are at Benchmark School.

What Benchmark students do every day is perform the same types of academic tasks that elementary students throughout the United States perform. The difference is that Benchmark teachers teach their students strategies, with extensive modeling and explanation of strategy use and of flexible tailoring of strategies to specific situations. There is no modeling of the application of a fixed number of strategies in a fixed sequence at fixed points during learning as is involved in teaching of SQ3R.

What is more, Benchmark teaching has a great resemblance to other innovative teaching now being deployed and studied. For instance, Gerald Duffy and Laura Roehler (e.g., Duffy & Roehler, 1990) are teaching teachers in Traverse City, Michigan, to instruct children to deploy strategies as the reading task demands rather than in some predetermined fashion. Another example comes from Montgomery County Schools, Maryland. That district has developed a program of strategy instruction for reading that involves teaching children a set of strategies (predicting, imagery, checking, questioning for clarification, summarizing) that are to be applied flexibly to reading. Daily reading group consists of applying these strategies to the selection of the day. Thus, students make predictions, generate images, check their understanding, seek clarification, and summarize as they go through a story. Although evaluations of this approach are far from complete or definitive at this time, preliminary (i.e., "eyeball") analyses of quasiexperimental data suggest the Montgomery County approach leads to better achievement gains than traditional Montgomery County reading-group instruction (T. Schuder, personal communication, May 1990). If the apparent positive effect in Montgomery County holds up, it will be impressive, because the comparison or control group represents students from one of the nation's most heralded school districts with respect both to instructional innovation and high student achievement.

Palincsar (1990; Chap. 9 in this volume by Palincsar et al.) refers to her new approach to reading comprehension as collaborative problem solving, because teachers and students work together to figure out which strategies to apply and how to adapt these to particular tasks. This approach is similar to the teaching method used in Ms. Wile's class, Montgomery County, and Traverse City. Palincsar (1990) reported comprehension advantages in a collaborative problem-solving condition relative to when students were taught strategies using a more rigid approach to comprehension instruction—one favored during the 1980s by Palincsar—reciprocal teaching. Apparently, collaborative problem solving's maiden flight was an impressive one, soaring higher than an intervention known to produce reading comprehension benefits (i.e., reciprocal instruction) (Lysynchuk et al., 1990; Palincsar & Brown, 1984), rather than simply outdistancing a no-strategy control alternative.

In short, there is reason to believe that an important breakthrough in how to conduct strategy instruction is being researched and developed in a number of settings—teaching students to coordinate use of a number of strategies, each of which contributes to overall comprehension. A natural question that follows is how educators in general might learn how to be strategy teachers.

Developing Professionals Who Promote Good Information Processing in Their Students

How is it tht Ms. Wile came to teach the way she does? How is it that she is already doing what the very best minds in educational research and comprehension instruction seem to be only now inventing? Determining whether other professionals can be taught to teach like her or in a fashion consistent with the good information processor model is an important research issue for the 1990s.

Ms. Wile has spend the last three years immersed in strategy instruction at Benchmark. She has had many opportunities to learn about strategy instruction, both from others and from trying to teach it herself. For instance, Pressley et al. (in press) included questions about factors in the school that supported learning about how to teach strategies. Over half the teachers endorsed each of nine resources available at the school: interaction with other teachers (97% endorsement); reading and reacting to manuscripts written about the school by school staff (87%); reading professional articles (87%); monthly inservice meetings with outside experts (81%); interaction with supervisors (81%); interaction with the school director (81%); observing other teachers (74%); teaching team meetings and other staff-sharing meetings (68%); and attending the school's weekly research seminar, which involves the school staff reacting to professional articles and presentations (65%).

Pressley et al. (in press) were able to determine that most of what was learned about strategy instruction occurred during the first 3 years at the school. In particular, there were clear differences in understanding of how strategy instruction can and should proceed between teachers in their first 3 years at the school and those with more experience. These data and informal interactions with the staff suggest that it takes a while "to get the hang of" strategy instruction, but that it can be accomplished in 2 to 3 years. Notably, many of the Benchmark teachers had no previous teaching experience, including Ms. Wile, so that these 2 to 3 years constitute their entire hands-on career in education.

That several years of practice with strategy instruction can produce classroom competence is an issue that is being considered seriously in several training programs. For instance, at Michigan State, Gerald Duffy supervises an undergraduate teacher training program that involves students spending 1 day a week in a school for 2 years.

During this time students have many opportunities to practice direct explanation approaches to strategic teaching, starting with one-on-one tutoring, eventually teaching larger groups of students. They also participate in classes and seminars at the school so that there is substantial instruction, discussion, and feedback about strategy teaching. The research produced by Duffy and his associates in conjunction with this type of student teaching confirms that a rich understanding of teaching is anything but complete after a semester (Herrmann, 1987) or even a year of practice (Roehler, Duffy, Herrmann, Conley, & Johnson, 1988). There is preliminary evidence, however, that student teachers at Michigan State who have more coherent conceptions of teaching, in fact, do teach better (Roehler et al., 1988).

The Kansas Institute for the Study of Learning Disabilities is also making progress in understanding what is required to create strategy teachers. They have had years of experience in preparing strategy teachers via inservice education, developing an inservice approach that is much more long term than traditional models. They schedule training in a school system for several years, with teachers practicing what they have learned between inservice sessions, which are a minimum of 2 months apart. The ideal is four to six such sessions during the first year of learning how to be a strategy teacher. There are follow-ups in subsequent years. Because the data are so clear that certainty of student gains is highly correlated with amount of staff training, the Kansas institute will only agree to train when a school system agrees to long-term, systematic inservice training. (See Schumaker and Clark, in press, for a detailed description of the extensive, multicomponent inservices provided by the Kansas group.)

More relevant here, the Kansas Learning Disabilities Institute has developed a position on preservice teacher education in light of their previous preservice education experiences and their inservice program. Although they recommend a comprehensive program, at its heart is a sequence of practicum experiences. The first requires a half hour of strategy teaching daily by the student enrolled in a practicum, continuing for 6 to 10 weeks. additional practica are given, with each of these involving extensive instruction for 8 to 10 weeks—the minimum period of time required to teach a strategy to the point of generalized deployment using the Kansas approach. Throughout this process, student teachers learn how to model and explain strategies, followed by instruction in how to use scaffolded teaching of procedures with their students. Student teachers also learn how to be strategy coaches. Tutees with learning disabilities learn strategies so well that they can explain the procedures and why they work; such reflective understanding permits the tutees to generalize the strategies they learned to actual school tasks presented in the regular classroom. Lenz and Deshler (in press) believe that to become a strategy teacher, the practice in teaching strategies with reflection and feedback is absolutely essential. Their position regarding the development of reflective teaching practitioners is much like Schön's (1987) position on the development of professional expertise in general. It should be emphasized that the Lenz and Deshler (in press) article is the most complete commentary currently available on how to develop strategy-oriented teachers, and all who are interested in developing strategic teachers should read it.

All of the emerging strategy-teacher preparation models have in common an emphasis on the practice of strategy teaching over extended periods of time. Moreover, the philosophy of these programs centers around the development of thoughtful professionals who will become strategic themselves as professional educators. Lenz and Deshler (in press) stated it well when they described what it meant to prepare a teacher to be a *strategist*:

> [Such] a teacher preparation program . . . has . . . as its primary goal . . . that teachers should be guided in how to think about learning and instruction as well as in how to make decisions about the integration of knowledge related to student characteristics, instructional theories, and intervention methodologies. In short, just as the strategies instructional approach is designed to teach mildly-handicapped students how to effectively shift from one strategy to another, abandon inappropriate strategies, process information using one strategy and then select another for the next phase of problem solving, or consider several processing approaches in rapid succession to arrive at a problem's solution, similarly, teachers are also prepared to scope out the parameters of an instructional problem, select an intervention stratgegy, apply the proposed solution, monitor the effectiveness of the procedure, make necessary adaptations or reject the procedure altogether, and select alternative instructional strategies. The focus of preparation for such a teacher is not a general awareness of a variety of approaches nor is the emphasis on training of one approach; rather the focus is on the acquisition and integration of teaching routines that cut across various instructional approaches and curriculum areas.

Strategy instructional researchers and theorists are giving serious thought about how to train teachers and what it means to be an information-processing–oriented teacher. Such an approach to teacher education deserves attention, if for no other reason than the high approval ratings given to it by teachers who have experienced such training (Pressley et al., in press; Schumaker & Clark, in press).

Closing Comments

The generally positive tone of this chapter should not lull the reader into forgetting our introductory caveats: Definitive assessment and treatment of children with learning disabilities (LD) is far from a fait accompli largely because it is so complicated. This theme was developed in more depth by Borkowski et al. (1989), who outlined some of the obstacles that are often encountered in teaching strategies to students with LD. Two components often prove especially difficult to modify or work around—one is principally a "nature" factor (neurological integrity) and the other is more a product of "nurture" (conceptual knowledge).

Neurological Integrity

Assessment.   At least some deficiencies traditionally considered to be learning disabilities, such as dyslexia, are associated with brain abnormalities (e.g., Galaburda, Rosen, & Sherman, 1989). More will be learned about the relative neural integrity of students with learning disabilities as techniques such as positron-emission tomography and nuclear magnetic resonance imaging become refined, cheaper, and more widely used. Even if neural differences between learners with learning disabilities and normal learners can be established, however, progress in understanding and assessing learning disabilities based on these differences is going to be slow. At this time, there is not even a complete theory of the "neural substrate" for fundamental categories such as memory and attention (e.g., Churchland, 1986, especially Chaps. 4 & 5; Churchland & Sejnowski, 1989). That is, our understanding of how particular areas of the brain support particular cognitive functions is not sufficiently refined to make anything more than gross estimates as to how particular brain differences determine differences at the behavioral and cognitive levels. For instance, is the neural substrate for two seemingly related strategies, such as verbal elaboration (i.e., embellishing to-be-learned material with verbal associations) and imagery elaboration (i.e., embellishing to-be-learned materials with visual associations), similar or different? Without such fundamental understanding of these neurological substrates for learning, explaining and identifying differences in learning, intelligence, problem solving, and memory will not be possible, nor will it be feasible to devise sensitive differential treatments for students with learning disabilities.

Treatment.   No one doubts that, to some extent, the integrity of the brain is essential for the success of cognitive interventions. For instance, substantial short-term memory capacity is required for execution of many of the academic strategies; students limited in their short-term memory capacity due to congenital deficiency or neural insult will likely experience difficulty carrying out many capacity-demanding strategies and cognitive functions (see Baddeley, 1986, especially Chaps. 3–6). Unfortunately, however, prediction of treatment effects based on brain characteristics of students with learning disabilities is not at all well developed. It will be a long time before large numbers of intervention outcomes are understood in relation to differences in neurological status.

Conceptual Knowledge

Assessment.   The long-term learning problems of children with learning disabilities take their toll on the accumulation of conceptual knowledge. Children who learn less from each daily lesson end up with less global and specific knowledge about the world around them. This is not to suggest, however, that children with learning disabilities are fundamentally impoverished with respect to long-term conceptual knowledge. Indeed, the best guess is that their long-term storage capacities do not differ from those of normal learners (Worden, 1983). One possibility is that children with learning disabilities lack long-term knowledge of information studied intentionally (such as much of the academic content taught in school), at least relative to their peers. Anyone who has ever interacted with children who have learning disabilities knows that, like all humans, children with learning disabilities know a great deal about their world. The world affords many opportunities for incidental learning, with all relevant evidence suggesting that differences between students with learning disabilities and normal students for incidental learning are very small (if they exist at all) compared to differences in intentional learning between these two groups (e.g., Tarver, 1981). The question then becomes a matter of what kinds of information different types of children possess, relative to what information they need to know to function in the modern world (e.g., Hirsch, 1987).

The type of prior knowledge deemed critical for today's students is a matter of contemporary debate (e.g., Simonson & Walker, 1988). It seems unlikely that there will be any broad base of agreement in the near future about what should be included in a valid test of necessary prior knowledge. We are more optimistic about informal assessment in this arena, believing teachers can often gauge how much their students might know about a particular topic. It is critical that teachers be aware of conceptual information known and not known by their students, because many intellectual processes that children can be taught (e.g., comprehension strategies) depend on the possession of relevant prior knowledge (Pressley et al., 1987). Thus, activating background knowledge, an important part of effective comprehension (Hansen & Pearson, 1983) is possible only if there is prior knowledge to activate. In fact, "new" content often is not understood at all when such knowledge is lacking (e.g., Anderson & Pearson, 1984). A teacher who is sensitive to the prior knowledge of his or her students is in a position to steer students away from heavily prior knowledge–dependent strategies when the students are working in topic areas that are unfamiliar to them.

Treatment. Whenever one set of content information is selected over another for instructional purposes, there will always be at least one group that will have legitimate claim that its point of view was ignored. Anyone proposing a content-specific curriculum will be a cultural imperialist to someone. Nonetheless, that students with learning disabilities can learn content both incidentally and intentionally (albeit their intentional learning is often less efficient than that of normals)—and that other academic performances are often improved when learners can relate information to extensive prior knowledge—makes it obvious that someone should play the cultural imperialist and assure that students with learning disabilities receive consistently rich presentations of academic information.

One of the most important reasons to teach strategies that increase efficient study of academic content is to increase learning for the long term. One "side effect" of many forms of strategy instruction and other teaching that promotes good information processing is that the knowledge base increases. Every lesson that is learned better than it would have been without the cognitive intervention increases some parts of the student's conceptual knowledge over what it would have been without the intervention.

Final Comment

A volume such as this is possible because of recent important advances in the assessment and treatment of learning disabilities. Nonetheless, there is much left to accomplish, with new challenges and potential bottlenecks made apparent by contemporary models of performance and instruction, such as the good information processor model. Based on the intervention programs discussed in this volume or covered briefly in this chapter, there is little doubt we know a great deal about how to improve the cognitive functioning of children with learning disabilities. Moreover, the authors represented in this volume are determined that we will know more about learning disabilities in the future.

References

Anderson, R. C., & Pearson, P. D. (1984). A schema-theoretic view of basic processes in reading comprehension. In P. D. Pearson, M. Kamil, R. Barr, & P. Mosenthal (Eds.), *Handbook of reading research* (pp. 255–291). New York: Longman.

Baddeley, A. (1986). *Working memory.* Oxford, England: Oxford University Press.

Borkowski, J. G. (1990, May). *Moving metacognition into the classroom.* Presented at the Cognitive Research for Instructional Innovation Conference, University of Maryland, College Park.

Borkowski, J. G., Carr, M., Rellinger, E., & Pressley, M. (1990). Self-regulated cognition: Interdependence of metacognition, attributions, and self-esteem. In B. F. Jones & L. Idol (Eds.), *Dimensions of thinking and cognitive instruction* (pp. 53–92). Hillsdale, NJ: Erlbaum.

Borkowski, J. G., Schneider, W., & Pressley, M. (1989). The challenges of teaching good information processing to learning disabled students. *International Journal of Disability, Development, and Education, 36,* 169–185.

Chi, M. T. H., & Bassok, M. (1989). Learning from examples via self-explanations. In L. B. Resnick (Ed.), *Knowing, learning, and instruction: Essays in honor of Robert Glaser* (pp. 251–282). Hillsdale, NJ: Erlbaum.

Churchland, P. S. (1986). *Neurophilosophy.* Cambridge, MA: MIT Press.

Churchland, P. S., & Sejnowski, T. J. (1989). Neural representation and neural computation. In A. M. Galaburda (Ed.), *From reading to neurons* (pp. 217–254). Cambridge, MA: MIT Press.

Clifford, M. M. (1984). Thoughts on a theory of constructive failure. *Educational Psychologist, 19,* 108–120.

Deshler, D. D., & Lenz, B. K. (in press). The strategies instructional approach. *International Journal of Disability, Development, and Education.*

Deshler, D. D., & Schumaker, J. B. (1988). An instructional model for teaching students how to learn. In J. L. Graden, J. E. Zins, & M. J. Curtis (Eds.), *Alternative educational delivery systems: Enhancing instructional options for all students* (pp. 391–411). Washington, DC: National Association of School Psychologists.

Duffy, G. G., & Roehler, L. (1990, April). *Reading strategy instruction: Intricacies and implications.* Presented at the annual meeting of the American Educational Research Association, Boston.

Duffy, G. G., Roehler, L. R., Sivan, E., Rackliffe, G., Book, C., Meloth, M., Vavrus, L., Wesselman, R., Putnam, J., & Basiri, D. (1987). The effects of explaining the reasoning associated with using reading strategies. *Reading Research Quarterly, 16,* 403–411.

Forrest-Pressley, D. L., & Gilles, L. A. (1983). Children's flexible use of strategies during reading. In M. Pressley & J. R. Levin (Eds.), *Cognitive strategy research: Educational applications* (pp. 123–156). New York: Springer-Verlag.

Galaburda, A. M., Rosen, G. D., & Sherman, G. F. (1989). The neural origin of developmental dyslexia: Implications for medicine, neurology, and cognition. In A. M. Galaburda (Ed.), *From reading to neurons* (pp. 377–388). Cambridge, MA: MIT Press.

Gaskins, I. W., & Elliot, T. (Eds.). (1991). *The Benchmark model of strategy instruction: A manual for teachers.* Cambridge, MA: Brookline.

Hansen, J., & Pearson, P. D. (1983). An instructional study: Improving the inferential comprehension of fourth-grade good and poor readers. *Journal of Educational Psychology, 75,* 821–829.

Herrmann, B. A. (1987, April). *The relationships between teacher education and prospective teachers' developing knowledge structures for reading and reading instruction.* Presented at the annual meeting of the American Education Research Association, Washington, DC.

Hirsch, E. D., Jr. (1987). *Cultural literacy: What every American needs to know.* Boston: Houghton Mifflin.

Hooper, S. R., & Willis, W. G. (1988). *Learning disability subtyping: Neuropsychological foundations, conceptual models, and issues in clinical differentiation.* New York: Springer-Verlag.

Johns, J. L. (1982). The dimensions and uses of informal reading assessment. In J. J. Pikulski & T. Shanahan (Eds.), *Approaches to the informal evaluation of reading* (pp. 1–11). Newark, DE: International Reading Association.

Lenz, B. K., & Deshler, D. D. (in press). Using the principles of strategy instruction as the underpinnings of an effective preservice teacher education model. *Teacher Education and Special Education.*

Lysynchuk, L. M., Pressley, M., & Vye, N. J. (1990). Reciprocal instruction improves standardized reading comprehension performance in poor grade-school comprehenders. *Elementary School Journal, 90,* 469–484.

Meltzer, L. J. (1987). *Surveys of problem-solving & educational skills.* Cambridge, MA: Educators Publishing Service.

Meltzer, L. J. (1990). Problem-solving strategies and academic performance in learning disabled students: Do subtypes exist? In L. Feagans, E. J. Short, & L. J. Meltzer (Eds.), *Learning disabilities subtypes.* Hillsdale, NJ: Erlbaum.

Meltzer, L. J., Solomon, B., Fenton, T., & Levine, M. D. (1989). A developmental study of problem-solving strategies in children with learning difficulties. *Journal of Applied Developmental Psychology, 10,* 171–193.

O'Sullivan, J. T., & Pressley, M. (1984). Completeness of instruction and strategy transfer. *Journal of Experimental Child Psychology, 38,* 275–288.

Palincsar, A. S. (1990, April). *Examining the differential effects of teacher-versus student-controlled activity in comprehension instruction.* Presented at the annual meeting of the American Educational Research Association, Boston.

Palincsar, A. S., & Brown, A. L. (1984). Reciprocal teaching of comprehension-fostering and comprehension-monitoring activities. *Cognition and Instruction, 1,* 117–175.

Pressley, M. (1986). The relevance of the good strategy user model to the teaching of mathematics. *Educational Psychologist, 21,* 139–161.

Pressley, M., Borkowski, J. G., & O'Sullivan, J. T. (1984). Memory strategy instruction is made of this: Metamemory and durable strategy use. *Educational Psychologist, 19*, 94–107.

Pressley, M., Borkowski, J. G., & O'Sullivan, J. T. (1985). Children's metamemory and the teaching of memory strategies. In D. L. Forrest-Pressley, G. E. MacKinnon, & T. G. Waller (Eds.), *Metacognition, cognition, and human performance* (pp. 111–153). Orlando, FL: Academic Press.

Pressley, M., Borkowski, J. G., & Schneider, W. (1987). Cognitive strategies: Good strategy users coordinate metacognition and knowledge. In R. Vasta & G. Whitehurst (Eds.), *Annals of child development* (Vol. 5, pp. 89–129). Greenwich, CT: JAI Press.

Pressley, M., Borkowski, J. G., & Schneider, W. (1989). Good information processing: What it is and how education can promote it. *International Journal of Educational Research, 13*, 857–867.

Pressley, M., Forrest-Pressley, D., & Elliott-Faust, D. J. (1988). What is strategy instructional enrichment and how to study it: Illustrations from research on children's prose memory and comprehension. In F. E. Weinert & M. Perlmutter (Eds.), *Memory development: Universal changes and individual differences* (pp. 101–130). Hillsdale, NJ: Erlbaum.

Pressley, M., Gaskins, I. W., Cunicelli, E. A., Burdick, N. A., Schaub-Matt, M., Lee, D. S., & Powell, N. (1991). Strategy instruction at Benchmark School: A faculty interview study. *Learning Disabilities Quarterly, 14*, 19–48.

Pressley, M., Gaskins, I. W., Wile, D., Cunicelli, E. A., Sheridan, J. (1991). Teaching literacy strategies across the curriculum: A case study at Benchmark School. In J. Zutell & S. McCormick (Eds.), *Learner factors/teacher factors: Issues in literacy research and instruction, 40th Yearbook of the National Reading Conference* (pp. 219–228). Chicago: National Reading Conference.

Pressley, M., Goodchild, F., Fleet, J., Zajchowski, R., & Evans, E. D. (1989). The challenges of classroom strategy instruction. *Elementary School Journal, 89*, 301–342.

Pressley, M., Johnson, C. J., Symons, S., McGoldrick, J. A., & Kurita, J. A. (1989). Strategies that improve children's memory and comprehension of text. *Elementary School Journal, 90*, 3–32.

Pressley, M., Woloshyn, V., Lysynchuk, L. M., Martin, V., Wood, E., & Willoughby, T. (1990). A primer of research on congitive stragegy instruction: The important issues and how to address them. *Educational Psychology Review, 2*, 1–58.

Roehler, L. R., Duffy, G. G., Herrmann, B. A., Conley, M., & Johnson, J. (1988). Knowledge structures as evidence of the "personal": Bridging the gap from thought to practice. *Journal of Curriculum Studies, 20*, 159–165.

Schmidt, J. L., Deshler, D. D., Schumaker, J. B., & Alley, G. R. (1989). Effects of generalization instruction on the written language performance of adolescence with learning disabilities in the mainstream classroom. *Journal of Reading, Writing, and Learning Disabilities, 4*, 291–309.

Schneider, W., & Pressley, M. (1989). *Memory development between 2 and 20.* New York & Berlin: Springer-Verlag.

Schön, D. A. (1987). *Educating the reflective practitioner.* San Francisco: Jossey-Bass.

Schumaker, J. B., & Clark, F. L. (in press). Achieving implementation of strategy instruction through effective inservice education. *Teacher Education and Special Education.*

Simonson, R., & Walker, S. (1988). *The Greywolf annual five: Multicultural literacy.* St. Paul, MN: Greywolf.

Tarver, S. G. (1981). Underselective attention in learning-disabled children: Some reconceptualizations of old hypotheses. *Experimental Education Quarterly, 2,* 25–35.

Vygotsky, L. S. (1978). *Mind in society: The development of higher psychological processes* (M. Cole, V. John-Steiner, S. Scribner, & E. Souberman, Eds. & Trans.). Cambridge, MA: Harvard University Press.

Weiner, B. (1979). A theory of motivation for some classroom experiences. *Journal of Educational Psychology, 71,* 3–25.

Worden, P. E. (1983). Memory strategy instruction with learning disabled. In M. Pressley & J. R. Levin (Eds.), *Cognitive strategy research: Psychological foundations* (pp. 129–153). New York: Springer-Verlag.

Index

Aaron, P. G., 225
Abductive learning, 183, 185
Abikoff, H., 235
Accuracy, in word retrieval, 157–158
Achievement
    automaticity and problem solving and, 122–123
    problem-solving strategies as predictors of, 120–122
Achievement efforts, and achievement-related beliefs, 197–199
Achievement-related beliefs
    aggressive behavior and, 203–207
    and different types of goals, 210–212
    goal setting and, 209
    impact on achievement efforts, 197–199
    inattentive/hyperactive behavior and, 203–207
    individual differences among children with learning disabilities, 201–203
    learning disabilities and, 195–196, 199–201
    sex differences in, 202–203
    strategy instruction integrated with attribution retraining, 207–209
    treatment and teaching recommendations, 207–214
    verbalizing strategies aloud and, 209–210
    viewing other children perform pertinent skills and strategies, 210
Ackerman, P., 99, 230, 235, 295, 297, 300
Adams, A., 252
Adams, P. A., 46
ADD. See Attention deficit disorder (ADD)
ADDH. See Attention deficit disorder with hyperactivity (ADDH)
ADDnoH. See Attention deficit disorder without hyperactivity (ADDnoH)
Adult-child interactions, Vygotsky's view of, 31–33, 35
AFT model. See Assessment for Teaching (AFT) model
Aggressive behavior and achievement-related beliefs, 203–207
AIMS. See Assessments for Integration into Mainstream Settings (AIMS)
Alexander, P. A., 280
Allen, R. D., 228
Allen, R. R., 170
Alley, D., 175
Alley, G. R., 98, 274, 326, 331, 343, 345, 366
Allington, R. L., 250, 251
Alves, A., 48
Alvy, K. T., 171
American Psychiatric Association, 223, 227
Ames, C., 201, 210, 211, 212

Ames, R., 211
Anastasi, A., 95
Anastopoulos, A. D., 199
Anderson, C. A., 199, 208
Anderson, J. C., 229, 230, 232
Anderson, L., 273
Anderson, L. M., 259
Anderson, R. C., 373
Anderson-Inman, L., 275
Andrews, G. R., 199
Anhald, J. M., 230
Anhalt, J., 295
Appelbaum, M. I., 203
Applebee, A., 278, 287
Archer, J., 201, 210, 211, 212
Asarnow, J., 210, 214, 253
Asch, S. E., 171
Assessment. *See also* names of spe-
cific assessment instruments
    Assessment for Teaching (AFT)
        model, 103, 104, 111–113, 294,
        307, 307, 309–316
    assisted assessment, 15, 103,
        108–110
    automaticity and, 96, 97, 102–
        103
    conceptual knowledge and,
        372–373
    from constructivist perspec-
        tive, 15
    continuum of, 103–104
    curriculum-based assessment,
        103, 104, 110–111
    dynamic assessment, 96–97,
        104–108
    formal assessment, 359–362
    goals of, 94
    Good Information Processor
        model and, 359–363
    ideal system for, 97
    informal assessment, 362–363
    integration with classroom
        instruction, 125–129
    and interactions of strategy use
        with motivation and self-con-
        cept, 100–102
    IQ used in, 95–96

    learning potential assessment
        device, 103, 105–106
    of learning strategies, 94–103
    of mathematics abilities, 300–
        303, 307–312
    metacognition and, 96, 97
    neurological integrity and, 371
    of organizational strategies,
        123–125
    process assessment, 107–108
    of reading instruction, 263–264
    setting demands and, 328–331
    and strategy use in students
        with learning disabilities,
        98–100
    of study skills, 123–125
    *Surveys of Problem-Solving
        and Educational Skills*, 108,
        111–120, 123
    *Surveys of Problem-Solving
        and Educational Skills*
        (SPES), 361
    of word-retrieval, 156
    of writing strategies, 283–287
Assessment for Teaching (AFT)
    model, 94, 103, 104, 111–113, 294,
    307, 309–316
*Assessments for Integration into
    Mainstream Settings* (AIMS), 333
Assisted assessment, 15, 103,
    108–110
Attention deficit disorder (ADD)
    definitional issues, 222–225
    distinguished from learning dis-
        abilities, 221–231, 234
    distinguished from opposi-
        tional/conduct disorder,
        221–222, 231–234
    historical perspective on, 226–
        227
    nature of association between
        learning disabilities and,
        229–231
    prevalence of, 221, 228–229
    subtypes of, 227–228
Attention deficit disorder with hy-
    peractivity (ADDH), 227–228, 229

Attention deficit disorder without
hyperactivity (ADDnoH), 227–228,
229
Attribution retraining for achievement-related beliefs, 207–209
Attributions
achievement and, 197
strategy use and, 100–102
Atwell, N., 189, 190
August, D. L., 249
August, G. J., 229
Augustine, D., 272
Austin, G. A., 183
Austin, T. T., 170
Automaticity
assessment and, 96, 97
mathematics assessment of,
303–306
mathematics strategy instruction and, 313–314
problem solving and academic
achievement and, 122–123
strategic language use and, 178
strategic learning and, 102–103
strategy effort and, 28–29
word-retrieval and, 146–147

Backman, J., 145
Baddeley, A., 372
Baker, J. G., 63
Baker, L., 175
Ballew, H., 315
Bally, H., 146
Baltes, P. B., 197
Bandura, A., 197, 209, 210, 211, 282
Banerji, R., 172
Barclay, C. R., 27
Barkley, R. A., 222, 227, 233, 234
Barron, R. W., 151
Bartlett, 8
Bassok, M., 357
Bauer, R., 63, 153
Baumann, J. F., 252
Bax, U., 226
Beaugrande, R. de, 272
Beck, I. L., 149, 152, 153, 154, 157,
159

Becker-Caplan, L., 175
Beckwith, L., 38n
Bednarczyk, A. M., 278
"Behavioral biology," 16
Behaviorism, as approach to learn-
ing disabilities, 6–7
Bell, J. A., 27
Bender, L., 226
Bender, M. E., 206
Benson, F., 298
Benson, N. J., 150
Bereiter, C., 248, 272, 273, 276
Bernstein, D. K., 175
Berry, C. A., 228
Berry, P. A., 228, 229
Biederman, J., 233
Billow, R. M., 172
Biological constructivism, 10–11
Bird, H. R., 232
Bisanz, J., 7
Blanchet, A., 176
Blandford, B., 275
Blashfield, R., 150
Blind children, 33–34
Bloom, B. L., 344
Blum, L. H., 41
BNT. *See Boston Naming Test* (BNT)
Boder, E., 150
Boersma, F. J., 200
Borden, S., 151
Borkowski, J. G., 25, 27, 61, 63, 65,
98, 102, 114, 116, 199, 206, 207,
208, 209, 249, 327, 357, 358, 371
Boston Naming Test (BNT), 147, 304
Bovet, M., 11
Bow, S. J., 41
Bowers, P., 144
Bowey, J. A., 151
Boyer-Schick, K., 273
Boyle, M., 233
Bradley, L., 151, 158
Bransford, J. D., 2, 18, 25, 98, 249,
313
Braswell, L., 214
Braunbeck-Price, R., 171
Broadbent, 8
Brody, G. H., 40

Brooks, L. R., 151
Brooks, R., 298
Brophy, J., 47, 48, 204
Brown, A. L., 2, 9, 12, 14, 16, 18, 25, 26, 27, 61, 63, 65, 75, 93, 98, 109, 115, 116, 126, 150, 199, 248, 249, 250, 257, 259, 280, 286, 287, 327, 330, 363, 367
Brown, I. S., 229
Brown, K. L., 170
Brown, V., 302
Bruck, M., 145
Bruner, J. S., 6, 18, 32, 173, 183, 187
Bryan, T., 46, 200
Bryant, P. E., 151, 158
Bryson, S. E., 151
Buhrmester, D., 233
Burgemeister, B. B., 41
Burleson, B., 171
Butkowsky, I. S., 28, 63, 101, 195, 197, 200
Butler, R., 212
Butterfield, E. C., 8
Byrne, B. M., 197

Caldwell Inventory of Home Stimulation, 39
Calvino, I., 159
Cameron, A. M., 197
Campbell, S. B., 43, 50, 51
Campione, J. C., 2, 14, 15, 18, 25, 63, 75, 93, 98, 103, 104, 108, 109, 115, 150, 249, 280, 330
Canino, G., 232
Cantwell, D. P., 229
Cariglia-Bull, T., 2, 61, 98, 180, 327
Carlson, K., 227
Carnine, D. W., 153, 252
Carpenter, T., 315
Carr, M., 63, 114, 199, 357
Cattell, M., 144
Catts, H., 38
Cavanaugh, J. C., 116
Cawley, J. F., 315
Cazden, C., 169, 263
CBA. *See* Curriculum-based assessment (CBA)

CBM. *See* Cognitive behavior modification (CBM)
Ceci, S. J., 63
Chall, J. S., 144, 145, 152, 344
Chandrasekaran, B., 183
Chapin, M., 209
Chapman, J. W., 200, 201, 200
Chapman, M., 197
Chatelanat, G., 107
Chazan, S., 200
Chi, M. T. H., 26, 80, 357
Chiang, B., 110
Christensen, S. L., 250, 332
Churchill, W., 130
Churchland, P. S., 371
Clark, E., 142
Clark, F. L., 172, 327, 331, 335, 369, 370
Clark, M. L., 41
Clark, R. A., 171
Classroom instruction. *See* Instruction
Clausen, L., 63, 197
Clements, S. D., 226
Clifford, M. M., 208, 357
Clift, R., 249
Coburn, T., 314
Cochran, K., 66
Cognitive behavior modification (CBM), 13, 253–254
Cognitive developmental instruction, 17–18
Cohen, S., 38n
Cohn, R., 299
Collaborative problem solving (CPS) for reading instruction, 259–266
Collins, J., 250
Columbia Mental Maturity Scale, 41
Colvin, G., 252
Communication
    automatization and, 178
    characteristics of, 168
    content knowledge and, 176–177
    decision making for strategic language use, 170

organization of behavior and, 178

pattern recognition and, 177–178

prerequisites for strategic language use, 176–178

problem solving for strategic language use, 169–170

as strategic action, 168–170

strategic language use and metalinguistic ability, 169

strategy development in, 171–172

Vygotsky's view of language, 32–33, 35

Communication-strategy instruction

abductive learning, 183, 185

deductive learning, 183, 184–185

direct implanting of knowledge, 183–184

effective strategy training for, 179–180

experimental learning, 183, 184

inductive learning, 183, 184

learning by analogy, 183, 185

Levels of Competence Model for, 180–186

macromodel for, 180–183

micromodel for, 186–188

minilessons for, 190

models and procedures for, 178–190

preteaching activities for, 189–190

Process Model for Strategy Development, 186–188

pullout therapy, 189

reasoning paradigms for, 183–185

settings and options for, 188–190

tutoring, 189

Compare-Diagnose-Operate revision strategy, 276

Compensation, 34–35, 52, 127–128

Conca, L., 25, 29

Conduct/oppositional disorder, distinguished from attention deficit disorder, 221–222, 231–234

Cone, T. E., 223, 224

Conley, M., 369

Connell, J. P., 205, 206

Conners, C. K., 205

Conners' Teacher Rating Scale, 205

Connolly, A. J., 43

Connor, F. P., 25

Constructivist theories

appropriate role for, 13–15

biological constructivism, 10–11

social constructivism, 11–13, 29–35

Control, locus of. *See* Locus of control

Cooley, W., 250

Cooney, J., 80, 81

Cooney, J. B., 62, 63, 209

Cooney, J. D., 75, 77

Cooperative learning, 14–15, 127

Corno, L., 212

Cort, R., 62

Corwin, R. B., 316

Costello, A. J., 227, 229, 232

Costello, E. J., 229, 232

Cowin, E., 224

Cox, P. D., 209, 210

CPS. *See* Collaborative problem solving (CPS)

Craik, 8

Crandall, V. C., 197

Crandall, V. J., 197

Cronbach, L. J., 152

Cross, D. R., 26, 27, 28, 256

Crossland, J., 152

Cullinan, D., 203

Cunicelli, E. A., 364

Cunningham, C. E., 41, 50

Cunningham, J., 315

Curriculum-based assessment (CBA), 103, 104, 110–111

Curtis, M. E., 144, 152, 153

Cuyler, J. S., 171

DACI. *See Divergent and Convergent Interview* (DACI)

Dale, E., 344
Dallego, M., 62, 63, 69
Daniels, D. H., 201
Dansereau, D. F., 76, 253
Darch, C., 252
Davis, J., 144, 146
Davis, Y. M., 248
Day, J. D., 249, 280, 330
Deaf children, 33–34
Debus, R. L., 199
Decision making for strategic lan-
    guage use, 170
Deductive learning, 183, 184–185
Delia, J., 171
DeLoache, J. S., 25
Demands. *See* Setting demands
Dempster, F. N., 28
Denckla, M. B., 28, 97, 102, 122, 141,
    144, 298, 304
Denhoff, E., 226
Deno, S. L., 93, 104, 110, 273
Deshler, D. D., 98, 128, 129, 172,
    175, 186, 254, 274, 280, 326, 327,
    328, 331, 335, 343, 345, 346, 365,
    366, 370
Deutchman, L., 275
Development, Vygotsky on, 30–33
Developmental dyscalculia, 299
Dewey, J., 295
*Diagnostic and Statistical Manual
    for Mental Disorders* (DSM), 223,
    227, 228, 231
*Diagnostic Test of Arithmetic Strat-
    egies* (DTAS), 302
Diener, C. I., 100, 101, 197
Direct explanation
    for reading instruction, 255–256
    of strategies, 128–129
Direct implanting of knowledge,
    183–184
Direct instruction for reading, 252–
    253
Disabilities. *See* Exceptionalities;
    Learning disabilities; Mathemat-
    ics disabilities; Reading disabili-
    ties
Ditton, P., 43

*Divergent and Convergent Inter-
    view* (DACI), 231
Dixon, R. C., 153
Dodge, K. A., 204
Doise, W., 18
Donahue, M., 200
Dorval, B., 48
Dreyfus, H., 173–174, 183
Dreyfus, S. E., 173–174, 183
Drummond, F., 200
DSM. *See Diagnostic and Statistical
    Manual for Mental Disorders*
    (DSM)
DTAS. *See Diagnostic Test of Arith-
    metic Strategies* (DTAS)
Duffy, G. G., 63, 128, 255, 256, 363,
    367, 368, 369
Dunn, L., 147
Dweck, C. S., 100, 101, 197, 198, 199,
    202, 209, 210, 211
Dyck, D. G., 209
Dykman, R. A., 99, 230, 235, 295
Dynamic assessment, 104–108
Dyscalculia, developmental, 299
Dyslexia, 142, 145–154, 157–158, 224,
    298. *See also* Reading disabilities

Eckroth, D., 183
Ecological approaches to learning
    disabilities, 15–18
Edelbrock, C., 227, 229, 232
Effective strategy training for com-
    munication, 179–180
Efficiency of strategy selection,
    114–115
Elawar, M. C., 212
Elkind, G. S., 232
Elliot, T., 364
Elliott, E. S., 210, 211
Elliott-Faust, D. J., 286, 287, 365
Ellis, A. W., 145
Ellis, E. S., 52, 186, 190, 328, 335
Ellis, H. D., 67
Embert, J., 63, 153
Emotional disturbance, 33
Englert, C., 14, 63, 273, 274, 275
Epstein, M. A., 232

Epstein, M. H., 203
Eribaum, V., 105
Estrada, M. T., 61, 327
Ethology, 15–16
Evaluation. *See* Assessment
Evans, E., 25, 277, 364
Everitt, B., 231
Evertson, C. M., 204
Ewers, C., 66
Exceptionalities, Vygotsky's view
    of, 33–35, 52
Executive Strategy training model,
    186
Experimental learning, 183, 184
Expert performance, 79–83
Expertise, development of, 173–174

FAF performance. *See* Fast, auto-
    matic, and fluent (FAF) per-
    formance
Faraone, A., 233
Farr, M., 80
Fast, automatic, and fluent (FAF)
    performance, 122
Feagans, L., 48
Fear, K., 273
Feedback
    achievement-related beliefs
        and, 211–212
    strategy utility and, 26–28
Feingold, I., 149, 152, 157
Felton, R. H., 229, 230
Fennema, E., 294
Fenton, R., 254
Fenton, T., xx, 99, 119, 120, 122, 361
Ferrara, R. A., 2, 18, 25, 63, 98
Feuerstein, R., 93, 103, 104, 105,
    106, 108
Fey, M. E., 151
Filler, J. W., 107
FIRST-Letter Mnemonic Strategy,
    335, 345
Fisher, F., 74
Fisher, S., 46
Flaugher, J., 40
Flavell, J. H., 12, 25, 171, 173, 249
Fleet, J., 25, 98, 277, 364

Fleischner, J., 25, 102, 295, 297, 300
Flesch, R., 344
Fletcher, J. M., 145n
Flexibility
    in application of rules, 151
    in sequencing, 366–368
    of strategy selection, 115
    in word-retrieval, 157–158
Flower, L., 272, 277
Fluency in word-retrieval, 157–158
Ford, C. E., 25
Ford, W., 297
Formal assessment, 359–362
Forman, E. A., 24, 32, 175
Fornarolo, G., 145
Forrest, T., 46
Forrest-Pressley, D., 365, 366
Foth, D., 69
Fowler, C., 74
Fowler, J. W., 199, 210
Freeman, S., 25
French, J. H., 150
French, L. A., 18
Freschi, R., 153
Freud, S., 8
Frith, U., 145
Frost, J., 152

Gadow, K. D., 203
Galaburda, A. M., 371
Gall, M., 329
Gallagher, J. M., 11n
Gallagher, M. C., 14
Gallistel, C. R., 297
Gardner, H., 93, 95, 105, 112
Garfinkel, B. D., 222, 229
Garner, R., 249, 280
Garnett, K., 25, 102, 295, 297, 300
Garofalo, J., 301
Gartrell, K. E., 209
Gaskins, I. W., 364
Gavelek, J. R., 9
Gearhart, M., 38, 45
Gelfand, H., 9n
Gelman, R., 297
Gelzheiser, L. M., 62, 78

Generalization
    and reading disabilities, 150–151
    teaching for, 365–366
Gerber, M. M., 25, 99, 175
German, D. J., 141, 154, 157, 158
Gersten, R., 252
Gerstmann, J., 299
Gestalt psychology, 8
Gettinger, M., 209
Ghatala, E. S., 27
Gholson, B., 173
Gickling, E. E., 326
Gilhooly, K. J., 170, 174
Gilles, L. A., 366
Ginsburg, H., 297, 299, 302
Giovenco, A., 253
Gittelman, R., 149, 152, 157, 228
Glaser, R., 80
Gleason, J. B., 143
Gleick, J., 234
Goals
    achievement-related beliefs and, 207, 210–212
    distal goals, 209
    learning goals, 209–210
    performance goals, 209–210
    proximal goals, 209
Goetz, T. E., 202
Goin, L., 313
Goldman, S., 63, 65, 180, 297, 301
Goldstein, K., 226, 299
Good, R. H., 104
Good, T., 47, 48
Good Information Processor model
    assessment and, 359–363
    components of, 358, 359
    description of, 356–358
    flexible sequencing and use of strategies, 366–368
    formal assessment and, 359–362
    informal assessment and, 362–363
    mature thinking and, 357–358
    professional development for teaching of, 368–370
    teaching for generalization and, 365–366
    teaching model for, 363–368
Good Strategy User model, 357
Goodchild, F., 25, 98, 101, 277, 364
Goodglass, H., 143, 145n, 147, 298, 304
Goodlad, J., 340
Goodman, J., 83, 85
Goodnow, J., 183, 314
Gottlieb, J., 48
Gottman, J., 206
Gough, P., 145
Gould, S. J., 234
Graden, J., 47
Grading practices, 340–343
Graham, S., xx, 25, 95, 96, 273, 274, 275, 276, 277, 278, 279, 280, 281, 282, 283, 284, 285, 286, 287, 288
Graves, A., 275
Gray, J. W., 29
Green, R. J., 43
Greenes, C., 314
Greenfield, P., 173
Greeno, J., 315
Gregg, S., 14, 274
Grice, H. P., 170
Grolnick, W. S., 213
Gruenenfelder, T. A., 27
Guttentag, R. E., 28

Hale, C., 61, 327
Hall, H. R., 158
Hall, R. J., 99
Hallahan, D. P., 175, 210, 343
Halperin, J. M., 228
Handicaps. *See* Exceptionalities
Hansen, J., 373
Hanson, A. R., 210
Hardwick, N., 149
Hare, V. C., 128
Harris, K. R., xx, 95, 96, 273, 274, 275, 276, 277, 278, 279, 280, 281, 282, 283, 285, 286, 287, 288
Harter, S., 197, 200, 205
Hartsfield, F., 204, 205, 207

Haskett, 202
Haslett, B., 168
Hasselbring, T., 313
Havertape, J. F., 326
Hayes, J., 272, 273, 277
Hayes-Roth, B., 75, 115
Hayes-Roth, F., 75, 115
Haynes, M. C., 47, 250
Haywood, H. C., 107
Head, H., 299
Hearing impairments. *See* Deaf
  children
Heller, J., 315
Heller, T., 233
Henker, B., 233
Henschen, 299
Herman, P. A., 153
Herrmann, B. A., 369
Herrmann, N. D., 63
Herzog, A., 200
Heshusius, L., 17
Heterogeneity
  in dyslexia, 150
  reading instruction and, 264
Hill, D., 277
Hinshaw, S. P., 233, 234
Hirsch, E. D., Jr., 372
Hiskey, M. S., 36
Hiskey-Nebraska, 36
Hodge, G. K., 204
Hoffman, M., 105
Hohman, L. B., 226
Holborow, P., 228, 229
Holcomb, P. J., 230
Hoogeboom, S., 314
Hooper, S. R., 360
Hoskins, B., 180
Howell, K. W., 331
Hresko, W. P., 9n, 13, 18, 124, 175,
  298, 299
Hudson, F. G., 100
Hughes, C. A., 345, 346, 348
Hutchinson, T., 302
Hynd, G. W., 227
Hyperactivity and achievement-
  related beliefs, 203–207

Inattentive/hyperactive behavior
  and achievement-related beliefs,
  203–207
Inductive learning, 183, 184
Informal assessment, 362–363
Information processing
  advantages of, 8–9
  as approach to learning disabili-
    ties, 7–10
  definition of, 8
  disadvantages of, 9
  Good Information Processor
    model, 355–370
  learning disabilities and, 99–
    100
  metacognition and, 12–13
  strategy instruction and pro-
    cessing differences, 69–72
Informed strategies for learning
  (ISL), for reading instruction,
  256
Inglis, S., 39
Inhelder, B., 11, 171
Instruction. *See also* Communication-
  strategy instruction; Mathematics
  strategy instruction; Reading
  instruction; Strategy instruction;
  Writing-strategy instruction
  achievement-related beliefs
    and, 212
  difficulties encountered in,
    371–373
  Good Information Processor
    model and, 363–368
  integration of assessment with,
    125–129
  Vygotsky's view of, 12, 52
*The Instructional Environment
  Scale* (TIES), 332–333
Intelligence. *See* IQ
IQ
  in assessment of learning dis-
    abilities, 95–96
  learning disabilities and, 223–
    224
  role in definition of learning
    disabilities, xx

ISL. *See* Informed strategies for learning (ISL)
Ivey, G., 62

Jacobs, J. E., 27, 249
Jagacinski, C. M., 212
Jastak, S., 303
Jenkins, J. R., 47, 110, 250
Jennings, D. L., 199, 208
Jensen, M. R., 93, 105
Jewett, J. P., 48
Johns, J. L., 362
Johns, M. S., 149
Johnson, C. J., 363
Johnson, D., 298
Johnson, J., 369
Johnson, M., 173, 177, 184
Johnson, M. B., 224
Johnston, M. B., 98
Jones, R. S., 63
Jones, W., 62

Kail, R., 7, 26, 143, 148, 154, 156n, 172
Kameenui, E. J., 153, 252
Kamhi, A. G., 151, 169
Kane, M. J., 287
Kaniel, S., 93, 105
Kaplan, E., 143, 147, 298, 304
Kaput, J., 316
Kastner, S. B., 29
Katkovsky, W., 197
Katz, R., 143, 148
Kavale, K. A., 100
Kazdin, A., 288
Keating, D., 293
Keenan, K., 233
Kendall, P. C., 214
Kennedy, B. S., 27
Kerr, M. M., 333
Kessler, M. D., 227
KeyMath Achievement Test, 43
Kintch, W., 259
Kistner, J. A., 27, 49, 63, 197, 200, 201, 202
Klare, G. R., 344
Klein, D. F., 228

Kline, S., 171
Klopp, K., 38n
Klorman, R., 233, 234
Kneedler, R. D., 210, 343
Knight-Arest, I., 13
Knutson, N., 96
Kolligan, J., 25
Kolligian, J., 61
Kosc, L., 298, 299
Kozleski, E., 71
Krager, J. M., 139, 221, 233
Krampen, G., 211, 212
Kratochwill, 107
Kriegsmann, E., 39
Kronick, D., 7
Kurita, J. A., 363
Kurtz, B. E., 25, 27

LaBerge, D., 102
Labov, W., 170
Lachman, J. L., 8
Lachman, R., 8
Lahey, B. B., 227, 228, 229
Lahey, M., 169
Lakoff, G., 173, 177, 183
Lambert, D. L., 333
Lambert, N. M., 228
Landau, S., 205
Langhorne, J. E., 231
Language. *See* Communication
Language-learning disabilities
    characteristics of, 168
    parent-child interaction and, 36–42, 45–46, 49–50
    strategy deficiencies and, 175–176
    strategy instruction for, 167, 178–190
LaPrade, K., 231
Larson, V. L., 175
Lasky, E. Z., 38n
LASSI. *See Learning and Study Strategies Inventory* (LASSI)
Laufer, M., 226
Law of parsimony and strategy instruction, 83–86
Learned helplessness, 101

Learning and Study Strategies Inventory (LASSI), 124
Learning by analogy, 183, 185
Learning disabilities. *See also* Language-learning disabilities; Mathematics disabilities; Reading disabilities; Strategy deficiencies
   achievement-related beliefs and, 195–196, 199–201
   behavioral approach to, 6–7
   biological constructivism and, 10–11
   characteristics of, 99–100, 225, 325–327
   conceptual knowledge and, 372–373
   constructivist theories of, 10–15
   current perspectives on, xix–xxi
   curriculum not geared for students with, 325–326
   definitional issues, 222–225
   difficulties encountered in instruction, 371–373
   distinguished from attention deficit disorder, 221–231, 234
   ecological approaches to, 15–18
   historical perspective on, 226–227
   individual differences in achievement-related beliefs in, 201–203
   information processing approach to, 7–10
   nature of association between attention deficit disorder and, 229–231
   neurological integrity and, 371–372
   parent-child interaction and, 36–46, 49–50
   postbehavioral perspectives on, 18
   prevalence of, 228–229
   problem-solving strategies and, 120
   production deficiency view of, 78
   social constructivism and, 11–13
   strategy deficiencies and, 24–29, 42–52, 98–100, 175–176
   strategy model of, 64–65
   strategy use and, 98–100
   teacher-student interaction and, 47–50
   Torgesen's view on, 23
Learning potential assessment device (LPAD), 103, 105–106
Lee, W. M., 100
Lehtinen, L. E., 226
Leinhart, G., 250
Leiter International Performance Scale, 41
Leiter, R. G., 41
Lenz, B. K., 172, 254, 326, 327, 328, 331, 335, 366, 370
Leonard, L. B., 143, 148, 154, 156n, 157, 159, 172
Lerner, J. W., 297
Lester, F. J., 301
Levels of Competence Model for communication-strategy instruction, 180–186
LeVerrier, L., 197
Levers, S. R., 27
Levin, J. R., 27, 63, 66, 72, 77, 78, 153, 281
Levine, M. D., xx, 99, 254, 298, 361
Lewin, K., 330
Lexical development and word-retrieval, 147–149
Liberman, A. M. 151
Liberman, I., 74, 142, 148, 151, 224
Licht, B. G., 24, 25, 26, 27, 28, 35, 49, 63, 100, 101, 114, 195, 197, 198, 199, 200, 201, 202, 204
Lichter, A., 14
Lidz, C., 96, 104, 104n, 105
Lincoln, A., 200
Lindauer, B. K., 25
Linden, J. D., 199
Linguistic perspectives on mathematics disabilities, 297–298
Linn, R. T., 204
Lipson, M. Y., 26, 95, 256

Lloyd, J. W., 203, 210, 275, 343
Loban, W., 168
Locus of control, 197, 205
Lodico, M. G., 27
Loney, J., 205, 231, 233
Lord, C., 293
Lorenz, K. Z., 15
Lorge, I., 41
Lorsbach, T. C., 29
Lovett, M. W., 149, 150, 151, 152
Low, A. A., 299
Low-achieving students, teacher
    interaction with, 47
Lundberg, I., 152
Luria, A. R., 253, 299
Lysynchuk, L. M., 2, 363, 367

Mac Iver, D., 202
MacArthur, C., 273, 274, 275, 276,
    283, 284, 285
MacKeith, R. C., 226
MacLean, M., 151–152
Macromodel for communication-
    strategy instruction, 180–183
Malkus, K., 119, 122
Mandelbaum, S. E., 186, 188
Mandler, G., 5, 8, 16, 69
Mann, V. A., 224
Marfo, K., 38, 45, 46
Mark, L., 74
Marsh, H. W., 197
Marshall, K. J., 343
Marston, D. B., 93, 104, 110, 126, 273
Martin, S. M., 14
Martin, V., 2
Mastroperi, M. A., 63
Mastropieri, M. A., 77
Mathematics
    automaticity for, 122–123, 303–
        306
    problem-solving strategies for,
        121–123, 314–315
    in Survey of Educational Skills,
        119
Mathematics assessment
    assessment for teaching (AFT)
        model of, 307, 309–316

of automaticity, language, and
    cognitive strategies, 303–306
case summary of, 307–309
commonly used math tests,
    302–303
developmental approach to,
    300–303
Mathematics disabilities
    cognitive and developmental
        perspectives on, 297
    conceptual perspectives on,
        296–300
    current issues in, 294–296
    interdisciplinary approach to,
        293–294
    linguistic perspectives on,
        297–298
    neuropsychological perspec-
        tives on, 298–300
Mathematics strategy instruction
    from assessment to teaching,
        307
    automaticity and, 313–314
    case summary of, 307–309
    goals for, 295
    standards for, 295–296
    word problems and, 314–315
Mathews, S., 302
Mathinos, D. A., 175
Matthews, F., 46
Mattingly, I. G., 151
Mattis, S., 150
MBD. *See* Minimal brain dysfunc-
    tion (MBD)
McClure, S., 48
McDaniel, M. A., 153
McElroy, K., 275
McEntire, E., 302
McGauvran, M. E., 261
McGee, R., 229, 230, 233
McGill-Franzen, A., 250, 251
McGillicuddy-DeLisi, A. V., 40
McGinley, W., 248
McGoldrick, J. A., 363
McGregor, K. K., 143, 148, 154, 157,
    159
McKeown, M. G., 149, 153, 159

McKinley, N. L., 175
McKinney, J. D., 48, 203, 343
McLoone, B. B., 63
McVey, K. A., 27
Mecklenburg, C., 47
Meichenbaum, D., 83, 85, 175, 210, 214, 253
Meltzer, L. J., xx, xxi, 2, 3, 15, 97, 99, 103, 108, 111, 112, 113, 115, 116, 119, 120, 122, 149, 254, 294, 297, 304, 361
Mental retardation, 33, 34, 45
Menyuk, P., 169
Mercer, C., 345
Metacognition
    assessment and, 96, 97
    constructivism and, 12, 14
    information processing and, 12–13
    learning disabilities and, 98
    mature thinking and, 357
    and motivation and self-concept, 100–102
    reading achievement and, 249
    self-monitoring and self-checking strategies, 115–116
    strategy deficiencies and, 25–26
Metalinguistic ability, 169
Method replacement, 81
Methylphenidate (MPH), 233–234
Metropolitan Reading Achievement Test, 261
Meyer, A., 226
Meyers, J., 105, 107, 108
Michals, D., 99, 100, 297
Michel, G., 146
Micromodel for communication-strategy instruction, 186–188
Milich, R., 205, 231, 233
Miller, D. J., 27
Miller, G. E., 253
Miller, R., 105
Mills, B., 39
Milstead, M., 61, 327
Minick, N., 30n, 32
Minilessons for communication-strategy instruction, 190

Minimal brain dysfunction (MBD), 226–227, 299
Mirkin, P. K., 110, 273
Moely, B., 62, 63, 69
Moffitt, T., 230
Montague, M., 275
Moran, M. R., 275, 340
Morgan, D. P., 48
Morris, R., 146, 150
Morrison, F. J., 151, 293
Moser, J., 315
Motivation. *See* Achievement-related beliefs
Moynahan, E., 27
MPH. *See* Methylphenidate (MPH)
Multidimensional Measure of Children's Perceptions of Control, 205
Murphy, H., 62
Murphy, L. A., 143
Myklebust, H., 298

Nachtman, W., 43
Nagel, D., 335, 345
Nagy, W. E., 153
Nation, J. R., 209
National Council of Teachers of Mathematics (NCTM), 294, 295
Naus, M. J., 26
NCTM. *See* National Council of Teachers of Mathematics (NCTM)
Neisser, U., 9, 16, 173
Nelson, C. M., 333
Nerlove, H., 171
Neurological integrity, 371–372
Neuropsychological perspectives on mathematics disabilities, 298–300
Newell, A., 72
Newman, J. P., 204
Newman, R. S., 27
Nicholls, J. G., 210, 211, 212
Nippold, M. A., 171, 172
Nolen, S. B., 211
Nolet, V., 96
"Notion of specificity," 64
Novel compound formation, 141–142
Novoa, L., 146n

Nurss, J. R., 261
Nuzum, 25

Obregon, M., 146, 147
Offord, D. R., 233
Ogleby, D. M., 99
Ogonowski, M., 119, 122
Oka, E. R., 64, 65, 180, 249
Oldfield, R. C., 144
Olds, J., 150
Oliver, R., 173
Olson, R., 152
Omanson, R. C., 153, 159
Oppositional/conduct disorder dis-
    tinguished from attention deficit
    disorder, 221–222, 231–234
Organization of communication
    behavior, 178
Organizational strategies, assess-
    ment of, 123–125
Ornstein, P. A., 26
Osborne, M., 197
O'Sullivan, J. T., 357, 365
O'Sullivan, R., 250
Overholser, J. D., 77
Ovrut, M., 146
Owen, R. W., 46
Owings, R. A., 249
Ozkaragoz, T., 63, 197

Paine, S., 275
Palincsar, A. S., 9, 14, 32, 61, 63, 65,
    109, 116, 126, 127, 199, 248, 250,
    257, 259, 262, 280, 327, 363, 367
Palmer, D. J., 43, 200
Palmer, D. R., 124
Palmer, S. M., 151
Parent-child interaction
    language impairment and, 36–
    42, 45–46, 49–50
    learning disabilities and, 42–46,
    49–50
    strategy deficiencies and,
    36–46, 49–50
Paris, S. G., 25, 26, 27, 28, 64, 65, 95,
    98, 102, 180, 249, 256
Parmalee, A., 38n

Parsimony, law of, 83–85
Pashley, B., 199
Patashnick, J., 211
Patching, W., 252
Patel, R. K., 151
Paternite, C. E., 231
Pattern recognition and strategic
    language use, 177–178
Pattison-Gordon, L., 316
Peabody Picture Vocabulary Test,
    147
Pear, J., 275
Pearl, R., 28, 46, 199, 200
Pearson, P. D., 14, 373
Peckham, P. D., 202
Pelham, W. E., 25, 206, 228
Pellegrini, A. D., 40
Pellegrino, J., 63, 65
Perfetti, C. A., 144, 147, 149, 159
Perry, N., 63
Peters, J. E., 226
Peterson, O. P., 152
Peterson, P. L., 199, 210
Pfiffer, J., 105
Phillips, S., 225
Phonology-based studies of reading
    disabilities, 151–152
Piaget, J., 8, 10–11, 12, 13, 14, 30,
    171, 173, 295
Pierce, C. S., 183, 185
Pistono, K. S., 25
Pollatsek, A., 143
Polya, G., 295, 301
Poplin, M. S., 13, 14, 18, 248, 259
Poteet, J., 273
Powell, J. S., 153
Preller, D., 288
Pressley, M., 2, 25, 26, 27, 28, 61, 63,
    64, 72, 98, 101, 102, 114, 124, 153,
    180, 249, 276, 277, 278, 279, 280,
    281, 282, 285, 286, 287, 288, 297,
    327, 357, 358, 361, 363, 364, 365,
    366, 368, 370, 373
Preteaching activities for commu-
    nication-strategy instruction,
    189–190
Pritchett, E. M., 43

Problem solving
    automaticity and academic
        achievement and, 122–123
    learning disabilities and, 99–100
    math word problems, 314–315
    mathematics assessment and,
        301–302
    as predictors of academic
        achievement, 120–122
    in reading instruction, 259–266
    for strategic language use, 169–
        170
    in students with and without
        learning disabilities, 120
    *Surveys of Problem-Solving
        and Educational Skills*
        (SPES), 108, 111–120, 123,
        304, 310, 311, 361
Process elimination, 81
*Process Model for Strategy Develop-
    ment,* 186–188
Pullout therapy, 189
Purcell, L., 250
Putallaz, M., 206
Putnam, M. L., 334, 335, 345, 346

RAN. *See Rapid Automatized Nam-
    ing Test* (RAN)
Rand, V., 93, 105
Ransby, M. J., 149, 151
Raphael, T., 273, 274, 275
Rapid Alternating Stimulus Test
    (RAS), 304, 305, 310, 311
Rapid Automatized Naming Test
    (RAN), 304, 310, 311
Rapin, I., 150
RAS. *See Rapid Alternating Stim-
    ulus Test* (RAS)
Rathgeber, A., 69
Reading
    automaticity for, 122–123
    collaborative problem solving
        for, 259–266
    directed learning for, 259–266
    problem-solving strategies for,
        120–123

    self-regulation in, 249
    strategy instruction for, 65
    in Survey of Educational Skills,
        118
    word-retrieval and, 142–149
Reading comprehension, 153
Reading disabilities
    general intervention studies on,
        149–154
    generalization and, 150–151
    heterogeneity in dyslexia, 150
    phonology-based studies of,
        151–152
    semantic-based vocabulary
        studies of, 152–154
    and speech and language diffi-
        culties, 224–225
Reading instruction
    assessment of response to, 263–
        264
    cognitive behavior modification
        for, 253–254
    comparison of three models of
        strategy instruction for, 258–
        266
    direct explanation for, 255–256
    direct instruction for, 252–253
    ease of implementation, 262–
        263
    goals for, 247–248
    heterogeneity and, 264
    informed strategies for learn-
        ing, 256
    nature of, for poor readers,
        250–251
    participation structure, 263
    reciprocal teaching for, 257,
        259–266
    strategies intervention model
        for, 254–255
    strategy instruction for, 251–266
Reasoning paradigms, for commu-
    nication-strategy instruction,
    183–185
Recall
    as function of encoding effort,
        67–68

processing differences and, 69–73
rehearsal and, 78–80
strategies for non-LD versus LD students, 75–78
Reciprocal teaching, 14, 109, 257, 259–266
Reduction to rule, 81
Reeve, R. A., 25, 26, 27, 286
Reeves, J. C., 232
Reid, D. K., 6, 9n, 10, 11n, 13, 14n, 15, 17, 18, 124, 125–126, 175, 298, 299
Reid, M. K., 98, 199, 206, 207, 208, 209
Reis, R., 249
Reisman, F., 302
Rellinger, E., 114, 357
Renick, M. J., 200
Rentiers, K. A., 253
Reordering, 81
Reppucci, N. D., 197
Resnick, D. P., 247
Resnick, L. B., 247, 297
Restle, F., 172
Results to answers, 81
Reynolds, C. R., 223, 224, 277
Rhine, B., 80
Rice, J. M., 210
Richey, D. D., 48
Richness in word-retrieval, 158
Rickarts, C., 29
Riegel, R. H., 329
Riley, M., 315
Ripich, D. N., 175
Robbins, F., 202
Robinson, E. J., 229
Rock, D. A., 40
Roditi, B., 102, 103, 111, 119, 146, 294, 297, 303, 315
Rodriguiz, I. A., 67
Roehler, L. R., 256, 367, 369
Rogers, C. M., 200
Rogers, H., 200
Rogoff, B., 24, 29, 30
Rohrkemper, M. M., 204
Rommetveit, R., 262

Rosen, G. D., 371
Rosenholtz, S. J., 202, 211
Ross, A. D., 25
Ross, G., 32
Rotella, T., 152
Rourke, B. P., 227
Rubin, H., 142, 148, 152
Rubio-Stipec, M., 232
Rudel, R., 29, 97, 102, 122, 141, 142, 144, 145n, 228, 298, 304
Russell, S. J., 297, 316
Rutter, M., 223, 231, 232
Ryan, E. B., 63, 99, 151, 253, 278
Ryan, R. M., 213
Ryckman, D. B., 202

Sabornie, E. J., 328
Safer, D. J., 139, 221, 228, 233
Saklofske, D. H., 200
SAMI. *See Sequential Assessment of Mathematics Inventories* (SAMI)
Sammarco, J. G., 36, 37, 38, 40, 41, 42, 43, 46
Samuels, S. J., 102
Sanborn, M. E., 48
Sandberg, S. T., 231, 232
Sandoval, J., 228
Satz, P., 150
Saudargas, R. A., 48
Saving partial results, 81
Sawatsky, D., 63
Sawyer, R., 277, 281
Scaffolding, 127–128
Scanlon, D. M., 152, 224
Scardamalia, M., 248, 272, 273, 276
Schachar, R., 231, 232
Schaughency, E. A., 227, 228
Scheffel, D. L., 41, 42
Schiffman, H. R., 173
Schlick, A. R., 329
Schmidt, J. L., 366
Schneider, P., 38, 45
Schneider, W., 98, 102, 230, 249, 357, 358
Schoeheimer, J., 224
Schoenfeld, A., 295

Scholnick, E., 293
Schön, D. A., 370
School Survival Skills (SSS) Program, 333–334
Schuder, T., 367
Schulte, A. C., 124
Schumaker, J. B., 98, 128, 129, 172, 186, 254, 275, 276, 277, 280, 326, 327, 328, 331, 335, 340, 343, 345, 346, 348, 365, 366, 369, 370
Schunk, D. H., 197, 208, 209, 210
Schwartz, L., 152
Schwartz, S., 229, 273, 274, 275
Scott, K., 293
Scruggs, T. E., 63, 77, 87
Seabaugh, G., 275
Searle, J. R., 170
Secord, W., 168, 169, 175
SEDS. *See Survey of Educational Skills* (SEDS)
Segal, D., 142, 147, 148, 154, 156n, 157, 158
Seidenberg, M. S., 145
Seidenberg, P. L., 175
Sejnowski, T. J., 371
Self-concept and strategy use, 100–102
Self-efficacy, 197
Self-Perception Profile for Children, 205
Self-regulation
   in reading, 249
   for writing-strategy instruction, 274–275
Semantic-based vocabulary studies of reading disabilities, 152–154
Semantic mapping strategies, 364
Semel, E., 154, 158
Sequential Assessment of Mathematics Inventories (SAMI), 302
Sergeant, J., 230
Setting demand hierarchy system, 334–339
Setting demands
   assessment and, 328–331
   available methods for determining, 332–334

design of strategy instruction and, 345–350
example data set from study on, 339–345
future areas of study, 349–350
The Instructional Environment Scale (TIES), 332–333
School Survival Skills (SSS) Program, 333–334
setting demand hierarchy system, 334–339
Social Behavior Survival Program (SBS), 333
test directions, 343–344
test organization, 343
test questions, 344–345
testing and grading practices, 340–345
Severson, 107
Shankweiler, D., 74, 224
Shapiro, S., 63, 183, 197
Share, D. L., 229
Shavelson, R. J., 197, 262
Shaw, R., 225
Shaywitz, B. A., 221, 222, 223, 232
Shaywitz, S. E., 221, 222, 223, 225, 228, 232
Sheldon, J., 275
Sheldon-Wildgen, J., 340
Shelton, T. L., 199
Shelton, T. S., 249
Sheperd, M. J., 62
Sheridan, J., 364
Sherman, G. F., 371
Sherman, J. A., 340
Shiffrin, R. M., 230
Shifman, M. A., 107
Shinn, M. R., 93, 96, 104, 109, 110, 111
Shlechter, T. M., 16
Shonkoff, J., 298
Short, E. J., 63, 99, 278
Short, J., 253
Siegel, L. S., xx, 41, 95, 151
Sigel, I. E., 40, 41, 43, 46, 50, 293
Silliman, E. R., 168, 175
Silva, P. A., 229, 233

Silver, E., 316
Simmonds, E. P. M., 188
Simon, C. S., 175
Simonson, R., 372
Simpson, C., 202, 211
Sinclair, H., 11
Singer, H. D., 299
Singer, M. T., 43
Sison, C. E., 158
Skills, definition of, 95
Skinner, B. F., 6n
Skinner, E. A., 197
Slate, J. R., 48
Slavin, R. E., 211
Smiley, S. S., 249
Smirnov, A. A., 28
Smith, A., 232
Smith, M. D., 200
Smith, T., 249
Snyder, B. L., 2, 61, 98, 180, 327
Social Behavior Survival Program
  (SBS), 333
Social constructivism, 11–13, 29–35,
  50–52
Solomon, B., xx, 99, 120, 122, 254,
  361
Somberg, D. R., 204
Spear, L. C., 63, 65
Specificity, notion of, 64
Speece, D. L., 203
Spelling in *Survey of Educational
  Skills,* 119
SPES. *See Surveys of Problem-Solv-
  ing and Educational Skills* (SPES)
Spinelli, F. M., 175
Spitzer, R., 227
Spring, C., 144, 146
SPRS. *See Survey of Problem-Solv-
  ing Skills* (SPRS)
SQ3R, 366–368
SSS Program. *See School Survival
  Skills* (SSS) *Program*
Stacey, R., 157
Stanovich, K. E., 64, 145, 151
Steffy, R., 144
Stegink, P., 71
Stein, B. S., 249

Steinberg, E., 63
Stempniak, M., 229
Stern, P., 262
Sternberg, R. J., 25, 61, 63, 65, 93,
  95, 98, 102, 105, 112, 115, 151, 153
Sternberg, S., 230
Stevens, D. D., 248
Stevenson, H. W., 173
Still, G. F., 226
Stipek, D. J., 48, 201
Stoddard, B., 276
Stolz, L. M., 46
Stone, A., 297
Stone, C. A., 12, 14, 32, 33, 37, 38,
  52, 99, 100, 127, 128, 175, 248
Stowe, M. L., 43
Strang, L., 200
Strategies intervention model for
  reading instruction, 254–255
Strategy
  in communication, 168–170
  definition of, 62, 95, 172–173
  relationship to skills, 95
Strategy application
  methods of, 115
  styles of, 115–116
Strategy deficiencies
  automaticity and strategy
    effort, 28–29
  characterizations of, 25–26
  and consequences of previous
    behavior, 26–28
  continuum of, 62
  future research on, 51–52
  integrated view of, 29
  language impairment and, 36–
    42, 45–46
  language-learning disabilities
    and, 175–176
  learning disabilities and, 24–29,
    42–52, 98–100, 175–176
  low-achieving students and, 47
  metacognition and, 25–26
  motivational factors and, 23–24
  parent-child interaction and,
    36–46, 49–50
  processing inefficiencies and, 24

social constructivist perspective on, 29–35, 50–52
social factors in the etiology of, 35–49
teacher-child interaction and, 46–50
Vygotsky on childhood exceptionalities, 33–34, 52
Vygotsky on the nature and path of development, 30–33
Strategy development, in communication, 171–172
Strategy effort, and automaticity, 28–29
Strategy execution deficiencies, 25
Strategy explanations, 116, 119–123, 128–129
Strategy instruction
abductive learning, 183, 185
for achievement-related beliefs, 207–209
advantages of strategy model for, 64–65
challenging component of, 129–130
communication-strategy instruction, 167, 178–190
comparable performance versus comparable strategies, 72, 74–75
comparable strategy use and performance differences, 78–80
as continuum, 65–66
deductive learning, 183, 184–185
definition of strategy, 62
different purposes of strategies, 85, 87
direct explanations of strategies, 128–129
direct implanting of knowledge, 183–184
experimental learning, 183, 184
expert performance and strategy transformation, 79–83
goals of, 61, 327–328
good strategies for non-LD versus LD students, 75–78
inductive learning, 183, 184
integration of assessment with, 126–129
law of parsimony and, 83–86
learning by analogy, 183, 185
in mathematics, 307–316
principles of, 66–87
processing differences and, 69–73
professional development for, 368–370
rationale of, 63–64
for reading, 247–266
setting demands and, 345–350
stepwise process for, 128
student's capacity and, 66–69
Vygotskian approach to, 127–128
for writing, 271–288
Strategy selection
efficiency of, 114–115
flexibility of, 115
Strategy selection deficiencies, 25
Strategy transformation, 79–83
Strategy use
assessment of, 94–103
automaticity and, 102–103
and consequences of previous behavior, 26–28
decision making for strategic language use, 170
expertise and, 173–174
flexible sequencing and, 366–368
in language and metalinguistic ability, 169
learning disabilities and, 98–100
motivation and, 100–102
problem solving for strategic language use, 169–170
self-concept and, 100–102
Strauss, A. A., 226
Strauss, N. L., 202
Stubbs, M., 170
Study skills, assessment of, 123–125
Subtle dysnomia, 142, 144

Survey of Educational Skills
(SEDS), 113, 116, 118–119, 304, 310
Survey of Problem-Solving Skills
(SPRS), 113, 116, 117, 304
*Surveys of Problem-Solving and
Educational Skills* (SPES), 108,
111–120, 123, 304, 310, 311, 361
Swanson, H. L., xx, 2, 7, 9n, 16, 23,
25, 26, 27, 29, 48, 52, 61, 62, 63,
64, 66, 67, 68, 69, 70, 74, 75, 76, 77,
78, 80, 83, 84, 97, 99, 100, 130,
173, 174, 175, 176, 179, 190, 249,
251, 297
Swanson, L. B., 144, 146
Swassing, R., 277
Swenson, C., 204
Symons, S., 2, 61, 98, 101, 180, 327,
363
Szatmari, P., 233

Tarver, S. G., 372
Tate, E., 144
Taylor, E. A., 223, 231
Teacher-child interaction
achievement-related beliefs
and, 211–212
learning disabilities and, 47–50
low-achieving students and, 47
in reading instruction for poor
readers, 250–251
strategy deficiencies and, 46–50
Test of Mathematical Abilities
(TOMA), 302, 303
Test-Taking Strategy, 345, 346–348
Testing practices, 340–345
Text analysis, 364
Thiele, C., 204
Thomas, A., 195, 199
Thomas, C., 273, 274
Thomas, C. C., 14
Thomas, R. L., 67
Thompson, C. K., 158
Thompson, R. H., 48
Thompson, V. P., 326
Thorley, G., 231
Thorndike, R. L., 223
Thurlow, M. L., 47, 250, 329

Tierney, R. J., 248
TIES. *See The Instructional Envi-
ronment Scale* (TIES)
Tindal, G. A., 93, 104, 110, 126
Tippets, E., 273
Toglia, M. P., 16
Tollison, P., 43, 46, 200
TOMA. *See Test of Mathematical
Abilities* (TOMA)
Torgesen, J. K., xx, 2, 23, 24, 25, 26,
35, 62, 69, 70, 98, 100, 101, 114,
151, 195, 199
Trites, R. L., 231
Tsuang, M., 233
Tunmer, W., 145
Turner, J. C., 95
Turner, L. A., 199
Tutoring, 189
Tyroler, J. J., 229
Tzuriel, D., 93, 105

U-ADD. *See* Undifferentiated atten-
tion disorder (U-ADD)
Undifferentiated attention disorder
(U-ADD), 227
Unit building, 81
U.S. Office of Education, 223

Vallasi, G. A., 183
Van Baal, M., 230
Van der Meere, J., 230
Van der Spuy, H. I. J., 41
VanDijk, T. A., 259
Vellutino, F. R., 145n, 152, 224
Vetter, A., 275
Visual impairments. *See* Blind chil-
dren
Vitale, P. A., 48
Vocabulary
levels of word knowledge, 159–
160
reading disabilities and, 152–154
word-retrieval and, 147–149
Vogel, S. A., 151, 202
Voth, T., 275
Vye, N. J., 363

Vygotsky, L. S., 8, 10, 11–12, 14, 15, 24, 30–35, 31n, 36, 47, 50, 52, 85, 95, 106, 127–128, 253, 295, 362

Wagner, R. K., 102, 151
Wagoner, S., 249
Walker, H. M., 333
Walker, S., 372
Wallace, L., 275
Wallach, G., 169
Wansart, W. L., 175
Ward, M., 277
Warner, M. M., 98, 274, 326, 331, 343, 344, 345
Warren-Chaplin, P. M., 151
Wasik, B. A., 95
Wechsler, D., 40, 43, 223, 303
Wechsler Intelligence Scale for Children, 43
Wechsler Intelligence Scale for Children–Revised (WISC–R), 223, 303
Wechsler Preschool and Primary Scale of Intelligence, 40
Weed, K. A., 253
Weiner, B., 197, 358
Weinstein, C. E., 124
Weinstein, M. L., 299
Weintraub, S., 147, 304
Weisz, J. R., 197
Well, A. D., 143
Wellman, H. M., 25
Wells, G., 170
Wender, P., 222
Werker, J. F., 151
Werner, H., 226
Werry, J. S., 232
Wertlieb, D., 293
Wertsch, J. V., 12, 14, 30, 30n, 32, 36, 37, 43
Weyhing, R. S., 63, 199
Whalen, C. K., 222, 233
White, K., 48, 202
Wide Range Achievement Tests (WRAT), 303
Wieselberg, M., 231

Wiig, E. H., 154, 158, 168, 169, 171, 172, 173, 175, 180, 181, 186, 187, 188, 189
Wile, D., 364, 365, 367, 368
Wilkinson, G., 303
Williams, S., 229, 230, 233
Willis, W. G., 360
Willoughby, T., 2
Willows, D. M., 28, 63, 101, 195, 197, 200
Wilson, L. R., 223, 224
Wingfield, A., 144
Winn, J. A., 248
Winne, P. H., 200
Winograd, P., 98, 102, 128
WISC–R. *See Wechsler Intelligence Scale for Children–Revised* (WISC–R)
Wise, B., 152
Wixson, K. K., 26, 95
Wolf, M., 97, 102, 142, 143, 144, 145n, 146, 146n, 147, 156, 157, 158, 298, 303, 304
Wolff, P., 146
Woloshyn, V., 2, 98
Wong, B. Y. L., xx, 25, 52, 62, 63, 69, 78, 200, 249, 273, 275, 276, 279, 286
Wong, R., 63, 69
Wood, D., 32
Wood, E., 2
Wood, F. B., 229
Woodcock, R. W., 224
Woodcock-Johnson Psycho-Educational Battery, 224
Woodland, M. J., 200
Woolston, J. L., 232
"Word Wizard" approach, 153, 159
Word-retrieval
    accuracy in, 157–158
    assessment of, 156
    automaticity rate and, 146–147
    flexibility in, 157–158
    fluency in, 157–158
    intervention program for word-retrieval deficits, 155–159
    phonology-based studies of, 152

reading processes and, 142–149
richness in, 158
semantic-based studies of, 154
sources of difficulties in, 154
vocabulary and lexical development, 147–149
Worden, P. E., 69, 372
WRAT. *See Wide Range Achievement Tests* (WRAT)
Writing, in Survey of Educational Skills, 118
Writing-strategy instruction
applications in school-based settings, 287–288
cognitive, behavioral, and affective measures for, 283–284
components analyses for, 280–282
components, characteristics, and procedures for, 279–280
editing and revising in, 276
evaluation of writing strategies, 283–287
evidence on how students use a strategy, 284–285
field-tested writing strategies for, 274–276

individual differences and, 85–286
maintenance and generalization in, 286–287
planning strategies in, 275
rationale for, 272–274
self-regulation procedures for, 274–275
sentence and paragraph production in, 275
social validity and, 287–288
strategy selection in, 276–279
Wulbert, M., 39, 51

Ysseldyke, J. E., 47, 48, 250, 329, 332

Zajchowski, R., 25, 277, 364
Zametkin, A., 232
Zigmond, N., 250
Zimmerman, D., 46
Zimmerman, S. A., 124
Zinchenko, P. I., 28
Zinkgraff, S., 200
Zone of proximal development (ZPD), 12, 32, 106, 109, 128
ZPD. *See* Zone of proximal development (ZPD)
Zucker, S. F., 63

NATIONAL UNIVERSITY
LIBRARY RIVERSIDE